David Bradley sets out to discover how Elizabethan theatre companies prepared plays for performance: how playwrights understood the composition of the actor-companies they wrote for, how actors followed their directions for entrances and exits, and what happened when plays were adapted for changes in personnel or for other companies. For his study, Bradley has evaluated documents which survived from the records of Stage Revisers (or Plotters as they were known). Bradley's evidence includes seven theatre plots and seventeen manuscript plays, some from theatre productions which took place at the Shakespearean playhouse, the Rose Theatre. The Stage Revisers worked from plots or lists which indicated the action taking place on stage, the props needed, costume changes, and the actors who should appear.

Of the surviving material, only one work, *The Battle of Alcazar* (published in 1594 and revived at the Rose Theatre in 1599), by George Peele, is represented by both a plot list and a printed version of the play. This places the play in a unique position to be used by Bradley as a test case to formulate and analyse the rules which governed the composition of the text and its reconstruction on stage. Beyond an examination of one work, Bradley's conclusions can be extrapolated to expand our understanding of other companies and their repertoires in the Elizabethan theatre.

The book contains reproductions of the extant plots of the period, an appendix listing playwrights, plays, theatre companies, and the number of actors needed for performance, and an extensive bibliography.

From text to performance in the Elizabethan theatre

From text to performance in the Elizabethan theatre

Preparing the play for the stage

DAVID BRADLEY
Professor of English, Monash University

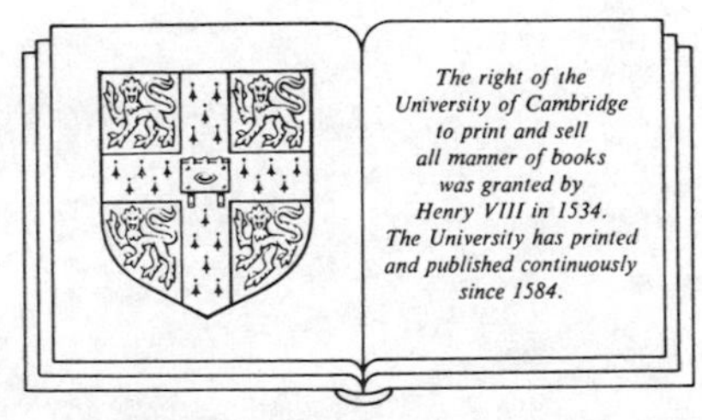

CAMBRIDGE UNIVERSITY PRESS
Cambridge New York Port Chester
Melbourne Sydney

Published by the Press Syndicate of the University of Cambridge
The Pitt Building, Trumpington Street, Cambridge CB2 1RP
40 West 20th Street, New York, NY 10011-4211, USA
10 Stamford Road, Oakleigh, Melbourne 3166, Australia

First published 1992

Printed in Great Britain at the University Press, Cambridge

British Library cataloguing in publication data

Bradley, David
From text to Performance in the
Elizabethan theatre:
preparing the play for the stage.
I. England. Theatre, history
I. Title
792.0942

Library of Congress cataloguing in publication data

Bradley, David.
From text to Performance in the
Elizabethan theatre:
preparing the play for the stage/David Bradley.
p. cm.
Includes bibliographical references (p.) and index.
ISBN 0 521 39466x
1. Theater – England – History – 16th century. 2. English drama – Early modern and Elizabethan, 1558–1603 – History and criticism.
3. Plots (Drama, novel. etc.) I. Title.
PN2589.B73 1991
792'.0942'09031–dc20 90-28477
CIP

ISBN 0 521 39466x hardback

UP

Contents

Illustrations

The Plots are reproduced from W. W. Greg, *Dramatic Documents of the Elizabethan Playhouses* (Oxford, 1931) by kind permission of Oxford University Press.

Acknowledgments

In its long development from a theatrical experiment to a detailed textual study, this work has acquired more debts than I can adequately acknowledge. I wish to remember Professor Keith Macartney and Jeana I. D. Tweedie, who taught me all I know about directing in student theatre; Les Frith, Josh Reynolds, and the men of St George's College in the University of Western Australia, who helped build the original fit-up tiring-house out of jarrah posts, and the actors who turned it into a thing of magic, until its bolts burst under its immense weight; Professor Allan Edwards, who perpetuated the idea in the design of the New Fortune Theatre, and first drew my attention to the importance of *Alcazar*; the Research Assistants who have helped me and checked my findings: Delwyn Schoebel, Sujatha Pannell, Dr Iain Topliss, Pam Keightley, Andrew Griffiths, Peter Neyland, Dr Mimi Colligan, and most of all the ever-dependable Lorraine Bullock. My grateful thanks are due to the staff of the British Library, the Bodleian, the Cambridge University Library and Dulwich College, for their unfailing courtesy and helpfulness, and especially to the technical staff of the British Library Manuscript Room who helped me to examine the Plots under very strong magnification.

I am much obliged to the Council of Monash University for periods of research leave and a timely grant in aid; to Professors Molly Mahood and David Bevington, whose generous interest and comments have saved me from some inattentions and idiocies; to Ms Victoria Cooper, Mrs Jean Field, and the readers for Cambridge University Press for their many helpful suggestions; to the late Professor Arthur Brown, the friendliest guide through the mysteries of bibliography, and willing to tolerate, if hardly to share, my frequent scepticism; to my other colleagues in the department of English, especially Professor Clive Probyn and Dr Harold Love, who have kindly read the script, but have no responsibility for its faults, and above all to the secretarial staff, and in particular to Mrs Barbara Calton and Mrs Doreen Dougherty who have laboured cheerfully, far beyond the call of duty.

I must acknowledge the great debt I owe, together with the whole world of scholarship to Sir Walter Greg, who is here cast in the role of antagonist, but without whose towering editorial achievement few of the documents discussed in this study would have been available for criticism. I am indebted to Oxford University Press for their kind permission to reproduce Greg's transcriptions of the Plots from his *Dramatic Documents from the Elizabethan Playhouse*, 2 vols. (Oxford, 1931). The skeleton plans have been prepared with the help of Victoria Bradley, Philip Scamp and the Monash University Department of Geography. Lastly, things deeper than thanks go to my sternest critic and steadfast source of encouragement, Jocelyn, my wife, to whom this book is dedicated.

Introduction

If we are to take the fullest advantage of the exciting discovery of the sites of the Rose and Globe theatres, and of the building of the Globe replica, in reconstructing the conditions of Elizabethan playing, we shall need to understand more than we do at present about the documents made ready in those theatres for preparing and governing performances: the prompt-book, the cast-list, and the Plot. The aim of this study is to rescue the theatre Plots from the critical neglect they have fallen into, to interpret their function as working documents of the stage, and to explain the witness they bear to the way the dramatists of the age understood their craft and the requirements of the companies of men and boys for whom they wrote. The seven extant Plots were all associated with the Rose theatre and the companies that played there in the 1590s under the management of Philip Henslowe and his son-in-law, the famous actor Edward Alleyn. They were reproduced in photo-facsimile in Sir Walter Greg's edition, *Dramatic Documents from the Elizabethan Playhouses*, 2 vols. (Oxford, 1931), and are reproduced in his transliteration in chapters 5 and 6 of the present work.

We do not know how performances in the Elizabethan theatre were actually directed, or who directed them. We may gather from the prologue to Jonson's *Bartholomew Fair* that the author himself was sometimes in the tiring-house during the play, but whether playwrights regularly directed their own works is a matter for speculation. Certainly it cannot have been the common case at the Rose towards the turn of the century. The Admiral's Men were then embarking on a number of revivals of plays whose authors had been dead for some years, and commissioning others from free-lance writers.

In the preparation of the eighteen or so extant prompt-books, many seemingly magisterial hands have left their mark, but these we can rarely identify. Edward Knight is known to have been the Book-keeper and Stage-reviser for the King's Men in 1633, and had probably been so since 1625. His hand can be found on several manuscripts, but if he was also charged with constructing Plots, none survive. The known work of the scrivener, Ralph Crane, for the King's Men, is principally scribal, and may or may not identify him as a theatre functionary. Thomas Vincent was Book-keeper or Prompter of an earlier Shakespearean company, but unless he was himself the Vincent who appears in the Plot of *2 Seven Deadly Sins* we cannot trace him in the written record.

It is not certain that the office of Book-keeper was also that of prompter, although that appears to have been so in the Restoration theatre. Several hands at a time may be co-operatively seen at work on early manuscript prompt-books, sometimes including those of one or more authors, but, the general director of affairs, whether we call him by the name of Stage-reviser or Plotter, was most probably the man who made out the Plot, the ground-plan of the action to be performed. Anthony Munday, playwright, balladist, translator, and composer of interminable Romances, is called 'our best Plotter' in Francis Meres's *Palladis Tamia* (1598). He was the scribe of the manuscripts of *Sir Thomas More* and *John a Kent and John a Cumber*, and in several plays is satirised as a theatrical Jack-of-all-trades. He certainly had connections as a playwright with the Admiral's Men at the Rose at about the time the Plots were composed, but we have no Plot in his hand, and whether he was in the regular employ of any company is uncertain. In one case, however, the connection between plotting and revision can be made: the principal Stage-reviser of the Book of *Sir Thomas More*, known as Hand C, has been identified as the Plotter who wrote the Plots of *2 Seven Deadly Sins* for Strange's Men and *Fortune's Tennis* for the Admiral's.[1]

It will make little difference whether we regard the Stage-reviser, the Book-keeper, the Prompter, and the Plotter as one man or a committee. In the following discussion I propose, for the sake of simplicity, to call this composite character the Plotter or the Stage-reviser indifferently. The prompt-book, or simply 'Book', as theatre terminology had it, must always have been the final authority for directing a performance, whether or not it was the same book as that actually in the hands of the prompter, but there are strong grounds for believing that any production of an Elizabethan play initially involved the making out of a Plot.

Of the seven Plots that have survived, three are badly decayed and two so fragmentary as to be almost uninterpretable. One exists only in a transcript made by Steevens, printed in the so-called Variorum Shakespeare of 1802, and probably contains a number of inaccuracies and omissions. The texts of the plays represented by the Plots have disappeared in every case but one – that of Peele's *The Tragicall Battell of Alcazar in Barbarie*. The interpretation of the relationship between the Plot and the text of *Alcazar* will therefore be the focus of our enquiry.

The text of Peele's play was printed by Edward Allde in 1594, and is said on its title page to have been 'sundrie times plaid by the Lord high Admirall his seruants'. The date of its composition is certainly much earlier, probably soon after 1588, but we have no record of its performance before it passed into the hands of Lord Strange's Men, by whom, if it is the *mulomurco* or *mvlo mvlluco* recorded in Henslowe's Diary, as I believe it surely must have been, it was played fourteen times between February 1591 and January 1593.[2] The Plot was made for a performance some years later, probably some time between 1598 and 1601. In that revival, Muly Molocco (Abdelmelec) was played by Thomas Downton and the part of his villainous rival, Muly Mahamet, by Edward Alleyn. Alleyn's presence in the Plot, although it provokes some doubts about the dating, is the link that binds the documents together, for he was also associated with Strange's Men in 1591, while retaining a separate allegiance as an Admiral's man, until 1594, and was still a leading member of the Admiral's company in 1598, even though it is believed that he had temporarily ceased playing.[3] The Plot of *Alcazar* thus offers the only first-hand evidence upon which an interpretation of the Plots, and thus of the Plotter's behaviour in general, can be based. I hope to show that the text, too, is uniquely informative when studied in the light of the Plot.

The interpretation of the relationship of the two documents is, however, full of difficulties both of fact and logic. First, the documents are far apart in time and a direct relationship between them appears *prima facie* to be improbable. The Plot preserves a record of the first four acts of the play, but is badly damaged in the right-hand column which contains the third and fourth acts. That column must, therefore, itself, be reconstructed. While the first two acts correspond reasonably closely with the text, enough remains of the third and fourth to make it quite certain that they diverge strikingly in a number of instances. It is, nevertheless, possible to reconstruct the Plot with a fair degree of probability from the text. But when we attempt to interpret the apparent imperfections of the text by comparison with the Plot we are necessarily involved in circularity of argument and our conclusions will be so much the less certain.

The attempt was first undertaken by Sir Walter Greg in *Two Elizabethan Stage Abridgements: Alcazar and Orlando* (1923), with the intention of offering convincing independent evidence of the bad Quarto theory, and his arguments have ever since remained a cornerstone of textual bibliography. His judgment of the text, by comparison with the Plot was that it represents a version of the play:

> drastically cut down by the reduction and omission of spectacles, elimination and doubling of parts, suppression of spectacular shows, for representation in a limited time by a comparatively small cast, with a minimum of theatrical paraphernalia. No scenes have been wholly excised (at any rate from the first four acts) and there is no evidence of matter having been added or of the remaining portion of the text having been tampered with or seriously corrupted. All indications point to the adaptation having been deliberately made for a special purpose or occasion in what one would *a priori* suppose to have been the normal manner.[4]

Such was the authority of Greg's promotion of the new bibliography that in the preface to the Yale facsimile of the Shakespeare First Folio in 1954, Professor C.T. Prouty, who had been sceptical of the bad Quarto theory, accepted the case about *Alcazar* and *Orlando* as 'a matter of definite knowledge'. John Yoklavitch, in Prouty's Yale edition of Peele's plays, went even further and adopted into his edition some of the directions from the Plot, and even some of Greg's reconstructions and criticisms, as if they had independent textual authority. The unfortunate effect of Greg's hypothesis was, however, to divorce the Plot and the text of *Alcazar* from their seemingly close relationship, and to render the Plot – and, in consequence, all the other Plots – dumb.

In combating his arguments I shall no doubt arouse the scepticism of scholars who have internalised the orthodox bibliographical theories of the last seventy years without re-examining what I believe to be one of their more spectacular misapplications. I shall also try the patience of readers whose interest is in the theatrical outcomes. To them I can only apologise, for, if the evidence of regular theatrical practice is to be more convincing than the bibliographical arguments that confront it, the arguments for it must be equally stringent, and must be shown to operate for the great majority of texts. We shall therefore be seeking in many different directions for evidence of the limiting conditions and conventions to which the playwrights of the Great Stage conformed their imaginations; seeking, that is to say, the internalised rules of their craft.

Greg was, of course, well aware of the circularity of his arguments about the text of *Alcazar*, and attempted to find external support for them by a comparison of the allegedly corrupt and shortened text of Greene's *Orlando Furioso* with Edward Alleyn's acting scroll for the part of Orlando, of which a good portion is preserved. The discrepancies between these documents, however, are not great enough to hang an independent theory about the text of *Orlando* upon, without risking some very rash literary judgments, and the interpretation of that text requires support, in turn, from the supposition that *Alcazar* already illustrates the stigmata of a shortened text and a reduced acting cast, even though shortened in a different manner and with a different object in mind.

The quasi-scientific prestige of the new developments in bibliographical method no doubt contributed to the overwhelming success of these circular arguments, but Greg himself knew that their application was illogical. He at first regarded his demonstration that *Alcazar* was a text reduced for performance by twelve actors as little better than a game, and revealed in an inconspicuous footnote that, even as a game, it will not work. The difficulties in generating evidence of the working principles of the Elizabethan theatre nevertheless spring immediately from the general acceptance of Greg's illusory casting of the Quarto text for twelve men.

In attempting to escape from the shadow of bibliographical authority, perhaps we should remind ourselves of the most elementary question that can be raised about Elizabethan playscripts: does not the almost universal absence of expected instructions for performance or production in the early printed texts and the surviving manuscripts suggest the probable existence of widely understood mimetic conventions that must have compensated for their lack of magisterial detail? At the very simplest level of observation, we see, throughout the period, an arrangement of the text by which the action is divided into very short segments, or scenes, and the story told by the sequential appearance and disappearance of groups of characters. As this is not a necessary method of building a play, we may ask why it should have persisted as a structural principle, almost without exception, for the whole period during which the particular architecture of the Great Stage endured.

Universally characteristic of both printed texts and manuscripts is the extreme meagreness of their stage directions, their frequent failure to mark segments of the action, including entrances and exits, their almost total silence in registering indications of time and place, and their complete indifference about stage-positioning and the working of spectacular effects. Even in copies that have undoubtedly served as prompt-books, description of detail necessary for the realisation of the action is often omitted. The direction of exits, whether by the left or right door, is never recorded, and, except for one late printed play, directional entrances also are wholly lacking. May we not infer, from the very absence of such information, the existence of a regular and universal method of theatrical interpretation that allowed the texts to achieve their proper effect in performance?

Two obvious and interconnected considerations are involved in the quest for an answer. One is the response of both playwright and actors to the physical structure of the Elizabethan theatre itself; the other, the casting of the plays according to the usages governing the employment, availability, and status of actors. These are the major influences on the practical shaping of the text as we have it on the page, on the playwrights' imaginative handling of time and place, and on the structuring of the dramatic narrative.

The replica of Shakespeare's Globe itself will be of no greater informative value than any other experimental stage-setting for Shakespeare, unless we can re-create, at the same time, an approximation of the model of the pre-Commonwealth companies for whose use it was designed. Professor T. W. Baldwin's study of the records of the later King's Men in *The Organisation and Personnel of the Shakespearean Company* (1927) showed the importance for our understanding of Elizabethan working methods of the joint-stock arrangements of the major companies. My own study is much indebted to it. But Baldwin followed the more engaging speculations of reconstructing the actor-lists of Shakespeare's plays as they were performed in his own lifetime, and his work did little to refute the general suspicion of authorial ignorance or whimsicality that is one of the residual, unexplained myths of bibliographical inference.

Editors, whose object has been to recover the true original text of their authors through the study of the imperfections of its transmission, have sought their evidence in the printing-house, rather than in the gaudy and unreliable theatre, and have established their picture of theatrical practice from the assumed regularity of compositors' habits. This kind of evidence is now open to challenge on its own terms, but its implications have long seemed improbable to theatre directors and to some literary scholars. It has led us to believe in a race of otherwise incomparable artists who were ignorant of the basic mechanics of their stage and of the capacities of the companies of actors with which they worked; who were liable in the heat of composition to make absurd demands, well aware in their sober fit that the cast available would fail miserably to support them; who commonly composed up to twice as many blank verse lines as could be spoken in the time available and then indifferently left to the company the task of discarding the poetic flesh and discovering the dramatic bones beneath. In the absence of any known limits to the artists' freedom, some scholars have cautiously accepted the assumption that, whatever may be said of others, Shakespeare was a skilled professional craftsman who could fit the needs of his theatre and his company so expertly that his comrades scarcely recalled having seen a line crossed out in his papers. Baldwin concluded from his study of the King's Men after the time of Shakespeare's death that, in that company at least, 'the play was regularly fitted to the company not the company to the play'.[5]

Some of the seventeen or eighteen manuscript plays which, in various states of preservation, carry evidence of preparation for performance, do suggest that the Plotter's primary task was the fitting of the play to the company, but in these he seems to be chiefly concerned with the minor members of the company and in only one case (that of Massinger's *Believe as You List*) can we generate a record of the actors that is convincingly complete. In the Plots the casts are more fully listed, but, as we have seen, there is only one that bears a close relation to an extant text against which its evidence may be tested. The evidence of both the Plots and the manuscripts is thus uninterpretable without external confirmation of the actual composition of the companies: that is to say, without our having a fair idea of the answer before we begin.

We must therefore go round about and attempt to generate evidence of cast sizes and company composition from the texts themselves, to test that evidence by offering an explanation of the constraints that bear upon the behaviour of the Plotter of *Alcazar*, and to formulate the fewest and simplest rules that may be seen to govern his responses to the extant text of that play. If these explanations win acceptance and may be seen, as I believe they may, to function generally, a new way forward will be opened for the understanding of Elizabethan theatre-craft.

Two other major obstacles stand in the way of our enquiry and force upon it a degree of circularity. The first is the mismatch between the actual practice of Elizabethan writers and the universal lip-service they paid to neo-classical dramatic ideas. It is curious that the finest players in Europe, performing at Court before the most sophisticated and learned audience England has ever known, left no independent body of theory. They looked over their shoulders at the principles of classical decorum and of the unities of time, place, and action, but for the most part they did otherwise. They spoke of Acts, but they wrote in Scenes. From this innocent habit has descended a long line of scholarly misconception of their working principles.

The five-act structure of Roman tragedy was certainly well known in the sixteenth century. It was imitated in academic drama and in some plays of the the children's companies, but it is doubtful if any playwright of the period had internalised it as a working imaginative principle, and in the plays of the public theatre it was of little moment until 1608.[6] In that year the King's Men took over the Blackfriars theatre and adopted some of the practices of the children, including the punctuation of the action by musical interludes. These do commonly divide the action into five segments, but, both in the manuscripts, where act divisions are arbitrarily shifted, and in the printed plays, as the sporadic marking into acts in the Shakespeare First Folio show, act divisions are made, for the most part, merely for convenience or as nostalgic gestures towards classical respectability. Even in the early plays of the University Wits, in which a five-act division was sometimes reinforced with dumb-shows or choruses, the dominant structural principle of the drama was, and remained, the scene, the sequence of action between two points at which the stage lay momentarily empty. By 1625 the customs of Blackfriars had been adopted at the Phoenix and other private theatres and the majority of plays published thereafter show division into acts.

Ben Jonson divided the plays in his *Works* (1616) into acts and noted the scenes eccentrically in the continental manner. He attempted to impose on his plays, and on his audience, principles of classical decorum derived somewhat slavishly from Horace's *Ars Poetica*. But even he rarely managed to achieve a true unity of time. His innovative creation of a unity of place in *The Alchemist*, figuring the stage for four acts as the interior of a single house, and, for the fifth act, as its exterior, did not depart from the fundamental structural division of the play into scenes in the sense in which his contemporaries would have understood them. His invention was not understood, and remained un-imitated for many years.

The second major obstacle is the sheer diversity of the material itself, the uncertainty of its provenance, and the imperfections of its transmission. There is also, one might add, the occasional difficulty of laying hands on the crucial evidence. Edited texts are nearly always misleading in some essential detail for our present purposes. The labours of the best and most conscientious editors inevitably obscure some element of the working principles. Editors may not now have the confidence of Malone who regarded the stage directions as wholly under his control, but even Greg declared: 'the editor has nothing to do with the technicalities of the ancient stage'.[7] The process, indeed, began contemporaneously, not only with wholesale regularisation in the printing houses and further 'unconscious' editing by compositors. Jonson's careful edition of his own plays revises the playtexts, and regularises the stage directions in such a way as to remove the evidence of any marking-up for performance they may have carried.

The rival volume, the Shakespeare First Folio (1623), has been shown to contain much revision of a similar kind, but it purported to represent 'the true and perfect coppie' from the hand of a master whose 'mind and hand went together' and who wrote with such ease that 'we have scarce received from him a blot in his papers'. This loyal assertion by Shakespeare's fellows of his effortless expertise in his craft set running the hare of subsequent editorial ambition to reconstruct for readers the original texts of the plays, 'perfect in their numbers as he conceived them', of which ambition the volume produced from Jaggard's printing-house had clearly fallen somewhat short.

There has been much dispute about the nature of the manuscript copy underlying the thirty-six plays printed in the First Folio. McKerrow thought the plays were generally printed from the author's original drafts, but subsequent research has suggested widely various origins. W. W. Greg's summary in *The Shakespeare First Folio* (1955) is not undisputed, but it serves as a convenient account of the possible diversity of material we have to deal with. He argues that of the twenty-two plays first appearing in the Folio, eight were printed directly from Shakespeare's foul papers. Most of these are likely to have undergone annotation in various degrees by the Book-keeper. *Coriolanus* and *Antony and Cleopatra* in particular are held to show careful preparation for production. The extent to which playhouse annotation has been retained or ignored in the printing must, however, remain uncertain. Three others in this class, *Measure for Measure*, *The Winter's Tale*, and *The Tempest* are thought to be transcripts made from Shakespeare's autograph by the scrivener Ralph Crane. Of these, however, *The Winter's Tale* is furnished with massed entries, untypical of playhouse use, and *The Tempest* with unusually elaborate stage-directions. The former suggests preparation for a private patron rather than for prompt copy; the latter is sometimes thought to have been annotated by Shakespeare with greater care than usual because of his absence from the London scene. The other plays in this group are: *A Comedy of Errors*, *The Taming of the Shrew*, *Henry V*, *All's Well that Ends Well*, *Timon of Athens* (unfinished), and *Henry VIII*. None is believed to have served as prompt copy.

Authorial fair copies that had served directly as prompt-books are thought to underlie the Folio texts of *1 Henry VI*, *Julius Caesar*, and *King John*, which all appear for the first time. To these may be added *2 Henry VI* and *3 Henry VI*, versions of which had previously appeared in the *Contention* volumes. Six other plays are held to be printed from non-autograph prompt copy or from transcripts of the prompt-book: *The Two Gentlemen of Verona*, *Twelfth Night*, *As You Like It*, *Macbeth*, *Cymbeline*, and *The Merry Wives of Windsor*. Only the last had previously appeared, in a shorter, variant version. The remaining fourteen plays were printed from copies of pre-existing Quarto editions, some after having been collated in varying degrees of thoroughness either with the author's foul papers or with the official prompt-book. We should, indeed, be treading like Agag before the Lord in attempting to derive any normative picture of dramatic composition or theatrical practice from the internal evidence of the First Folio.

The prospect is little better with the ten earlier Quartos believed with varying degrees of assurance to have been printed directly from Shakespeare's foul papers. These are *Titus Andronicus*, *Love's Labours Lost*, *Romeo and Juliet* Q. 2, *Richard II*, *A Midsummer Night's Dream*, *The Merchant of Venice*, *1 & 2 Henry IV*, *Much Ado about Nothing*, and *Hamlet* Q. 2.

It might seem that we are on firmer ground with the six so-called 'bad' Quartos: *The Contention*, *The True Tragedy*, *Romeo and Juliet* Q. 1, *Henry V*, *The Merry Wives of Windsor*, and *Hamlet* Q. 1. These are all short versions of the plays as printed in the Folio, sometimes containing only half as many lines as the 'original' versions, but believed to derive from playhouse copies. There is, thus, a chance that they retain more evidence of actual performance than the author's manuscript might do, and they often retain textual readings and stage directions that are of use in reconstructing or validating the copy-texts chosen by editors.

Despite the occasionally more elaborate stage-directions of the shorter versions, particularly those of Q. 1 of *Romeo and Juliet*, current theories, deriving from Pollard and Wilson's identification of four of these texts as 'bad' Quartos in 1919, have explained their composition as having taken place by a process of memorial reconstruction.[8] The need for such reconstruction is usually thought to have arisen in exceptional circumstances, such as the loss of the company's licensed playbook during country touring, necessitating its re-vamping either directly from memory, or from a combination of the recall of the stage action together with the actors' parts. Reconstruction from memory alone may have come about through the venal action of players recalling as much of the performed text as they could for sale to a publisher. The theory of the pirating of texts by reporters in the audience with the aid of stenography has proved less enduring, but is, no doubt, still believed by many.

Professor C. T. Prouty made a valiant, and, I believe, convincing, attempt to show that the *Contention* versions could reasonably be read not as corrupt, memorised versions of *2 & 3 Henry VI*, but as versions forerunning the form in which those plays appear in the Folio.[9] More recently, Professor J. K. Walton has argued that the prestige of the bibliographical method is overrated in distinguishing the stigmata of good and bad texts, and that all arguments in fact proceed from the assumption that a 'bad' Quarto text is greatly inferior in literary quality. The case against the possibility that these versions may be Shakespeare's first drafts is thus derived chiefly from the literary judgment that they are so 'degenerate' that they could not conceivably have been written by him.[10]

The case for revision in either direction could be proved only by the convincing demonstration that a single reading in one version *must*, beyond any possibility of alternative explanation, have preceded the reading in the other. On literary grounds alone, this kind of evidence is exceedingly difficult to produce. Prouty's case for the precedence of the *Contention* plays appeared to fail on the garbled genealogy of the Duke of

York, which introduces Edmund Mortimer among the seven sons of Edward III, but his demonstration of the possibility of a heavily revised manuscript having misled the compositor is no better and no worse in logic than the invocation of an exactly similar set of circumstances by the proponents of the bad Quarto theory to explain anomalies in the good texts. For the maintenance of their arguments, as Hardin Craig observed, 'a reporter is always conveniently at hand for the removal of any obstacle that stands in need of removal'.[11] Certainly it is hard to believe that Shakespeare could ever have written the garbled nonsense of the 'To be or not to be' soliloquy as it appears in *Hamlet* Q. 1, but is it not equally inconceivable that the memories of the supposed reporters of *Romeo and Juliet*, who, it is necessary to believe, were Paris and Romeo, should have failed utterly in the very scene in which they are on stage together? Were the enthusiasts who paid their sixpences for the Elizabethan equivalent of French's Acting Editions unlikely to notice the gross deception, if any had been intended? The late Margaret Webster, the only director I know who had taken the trouble to study the bad Quarto theory, used to observe that it involved the supposition that the actors who are identified as reporters had, uncharacteristically, in nearly every case forgotten their cues.

It would take us beyond all reasonable bounds to attempt in this study a survey of the textual questions raised by the bad Quartos, but, as we shall be much concerned with the texts that are supposed to have offered the proof of the existence of such a class of memorially reconstructed plays, I must at least foreshadow the direction in which the arguments of the following pages appear to lead. My belief is that the evidence so far produced for memorial reconstruction is unconvincing and vulnerable in fact and logic. In two cases, those of *Henry V* and *Hamlet*, however, the argument is at least a tempting explanation of the state of the texts. *Henry V* Q. 1, was, of course, the text on which Pollard and Wilson based their theory, and this text alone, in the garbled language and the transposed endings of the scenes in the French camp, satisfies the criterion proposed above of demonstrating a direction of derivation (in which Q is the debtor) that appears to be unassailable. That the choruses, the Duke of Burgundy's oration, and others of the great speeches left no trace in the reporter's memory, however, admits at least the possibility that the Folio text (as the internal evidence itself suggests) had undergone one or more revisions from a common, lost original. An area of doubt must, therefore, always be allowed. It is of interest that Dr Gary Taylor, the editor of the New Oxford edition, appears to believe strongly enough in the existence of an Ur-*Henry V*, to have retained Q's Bourbon in his text in places where, in the Folio, he has been replaced by the Dauphin.

Romeo and Juliet, on the other hand, shows examples of the contrary kind that appear to establish the precedence of the Q. 1 text. It is hard to imagine, for instance, how Q. 1's exact rendering of a Ciceronian apothegm that is rhetorically flourished beyond recognition in Q. 2 (I, i, 124 ff.) could have been restored by the kind of mechanical recall that is attributed to reporters' memories.[12] *The Merry Wives* Q gives evidence of an alternative arrangement of scenes, which, on the hypotheses I advance below, also entails that the Folio is the debtor, and the *Contention* plays have examples of rearranged castings and stage dispositions, as, for example, for the murder of Duke Humphrey of Gloucester, which suggest that they were written or rewritten for another theatre and another company. What is not often enough insisted upon is that whatever the direction of the revision may have been, more is involved than the operation of faulty memory or the casual errors and corrections of the printing-house. Some kind of deliberate theatrical intervention has occurred in every case.

The idea that Shakespeare's plays may have existed in several *authorial* versions is too close to the idea of continuous copy to be of comfort to editors, and has, on the whole, been opposed by bibliographers. McKerrow's view has not found general favour:

> It is very doubtful whether, especially in the earlier plays, there ever existed any written 'final form'. Shakespeare as an active member of a theatrical company would, at any rate in his younger days, have been concerned with producing, not plays for the study, but material for his company to perform on the stage, and there can be little doubt that his lines would be subject to modification in the light of actual performance.[13]

This view, so conformable to the practice of the modern theatre, is regarded by Professor Honigmann as somewhat radical. He preferred to re-state it in the following way, believing that Shakespeare, like any other author, may well have introduced many small changes in the process of copying his own work:

> I envisage ... two copies of a play, each in the author's hand, disagreeing in both substantive and indifferent readings: the play being regarded as 'finished' by Shakespeare in each version though not therefore beyond the reach of afterthoughts.[14]

The argument had earlier been proposed by Greg as a solution to the alternative texts of *Othello*, and has since been developed, most notably by Steven Urkowitz, in relation to the formerly suspect Q of *King Lear*.

Bibliographical studies of the copy underlying Elizabethan printed texts have thus shown it to be, as Fredson Bowers suggests, 'of every conceivable variety'.[15] Even were we faced with only the thirteen general types into which Bowers divides its possible origins, and those identified by undisputed demonstration, we should appear to be on very unsure ground in deriving from them any principles of practical composition and theatrical usage. It is not surprising that theories accounting for the relationship of variant texts have been derived, in the absence of external evidence of customary practice, from probabilities of scribal transmission and the habits of compositors that are at least amenable to quantification and methodical analysis.

The full crudity of the resultant picture of the methods of the theatre is wisely left in decent obscurity by respectable bibliographers, but Alfred Hart's numerate but quite contradictory analysis of the bad Quarto problem in *Stolne and Surreptitious Copies* (1942) faced the unpalatable facts with cheerful abandon. Hart estimated that the average length of a play of the period was about 2,300 lines – the number that can be spoken in the two hours' traffic of the stage – and assumed that the plays of Shakespeare and Ben Jonson, many of which are more than 1,200 lines (an hour's playing-time) longer, must have been cut down in performance. He thus believed that the bad Quartos were memorial reconstructions of these cut versions. The first draft theory appeared to him nonsensical on the grounds that Shakespeare could surely not have taken the trouble to revise in such minute detail, making over 2,000 petty corrections and additions in the texts of *Romeo and Juliet* and *The True Tragedy*, doubling the number of classical allusions and trebling the number of similes, besides adding much amplificatory material unnecessary to sense or context. In defending this view he writes:

> If a stage-manager excised from *3 Henry VI* all the passages not present in any form in *True Tragedy*, and retained also such other portions of Shakespeare's play as were necessary to the story but were differently expressed in the quarto, he would have an excellent acting version of about 2,200 to 2,300 lines. On the other hand, if he collected all the seven or eight hundred lines excised, he would discover that the story and plot had entirely disappeared; there would remain a heterogeneous assortment of disconnected extracts such as are found in a dictionary of quotations, e.g. excursions into practical philosophy and wisdom, general reflections on life, character and conduct, moralizing and ethics, similes, overworked metaphors, comments, asides, out-of-date topical matter, at times short episodes, some parade of learning, classical allusions, amplificatory detail, repetition of what is stated in the context, etc. However admirably they read, most of them carry little reference directly to fable, plot or action, and many could be fitted almost equally well in a suitable portion of another play.[16]

Hart does not appear to have noticed that if one stands this view on its head it implies that Shakespeare's originals were filled out with irrelevant and tawdry material which he must have composed in the sure expectation that it would be jettisoned in performance. Alas, poor Shakespeare! Hart bolsters his argument, however, by reference to Greg's supposed proof of the bad Quarto theory in *Alcazar and Orlando* which itself is based upon literary judgments about the printed text of *Orlando Furioso* no less dubious, if rather better concealed. 'Dr Greg has shown', he writes,

> that the players struck out long passages of Orlando's part which was stuffed with similes and classical allusions; but of 108 such passages in this part alone, necessity compelled them to keep 51 if they were to have any play left. Even after this severe pruning of poetic exuberance and a plentiful dilution of comic interpolation to make Greene's classical bombast palatable to their audience, they were compelled to present a play one fourth of which consisted of mythological embroidery.[17]

The literary implications of Hart's characteristic computation are rather unfair to Greg, who did not regard *Orlando* as a normally produced theatrical script and had a somewhat higher opinion of the popular appeal of Greene's rhetoric.

The theory of the unprofessional or insouciant Elizabethan author is, however, crucial to Greg's interpretation of the prompter's behaviour, both in the Plots and the manuscript plays. In summarising the evidence in *Alcazar and Orlando*, he writes:

> the author...demands attendants, courtiers, guards, a whole army perhaps; the plotter, bound by material limitations, allots what minor actors he can afford, but no one troubles to alter the prompt-copy, especially as the provision will vary from time to time according to the number of hired men and boys which the state of the company finances allows.[18]

This statement seems at first view strictly in accord with the bibliographical facts, but has, I believe, several implications that distort the true picture of the activities of the Plotter and his relationship with the dramatist and the company.

In the manuscript prompt-books there are, indeed, passages marked for deletion but not completely struck out, and there are alterations to the cast anticipated by the dramatist that mostly concern only the minor members of the company, but the implication that the cast available to a Plotter varied in size according to the degree of a company's financial success appears to be unsupported by external evidence and cannot be derived from the textual evidence itself.

It is difficult to tell how far Greg assumed that Elizabethan acting companies operated under something like the conditions of modern commercial managements, hiring actors as need arose to fit the casting requirements of plays acquired *ad hoc*. It would certainly be unjust to suppose that he believed, like Hart, that dramatists wrote, as their modern counterparts may sometimes do, with imaginations untrammelled by the sober considerations of theatre economics. The extremes of the modern theatre cannot be paralleled: there are no plays of the Elizabethan period with casts of two, and none with casts of two hundred. The common practice of doubling roles is itself an indication that the artistic freedom of the playwright was not unrestricted.

The most complete evidence we have of the workings of a theatrical company comes from Henslowe's Diary and the papers associated with it in the Alleyn collection at Dulwich College, and, once again, we are deeply indebted to Greg's edition of 1911. From these, it is true, one may derive the impression that companies of which Henslowe was the financier did conduct their business in something like the modern manner. In the Admiral's Men and other companies, actors, even some who appear to be among the major members, are recorded in the Diary as bonded to or hired by Henslowe personally for short periods. Plays were acquired from authors, who, although sometimes commissioned, as was Daborne, or employed under contract, as was Heywood, appear often to have submitted their work independently. The extant Plots, moreover, of which six out of the seven belonged to the Admiral's Men, reveal total casts varying in size between twenty and thirty. Certainly actors moved quite frequently from one company to another throughout the period, as boys grew into hired men and hired men into Masters, or as companies were forced to break and disband through financial hardship or the deaths of their patrons. Some dramatists, even writers of repute, like Ben Jonson, appear to have worked as free-lances for any company that would pay. The corollary cannot wholly be discounted that the Plotter's business, like the business of a modern producer, was to hire his cast to fit the play.

The company structure was, however, almost certainly perceived in a rather different way by contemporaries, and the textual evidence may be interpreted in another way. Even in Henslowe's companies, hired men were not engaged play by play but for periods of two years or more. The 'breaking' of a company was a serious matter and resulted in the actors losing their repertory. In the most stable company of which we have record, the Chamberlain's-King's Men, boys were engaged under conditions of apprenticeship and, as Baldwin has shown, often remained, first as hired men, then as master actors, and finally as sharers in the same company for the whole of their career. The Admiral's Men, even though dependent on a capitalist financier, maintained a very similar structure for ten years. I believe, as the figures of company composition in chapter 2 will show, that the perception of company organisation as an hierarchical, joint-stock organisation of fixed composition must have been general. Outside the Revels companies and the companies of children, it was the norm until well into the third decade of the seventeenth century, and must have furnished known limits of personnel, in the light of which dramatists were able to construct their plays with some assurance of their demands being met.

Most major playwrights worked closely for long periods with single companies. The King's Men's regular succession of master dramatists – Shakespeare, Fletcher, Massinger, and Shirley – is without parallel, but free-lance writers, too, must have been familiar enough with the composition of the companies to whom they expected to sell their plays. Even Clavell, the repentant highwayman turned playwright, made a singularly precise count of the cast available to him in *The Soddered Citizen*.

The casting of the play was undoubtedly the first concern of the Plotter or Stage-reviser, just as it is of any modern producer. The curiosity is, as Greg observes, that, in the manuscript plays, he appears not to be concerned with the filling of the major roles, but only with the allocation of minor parts. In the Plots his record of the actors, in so far as he needs to record their names at all, appears to be fairly complete. In both cases, minor actors are those most heavily involved in doubling roles and are kept more careful track of. On occasion, however, the Plotter is clearly attempting to meet the demands of a text that runs beyond his cast's capacity. The hard-pressed Plotter of *Frederick and Basilea* has to call in the gatherers from the theatre doors to provide a group of 'conspirators'. In a scene of *The Dead Man's Fortune* the Plotter calls on the tire-man as an attendant. To make a splendid show of conquered races for the last scene of *1 Tamar Cam* he enlists, it seems, every hanger-on in the theatre, including even one man and a number of boys whose names he does not know. We cannot be sure whether in any instance he called in some particular actor not normally a member of the company to fill a speaking role, but the consistency of the casts of the two latest Plots, together with what we know of the Admiral's Men from external records, suggests that he did not. It is a reasonable guess that the theatre functionaries called in to swell the scene were all mute and thought of quite separately from the acting cast, even though, in *1 Tamar Cam*, the whole of the acting cast, with the exception of the clown, is also on stage in the last scene.

The manuscript prompt-books appear to present a less methodical record than the Plots. They are not, of course, all of a kind: they have varied histories, they show a wide diversity of stages of preparation for performance, they are not all certainly the finished prompt-books of the companies by whom they were first played. Some, like those in the collection B.M. MS. Egerton 1992 and that of *Sir Thomas More*, have been patchily annotated and revised for revivals. In the prompt-book the Plotter or Stage-reviser is concerned with a multiplicity of things besides the management of the cast. He himself makes additions and deletions to the text; he may also note passages that are to be rewritten by others; he attempts to bring the script into conformity with the demands of the censor; he rewrites stage-directions and places them more prominently; he sometimes provides readying notes for actors well in advance of the point at which they are to enter; he occasionally makes notes for the provision of furniture and properties and, in a single instance, for the working of the trap-door; he marks in music cues, especially for the initial entrances to a scene; he may even rearrange the author's scene division.

He is, indeed, a *Johannes factotum*, but, while one of his major concerns is still quite clearly the fitting together of the text and the cast, his listing of actors' names gives the impression of being random and sporadic. We sometimes pick up the names of major actors from readying notes, or, in the case of *Believe as You List*, from a 'properties' list attached to the manuscript;[19] but when roles are allocated in the text itself, it is the minor members of the company who are principally involved. Doubling of roles is often indicated, but a puzzling feature is that actors are sometimes listed only at their second or subsequent appearance in a role, and thus we cannot be sure that the single appearance of an actor's name is anything other than an inscrutable *aide-memoire* by the Plotter to himself.

It is also true, as Greg observes, that in the prompt-books, there are, indeed, passages marked for deletion but not completely struck out, and, there are alterations to the cast anticipated by the dramatist that appear to show a desire to economise. Greg's notion of the maintenance of a 'recoverable' text, depending on the financial fortunes of the company, might thus be justified, even if it carries the rather surprising implication that the good texts of Shakespeare may have achieved adequate representation on the stage only when the King's Men were flush enough to afford it. On occasion, also, large groups of characters are deleted altogether, as in the manuscript of *Sir John van Olden Barnavelt*, where the Plotter has removed a direction for the procession of the whole of the Arminian party across the stage. Conversely, in the Folio text of *2 Henry VI*, Shakespeare's direction *Enter multitudes* has been transmitted from the prompt-book into print. As this is most unlikely to have been a functional direction, the possibilities are either that the Plotter left it standing as a kind of theatrical joke, deriving from the source material and referring to the five or six actors who were available to represent Jack Cade's party, or that he adopted the expedient of the Plotter of *1 Tamar Cam* and called in all the stage-hands and attendants. If the latter, why did not the Plotter of *Barnavelt* do likewise?

Happily we have external information suggestive of an answer, for the *Barnavelt* Plotter was working on material hastily thrown together, on the very heels of startling events in the Netherlands in 1619, by two dramatists who appear to have divided the available pamphlets relating to the execution of the great Dutch statesman, Barnavelt, between them. As a result, although the two, Fletcher and Massinger, had no doubt sketched out the general lines of the action in conference, their casts of characters, as they handed in their written-up scenes, were not quite synchronised. The Plotter, in this case, had the task not only of allocating the roles to particular actors (fitting the company to the play) but of revising the text (fitting the play to the company).[20] Far from behaving as though he could call on any number of supers and attendants, he carefully shapes the text to the available cast, creating, as he does so, some amusing but passable anomalies. The Arminian procession has to go because the Arminian party itself has been forced to dwindle for lack of actors. That change may, indeed, have been influenced by the censor, for the playwrights, understandably, had mistaken James's policy in the Netherlands and had swung their sympathies towards the wrong party strongly enough to have provoked the temporary inhibition of the performance by the Bishop of London. From the colonels and captains of Prince Maurice's army, however, the colonels still had to be removed for reasons of casting, leaving his remaining army identified anachronistically as *English* captains. For the execution at the end, the Plotter clearly felt it needful to retain the dramatists' crowd scene, but, having insufficient men, and requiring citizens who speak, he does not adopt the expedient of the Plotter of *1 Tamar Cam*: he swallows an improbability and brings on the boys.

If the Plotter's purposes are not understood, generalisations about the textual evidence of the manuscript plays – what one might suppose to be the bibliographical hard facts – can be as seriously misleading as the evidence to be derived from printed texts. Those purposes are likely to be as various in detail as the manuscripts and Plots that reveal them, but we may be sure that they all have one thing in common: they are all concerned with fitting together the play with an available cast of actors *that is in some sense finite*. The Plotter of *Barnavelt* would have found ready sympathy from the author who apologised to his audience for representing the battle of Agincourt with

> Five or six most vile and ragged foils
> Right ill-disposed in brawl ridiculous.

In order to estimate cast sizes, we shall pay particular attention to the rules and conditions under which actors double. But it is once again a curiosity of the enquiry that, if the documents we are concerned with had been lost, there would remain almost no trace in the literature of the period of the practice of doubling in the professional theatre. One man in his time may have played many parts, but that he may have played them in the same play is, as far as I have been able to discover, never suggested by the commonplace trope. There is the story of Tarleton having played the parts of both Dick and the Justice in *The Famous Victories of Henry V*, but this, of course, was memorable as an absurd feat of improvised clowning, for the two characters are on stage simultaneously. Bottom wants to double as the Lion in Shakespeare's glorious parody of an amateur troupe, but even he is restrained. For amateur players, however, publishers did produce texts offered for small casts that show, not always accurately, a proposed doubling pattern. Only two of these can be dated later than the opening of the Theatre in 1576: *Mucedorus* and *The Fair Maid of the West*. Professor Bevington seems to have believed, if I read him aright in *From 'Mankind' to Marlowe*, that such plays were printed for the use of professional troupes, although it seems doubtful if publishers would have found much of a market in that.[21] But he demonstrated convincingly, with the help of the later Plots, that the doubling of roles, firmly established in the Morality drama, was inherited as a native tradition of dramatic construction by the later theatre.

Soon after 1576 the city companies grew much larger than the four or six men and a boy or two who are assumed to have performed the Moralities, and the practical need for the doubling of roles became less intense; but the habit of representing the many by the few, and of writing plays in which the characters outnumbered the available actors, remained the natural mode for dramatists. We are here, however, no closer to precise numbers, and although I believe Bevington to be substantially correct, there is no convincing evidence outside the texts themselves that will tell us so. It may even be that he was misled about some early texts by the wily publishers, and that the analogy suggested by the four men and a boy who appear as the Cardinal's Men to play *Wit and Wisdom* in the manuscript play of *Sir Thomas More* is a creation forced upon the author by the casting exigencies of the latter play, just as the company of Sir Oliver Owlett's Men in *Histriomastix* is an entirely fanciful group who cannot even themselves tell how many they are.

Finally there are travellers' tales. In 1599, Dr Thomas Platter of Basle saw *Julius Caesar* played in London by 'approximately fifteen actors' (*mitt ohnegefahr 15 personen*).[22] The play-texts, imperfect though we have seen their testimony to be, may be used to reveal minimum casts, simply by counting the greatest number of actors on stage at any one moment. For *Julius Caesar* the number is, indeed, fifteen. This tells us little in itself, for, as Professor W. F. Ringler has shown in his casting analysis of several of Shakespeare's middle-period plays, the total needed for *Julius Caesar*, according to his method of counting, is sixteen.[23]

Basing his observations on Platter's journal, however, Ringler paved the way for the generation of information about the size of acting companies from the texts themselves. He took as his working principles only two propositions:

(i) that plural calls in the stage directions may be satisfied with the appearance of two actors,

(ii) that an actor does not leave the stage at the end of the scene and re-enter it immediately, either in a doubled role or in his own person, unless for some reason of the fable. This principle had been observed in the plays of the Shakespeare First Folio by William Poel.

Ringler thus arrived at a figure for a minimum cast that is one degree more sophisticated than the count of the greatest concentration of actors in a scene: a total derived from two or three scenes together where actors are blocked from re-entering or doubling by his second proposition.

It should be noted that if Ringler's second proposition is true for the post-Morality drama, as I believe it is, a marked change in dramatic perception must have occurred with the building of Burbage's Theatre. Bevington observed that actors in some Morality plays exit and re-enter, sometimes in changed roles, or at least with new names, without any intervening action having taken place. The sense of the personal identity of the actor must have been very slight, and the co-operation of the audience in the allegory very strong, if a quick change of beard, cap or cloak was understood as introducing a new character. Dr Leonard Glickfield has argued that the most developed Moralities even show a pattern of 'configurative doubling', that is to say, doubling in which the actor is intended to remain recognisably involved in his first role while doubling in his second. The characters are thus understood to be superimposed one upon the other for the purpose of making the allegorical point.[24]

It is diverting, as Peter Brook's celebrated production of *A Midsummer Night's Dream* demonstrated, to apply this convention of theatrical perception to the later secular drama, but his much-praised doubling of Theseus and Hippolyta with Oberon and Titania violates Ringler's second proposition and appeared to lead to no fresh insights. That this kind of symbolic inconsequentiality was not the practice of the secular Renaissance theatre requires only a moment's reflection on the frequency of disguise plots in both comedy and tragedy. A convention by which some of the characters on stage are disguised, but must, for the purposes of the story, be recognisably constant in their primary roles, while others, doubling in secondary roles, are in fact recognisable but asking to be taken as someone else would be mind-stoppingly confusing. The consequence is that in disguise plots there is very little doubling, except in the most minor roles.[25] The corollary is that Elizabethan actors, when doubling, attempted to conceal their original identity from the audience as far as possible.

Ringler followed Greg in assuming that boys may have doubled in adult male roles, and, counting in this way, found support for Platter's figure in a number of Shakespeare's middle-period plays. His inferences, however, fell short of a 'whole-field' investigation, just as Hardin Craig claimed those of the textual critics had done in the case of the bad Quartos, and although he was able to arrive at some true and amusing conclusions – such as that Titania's train in *A Midsummer Night's Dream* must have been composed largely of men – this aspect of his theory fails in extension.[26] It will not work for Shakespeare's plays outside this period, or for plays by other dramatists or other companies, except sporadically and by accident.

The alternative assumption, which, in my view, is the only one in accordance with the evidence of the Plots and with theatrical common sense, is that boys did not normally double with men, except in situations of extreme stress. A boy of thirteen years, young enough to play women's roles, simply does not *look* like a man, nor could he be expected to engage in the tasks of porterage that often fall to the adult cast. Any too hard-and-fast rule may, however, be out of place. We know that boys bred up as apprentices with the King's Men did stay with the company as men and that there may have been a period for each when the sex of the roles assigned to them was uncertain. In the Admiral's Plot of *Alcazar*, Dick Jubie doubles as a Queen and a Portuguese nobleman. The Young Lords in *All's Well that Ends Well* are almost certainly so called because it was necessary to allot the roles to boys. In the Plot of *1 Tamar Cam* (1602), Thomas Parsons, who had played only a Fury in *Alcazar*, two or three years earlier, and was then almost certainly a little boy, now plays an attendant, a guard and a spirit in the early scenes, but he may double as a nurse and finally turns up in the grand procession of peoples at the end as an Hermaphrodite. The cast-lists of the King's Men do not reveal such intermediate stages, but this may be because the accepted dating of the lists has been arrived at partly by observing the points at which boys begin to play adult roles.

If, then, we add one further proposition to Ringler's original two, namely:

(iii) that boys do not normally double in adult male roles,

we have an hypothesis, based on the simplest observations available to common sense, that will allow us to generate information from the playtexts themselves and to discover the limiting conditions under which the dramatists and the actors worked. The method is simply to invite the reader to turn Plotter and to work on the texts in the manner in which the Plots show him to have worked, but, as it were, in reverse. We are seeking the very information that was known to him when he began: that is to say, the actual composition of his company. Once again, there might seem to be very little chance of success. Given the great variety of origins posited for the texts, a 'block-buster' logic of this kind might well appear doomed to fail from the outset. It depends on the assumption that dramatists could and did *anticipate* the way in which the roles they created would be doubled in performance and wrote precisely to that prescription: that is to say, that they knew as well as the Plotter the composition of the company they were writing for.

There is, indeed, some tenuous external evidence that this was sometimes the case. Malone Society editors have observed in some prompt-books manuscript evidence suggesting that the author and the Plotter collaborated in the final sorting out of the roles. In addition there is the unique 'doodle' of a Plot on a scrap of paper in the Alleyn collection, made by Robert Shaa in November 1599 while listening to a reading of a play about the flight and capture of the Duke of Buckingham and the landing of Henry Richmond.[27] If Shaa's intention was anything other than daydreaming, it must have been to make a count of the cast. In this we have at least a faint suggestion that practical theatre men of the time followed the course I am about to ask the reader to consider.

By adopting Shaa's method we can discover in every play-text a 'limiting' scene or group of scenes that allows us to propose a numerical composition for the company for whom it was written. The results of the exercise, based only on the three propositions above, turn out to be statistically significant beyond the possibility of mere chance. I give an account of my findings up to 1642 in chapter 2, and list the figures for the casts of public theatre plays up to 1625 in the appendix. They may be repeated and checked by any reader with the time and patience to do so. Life being short, the figures are not, in all respects, as accurate as I should like, and there is, of course, a large element of subjectivity involved, partly owing to the maddening vagueness of the Elizabethans when using figures, and partly owing to the errors and corruptions in the texts themselves, but I believe they will stand up in the gross as objective facts.

The way in which doubling patterns may be derived from the texts, however, depends upon the peculiar logic imposed on Elizabethan dramatic construction by the form of the theatre itself. Much remains in dispute and much remains to be discovered about the architectural detail of particular theatres, but we may here take a short cut. On general principles, as well as on the evidence of the extant builders' contracts and of Wright's memory late in the century, we may assume the *stages* of the London theatres to have been constructed one on the model of another.[28] With the difference, perhaps, of a tower and a larger-than-usual discovery space at the Curtain, a 'tarrass' at the Swan, the absence of posts and 'heavens' at the Hope, a square auditorium at the Fortune (whose stage was certainly modelled on that of the first Globe), and a more than usually elaborate balcony at the Blackfriars, the basic form of the stages, stripped of the particular architecture of their tiring-house façades, was that of a large platform entered by a door on either side, with an upper and a lower discovery space in between. In essentials they reproduced the conditions of the market-place stages commonly seen in illustrations, and might have been replaced, as perhaps they were when country touring made it imperative, by two carpets slung on a pole beneath a balcony.

In its permanent and more sophisticated architectural forms, with or without the addition of flying machinery and trap-doors, this simple machine was, nevertheless, a powerful creator of illusion, and might have been adapted to a variety of theatrical modes. It differs in few essential respects from the stages of Greece and Rome and might have accommodated an imitative classical drama, observing the unities of time and action. It could be imagined both as the interior and exterior of a house and adapted to a kind of social realism employing the unity of place. With the help of scenic cloths, it was adapted towards the end of the period to local place realism. But experiments made in these directions brought about no fundamental revolution in style. Plays continued to be constructed on the principle of the alternation of groups of characters entering and leaving the stage to play episodes of no great length, and creating by their movement an illusion of a world, just outside the range of the audience's vision, in which time and place flowed with imaginative freedom at the bidding of the spoken word.

That there was a strict logic to the illusions this vanished stage was used to create is indeed the reason why we are able to return a statistically probable answer from the unlikely enterprise of counting actors in texts of widely diverse origin. The long endurance of the convention is, however, surprising, and arose, perhaps, from the conservatism of the players' organisations. These were tending to break down towards the end of the period as shares accumulated in fewer hands and younger actors were increasingly excluded from the profits of joint-stock partnership. But the King's Men, at least, appear to have maintained a complement of sharers, masters, and hired men, which, through many changes of personnel, and with occasional depletions from plague, remained virtually constant, from their foundation as the Chamberlain's Men in 1594, for forty-six years.

At the Restoration, the native tradition of performance by corporate associations of men and boys was briefly re-established.[29] The need to find an immediate repertory from the store of pre-revolutionary plays ensured that the size and perhaps the organisation of the new companies established by the royal patentees, Davenant and Killigrew, remained much as before, and new plays continued to be written to something like the old prescription. Even the innovation of scenery, as plays such as Ravenscroft's *The Careless Lovers* (1673) show, did not, for a time, create a revolution in play-making. The illusions created by the opposing doors of the great stage took time to fade from the imagination and practice of the writers of the new age, but the old company structure succumbed almost at once with the first appearance of women in female roles and the consequent destruction of the apprenticeship system. The co-operative joint-stock associations, moreover, were soon replaced, under the powers of the patentees, by a dominantly entrepreneurial system of managership. The new conditions of Restoration staging and theatre organisation were, no doubt, merely the logical outcome of the directions in which late Caroline theatre had been moving, but, once established, they became an almost impenetrable barrier behind which the methods of the giants of the former age could no longer be discerned or their purposes understood. It was not only the changed taste of the new age that soon dictated the wholesale rewriting of the plays that were still, in some sense, venerated as English classics.

1

The logic of entrances

All actors know the importance of entrances, but anyone who has experimented with productions on models of the Elizabethan scaffold comes to recognise their meaning in a particularly acute way. It is not an exaggeration to say that the action of an Elizabethan play *consists* of entrances. They are the means by which the story is told; the controllers of the illusion of time and place; the sign-posts for the understanding of the plot. There is nothing very strange in this: directors of cinema and television use the technique of cutting from one group of characters to another to tell a story in precisely the same way, but neither the Elizabethan playwright nor the Plotter enjoyed the freedom of the camera; their characters had to walk on and off stage in successive groups, rather, it sometimes seems, like the figures on a German town-hall clock.

What the actors were to do when they got on stage and how they were to make their exits appear to be matters of less concern to the Plotter, at any rate as far as making a record went. These matters appear to have been governed largely by the spoken text. Some Plots do not mark exits at all, and, even in prompt-books, exits are frequently overlooked, just as they often are in printed texts. Stage action is almost never described, although in many cases it must have been elaborate: the Plotter merely records the entrancces and the properties that are to be carried on. In the Plot of *Alcazar*, for example, the fourth dumb-show is clearly an elaborate scene. The square backets in the text below represent the Plotter's deletions; the words within curly brackets are conjectural.

Enter the Presenter : to him :
{4} Domb shew
Enter a {ba}nquett br{ought} in by
mr Hunt & w. Cartwr{ight : to} the
banqvett enter Sebastian : Muly
mahamet Duke of Auero : & Stukeley
to them De{a}th :& {3} F{uries} mr
Sam Ro: Tailor {George &} Parson{s }
one wth blood to Dy{ppe li}ghts : one
{w}th Dead mens head{s} in dishes : an{o}ther
{w}th Dead mens bon{es} to the{m} w{ar}
{w. kenda}ll [D] {weapons : Dick} Jub{ie}
{& a}Furie {wth bloody clothes} exeunt

But it is only from the Presenter's speech in the text that we are able to make anything of the spectacle:

> Now hardned is this haplesse heathen prince,
> And strengthned by the armes of Portugall,
> This Moore, this murtherer of his progenie.
> And warre and weapons now, and bloud and death
> Wait on the counsels of this cursed king:
> And to a bloudie banket he inuites
> The braue Sebastian and his noble peeres.

The Plotter of *Alcazar* is, nevertheless, uncommonly informative. He does occasionally locate characters on stage, as when he records the ghosts of Muly Mahamet's victims 'lying' (or crying) 'behind the Curtaines', or when he places the Moore's pages 'on each side' of his chariot; or, if Greg's reconstruction of the last scene is correct, when he indicates the mood of an entrance with 'Enter by Torchlight.' Otherwise his object appears to be to marshall his actors on to the stage, to fill and empty the scene, and to keep track, as he does so, of the actors who are in use and those who are still available in the tiring-house. Usually he will employ the standard formulas of stage directions also found in all the texts : 'Enter ... ; to him ... ; to them ... ; exeunt'. He uses 'manet the rest', or 'manet ...' followed by a character name, after medial exits, and, for re-entrances of the same character, the unusual: 'enter ... a gaine', which is also to be found in the prompt-book of *Believe as You List*. Above all, he twice assembles confronting groups of characters with the expression: 'At one dore ... and at another ... ' and thus gives us the clue to the possibility of meeting with success in plotting from the texts.

William Poel long ago advocated the advantages of restoring Shakespeare to his native scaffold. There is no doubt that much Shakespearean dialogue goes blank on a scenic, proscenium stage, where it has ceased to be functional, but comes alive in such productions when it is subliminally understood as a guide to the working of the illusions of time and place. My own attempts to follow Poel's lead with student productions in the fifties in the great hall of the University of Western Australia, however, involved at first a somewhat painful revision of my expectations. The absence of scenery on our fit-up imitation of the Swan stage, I was, of course, prepared for, but all the things a conscientious young director who had read up his Granville Barker and Wilson Knight then came prepared with to the theatre – the careful plotting of a variety of entrances; the choreographed groupings; the tailoring of the text and the transposition and running together of scenes in order to build up tension in the manner of a well made play – simply had to be thrown into the waste-paper basket.

The stage itself imposed its own order and discipline on the performance. The two great doors through which successive files of actors had to march on, now from one side, now from the other, came to seem like inexorable logicians, the guardians of unalterable theatrical law. It was they who demanded that the text, cut and stitched together so carefully to make the action flow and the poetry to sing on a proscenium stage, be restored, because, in their view of the matter, it was functional and necessary. They re-imposed upon the play its original shape, which I had been at such pains to replace with false inventions of my own. It was they who insisted that the action had to flow continuously and that an interval was permissible only with their sternest disapproval. As one grew to understand them better, they plainly told me I was irrelevant.

Was it then possible that, after the prompt-book had been finalised, the directions it contained, so cryptic and even defective by modern standards, might have served with very little intervention to direct the performance? Could the universal reticence of Elizabethan stage-directions be taken to indicate that regular conventions of entrances, exits, and stage-groupings existed, and were so well understood that they needed only the barest recording?

Even Alleyn's part for Orlando, which appears to have been annotated in his own hand, contains none of the positional markings and scribbled annotations that are typical of a modern player's script. It is as reticent as the other documents of theatre, except for the few directions such as 'N. victus' and 'Oliver victus', which are necessary as action-cues for Orlando's speeches.[1] The laconic directions 'pugnant' that usher in the duels are far short of the elaborate directions in Q: 'He fighteth first with one and then with another, and ouercomes them both', and 'They fight a good while and then breath.' But there is no cue at all for Orlando's disguised, silent entry into the final scene about thirty-seven lines after it begins. Alleyn need have been able to carry in his head no more than a modern actor, but, in order to make a correct entrance here, he must clearly have been able to *hear* the dialogue and to follow its drift, for the direction for his entrance in the text is placed merely for convenience between speeches, and Orlando's first lines reply to words uttered before that point.

A theatre that worked by well-understood convention and the intelligent co-operation of the actors with the implications of the spoken text itself may seem to be a fantasy, but I believe it to be closer in accord with the evidence we have than any model provided by the practice of the director-dominated theatre of later times. What gives it credibility is the general testimony to a stage that was entered through two doors, or from two sides.

This testimony probably now needs no defence, but at the time I began my investigation the theories of Professor Leslie Hotson,[2] and, in particular, his notion of composite locational staging in the public theatre were gaining some acceptance. Although based on evidence about the contemporary Spanish theatre that has not stood the test of subsequent enquiry, it could not then be confidently refuted, and even won some measure of assent in the picture of standing set-pieces placed on the outer stage that Professor Glynne Wickham espoused in his *Early English Stages* (1963).

Such a kind of staging was not, of course, unknown. It exists in the early play *The Most Virtuous and Godly Susanna*, in the plays of Lyly written for Paul's Boys, in University plays and in the late Morality *Liberality and Prodigality*. The stage-directions of the latter indicate very clearly that it was designed to be played on an arena stage surrounded by 'sedes' or locations, but both the form of those directions, and their logic, according to Ringler's propositions, distinguish them very sharply from the directions in the public-theatre texts. That they had not been so distinguished is perhaps to be accounted for on two grounds. First, that it is commonly assumed that about four-fifths of the plays of the period have been lost to us, so that generalisations appearing to limit the possible variety and scope of theatrical innovation are suspect. Second, that the soberest scholars have been reluctant to submit their imaginations to the discipline of the evidence, and wholly to discard nineteenth-century concepts of a theatre whose stock-in-trade is scenic effect and novelty. For how could it have been possible that the adult companies followed, for fifty years, methods that were more austere and less innovative and spectacular than those of the children's theatres and the academies, in whose productions multiple scene-setting and even elaborate painted houses were sometimes employed? Nevertheless, I believe that such was the case. Was Ben Jonson declaring contempt for the tastes of his audience or received opinion about the proper ends of the drama when he told them:

> I'd have you wise
> Much rather by your ears than by your eyes?[3]

At any rate, the dramatists at the Phoenix and later Blackfriars, contrasting their practice with the spectacles at the Red Bull and Paris Garden, frequently echoed his view.

The public stage, of course, lacked neither novelty nor striking inventions. Within the discovery-space between the entrance doors, scenic effects were, to a limited extent, achieved. These were provided by large movable properties, and perhaps, on occasion, by painted hangings, but the properties called for are remarkably few and remarkably standard. Their number is virtually exhausted by the Inventory lists of the Admiral's Men recorded in Henslowe's Diary for 1598, and they were clearly used time and again is successive plays.[4] The larger items, the grassy banks, tombs, altars, rocks, shop-counters, and 'degrees' for the senate house, were commonly set up behind the curtain and revealed when required. Interiors are sometimes suggested by initial 'revealings' behind the curtains and texts sometimes specify who is to draw them. Beds, too, are sometimes revealed within the central opening, but sometimes they are 'thrust out' with their occupants. Studies may have been more elaborately composed, for the direction 'Enter in his study' is rather common, but there are instances where the study is clearly 'above' or indicated by properties carried onto the outer stage itself. Thrones and chairs of state may often have been revealed in the inner stage, although they, too, are sometimes carried on. Entrances and exits by trap-door ('the ground') are often implied in the texts, and may have served oftener than we can detect to represent prison scenes, although there is sometimes mention of a 'grating' for that purpose. But traps, like the squeaking thrones that did, if rarely, descend 'the boys to please', may have been luxuries and can hardly have existed in all theatres and inn-yards.

Apart from these more spectacular modes of entering and leaving the stage by flying upwards or sinking into the earth – effects that tended to be less and less employed as time advanced – the great mass of stage-directions bear witness to the dominance of my two great logicians, the stage doors. The common forms that record them are: 'Enter at one door ... and at the other'; 'Enter at one door ... and at another'; 'Enter at each side of the stage'; 'Enter severally'; 'Enter at either side.' Not all plays, of course, introduce simultaneous entrances of this kind, and in many the presence of doors goes unnoticed, unless they must be locked, or unless a character enters 'listening at the door' or the like. In the fifteen manuscript plays regarded by Greg as undoubted prompt copies, seven contain the wording 'at one door ... and another' and four of the seven also have the more positive form 'at one door ... and at the other'. To these we may add *The Soddered Citizen* which was annotated by Knight, and must have been considered for prompt use, whether or not it was ever used. The early play *John a Kent and John a Cumber*, which is in Munday's hand, employs both forms, as do many printed texts. It is of interest to note that the manuscript of Fletcher's *The Honest Man's Fortune*, which is in Knight's hand throughout, contains references to the two doors that are obliterated in the revised directions of the 1647 Folio. That other prompt copies are silent about the existence of the doors is simply because they contain no simultaneous entrances.

There exist, nevertheless, a few directions that suggest the use of three doors. They occur in the 1615 Q of Heywood's *If You Know Not Me You Know Nobody*, in *Eastward Ho* (I, i), in the prologue to *A Warning for Fair Women*, in *Patient Grissel* (III, ii), and in Heywood's *The English Traveller*. The prologue to Munday's *The Downfall of Robert Earl of Huntingdon* begins with the direction: 'At every door all the Players run out.' At the Red Bull multiple entrances seem to have been not infrequent: it appears to have been possible to enter that stage from beneath, or 'at every corner'. The Plot of *2 Seven Deadly Sins* also records Gorboduc's entry 'in the midst between' his two sons. This may imply an entrance through a central door, because Ferrex and Porrex have entered 'severall wayes', but it is doubtful, for there is already a tent permanently set up on stage with Henry VI asleep in it, and to this tent actors enter 'at one dore ... and at an other'.

The vagueness of Elizabethan usage does not allow us to assume with confidence that 'at another' and 'at the other' mean exactly the same thing, but we can reasonably conclude that simultaneous entrances from three or more directions were exceptional. Sometimes it is possible to observe a playwright coping with the resistance of the two-door structure to the illusion he wishes to create. In *The Silent Woman*, for example, Jonson has to set the scene for the gulling of Dawe and La Foole by having Truewit 'create' the geography of the house of the Collegiate ladies in which he is already standing and which the audience has so far understood in a different way:

Doe you obserue this gallerie, or rather lobby, indeed? Here are a couple of studies, at each end one ... DAW and LA-FOOLE, which of them comes out first, will I seize on; you two shall be the *chorus* behind the arras, and whip out between the *acts* and speak ...

Thus a programme for action is set up, in which the central entrance, or discovery space, will be used unconventionally when the normal entrance doors, temporarily representing 'studies', are 'blinded' and unavailable. No doubt it was able to pass without gross improbability because eavesdropping behind the arras is such a frequent theatrical trope. This play was written for the Children of the Revels at Whitefriars in 1609, but something like this passage would, I believe, have been necessary in any other theatre for directing the illusion of the domestic geography.[5]

Further analysis may perhaps be able to distinguish more closely the particular furnishings of different stages. It suffices to say that even if, in some theatres, there may have been two doors grouped together at each side of the stage, as directions such as 'Enter ... listening at the door' may seem to suggest, I have come across no suggestion that paired doors, if they existed, were ever distinguished from each other as *locations*.

In praising Jonson for having banished the imaginative excesses of the stage, Jasper Mayne's memorial verses, published in 1638, also, although less justly, pay tribute to his restoration of the proper discipline of its binary logic:[6]

Thy scene was free from monsters; no hard plot
Call'd down a God t'untie th'unlikely knot:
The stage was still a stage, two entrances
Were not two parts o'th world, disjoined by seas.
Thine were land tragedies, no prince was found
To swim a whole scene out, then o'th stage drown'd
Pitch'd fields, as Red Bull wars, still felt thy doom;
Thou laid'st no sieges to the music room.

However much classical sensibilities were strained by the free flowing of time and place that the two entrances permitted, the doors impose an imaginative logic upon the audience's expectations, even in 'pitch'd fields' and 'sieges', and often justify situations in Shakespeare where the unities are violently transgressed and which even the conventionless modern theatre cannot always rescue from absurdity.

In *Richard II*, for example, the telescoped time-scheme of the sequence between Bolingbroke's departure for exile and the report of his return to England fails markedly to satisfy our post-Ibsenite sense of probability. It is clearly quite deliberate on Shakespeare's part and no amount of editorial emendation can rectify it. It begins with Aumerle's report to Richard (I, i) that he has just taken his farewell of Bolingbroke 'at the next highway'. Bushy then enters as a messenger from Ely House to report Gaunt's grievous sickness, 'suddenly taken'. He has come 'post-haste', and the king leaves the stage praying (if hypocritically) that his party may make haste to arrive. Gaunt and York immediately enter as if in Ely House (II, i), impatiently awaiting the king's coming, and Richard shortly afterwards enters to his confrontation with his dying uncle. So far, the king's approach has been represented in natural time, that is, in not much less than the events represented would actually have taken, and the confrontation scene itself is played in real time. But after Gaunt is dead and the king has left the stage, Northumberland immediately pulls from his bosom treasonable correspondence reporting Bolingbroke's return to the English coast and his approaching arrival at Ravenspur, thus leaping the story over four years of his exile, when all the textual time signatures suggest that he has hardly had time to reach Rochester on his way to Dover.

I am not sure that this would not have strained credulity somewhat, even in 1597, but what makes it possible for a playwright to compose his story in this way, and to get on with the business, is precisely the imaginative importance given by the two doors to entrances and exits. Because the stage has been cleared once and a major entrance and two major exits have taken place, our imaginations may allow time to have elapsed, even though our information is that no lapse of time is possible.

The doors are thus the systole and diastole of the great heart-beat of the Elizabethan stage as it fills and empties, fills and empties, allowing our imaginations free play in the unoccupied spaces, until at the end the actors depart and the great platform lies bare. No wonder if, in the minds of both dramatists and spectators, it stood as the inevitable metaphor of life and death.

It is this heart-beat that assures us of the structural primacy of the scene. In printed plays and manuscripts, of course, the division into scenes often shows up less clearly than the division into acts. Scenes are the natural division points in the action and the registers of the passing of time. They do not need elaborate notation. A cleared stage may be indicated by the direction 'Exeunt' or 'Exeunt omnes', supported merely by the following direction for an entrance. Acts, on the other hand, require notation because they are *un*natural divisions. They register the arrival of a variety of interruptions to the narrative: the appearance of a dumb-show; an interlude of music; an unusually long pause. In authorial manuscripts, Stage-revisers often change the positions of acts in a seemingly arbitrary manner, without consideration of the continuities or pauses in the progress of the story. These interpolations may sometimes also be seen in the printed texts, as in the well-known direction in the Folio text of *A Midsummer Night's Dream* – 'They sleep all the Act' – where, after the exit of Oberon and Titania, the lovers must be left on-stage during the musical interlude introduced after 1608 into the unbroken sequence of the Quarto text. Scene breaks do show up in the Plots, in which they are distinguished as segments by the line ruled under each, and they are sometimes marked by Stage-revisers in prompt-books with the word 'clear'.

The influence of the scenic structure on the sense of place may have varied widely at the whim or need of the playwright, as Jasper Mayne's verses, among much other neo-classical commentary, suggest, but it was not just a matter of instructing the imaginations of the audience to picture Illyria or Elysium. Stage-revisers sometimes did make elaborate alterations to playwrights' scene divisions. The case of Heywood's *The Captives*, although a relatively late example, is instructive.

In this manuscript the reviser has added notes at all but one of the points where the stage is clear. He has added some not anticipated by the dramatist, obliterated two by the addition of sound cues and removed others by re-writing the text. Thus, the dramatist's '*Actus 2s Scena Pra.*' has been overborne by the reviser's '*Act* : *2 contynewed*', without 'clere' being marked; the reason being that, although the actors change, time and place are here continuous. '*Thunder*' also bridges II, i and II, ii for the same reason, and II, iii is heavily cut and run together with them. Heywood did not mark scenes for IV, iv and IV, v, for the stage is technically occupied on both occasions by the body, or more probably the dummy, of a murdered Friar; but the reviser has this time marked 'clere' in both places, for new actors enter and the scene is cleverly persuaded to change. Finally the reviser inserted a cleared stage at V, ii, where Heywood appears not to have intended it. The reasons are of interest.

Heywood carefully marked his scenes in the conventional way, at the points where the stage is actually empty. Because of the ingenious impression of locale created in this piece, however, the reviser has made things a little easier to follow by marking the scenes only at those points where the cleared stage corresponds with a change of place. In Acts IV and V there is an excellent comic invention by which, with the help of a ladder to the upper stage, the body of Friar John is twice removed and returned to the identical place on stage, to the consternation of his supposed and actual murderers. The audience is to imagine the body being hoisted over and left now on one side and now on the other of a wall (represented by the stage balcony) that divides the Lord D'Averne's courtyard from the Priory next door. Thus, although the body prevents the stage being technically clear, a new set of characters enters to it in each of its imagined locations and the Plotter marks a scene.

In Act V, however, it appears from the continuous succession of entrances and exits that the dramatist had abandoned his imaginary wall and he brings in his Friars for their final entrance to what the reviser clearly felt to be the 'wrong' side, the Lord D'Averne's courtyard. At some small sacrifice to the characterisation, the Plotter can avoid this minor break in the illusion of place simply by clearing the stage, and he does so, thus seeming to return the Friars to their own domain.

There could be no surer indication that the logic of the entrances exerted its influence on the sense of place as much as upon that of time. It is small wonder that the popular playwrights of the age, with such a co-operative illusion machine at their disposal, should have felt no need for the more consistent observance of the unities that Jonson dogmatically strove to impose upon his art and his audience. If a theory had been demanded of them they would, no doubt, have pointed to the theatre and said 'Look about you.' Dekker's advice to gallants in Paul's Walk speaks for them:

And first observe your doors of entrance, and your *Exit*, not much unlike the plaiers at the Theaters, keeping your *Decorum*, even in phantasticality. As for example: if you prove to be a *Northerne* Gentelman, I would wish you to passe through the North doore, more often (especially) than any of the other: and so according to your countries, take note of your entrances.[7]

Dekker's doors are the doors of St Pauls, not of the theatre, but his satiric picture of the fantastics' behaviour bears witness to the decorum of place created by the entrance doors of the stage and tends to support the opinion of William Poel that

Actors understood the dramatists' structure and regarded it as their business to preserve it, for unless the plot [i.e. the fable or narrative line] were adhered to confusion would have arisen in the matter of entrances and easily caused the continuity of movement to be interrupted.[8]

The question remains, by what means did the actors themselves understand the stage-directions? An actor might reasonably ask: 'Enter at one door. Yes. But at *which*?' Hardly a single manuscript or printed text can answer. Rare directions are given when for some reason of plot characters must pass each other on their paths on and off the stage, but none of those that I have found mark whether the left or right door is involved. Alleyn's actor's scroll, like the Plots, notes entrances with properties, such as 'Enter wth a mans legge', but gives no clue as to their direction. The only example of directional entrances I have found is in Thomas Nabbes's *Covent Garden*, printed in 1632, for which I shall offer an explanation presently.

Are we here again in the presence of a convention so well understood that it requires no noting? It is suggestive of a positive answer that the directions for 'revealings' in and exits through the discovery space are often specific and circumstantial, and thus imply, as does Truewit's speech quoted above, that this was the exceptional mode of access to the stage. One discovers in performance that actors are, indeed, easily able to follow what Dekker calls the *decorum* – that is, the imaginative logic – that the doors impose on the audience's expectations, but in reverse. The tiring-house where the actors await their cues is simply a looking-glass world. Frantic though they may be with changes of costume and the collecting of properties, so long as they can hear what is happening on stage, they are still participating in that logic, and truly involved in *play*.

For the most part dramatic narratives are so constructed that the sense of place enables an actor to follow a simple rule that he re-enters the stage through the door he last left by. That ensures, as Dekker says, that on the whole – 'more often (especially)' – he becomes identified with his entering side. But as the illusion of place changes this logic evaporates from time to time and the actor has to think again.

The major actors, at least, had time to reflect between entrances. William Poel accurately observed that of the plays written wholly by Shakespeare, with the exception of *The Tempest*, 'all are so constructed that characters who leave the stage at the end of one episode are never the first to re-appear...nor even does a character who ends one of the acts marked in the folio ever begin one that follows'.[9] This is also generally true of the public plays of the period as a whole, except that 'immediate' re-entry after an act break becomes more frequent as the intervals for music became more firmly established after 1608. Minor actors may have had to listen more intently to prepare for their entrances in doubled roles, but, once on stage, the logic of the dialogue will commonly direct the direction of their exit.

The way in which actors can follow almost automatically the place-logic of entrances may be illustrated from the sequence from *Richard II*, previously discussed. Working backwards, we see that in the second scene (II, i) Gaunt's death is reported almost immediately after his exit. Since the action is played in real time, we are persuaded to believe that Gaunt dies in the adjoining room. The geography of Ely House is thus imagined to consist of a door leading to Gaunt's bedchamber, an ante-chamber where the dialogue takes place, and a second door leading to the outer entrance. Which way round we see this arrangement will be determined by the door through which the king and his party leave the stage at the end of the previous scene. It will not matter much. Suppose he leaves by the left door. Gaunt and York must then enter from the right: otherwise they will appear to have met the king's party in the passage outside, as indeed they would actually have done.

The interior of Ely House itself is established as a location by Gaunt's entrance, in the manner well known to Dekker, and the actor playing Richard will immediately understand that if he is to visit that place he must come from the outside, that is, through the other door, which is, in this case, the door he last left by. The dialogue gives him every assistance, for although the direction in the Folio brings Gaunt on 'sicke', it mentions neither the sick-beds nor the litters introduced by modern directors, nor any attendants except York. His first words, 'Will the king come... ?', and York's reply, 'Vex not yourself, nor strive not with your breath', are natural signals to convey the anxiety of an old man feebly pacing with his brother's aid towards the door through which he expects the king to arrive.

At the end of the confrontation, Gaunt commands that he be conveyed to bed and he is helped off. Naturally this will be to the right, for the king's entrance has established the left entrance as the 'front' door. Northumberland almost immediately enters from the right to report Gaunt's death and only the most insensitive royal party could now use that door for their general exit: it would seem as if they had recklessly trampled over the old man's body.

The king's exit, and the subsequent exits of Northumberland, Ross, and Willoughby, will therefore be through the left door; but thereafter the illusion of Ely House is broken. In order to avoid a pause in the action, the enterer to the next scene must come through the right-hand door, Gaunt's door, and it will be as well if this is a character whose concerns are different enough from those of the previous scene to make a change of location instantly recognisable. It is, in fact, the queen. In this instance, the breaking of the illusion of place is very much eased by the dialogue of the three lords who remain on stage in II, i. By broadening the imaginative scope with lists of England's wrongs under Richard, and creating a sense of impending action off stage, their speeches tend strongly to delocalise the end of that scene.

Actors can commit to memory much more complicated directions than these, but in the conditions of Elizabethan repertory playing the logic of the doors must have been helpful and perhaps essential. In the month of January 1596, for example, the Admiral's Men played on every day except Sundays and presented fourteen plays. Six were given only one performance in the month and no play was presented more than four times. The shortest interval between the repetition of any single play was three days and the next shortest five. Although all except one were old plays, this record represents an achievement that would almost certainly be beyond the capacities of actors in the modern theatre. It can only have been made possible by reliance on well understood conventions of stage-behaviour such as those I have outlined above.

In these conditions it is easy to see why the experiment of Thomas Nabbes in *Covent Garden* (1633) was not repeated. This play, as the last words of the assembled cast declare, 'hath a new foundation'. It was a riposte to *The Weeding of Covent Garden* by Brome, Jonson's disciple and former servant, and was an attempt to outdo Brome's play in the observance of the unities of place and action, but appears to have received only a 'partiall allowance' on the stage.

Nabbes carefully marks in the direction of entrances from the right, middle, and left, and on the balcony, and contrives to clear his stage only at the act breaks, changing the location at those points. Thus, two acts represent the outside of Worthy's house, two its interior, and one the inside of a tavern. His description of the doors as 'scaenes' appears to be an interesting bit of antiquarianism: there is no suggestion of the actual use of scenery. The exterior of the house is established by the appearance of characters on the balcony, the interior by the middle entrance alone. The inside of the tavern is shown by entries solely through the left entrance, while the right door is reserved for the street and sparingly used in the first and third acts only. This unfamiliar convention puts great strain on the management of the story and cannot be consistently maintained. In Act III a vestige of Dekker's decorum is maintained when characters must leave the stage in different directions. The left door (the tavern door) is then used to suggest the *way* to the tavern, but the decorum is broken completely when Warrant is forced to enter as if in the street, on his way to the cutlers, through the middle door, entrances through which formerly established the interior of Worthy's house.

Jonson's lesson in maintaining a unity of place by 'revolving' the stage about a central point of interest (the alchemist's furnace; the fair-booths) as he does in *The Alchemist* and *Bartholomew Fair*, had not been learned, and perhaps could only have been achieved with the peculiar linearity of the rogues-and-gulls plots of those plays. Nabbes masters something like this technique in the first three acts of *Covent Garden*, but his unsuccessful attempt to solve the problem by the regular use of the middle entrance and the consequential need to indicate the direction of every entrance bear eloquent testimony to the inescapable imaginative dominance of the two-door convention.

On a stage where the progress of the story is advanced by the momentary clearing of the stage and where continuous playing is the rule, the provision of two or more sets of characters is not a matter of artistic choice but of necessity. The rule observed by Poel that whoever exits cannot immediately re-enter means, of course, that someone else must. Unity of action was therefore always certain to be a lost cause in this theatre, and, even in plays that seek to preserve it, the splitting of characters into groups or teams who alternate scene by scene is strikingly apparent. Although full-blown sub-plots are rare, there is, nevertheless, introduced into every Elizabethan play some subsidiary strand of interest or characterisation that diverges from the main issues, for the sake of allowing the actors to circulate and the story to be told. This is not to say that we should take no heed of Madeleine Doran's opinion – echoing Pope's great metaphor comparing Shakespeare's plays to Gothic cathedrals – that the lust for variousness, characteristic of medieval art, is at the root of Elizabethan theatrical taste; rather, it helps to explain why that taste was able to be silently indulged against the grain of all contemporary dramatic theory.[10] The dramatists could do no other than conduct their story by the alternation and linear suppression of groups of characters, which, as Bevington has shown, was a direct inheritance from the techniques of the psychomachia drama. Though largely de-allegorised, those techniques were now reinforced in the secular theatre by the very form of the stage itself.

The simplest method of separating major entrances was, of course, to call in the clown, 'like to the old Vice' of the Moralities. Manuscript evidence, such as the prompt-book of *John of Bordeaux*, suggests that early plays may sometimes have been handed over to the clown of the company, after the serious parts had been composed, for him to write in 'pleasant mirth' of his own devising. When a play was published this material might be disowned, as the publisher of *Tamburlaine* tells us he has removed 'some fond and frivolous gestures far unmeet for the matter'. A useful alternative to the clown is the display of a 'humour' character or group of characters (a technique perfected by Jonson) and often used to introduce topicality to remote settings or historical themes, as, for example, the display of the humours of Ancient Pistol in Shakespeare's *2 Henry IV*, or of the 'Roarers' in Marston's *The Insatiate Countess*, or of the fatuous exchanges of Fletcher's Executioners in the manuscript of *Sir John van Olden Barnavelt*. Unskilful writers, like the author of *Two Lamentable Tragedies*, might simply alternate two strands of action that have no connection in time or place, and none at all except that the contemporary London story and the Italian version of the Babes in the Wood alternately represented in that play are both concerned with the discovery of murder. Experienced writers, however, more commonly alternate groups of interconnected characters. These will have independent life-lines of interest, developed with various degrees of fullness, as, for example, the story of Lorenzo and Jessica in *The Merchant of Venice*, which may be taken to represent the smallest kind of sub-plot; or the madhouse episodes in *The Changeling*, which constitute an anecdote in parallel and contrast with the moral development of the main plot; or the Gloucester family in *King Lear*, whose history is fully explored and whose life-lines are interwoven, both in actuality and in the tightest thematic way, with those of the main characters.

The form of the stage thus gave rise to what we may call the 'extended' plot. It is really a misnomer, for the most part, to speak of 'sub-plots' or 'double-plots' in Elizabethan plays, and quite mistaken to maintain the nineteenth-century theory, still not quite extinct with modern critics, that the mixture of comedy and tragedy that the extended plot admitted, and indeed, invited, was a means of dividing interest in the theatre between the pit and the gallery.

If, then, it is reasonable to conclude that plotting an action by the alternation and suppression of groups was a virtual necessity, imposed upon the playwrights' imaginations by the two openings giving access to the stage, and enabling them to write, as their predecessors in the Moralities had done, for casts of characters much greater than the number of actors at their disposal, it is also possible to suggest some rules for the doubling of roles that will allow us to generate estimates of the size of the companies. We shall need, in fact, no more than Ringler's and Poel's two propositions, with the addition of a third (the probability that boys do not normally double as men).

Baldwin's conclusion that, in the company of the King's Men, 'the play was regularly fitted to the company', seems at first view less than reassuring, however, when we turn to the actual Plots associated with

Strange's Men and the Admiral's company. If we list the adult actors, there are, in the Plot of *Frederick and Basilea*, only twelve accounted for before it becomes necessary to call in the gatherers from the stage doors, and the cast never exceeds twelve. In *Tamar Cam*, sixteen players appear in addition to the boys, but two important members of the company take part only in the final two scenes, and gatherers are called in for the last in considerable numbers. The fragmentary Plots of *Troilus and Cressida* and *Fortune's Tennis* appear to list sixteen actors, but they are so damaged that any conclusion must be uncertain. In *Alcazar*, where the doubling is uncommonly fast and furious, no additional help is called for, but male roles are seemingly allotted to one boy and possibly to two. Even then there are absurdities in the doubling pattern, apparent without the help of the text, that show the company to have been particularly hard pressed. One thing is apparent, however, from the application of our propositions, namely that in all the reasonably complete Plots the cast is shown to be finite by the limiting scenes, and that as soon as a specific number of characters is blocked from entering by the operation of our three propositions, one or more actors must change roles.

It would be disastrous for our enterprise if there were evidence in the Plots of the 'splitting' of roles, that is, the sequential adoption of a single role by different actors. In the manuscript of *Believe as You List* this does, in fact, occur: the Plotter assigns three different actors at various times to the minor role of Demetrius, but he does this rather as a matter of convenience than necessity. The roles of the attendants in that play are scarcely characterised and easily reassigned. I believe splitting of roles to be exceptional. The Plots show no sign of it, even in situations of emergency. They do, however, show a practice I shall call 'dodging', that is, returning an actor to his original role after he has doubled in another. This practice may also be observed in the manuscripts and may be inferred from some printed plays in which, without it, senior actors would be underworked and idle for long periods while the hired men would be pressured beyond reason.

The curiosity of the Plot of *Alcazar* is, indeed, that although the Plotter is clearly very hard pressed, he frequently appears to have actors standing idle. He is forced to 'dodge' even some of his major actors, and to create minor absurdities. One of these is his doubling of the Spanish Ambassadors with the very Portuguese lords who are sent to fetch them. Yet four or five actors who might, according to our theory, have leaped to the colours at this point are unused. It was this semblance of plenty in the midst of dearth that confirmed Greg in his *a priori* assumption that the text of 1594 was a version of the play cut down for country touring, and that another, fuller version of the text and a larger cast had been available to the Plotter in 1598. He thus constructed a fanciful Plot for the 1594 cast consisting of twelve men and four boys, on the equally unbased assumption that such was the size of a touring company in the plague years. On this unstable foundation, which, in fact, breaks every one of our three rules, to the first two of which Greg himself assented, and which does not in actuality reduce the adult cast below fifteen, he proceeded to criticise the text by comparison with the Plot.

Astonishingly, Greg had overlooked the fact that in this play, where four distinct groups of actors alternate scene by scene, the first two representing Europeans and the others opposing factions of the kingdom of Morocco, one of the latter groups is always debarred from doubling in the European scenes, which are those most desperately in need of cast, because, as we are plainly told both in the text and in the Plot, they are black. In the Plot they are described as 'Moors', henchmen of the text's 'negro Moor', Muly Mahamet. Those of the other Moorish party are Berbers or Barbarians: that is to say, 'white', or as the Plot of *Tamar Cam* has it, 'olive-coloured' Moors. They do double freely in the Plot with Europeans. They are never described as 'Moors' in the Plot, and almost certainly not in the text. Their leader, Abdelmelec (Muly Molocco) is called 'this brave Barbarian lord'. The members of the black party double in the Plot's dumb-shows appropriately as devils, just as, in the text, they are first introduced as 'deuils coted in the shapes of men'.

When this inhibition is understood, many other aspects of the Plot become interpretable that were incomprehensible to Greg, and even its physical reconstruction becomes more plausible. Fragments of the decayed right-hand column of the Plot, for which Greg could find no place, turn out to fit naturally into an alternative reconstruction. The text of *Alcazar* then appears in another light. It has an almost unique characteristic among printed texts: it notes three doubled roles by retaining the original character names of the doubling actors in the speech-prefixes for their reappearance in secondary roles. Thus, Hercules and Jonas, English Captains, followers of the notorious Thomas Stukeley, are forced to turn into the disaffected Italian Captains who later murder him. Zareo, viceroy of Algiers and chief lieutenant of the white Barbarian party, is, likewise, forced to dodge as a minor member of the opposing Moorish forces. Although the scene is lost from the Plot, it is certain that, in the case of the English Captains, the Plotter would have had no recourse but to follow suit. In the case of Zareo, there is a discrepancy betwen the Plot and the text. The text clearly regards him as a Moor, that is to say, black-skinned, and doubles him in Muly Mahamet's party, where he does not properly belong, but the Plotter doubles him with a Portuguese lord. He must have been the readier to do so, because he cannot, or does not, provide a single Moor to accompany Zareo in the very first scene where the text calls for them rather conspicuously:

> *Sound Drummes and trumpets, and enter Abdilmelec with Calsepius Bassa and his gard, and Zareo a Moore with souldiers.*
> Alhaile Argerd Zareo and yee Moores,
> Salute the frontires of your natiue home

Greg was forced to the odd conclusion that, while his hypothetical reviser of the 1594 text for a small cast must have been even less able to provide the Moors, he had nevertheless continued to copy the author's lavish directions, and left standing in the text these conspicuous lines in which they are addressed.

It will now be convenient if I anticipate my own conclusion, which is that the behaviour both of the dramatist (or at least of the text of 1594) and of the Plotter is explicable in the light of the three propositions I have advanced, and that their understanding of the structural problems of presentation was virtually identical. The printed text shows itself to be so prescient that, if the Plotter were not working from that text, he was working from a text so close to it as makes little difference.

Apart from the addition of some spectacular effects, what he did was simply to change, in one seemingly trivial respect, the disposition of the cast as the playwright imagined it. He has kept the playwright's black Zareo *white*. For this he has to pay a remarkably heavy and complex penalty, including, finally, the omission of a whole scene; but the principles on which he did so are precisely those the dramatist would have understood. He wanted, presumably, as any modern director might do, to keep his team allegiances clear by colour co-ordinating his cast, and did not quite foresee the mess he would land in by attempting it. It is unlikely that he was of that number, like some critics of *Othello*, who are not able to stomach the idea of a noble Mauretanian being negroid, for the Elizabethans, as we shall see, if knowing not much about Morocco, had reason to know more about it than many modern scholars do. At any rate, the dramatist, whose principal sources were unknown to Greg, was less resistant than the bibliographer to the idea that not only his villain but also one of his minor heroes was a blackamoor.

What concerns us here is the notion of the prescient text. If the problem of *Alcazar* can be explained on the principles we have advanced, we have some justification for supposing that a great number of more sophisticated texts will also reveal the workings of a prescient author or the corrections of a Stage-reviser.

There are a few straws in the wind. In *2 Tamburlaine* V, i, appears the direction: *Enter ... with others, the two spare kings*, where it can be shown that in a sixteen-cast play, such as *Tamburlaine* elsewhere shows itself to be, the two kings are the only actors available. There can be no doubt that Clavell was making a count of his cast when there appears in the manuscript of *The Soddered Citizen* the direction: 'Enter 7 maskers and tread a solemn measure', where, again, the number accords with the probable cast of free actors revealed by plotting.

In the process of plotting, indications of casting in the texts that at first sight appear quite vague begin to take on precise significance, and frequently show dramatists making capital out of the very limitations of their craft. As Ringler pointed out, Bottom's calling acquaintance with the fairies in *A Midsummer Night's Dream*, when addressed to *Mounseer* Mustardseed and *Cavalary* Cobweb, played (as is most probable) by adult men, reads not as whimsical patronage, such as might be appropriate to children, but as sophisticated satire of another kind. The servant with the goose-look in *Macbeth* must certainly be a boy, as Macbeth calls him, for although the term is sometimes used to mean 'coward', all sixteen men in the cast, apart from the two attendants who enter with Macbeth, are fully occupied elsewhere, preparing to enter as Malcolm's soldiers.

The novel manner of attention to the text that this method of plotting induces, provides the student with scores of exciting insights into the working practices of the Elizabethan dramatist. In individual cases, these discoveries may, of course, be illusory, but in the gross they may be seen to have evidential value. There enters at the end of *Othello* a character called Gratiano. He is a Venetian of rank, but, as far as his function in the plot goes, might be almost anyone. He turns out to know Roderigo, to be well known to Iago, and is greeted by Othello as 'uncle'. He is none other than Brabantio's brother, and therefore almost certainly the actor who played Brabantio himself, reappearing in this most probable disguise which, even after his long absence from the stage, is needed to deflect the audience's recognition. Like many another character doubling in this situation he has the piquant duty of announcing his own demise in the former role.

2

Plotting from the texts

We may now begin to imitate the Plotter's methods, and our object will be to search for what I shall call 'limiting' scenes. Scenes may reveal the finite limitations of the cast at the playwright's disposal in two ways, either:

(a) where all the available cast is on stage, or,

(b) where there exist recognisable character continuities in two or three scenes together that block actors from changing roles.

The Plot of *Alcazar*, because it is incomplete, does not certainly show a limiting scene of the first kind, but it has several examples of the second. In the other three Plots of the Admiral's Men, it is clear that if one actor were subtracted from their limiting scenes, deficiencies would be created in other scenes and roles would have to be dodged. In *Alcazar* roles are already dodged, and we are therefore be justified in assuming that the cast is very hard pressed.

Moreover, *Alcazar* exhibits what I shall call 'crucial' scenes: points at which there is some strong restriction at work on the Plotter's freedom of movement that forces him to do something silly, or to reveal his predicament by leaving an unimportant error or an imperfectly made alteration standing in the Plot. In *Alcazar* we can often tell what has happened by comparison with the text; in the other Plots there is certainly evidence of changes of intention and we may sometimes suspect the existence of crucial scenes, but, in the absence of a story-line, they are for the most part uninterpretable. Crucial scenes also exist in the printed plays, and we shall also be on the look-out for those places where the playwright is forced in some indirect way to reveal his hand, but there may often be a large subjective element in their interpretation and they must, therefore, always be considered in the light of the limiting scenes.

Our aim in plotting, then, will be to seek for limiting and crucial scenes in the printed texts. Limiting scenes, of course, exist in every play. They are of greatest interest for our purpose when we find that the tightest possible doubling-pattern short of dodging coincides with the evidence of the minimum cast, that is to say, when the cast is worked as hard as it reasonably can be worked. Fortunately, such a result occurs, as we might expect, in the majority of plays written for the public theatre.[1] It is often harder to arrive at in plays with very large casts, or – what often amounts to the same thing – in plays written for the children's companies. In the latter, the absence both of a company hierarchy and of a division between boys and men also works against the need for tightly economical casting.

The plays of the early children's companies thus provide us to some degree with a control-group that confirms the postulates of our enquiry. That those of the later children's and Revels companies cannot be relied on as a truly scientific control is because a considerable number appear to involve twenty actors, divided as sixteen men and four women, which is also the commonest composition of the adult companies. Many of the plays of the children of Blackfriars passed into the possession of the King's Men, and may have been printed in versions revised for that company. This was certainly the case with *The Malcontent*. It is also likely that the children took over plays written for the adult companies, for, while a play with a cast larger than the number of actors available obviously could not be played without re-writing the text, some plays written for smaller casts might be performed by larger companies simply by easing out the doubling of roles.

Crucial scenes will not appear in printed texts as clearly as in the Plot of *Alcazar*; but they will be detectable when there are clear signs of an author writing himself out of difficulty: for example, by explaining in some oblique way the failure of an expected character or group of characters to appear, or by having to leave prisoners unattended on stage because he has no-one to guard them. The first of these crises occurs in *Believe As You List*, when Lentulus enters on an important mission from Rome. He is, perforce, unattended, and is allowed by the prescient dramatist to comment on the fact. The latter case occurs in Munday's *The Death of Robert Earl of Huntingdon*. When the queen is captured, she has, improbably, to be guarded by Matilda, because all the men available are temporarily moving off stage as bearers. On Leicester's re-entrance there is an attempt to naturalise the situation verbally by giving him the bluff query: 'Queen Elianor, are you a prisoner?'[2]

The working principles

The three propositions, then, that will enable us to liberate the information in the texts are:

(i) That plural calls for attendants may be satisfied by the appearance of two actors, unless the text clearly indicates otherwise.

(ii) That an actor who leaves the stage last in one scene will not normally re-enter at the beginning of the next.

(iii) That boys will not normally double with men. To which we may add that men will not normally play female roles.

The first two of these propositions are consistent with the evidence of the Plots, and the last, as far as we can see, with all but one. But it will be necessary to add two working principles, the first of which appears to be consistent with the evidence of two of the Plots, namely:

(iv) That if, in a single scene, the demands made on the cast suddenly swell out of proportion to those made by the next largest limiting scene, and beyond the evidence of cast size in any crucial scenes there may be, we may suspect the presence of gatherers or stand-ins.

This will, of course, be valid only if the extras are mutes. If we may believe the reminiscences of old plays in John Tatham's *Knavery in All Trades* (1664), it was a well-understood convention that mutes might be used for guards and attendants in the 1630s.[3] Some manuscript plays do offer faint confirmation of this, and, in my counting, the rule that mutes must be numbered in the regular cast if they appear in more than one scene may have swollen my cast counts unduly for some plays, at any rate after 1625. Speaking actors must always be counted as regular members of cast, but mutes are mentioned as early as the *Troilus* Plot, and gatherers who were presumably mute appear several times in *Frederick and Basilea*. I may sometimes have created limiting scenes by counting silent stand-ins as actors. The manuscript of *Believe as You List* (1631) shows, like that of *Barnavelt* (1619), that the King's Men made every effort to keep the regular cast fully employed in the minor roles, at the risk of some mild anomalies of allegiance, rather than calling in extras.

The second working principle cannot strictly speaking be derived from the Plots, but does not contradict their testimony:

(v) That speaking actors were not normally cast for two *alternating* roles in the same play.

That is to say, our actor-counts will ignore the possibility of actors 'dodging' roles, unless there is clear need of it. If this was not a normal working principle of the drama, our exercise would be bound to fail; no dramatist would have been able to calculate with any precision the actual resources of his company. Yet dodging does occur. The Plotter of *Alcazar* dodges many of his minor characters in and out of dumb-shows. That was probably common practice. But he also dodges two speaking actors. Most notably he casts Charles Massey in the roles of Zareo of Algiers and the Portuguese Duke of Barceles, and doubles the latter, most improbably, with the Spanish Ambassador *en passant*. It is likely that Massey was silent in the first of his European roles and possible that he was silent in the second, but, as a consequence of his appearance as an Ambassador, the Plotter has to omit the whole of the scene following in which Zareo reappears. The possibility of dodging must be kept in mind as a desperate recourse, but if such a disposition of cast were planned by a dramatist, the changes of roles would surely be allowed, as in *Alcazar*, only after considerable intervals. The splitting of speaking roles to be observed in *Believe as You List* is unique.

The method of plotting, then, will be to follow the application of our 'rules' to the printed texts and other documents as mechanically and objectively as possible. The actual method used by the Elizabethan Plotter does not make the information we are seeking conspicuous, nor did it need to, for he was in possession of that very information and his aim was to make the best sense he could of the text with the cast available to him.

In order to make the demands of the text visible to the eye, I have settled on a method of marking the progress of the action in the simplest possible way with the help of graph paper. On the vertical axis of the graph the actors are numbered from top to bottom. Only in rare cases do we know their names. The first entering character becomes Actor 1. His life-line in that character moves forward one square on the horizontal axis, as do the life-lines of any others who enter with him, who are listed as Actors 2, 3, 4, and so on. Boys are separated from men and listed separately. When any character leaves the stage, the life-lines of all other characters on stage are carried forward a further square, and likewise when another character enters the scene. When the stage is cleared, the scene-ending is marked by a vertical line down the whole page.

This method keeps track at a glance of which actors are on and off stage and who is available at any point to double. The next move is to double an actor in a newly appearing role at the first opportunity, according to our five rules, and to continue to do so whenever possible, until we arrive at the end and can check back to identify the limiting scene, or scenes. That scene in Elizabethan plays is not always, or even often, the last, but once it is identified a count of the minimum cast has been arrived at.

That, at least, is the theory, but it would, of course, become extremely tedious to follow slavishly through all the seemingly possible doublings that turn out at a later stage to be mutually exclusive. In practice it quickly becomes apparent that between five and ten of the leading actors will play single roles. They will be the most frequent enterers and will therefore be barred at some stage from doubling with nearly every other character. Their availability for doubling will become readily apparent when their life-line on the horizontal axis goes blank. Care is still needed, however, to make sure that these characters will not turn up again, for reasons of plot, in the final scene. If any have suffered a convenient demise, I mark them with discreet crosses, to show that they are now available to double if need be.

The horizontal axis does not give any sense of a time-continuum. Its extension indicates only the number of exits and entrances that have taken place. Very long scenes in which the characters all enter and exit together occupy only one square; short scenes in which there is much coming and going may occupy six or more and look more impressive to the eye. It is therefore necessary, when any scene ends with a soliloquy or a duologue, to mark in the number of lines spoken, in order to estimate whether any of the characters who have just left the stage have time to enter in doubled roles at the beginning of the next scene. In practice, one finds that this is never accomplished in less than twenty-five lines of dialogue, and that doubling characters have usually been off-stage for at least a scene before their appearance in a new role. That is, no doubt, because they have to make a change of costume and make-up. Characters adopting a comic disguise may sometimes make it in less, but this is not true doubling.

Estimating numbers

The Elizabethan mind seems to have shunned precise figures. It is always a joy to find a direction like 'Enter 2 Moores' in place of the usual 'two or three', 'five or six', 'as many as may be'. Perhaps even contemporary readers found this vagueness in playtexts amusing. In Act I of *Histriomastix* (1599), a rather poor skit of university or Inns of Court provenance, the players, led by the poet Posthaste, are listed as three in the stage direction, but four speak. Posthaste calls them 'half a dozen good fellows', but Clout replies reproachfully – 'Sir, we are but four or five.'[4] In plotting through the texts one sometimes has to make inspired guesses about this sort of numbering and an element of subjectivity cannot be ruled out. For this reason, and because of the operation of our rule iv above, concerning the occasional presence of gatherers, I have listed in every case a maximum as well as a minimum cast count, followed by a 'probable' reconciliation. The difference in most cases is only of a single digit, but the discrepancy often arises from quite complex chains of reasoning, which the grateful reader will, I am sure, forgive me for passing over in silence. The Plots themselves contain inaccuracies that allow us to be confident of a result only of plus or minus one.

Concerning the boys, my figures will probably be inconsistent. I began working on the assumption that although boys could not double as men, they may well have doubled within their own sphere, as women, juvenile pages, minor servants, and the like. That assumption is consistent with the Plots. I have since become convinced that in the later companies, after about 1600, boys rarely doubled. It is hard to justify this conviction rationally. As one becomes accustomed to watching the ways in which men are asked to change roles, the doubling of boys in many situations simply *feels* wrong. The point is, perhaps, that a stage boy is already in disguise, and to ask of him a versatility in deception that is not asked even of the men tempts one to exclaim, as Sir Thomas More does of the Cardinal's boy: 'And one boy play them all? bir Lady, hees loden.'[5] It is also worth reflecting that Elizabethan actors were rigged out not in specially designed stage clothes, but in the actual dress of the day. Women's costume must have been particularly time-consuming to put on and off, especially when it had to be of a kind that concealed the natural deficiencies of the wearer. But it also seems improbable that complex roles would have been demanded of the boys when in many plays even some of the hired men are virtually mute. At any rate, my figures for the boys will probably reflect inconsistencies that I have neither time nor wit enough to put straight. There may often have been many more boys in a company than were actually given parts in any particular play. With these reservations, the results of plotting are strikingly informative.

A straightforward example: Shakespeare's Richard II

The Folio text of *Richard II*, which has uncommonly precise stage-directions, provides a convenient illustration. The Plot is represented in skeleton form on p. 48, and may be followed reasonably well from any edition. As with almost any example one might choose, however, an edited version will always obscure some working principle of the text, and for a perfect view I must refer the reader to one of the Folio facsimile editions. Current theories of the Folio text hold it to be at least one stage of revision or collation removed from the prompt-book. Editors have chosen Q. 1 (1597) for their copy text as the version likely to be closest to Shakespeare's original, and have made eclectic collations of its vaguer stage-directions with those of the Folio. The management of the cast, however, is virtually identical in each. Apart from occasional doubts about the precise number and identity of the characters on stage, and given that it is accepted that the showing of Richard's abdication in IV, i, omitted in the Quarto, was an original part of the play, the same personages will have appeared in both.

One *caveat* is needed. Editorial insistence on the presence of soldiers and attendants, when the texts indicate enterers to a scene with an '&c.', or the direction 'others', or the like, is always distracting. There are only two soldiers in *Richard II* who are not lords, and only one under the rank of a knight. The dramatist's consciousness of the restriction is characteristically revealed in a crucial scene at III, iii, 51–3, when Bolingbroke, wishing to display his 'fair appointments' to the refugees in Flint Castle, orders his troops to march 'without the noise of threat'ning drum'. This silence cannot have been provoked by a crisis in the music department, for the scene opens 'with Drum and Colours'. But there are no troops. The audience is therefore directed in this tactful manner to imagine the forces off stage and just out of ear-shot.

The limiting scene in the Folio is the Parliament scene (IV, i). Here, according to our method of counting, the text may be fully satisfied with the appearance of thirteen adult actors, ten of whom are called on by name, the others being a Herald and Officers. Three more, the actors who played the Gardeners in the previous scene, are blocked from entering. The minimum number of men needed is therefore sixteen. All other stage-directions, implicit and overt, may be satisfied within that number, and it is also the probable maximum.

The boys are clearly additional. One of them (Young Percy) is already on stage. The three who play the Queen and her Ladies cannot be imagined to have changed into male costume within the space of the six lines of the Gardener's speech at the end of III, iv. Even if we assume an act break (for the Folio text is regularly divided into acts), these three would have the same problem at the scene break of IV, i, where they would have to reappear in their female roles within the space of thirteen lines. It is, I suppose, conceivable that the Duchess of Gloucester and the

Duchess of York might have been played by the same boy, since their appearances are eleven scenes apart, so our count of boys will be registered as five/six.

The really interesting point here is that, when we check back through the mutually exclusive doubling roles in the first three acts, it becomes clear that there are thirteen named and recognisable characters in play up to the end of II, i, and still four character roles of importance to be filled: Berkeley, Salisbury, the Welsh Captain, and Percy. If Bagot is not dodged as the Welsh Captain, one of the latter roles will have to be allotted to a juvenile. It is, of course, Percy who is chosen, perhaps because he stands in family relationship as son to Northumberland. In historical fact, as Shakespeare must have known, Henry Percy was at least as old, if not older than, Bolingbroke. We can see the playwright making capital out of the problem, both in lightening the atmosphere of this almost wholly serious play by the introduction of an up-and-coming young leader, and seizing the opportunity in *1 Henry IV* of developing Hotspur into a coeval antagonist to Prince Hal. At any rate, the casting of Percy is a sure sign that the adult cast of *Richard II* is no greater than sixteen.

Several other points deserve noting. First, that the doubling pattern shown on the plan is in this case almost unshakeable. Although there are few tell-tale signs of Shakespeare's working, it suggests a prescient author almost as clearly as the text of *Alcazar*. It would, indeed, be possible to reverse the doubling roles of Gaunt and Mowbray, but there are clear advantages in leaving the actor of Gaunt off stage for as long as possible. It is scarcely even possible to dodge roles, apart from those played by actor 10, but Gaunt might be kept in reserve to play the Abbot of Westminster if Bagot were to dodge in the role of Scroope in III, ii. Mowbray also appears to me likely to have doubled as Carlisle, because, like Gratiano, he will have the touching duty in IV, i of announcing his own death in the former role. Likewise, Bushy and Greene must almost certainly double as Gardeners, because the Officers in IV, i can hardly be other than Ross and Willoughby. As Gardeners, the 'caterpillars of the commonwealth' will be forced to hear, and express surprise at, the news of their execution in their former roles, and they will have no option later but to turn into Exton's servants and to be slain by their former king and master. Their case is very like that of Jonas and Hercules in *Alcazar*. The removal of their bodies will also be a problem for Sir Pierce of Exton and the Keeper (if the latter is still on stage), much like that of Muly Mahamet Seth's in disposing of the bodies in Peele's play. Shakespeare has partially written his way out of it, with the suggestion that the servants are to be hastily interred nearby ('Take hence the rest and give them buriall here'), for unless Exton has a posse of mutes the spectacle will perforce be far from dignified.

The Folio text also tidies up the Quarto in one small matter of interest to us. It is the purely mechanical observation of our rule that an actor who leaves the stage last in one scene does not normally appear at the beginning of the next. In I, i an unmotivated and improbable exit for Gaunt is noted about ten lines before the end. The reason is that he will appear simultaneously with the Duchess of Gloucester at the beginning of I, ii, a scene that represents their parting in different directions, presumably, as at first envisaged, from London. The note for Gaunt's exit may have been prompted in part by a Stage-reviser's inspiration to change the sense of *place* in II, i from London to Plashy, Woodstock's seat in Essex, which is given some prominence in the dialogue, and where the Duchess is later reported to have died. The dialogue will just, at a pinch, allow it.

In the Quarto, the omission of Richard's abdication from IV, i leaves no disturbance in the text, which is perfectly self-consistent without it. The effect, for our purposes, however, is to reduce the limiting scene to twelve. That this is not a true figure is revealed by the computation that the sequence of scenes from II, iii to III, ii involves fourteen, and probably fifteen, mutually exclusive roles, that is, characters who are blocked at some point from doubling with each other. Depending, then, on whom we assume to have been present at the lists at Coventry in I, iii, the probable cast for the Quarto is also sixteen. In the play-tables we should therefore have to list our findings as a minimum of fourteen, a maximum of fifteen, and an apparently illogical reconciliation, in this unusual case, of sixteen, plus five or six boys; for there is very little doubt that the casts of the Folio and the Quarto are actually identical.

It may finally be noted that Ross and Willoughby, the two lords who are suborned by Northumberland to become the first supporters of Bolingbroke, may be presumed to remain his lords throughout. They are still prominently named in the initial directions to II, iv, although they are already mute in that scene. Thereafter in the Folio their presence is noted only as 'attendants', 'lords', 'officers', or 'others': they have, as it were, become stage properties. In the Quarto they are never mentioned in the stage-directions and are named (as in the Folio) only once in the spoken text, but they speak the same lines and fall silent at the same point. There is no possibility that there was an intention to cut them from the cast, for they are certainly needed as presences, even though their characters have ceased to be of any interest. We shall have reason to recall their gradual demotion into mutes when we come to consider the case of the silent Portuguese lords in *Alcazar*.

The composition of the companies

Of the 344 of the plays of the public theatre from 1580–1642 I have been able to analyse in this manner, well over half (56 per cent) show a fairly certain count of sixteen actors. Fifty-three (15.4 per cent) show a cast of twelve; twenty-nine have fourteen; five have eight and ten precisely ten. Seventeen have casts well in excess of twenty. Seven fall into a doubtful category because their directions are too confused to be able to make any confident judgment upon. Plays in which a single scene

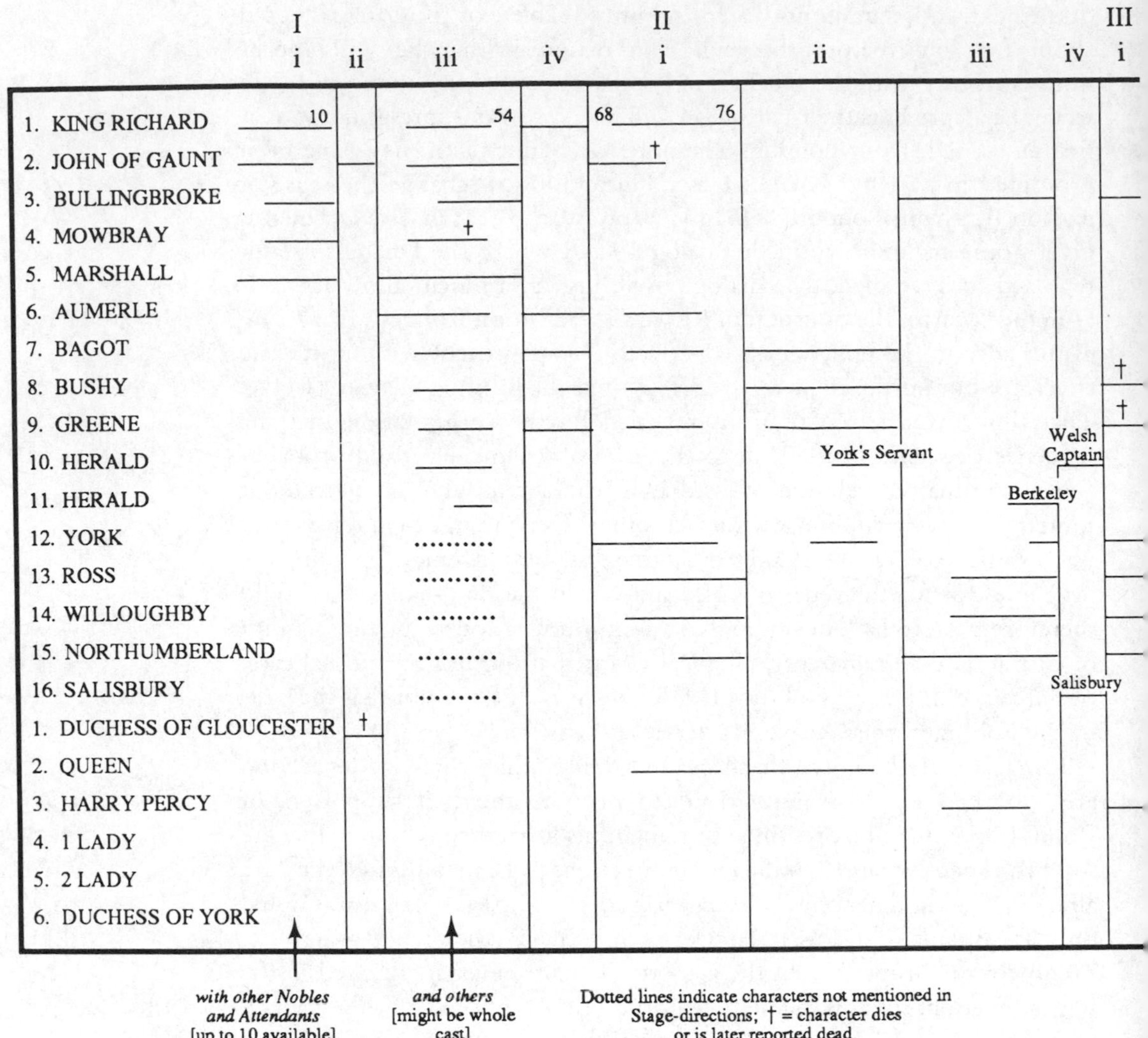

1 Skeleton cast plan of *The Life and Death of Richard II* (Folio text, 1623)

suddenly swells to exceed the otherwise reasonably precise record of the text, as in the plot of *Tamar Cam*, I have counted at the lower figure. There are thus thirty-five plays recorded as sixteen +. An example is Heywood's *1 If You Know Not Me You Know Nobody*, where, in the final scene the Mayoress enters attended by the Waits of London and the Beefeaters of the Tower. Some of these must be the theatre musicians. In all other cases, too, I have striven to be reductive to the smallest possible number, even when there are signs of discomfort in the narrative, as, for example, where changes of identity appear disconcertingly rapid but no scene is positively limiting. These casts are marked twelve +, and fourteen +, but, as in the case of *Richard II* Q. 1, many such plays were probably written for standard sixteen-cast performance. The manuscript of *Believe As You List* would at first also seem to fall into the twelve +

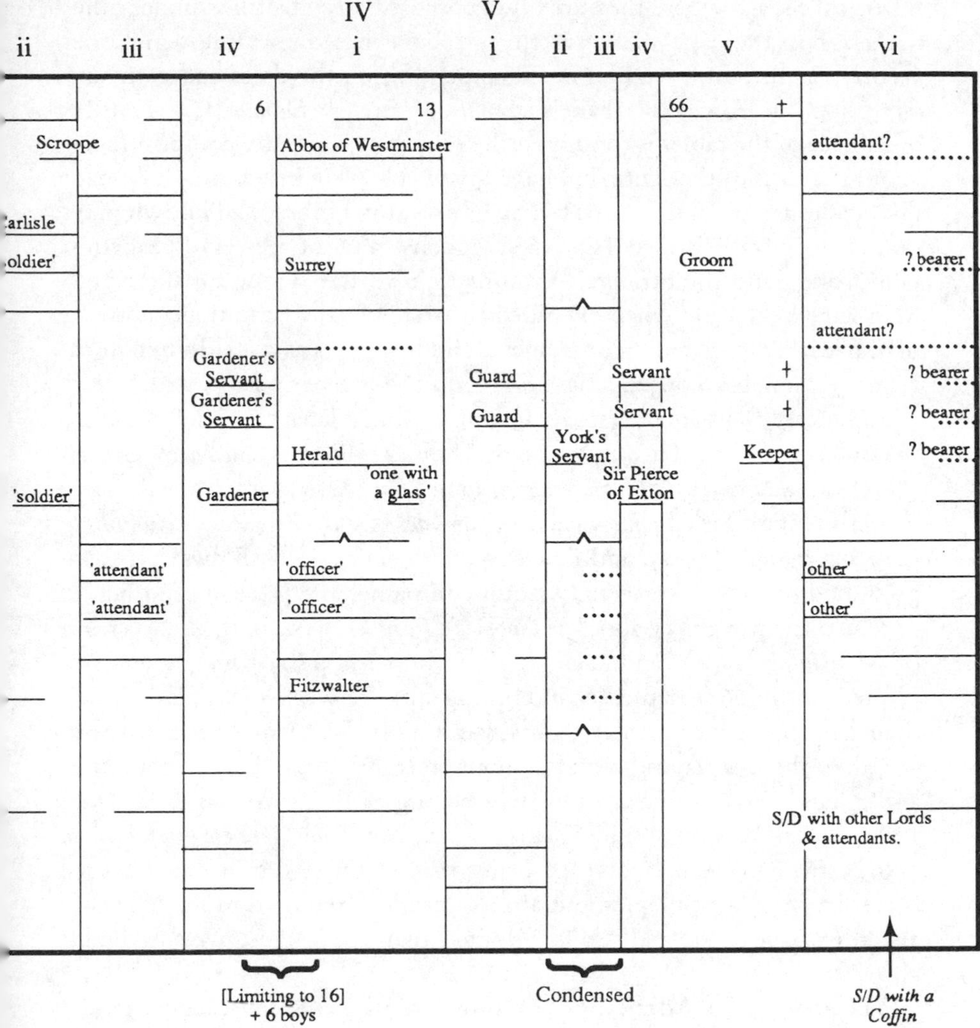

category, because it seems possible from the text that the Bondmen who are led away to be murdered at the end of II, i might have had time to double in the thirteen lines of Flaminius's soliloquy that end the scene. By experience one finds that the time is too short, and the Plotter's annotations reveal that they did not: the actual cast available was sixteen. There is no ten + category that I have discovered, because the record of ten-cast plays is uncommonly precise, involving very little doubling and showing variation only in the numbers (usually large) of boys. There are two late plays belonging to Beeston's boys that give an exact count of eleven men.

The figures are the more striking when divided between companies. Difficulties here arise mainly because of mis-ascription of companies on title pages and the scholarly jigsaw of dating and placing the plays in the historical record where they are often conjecturally identified under other names. For the sake of consistency, I have based the following brief account, and the play-tables in the appendix, on the dates and company ascriptions in Alfred Harbage's *Annals of English Drama, 975–1700.* As the object of the tables is to suggest the norms of company composition at about the turn of the century, I have given complete cast-listings of extant public-theatre plays up to 1625. The figures thus embrace all known plays of the Admiral's-Prince Henry's company and of Queen Elizabeth's, Pembroke's and the Strange's-Chamberlain's Men. Those for the King's Men vary very little when extended to 1642, but the conditions of others of the earlier and later companies were more various, although most return reasonably constant figures for quite long periods.

Eight-cast plays appear (with one or two much later exceptions), before the opening of the Theatre in 1576. They are: *Patient and Meek Grissell* (1559), *Cambises* (1561), *Horestes* (1567), *The Most Virtuous and Godly Susanna* (1569), *Sir Clyomon and Sir Clamydes* (1570), *The Rare Triumphs of Love and Fortune* (1582), and *Fedele and Fortunio* (1584). All these plays are presumed to have been acted by adult companies and were in print before 1590. To them we may add *The Cobbler's Prophecy* (1590), the first version of *Mucedorus* (1590), and *Guy, Earl of Warwick* (1593), which was not printed until 1661. A further interesting link between these plays is that their length is never greater than 1,800 lines or less than 1,220; that is to say, they share a playing-time of about an hour and a quarter to an hour and a half. Two doubtful cases may belong with them: Wilson's *Three Ladies of London* (1581) and Shakespeare's *The Two Gentlemen of Verona* (1593). Both appear capable of being played by fewer than ten actors, according to our principles, but almost certainly required more. They are also respectively 400 and 500 lines longer than the longest plays in the list above.

The plays of the Admiral's Men show a remarkable consistency. Of the thirty-six listed by Harbage as certain or probable Admiral's plays before 1603, of which a text or a Plot is extant, twenty-nine show casts of sixteen. The exceptions are *The Two Angry Women of Abingdon*, *The Wounds of Civil War*, *The Taming of A Shrew*, *Edward I*, *Doctor Faustus*, *Frederick and Basilea*, and *Old Fortunatus*. The Plot of *Alcazar*, of course, lists sixteen men, but uses its boys in addition in a way that would have made our count seventeen or eighteen if there had been an alternative text. The fragmentary Plots of *Troilus* and *Fortune's Tennis* must be considered doubtful, but are very probably also sixteen-cast. The Plot of *Frederick and Basilea* may well have been a sixteen-cast play, temporarily improvised as a twelve-cast by calling in gatherers. I do not know on what grounds Harbage places the twelve-cast play, *1 The Two Angry Women of Abingdon* as early as 1588. On the grounds of the maturity of its style, it is not likely to have been written much earlier than the date of its publication in 1599.

The Wounds of Civil War has a cast of well over twenty-four. It is possible that Lodge re-wrote the play for publication, restoring much of the historical material from Appian that he had been forced to simplify for public performance. *Edward I* probably consists of two plays joined together for publication and is a rather confused text, but as it stands its cast is also very large, including nine lords of Scotland who enter with their nine pages and a quartet of negro Moors who carry the Queen's litter into Wales.

Casts such as these could only have been furnished by the combined company of Strange's and Admiral's Men playing at the Theatre just prior to 1591. This company must also have played the *Contention* versions of Shakespeare's *Henry VI*, which also (*pace* the critics who have regarded them as reduced versions) exhibit casts of over twenty-four, well in excess of the casts of the Folio texts, although they, too, are abnormally large. *Doctor Faustus* is an odd case, only because the structure of the play allows very intensive doubling. The cast of Q. 1 cannot quite be reduced to twelve, but it may have been any number more. Similarly, the cast of the Q of 1616 is probably sixteen, but the count cannot be made with comfort. There is nothing in the casting that allows us to form any opinion about the primacy of either version. The difficulty of arriving at a more positive figure for *Old Fortunatus* arises simply from its confusing directions, which may result, as Chambers suggests, from Dekker's having 'boiled down' the original two-part play into one. Certainly something of the kind happened to the two parts of Munday's Robin Hood (Earl of Huntingdon) plays, but the second of these does in fact yield a precise figure, even though it is clearly made up of two plays that were originally of different cast sizes, thrust together. *Sir John Oldcastle* is another high-pressure oddity that must have involved even more dodging than the Plot of *Alcazar*, for there are a number of crucial scenes that strongly suggest a limited cast, and only I, i strictly requires gatherers.

Of the ten extant plays of this company after it passed into the patronage of Prince Henry in 1603, all are sixteen-cast: the two parts of *The Honest Whore*, *When You See Me You Know Me*, *The Whore of Babylon*, *The Roaring Girl*, *The Spanish Tragedy* (revised), *A Fair Quarrel*, *All's Lost by Lust*, *The Witch of Edmonton*, and *The Valiant Welshman*. The last is probably out of place, for it is shorter by a thousand lines than some others in the list, although *The Witch of Edmonton* is only 300 lines longer. *The World Tossed at Tennis*, most probably a 'device' to be played at Court, is much shorter still, but it, too, appears to exhibit a cast of sixteen, with the addition of more than the usual number of boys. The slight difficulty in accommodating *Sir John Oldcastle*, the revised *Spanish Tragedy*, and *The Whore of Babylon* to a cast of sixteen is troublesome, but the evidence that such was the custom of this company is convincing enough: 76 per cent of its known plays bear testimony to that number as its normal complement.

The plays of the Chamberlain's-King's company present the same fairly uniform picture of a sixteen-cast company from 1594 to 1642. Thirteen of the texts later than 1600 appear to be twelve-cast and a few late plays suggest casts of eighteen or nineteen, but without much certainty. There has undoubtedly been much mis-ascription of plays on title-pages and it is probable that at least some of the larger-cast plays should be allotted to one of the King's Revels companies rather than to the King's Men. Others may have been performed by two companies acting together. This was certainly the case with Heywood's *Ages* plays and may explain the large cast of *Henry VIII*.

The casts for the earlier plays of this company while under the patronage of Ferdinando, Lord Strange present some difficulties, largely because of uncertainties about the history and identification of the texts. The reasonably certain sixteen-cast plays among them are *Friar Bacon and Friar Bungay*, *The Jew of Malta*, *John a Kent and John a Cumber*, *A Looking Glass for London and England*, *Fair Em*, *John of Bordeaux*, *A Knack to Know a Knave*, *The Massacre at Paris*, and *Orlando Furioso*. In *Friar Bacon* a clear sixteen-cast emerges only by retaining the role of the King of Saxony. There are signs in the text that his deletion may have been intended. *The Jew of Malta* was not printed until 1633 and may have been revised by Heywood. *John a Kent* is a manuscript, and of good authority, but its association with Strange's depends on the rather improbable identification of it as *The Wise Man of West Chester* recorded in Henslowe's lists for 1594, while *The Massacre at Paris*, *John of Bordeaux*, and *Orlando Furioso* are all suspected of being corrupt and shortened versions. It would be rather silly to reckon *Orlando* as a seventeen-cast play on the grounds that a direction in the last scene calls for the entrance of the twelve peers of France, when Orlando, who, of course, is one of them, remains temporarily off stage; but its cast certainly cannot be reduced below sixteen, unless, as Greg whimsically proposed, the direction may be interpreted to call on only four or five.

Of the remainder, *The Spanish Tragedy* can be reckoned only as fourteen + in its earlier version, *The Comedy of Errors* (if it is to be identified as the Strange's play, *The Jealous Comedy*, in Henslowe's Diary) may be reduced to an absolute minimum of fourteen, and Q. 1 of *Richard III* can be played by twelve actors. The *Contention* quartos of the second and third parts of the *Henry VI* trilogy show casts in excess of twenty-four and probably much greater, while Shakespeare's *1 Henry VI* has a cast greater than twenty-five and is therefore almost certainly not the play of that name recorded by Henslowe.

The position of the company from 1594 until the end of the reign is of a settled composition of sixteen men. The difficulties here are very minor. *King John* calls for only twelve, as also does *All's Well that Ends Well*, except for the scene in which the Young Lords appear. *1 Henry IV* must be reckoned as fourteen +, although the uncompromising sixteen cast of *2 Henry IV* suggests that the ' + ' should be given its value. *The Merry Devil of Edmonton* is also in the twelve + category, and *Twelfth Night* may be played by fourteen because of the lack of pressure in its demands for attendant Lords. *Hamlet* Q. 1 is a twelve-cast play, but Q. 2 demands a minimum of sixteen.

Of the thirty-five known plays of this company between 1603 and Shakespeare's retirement from the theatre, twenty-five call precisely for a cast of sixteen men. One group from the remainder is of particular interest: *Philaster*, *A King and No King*, *The Maid's Tragedy*, *The Scornful Lady*, and *The Captain*. They are all from the atelier of Beaumont and Fletcher, and all have large numbers of boys, normally eight. In this they resemble *The Knight of the Burning Pestle*, *Cupid's Revenge*, *The Coxcomb*, and others played by the Children of the Queen's Revels. *The Scornful Lady* was most probably played by the Revels company at Porter's Hall as late as 1615. The title-page of Q. 1 (1616) attributes it to 'the Children of Her Maiesties Reuels in the Blacke Fryers', but, by the time of the appearance of Q. 2 (1625), it had passed to the King's Men and is described as 'now lately Acted by the Kings Maiesties seruants, at the Blacke Fryers'. We know from Keysar's deposition in the Court of Requests against the King's Men in 1610, some time after the transfer of the Blackfriars lease, that the Revels company consisted of 'eighteene or twentye persons all or most of them trayned up in that service, in the raigne of the late Queene Elizabeth for ten years together'.[6] It is possible, therefore, that all these plays were originally written for the Revels company and passed to the King's Men as a condition of the lease signed in 1608. If so, the conditions were slow to take effect. Plague having seriously interrupted playing for two years, they were probably not enforced until the Revels company dwindled and disbanded following the demolition of Porter's Hall. Some of the Revels company's other plays probably passed to the King's Men (as *The Coxcomb* did), through the Lady Elizabeth's Men. Another may have been *The Honest Man's Fortune* of which the Folio text (originally played, as Gerritsen has shown, by a combination of the Children of the Queen's Revels and the Lady Elizabeth's Men at Whitefriars in 1613), is a twelve-cast play, while the prompt-book prepared by Knight for the King's Men has a cast of sixteen.

For the remaining exceptions, *The Second Maiden's Tragedy* also exhibits a cast of exactly twelve, but has a smaller number of boys. *King Lear* and *The Fair Maid of the West* may perhaps have called for no more. *1 Jeronimo* and *The London Prodigal* can be reckoned only as fourteen +, but *Sejanus* and *Henry VIII* have much larger casts. The former was, of course, revised for publication, and the latter, as I have suggested, may have been connected with the joint company that performed Heywood's *Ages* plays at about the same time. But that is mere speculation. 67 per cent of the plays of this company up to 1625 yield a count of sixteen.

Five other companies briefly concern us: Queen Elizabeth's Men, Queen Anne's, The Lady Elizabeth's, Queen Henrietta's and Prince Charles's.

Queen Elizabeth's Men appear from their charter to have been formed as a twelve-cast company, but they must quickly have exceeded that number. All the plays that came to the press shortly after the company 'broke', in 1593 or 1594, are sixteen-cast: *Friar Bacon*, *A Looking Glass for London and England*, *King Leir*, *James IV*, *The Famous Victories of Henry V*, *The True Tragedy of Richard III*, *The Old Wives Tale* and *Selimus*. *The Troublesome Reign of King John* had already been published in 1591. *The Three Lords and Three Ladies of London*, assigned tentatively to the Queen's Men by Harbage, has a much larger cast, requiring at least thirty players and must have been written either for a joint performance or for a company of boys. *Sir Clyomon and Sir Clamydes* was not published until 1599 and was perhaps merely a survival from the bottom drawer. It is an eight-cast play.

The records of the Lady Elizabeth's suggest that it was, for at least part of its life, a smaller company. A number of the pieces more certainly attributed to it are twelve-cast plays, among them being *A Chaste Maid in Cheapside*, *The Honest Man's Fortune*, *Wit Without Money*, and *The Changeling*, but the company appears to have had a chequered history and many of its plays are of the standard kind.

Queen Anne's company, or more probably companies, presents the most confused picture. The company was originally formed in 1603 from Worcester's Men, whose two certain surviving plays have casts of between twelve and fourteen men and between five and seven boys. These are *How a Man May Choose a Good Wife From a Bad* and *A Woman Killed With Kindness*. The latter was later revived by Queen Anne's Men with a standard cast. Of the known Queen's plays after 1603, nineteen have a cast of sixteen men, and three others – *The Wise Woman of Hogsdon*, *The Fair Maid of the West* and *Swetnam the Woman Hater* – have casts that give a strict result of fourteen +, but are almost certainly designed for sixteen adult players. The remaining fourteen plays connected with the company have large casts of more than twenty-five. These plays are variously described on the title pages as belonging to Her Majesty's servants at The Red Bull, The Company of The Red Bull Revels, and the Children of the Queen's Revels, or else are known, like Heywood's *Ages* plays, to have been performed by combined companies.

It appears that there were at certain stages two Queen's companies, one of which normally played in the country but on occasion joined with its city counterpart. It is also probable that the children of these companies sometimes combined to perform separately at Court, without the men, as is suggested by plays such as *The Coxcomb* and Jonson's *Epicoene* which have eccentric total casts of sixteen or seventeen.

The Queen's plays with regular casts may be counted as *The Royal King and the Loyal Subject*, *Sir Thomas Wyatt*, *1 & 2 If You Know Not Me You Know Nobody* (part 1 with extras and musicians), *The Wise Woman of Hogsdon*, *Nobody and Somebody*, *The Rape of Lucrece*, *Fortune By Land and Sea*, *The Fair Maid of the West*, *Greene's Tu Quoque*, *Match Me In London*, *The White Devil*, *The Poor Man's Comfort*, *The Devil's Law Case*, *Swetnam the Woman Hater*, *Two Merry Milkmaids*, *The Virgin Martyr*, *The Costly*

Whore (the last three all ascribed to the Red Bull Revels), *The Maid of Honour*, and possibly *The Two Noble Ladies*.

The repertory of the Revels company is most likely identified by the casts of *The Travels of Three English Brothers*, *The Knight of the Burning Pestle*, *If It Be Not Good The Devil Is In't*, *The Tragedy of Byron*, *Cupid's Revenge*, *A Shoemaker A Gentleman*, and May's *The Heir*, which are all uniformly to be counted as above twenty, and mostly as twenty-five +. Heywood's *Ages* plays, *Henry VIII*, and *Dick of Devonshire* may also belong here. The later King's Revels company that appears to have had its origin from some section of this company after the Queen's death was typically much larger than this and in the late 1630s numbered more than thirty-five.

I am aware, of course, that in separating out the plays associated with Queen Anne's company in this way I am producing a result that strongly favours my own argument, but there appears to be no other way of giving an account of this company.

Queen Henrietta's was the heir of several companies and may have varied in size as the Lady Elizabeth's appears to have done, but its typical cast is one of exactly fourteen. Sixteen of the thirty-six plays of this company that I have been able to plot are of that composition, but there are six with casts of sixteen and about eight that give a cast of twelve or twelve +. Among the twelve-cast plays are *King John and the Fair Matilda*, *Love's Cruelty*, *The Ball*, *A Maidenhead Well Lost*, *The Example*, *The Opportunity*, and *The Hollander*. It is perhaps of interest that the livery lists for this company always include fourteen men, but as, until 1637, the lists also provide for fourteen King's Men, I do not know whether any significance attaches to the fact.

Finally, there is an interesting group of plays which do, indeed, appear to have a 'new foundation'. They have quite distinctive casts of ten men and about ten boys. Two of them, Shakerley Marmion's *Hollands Leaguer* and *A Fine Companion*, are ascribed on their title-pages to Prince Charles's (II) company, playing at Salisbury Court. A third, Shirley's *The Changes, or Love in a Maze*, is said (Q. 1632) to have been played by the company of His Majesty's Revels in the same theatre. Its prologue and epilogue pretty clearly reveal this to be correct as to place, but the casting tends to confirm the arguments of Adams and Bentley for regarding the company ascription as an error.[7] Further analysis of this distinctive company may be able to throw some light on Shirley's relationships with these companies and with Queen Henrietta's company at the Phoenix.

The plays with large casts to be found after 1603, are, I believe, to be attributed to the later Revels companies. Some of these companies were very large indeed, and must have included great numbers of boys. It is difficult to trace their history with any certainty. Such an exercise would take us too far afield in such a preliminary study as this, but one illustration may be of interest. Nathaniel Richards' play *The Tragedy of Messalina, the Roman Empress*, published in 1640, calls for at least eighteen men and fourteen boys. That it was played in something close to its printed form is vouched for by a partial cast-list giving the names of six of the men and three of the boys. It is also full of descriptive directions, without which the spoken text would not be fully comprehensible, and whose object was to spare the reader nothing of its noteworthy spectacles of bloodshed, lust, and balletic extravagance. Now, in the Mayor's Court Books of Norwich for March 1635, there is a record of a visit to that city by a company who were sent for so that their names might be taken.[8] Five of them appear in the cast of *Messalina* and two others are vouched for as players of the Revels by the diary of Thomas Crosfield, recording a visit to Oxford in 1634 by Richard Kendall, the wardrobe-keeper for that company. The Norwich record lists twenty-eight persons. Not all of them can have been actors. The list certainly includes two wardrobe-keepers, and others who may be 'necessary attendants', fencers, musicians, and the like. Two are vaguely identified as 'Maivrin' and 'Mistale'. But this is a crucially uncomfortable record for the commonly accepted history of the stage, for it implies that travelling companies, far from being small or reduced, might be of very great size.

G. E. Bentley was at pains to argue that the Norwich list included the actors of two troupes. His argument is rather unconvincingly based on the impression that there are eight or nine roles unassigned in *Messalina*.[9] In fact there are eleven speaking roles unassigned in the cast-list itself, and nineteen unassigned for the actual speaking cast. Moreover there are many extras involved. The text calls for six speaking boys, and, in addition, eight Furies in one scene and eight Bacchanals in another. At any rate, the twenty-eight members of the company at Norwich could not have played the last two scenes of Act V of Richards's play which unequivocally call for thirty-two actors and possibly even more. Even this great travelling group may have fallen somewhat short of the complete complement of the King's Revels as represented by its most notorious text. That the company could accommodate such a play, however, is shown by the one other known to be written for it: Brome's *The Queen and the Concubine*, which has an even larger total cast of thirty-six or more.

We may conclude that other large-cast plays such as *Dick of Devonshire* were not unplayable, as has sometimes been assumed, but created for companies that did exist, but to which we cannot assign a repertory with any great certainty. Or else they were deliberately composed for companies that combined together from time to time for some special reason.

Despite the variousness of the material that my rough logic has passed briefly under review, the picture that emerges, at least for the major companies, is one of remarkable constancy over quite long periods of time. If we take the five major companies, omitting Queen Henrietta's whose composition appears regularly to have been fourteen, we find that 68 per cent of their repertory yields a sufficiently constant numerical answer. The same figure turns up for the four major companies up to

1625. Over long periods of time their standard composition was of sixteen men. I believe we may be justified in regarding this as the perceived norm for the professional companies of the age.

Statistical evidence, like inferential argument, is convincing only as a whole field enquiry and merely establishes probabilities. It cannot be held to apply to any given play with certainty. Nevertheless it appears to me that the exceptional regularity with which sixteen-cast plays turn up in the repertory of the Admiral's Men at the Rose and the Fortune, justifies us in assuming that the Plot of *Alcazar* represents a performance in which the sixteen adult actors it clearly reveals were working under some abnormal kind of stress.

When the same rules are applied to the text of *Alcazar* as to other plays, however, it yields a probable limiting scene of sixteen, that is, if we assume that all the cast is called on stage in III, iv except for Abdelmelec, Zareo and Muly Mahamet Seth. Moreover, it twice exhibits groups of scenes that are limiting to fourteen, so that, if, as seems reasonable, Muly Mahamet and Sebastian did not double, the count of sixteen may be inferred three times. There are, even so, signs of crisis in the speech-prefixes where we find the enforced doubling of Jonas and Hercules as the Italian captains, the doubling of Zareo in the opposition Moorish party, and the probable excision of a Messenger in I, ii, all of which suggest a tight squeeze in filling the roles even with a cast of sixteen. It is clear, morover, that the dramatist could dispose of a much larger cast of boys than the Plotter, and that the latter is struggling to fill the stage and to re-create the spectacle demanded by the text. As the relationship of the two documents has been held to represent the very reverse of this situation, and the text of *Alcazar* to be a deliberately cut down version for a much reduced company on tour, it may be useful to make a digression at this stage to consider what evidence can be found of the ways in which companies actually met the problems of almost annual summer travelling, the depletions and financial hardships of the plague years, and the shifting and ageing of their membership.

3

The travelling companies

The belief that the major London companies were reduced in personnel when travelling in the provinces is probably an unshakeable myth of theatrical history. It has been a useful fiction helping to explain the existence of short texts of plays that are otherwise known in longer versions, and is a cornerstone of Greg's account of the text of *Alcazar*, which he regarded as having been reduced in the 'normal' way for country touring with a depleted cast.[1] It is frequently invoked by editors to account for the discrepancies between the named characters listed in the stage-directions of variant versions of printed plays, especially when the texts are otherwise closely parallel. But editorial calculations have been little more than guesswork and can rarely be seen to square with the probabilities of cast management outlined in the foregoing chapters. There is no convincing evidence for the belief that I have been able to discover, and much that points in the opposite direction. A brief survey of the question will nevertheless be useful in understanding how theatre companies perceived their own organisation, and will allow a little human colour into this rather arid and abstract discussion.

Professor J. T. Murray's collection of the Corporation records in *English Dramatic Companies. 1558–1642* (New York, 1910) tends to give the impression that the landscape of the Midlands and the southern counties of England was thickly and perpetually criss-crossed by the tracks of a multiplicity of travelling entertainers of all kinds. There were, first, the regular, licensed, provincial theatrical groups, whose life, when it had any continuity, was perpetually on the road, and who rarely if ever appeared in the metropolis. Alternating with their visits were those of amateur groups, as well as random collections of unemployed persons who might temporarily have found some kind of limited protection as players, and an apparent host of fencers, musicians, rope-dancers, acrobats, tumblers, mountebanks, puppeteers, and exhibitors of all kinds of marvels and grotesques. Intermixed with this wealth of diversions and not always clearly distinguishable from it are the relatively dignified progresses, sometimes made annually, and sometimes for several years together, of the companies under the protection of the crown and the lords of the Privy Council. These normally played, or at least had had their origins, in London.

It is highly plausible, as Dawson, Galloway, and Wasson have more recently argued of the records in Kent and East Anglia, that only a small fraction of the total dramatic activity appears in the registers of the corporations.[2] The absence or disappearance of the records in the towns through which the players must have passed on their way to the major centres is certainly suggestive. But, once again, the ordinances against players in years when few or no companies appeared in those towns where records exist (from which they infer a vast, feebly regulated incursion of annual entertainment) are susceptible of other interpretations. Such inferences, for example, almost certainly underrate the Puritan opposition to travelling players.

The strategies that existed for keeping this apparent wealth of proffered excitement under regular control were probably less diverse and makeshift than the impression created by the more spectacular embarrassments of the town authorities in applying them might suggest. We have, quite naturally, fuller accounts of the difficulties of the corporations than of their normal practices, but those difficulties, although exaggerated in the records of prevailingly Puritan towns such as Norwich, do not appear to have been unduly great. At Leicester, for example, where the records are reasonably full, Murray lists 59 visits by companies of all descriptions in the first 46 years up to 1576, and 228 in the following 66 years. On average, that is not much more than three a year. On thirty-eight of those occasions, moreover, companies were given a gratuity for leaving the town without performing. The figures also include a number of items that are probably more strictly concerned with bear-baiting than with dramatic performances. In addition to these, Murray records only a mere handful of other entertainments: an Italian motion and another puppet show, an exhibition of baboons under the licence of the Master of the Revels, some feats of activity, probably from the ubiquitous Peadle family, and the arrival of Mr Fenner, the King's Poet, who, however, was also persuaded with a gratuity to 'passe the Towne without playinge'.

The embarrassments of the town authorities were often real enough. The appearances of players were irregular and unpredictable. Fears of the spread of plague in large congregations of people were well founded. As frequently mentioned, and perhaps as serious, were the disruptions to the working week and the temptations offered by plays to the poor and unemployed to squander their substance, not to mention the damage to halls and buildings and more troublesome affrays and public disorders. In some towns, moreover, aldermen were bound to contribute to the gratuities paid, whether or not they attended the performances. To attend performances by the royal companies they might even be summoned by the corporation's mace-bearer, on penalty of a fine.

The means of regulation were nevertheless at the corporations' disposal and appear to have been more or less uniformly applied. Whether or not the towns were pestered by large numbers of fly-by-night performers must remain a matter of opinion. In the larger centres, and in the normal way, players were regularly bound to seek the approval of their visit from the authorities and to present their licence to the clerk for inspection and validation. An appropriate time for the visit (usually a few days, but sometimes extending to a fortnight) and a location for the performances would then be appointed. These matters appear to have been largely within the discretion of the corporation and recalcitrant actors might be, and were, summarily dealt with.[3] But, when, as very often happened, the townsmen wished to forbid the players' entry altogether, an ascending scale of possible clashes of authority becomes evident. A licence that merely guaranteed the protection of a noble patron might serve as a passport and save the actors from prosecution as rogues and vagabonds, but its potency seems to have depended on the status of the lord and his influence in the locality. It was another matter with a royal licence under the Great Seal authorising a company to play 'within anie towne halls or Moute halls or other convenient places within the liberties and freedome of anie ... Cittie, vniversitie, towne, or Boroughe whatsoever within our said Realmes and domynions' (King's Men's licence, 19 May 1603). With a passport such as this, actors could and, on occasion, did, flout the authority of the corporations. After the Restoration, Sir Henry Herbert declared in response to an ingenious argument advanced concerning one such licence by the Mayor of Maidstone, attempting to limit its effect to within the vicinity of the Court's progress, that this was 'such an interpretation as was never before given by any learned Gentleman'. Nevertheless, the corporations had made some headway before 1642 in excluding players from the town halls, in limiting their playing times, especially at night, and in enforcing the rules about Lent and the Sabbath. Herbert himself freed Norwich of the nuisance altogether by special dispensation in 1640. From the beginning of our period, the corporations had developed a diplomatic practice of paying companies to depart with a graduated scale of tips; but when a company insisted on its right to perform the townsmen had finally to appeal for whatever action they took against it to its patron or to the Privy Council.[4]

When allocated a playing-place, the players' custom was to charge for admission in the ordinary way, but, for their performances before the Mayor and civic dignitaries, for which, on occasion, no entrance money was collected, they were given a gratuity. It is reasonable to suppose that the size of the gratuity, being a very important component of a travelling company's income, also constituted a means of the corporation's control. Such rewards vary in amount, and possibly give us some clue to the size of the company, although it is as likely that in many cases they reflect the relative esteem in which the patrons of the companies were held. We are rarely informed of the number of plays presented. But that there is some basis in the assumption that the rewards relate to the size of the troupes is suggested by the fact that gratuities given for *not* playing bear about the same proportion between the companies as the gratuities for performances. Moreover, the sums given appear to vary around fixed basic amounts that change in each town from time to time according to the economic climate. Thus, at Coventry, between 1599 and 1602 a flat rate for a single civic performance seems to have been struck at 10*s*. Two companies – Derby's and Lincoln's – received a more generous payment of a mark (13*s*. 4*d*.), but the Queen's Men were paid 30*s*. For the following two years the rate appears to have been struck at just half that. Most companies received 5*s*. Worcester's and Lincoln's each received 6*s*. 8*d*. But the Admiral's got 20*s*., and the King's Men 40*s*. It should be noted that in these cases the payments to the larger companies are not multiples of those to the smaller and probably do not represent a greater number of plays performed. In other cases where we do know the number of plays, the companies seem to have been paid the same amount for each play, just as they would have been for performances at Court. Thus, it seems possible that the size of gratuities might provide an occasional clue to the depletion of the city companies when on tour, but the Queen's and the King's Men were invariably paid top rates, as were the Admiral's, except for the season 1592–3. The companies under royal patronage were welcomed at several towns with 'drynkynges' and farewelled with breakfasts at the corporations' expense. They could normally be assured of a gratuity of 30*s*. or £2. At the same time, however, there were regularly visiting companies that received less than the flat rate. Lord Ogle's players, for example, never received a reward of more than one mark, and at Gloucester, in 1596, got only 3*s*. 4*d*., twopence more than was spent on wine and sugar to welcome the Queen's Men in the same year.[5] Stafford's and Berkeley's companies, likewise, appear to have been near the bottom of the pecking order and to have been generally less liberally rewarded.

These purely provincial companies were almost certainly small, although they varied a good deal in composition. At Southampton in 1577 the clerk conveniently recorded numbers. These yield: Stafford's, 10; Clinton's, 6; Leicester's, 12; Bartlett's, 6; Delaware's, 10; Bath's, 11; Worcester's, 10. These totals are quite likely to be exact.[6] There is no reason to doubt that the Players of Downham who appear a number of times at Gawthorpe Hall in Lancashire and elsewhere between 1590 and 1596 were seven in number. We have very little information about the repertory of any of these companies. If, as seems probable, Berkeley's company, who played *What Mischief Worketh in the Mind of Man* at Bristol in 1578, was of comparable size, it is tempting to believe that these small provincial companies played Moralities, Romances, and Folk plays as their stock offerings, and possibly continued to do so for as long as they survived.[7]

Other small companies are recorded from time to time. Oxford's company at Bristol in 1581 had one man and nine boys. Richard Bradshaw's group, imprisoned at Banbury on 6 May 1633 for having forged a new date on an expired licence, seems to have been eight in number. This may also have been a children's company, for the arrested members speak of the principal, Edward Whiting, who was a Nottingham surgeon, as their 'master' and in one case as 'father' despite the fact that the acquaintance seems to have begun only six months before in Cornwall. Whiting, however, presumably did not act, nor did the saddest member of the group, Drew Turner, who confessed that he did 'nothing but drive the horse and beat the drum'. They carried a 'motion' or puppet show with them, and Bradshaw and Whiting were said to be in London seeking new recruits.[8] At Manchester in the plague year, 1637, there are records of three small companies being paid to avoid the town: Tho. Maskell and five others, another company of eight players, and Jon Costine with ten in his company.[9] These, too, were almost certainly puppeteers.

In these records we are approaching the lower stratum of the shifting population of vagabond entertainers. Beneath them still were those who managed, with forged or stolen papers, to eke out a desperate living one step ahead of the law. In 1583, Worcester's Men fell foul of such a group who stole, or otherwise came by, some of their papers at an inn and presented themselves as a licensed company to the clerk at Leicester. Three days later Worcester's themselves arrived, but, in the meantime, the clerk had spotted trouble. The indenture that the false company had shown spelt out the powers of the Master of the Revels. Among them was a clause: 'that none of their owne pretensed aucthoritye intrude themselves & presume to showe forth any suche playes, enterludes, tragedies, comedies, or showes in any places wthin this Realm, wthoute the ordlye allowance thereof vnder the hand of the sayd Edmund [Tilney]'. Worcester's themselves were therefore in some difficulty, for they were carrying only their passport from the Earl. They were asked not to play until the matter was cleared up, and offered an angel by the Mayor for their dinner. Ungratefully, they resisted, abused the Mayor in the public street and insisted on performing. The matter was only resolved by an unconditional apology from the stage and a promise by the Mayor that he would not refer the matter to their patron.

The sharp-eyed clerk had, however, also noticed an implication of Tilney's commission that was, no doubt, the ultimate recourse open to the corporations for controlling the players, and he inscribed it for future reference in the Hall Book. His comment is of importance for our argument and is worth noting. He wrote:

Nota. No play is to bee played, but such as is
allowed by the sayd Edmund, & his hand at the latter
end of the saide booke they doe play.[10]

Whether or not players were regularly required to submit licensed copies of their books to the provincial authorities I do not know. There appears to be no formal record of it at Leicester or elsewhere.[11] As with many aspects of tolerant Elizabethan administration, it was possibly a provision more honoured in the breach than the observance, but maintained as a fail-safe requirement that might be invoked to control seditious and obscene performances. The implication drawn by the clerk at Leicester, at any rate, was clearly that actors were expected to carry their licensed playbooks with them. The conditions under which the major companies played in London were not unknown or unrecognised in the provinces, and the writ of Tilney and his successors in the Revels Office pretty clearly ran throughout the kingdom.[12] It is an interesting question whether the London companies would have risked touring with an unlicensed text for very long, if they risked it at all, or whether they would have been eager to advertise their disregard of the Master's prerogative by offering such a text to the printer on their return.

The London touring companies were certainly often of greater size than any we have so far noted. Worcester's company, mentioned above at Leicester, was not small for 1583 and is recorded at Norwich in the same year, playing against the will of the corporation. There the players are recorded as 'James Tunstall Thomas Cook Edward Brown Willm Harrison & dyvers others to the number of x players of Interludes & servants as they say to the honorable therle of Worcester'. The four named players are probably those who attended to present the licence. Others of the ten are known from the Leicester list, which is presumably a copy of the licence itself. They are Richard Jones, Richard Andrews, Robert Browne, and Edward Alleyn. As the licence names eight sharers, the complete company was, I take it, at least fourteen strong.

At Plymouth in 1618 the Lady Elizabeth's players numbered twenty. Henslowe had 'broken' this company in about February 1615 by withdrawing its hired men. No doubt it had re-formed in the country. The licence of the Queen Anne's Revels company led by William Perry was copied by the clerk at Exeter in April 1624, and lists seven principals and 'the rest of their companie not exceeding the number of twentie'. At Norwich in February 1627, Ellis Guest appeared alone as the leader of Queen Henrietta's Men and presented their licence naming thirteen men. The rest of the company being still at Thetford, he was given a gratuity of forty shillings to stay away. This, too, must have been a company of some size. It may have been the 'greate Companie of players called the Cheefe Revells' recorded at Leicester in the following year.

As we saw in the previous chapter, the largest group recorded is George Stutville's King's Revels company at Norwich on 10 March 1635, totalling twenty-eight.[13] This may, indeed, have been an unusually large number for the road. Apparently it aroused some doubts on that score in the minds of the authorities. The players were sent for and their names taken 'to the end that … a certificate may be considered to be sent to the counsell'. The information having been provided, they were 'absolutely forbidden to play any longer in this City'.

The Norwich corporation was growing increasingly resistant to the visitations of the players and had been petitioning the Privy Council for some years to have them stopped altogether. It is not known whether Stutville's company had committed any misdemeanour, but it seems probable that the Norwich clerk had instructions to scrutinise the licences of visiting players for any irregularities.[14] In the same year he copied the patent of Daniel's Revels Company which was made out to 'Willm

Daniel, William Hart, John Townesend, Samuel Minion, Hugh Haughton, Thomas Doughton and the rest of their Company not exceedinge the number of ffifteene psons ... ' It cannot be certain whether the patent provides for fifteen or twenty-one people. The clerk at Coventry rather surprisingly added it up as seventeen ('William Daniell who brought a comission for the Revels vizt. for himself and 16 more in June last').[15] At any rate no fault seems to have been found with the composition of this company at Norwich, and the players were given a gratuity of ten shillings before being sent on their way.

Not all the names in the Stutville record can be those of regular actors. Musicians and other necessary attendants who would not be named on a normal patent must be included. The expression 'not exceeding', in patents, itself suggests that the Revels Office was aware of the disquiet caused by very large travelling groups. No doubt it was also possible for companies to pick up on their travels members who were of dubious character, or who might have fallen under the statute without the protection of the general provisions of a great troupe's licence.[16]

On 24 December 1624, as an addition to their travelling licence, the King's Men were furnished by Sir Henry Herbert with a letter of protection for the minor actors in the company, the boys, the musicians and attendants.[17] One of the latter, and the first named in the document, was their Book-keeper, Edward Knight. There are eighteen names altogether and the whole company must have been thirty-five strong. A similar licence was issued by the Lord Chamberlain in the plague year 1636. It is a curious confirmation of the resistance scholars have shown to the evidence for large travelling companies that Murray comments of this: 'The reason for the omission of the names of the principal actors of the company was, no doubt, because few of these intended to play in the provinces.'[18]

There is little reason, however, to suppose that the list is anything other than a complement to the normal travelling licence of the King's Men. The reason given for its issue, indeed, contradicts the idea that the company was somehow truncated. That is, that the company is 'to be prepared to attend his maiestie, and be nigh about the court this summer progress, in readines, when they shall be called upon to act before his maiestie'. Although this rather conventional clause may excite scepticism when employed by the Privy Council in defence of the London companies against the attacks of the City, there appears to me to be no cause to doubt its genuineness, certainly not in the present context. Preparedness to play at Court was what life for the major companies was all about. Neither in London nor in the provinces could such business be left to underlings. I have no doubt the whole company travelled, and, as we know that there were at least twelve principals not named in the Letter of Protection, the King's Men must have been as numerous on the road as Stutville's company.

The picture in the early 1590s, and in the year 1597, concerning the companies we are most concerned with – the Queen's, Admiral's, and Strange's – is, however, confusing and confused. It is one of a constant shifting and recombination of personnel, and a merging and separation of companies. All three of these companies appear from time to time in combination with others or with each other in the country records, and the combinations sometimes endured in London seasons (as did the Queen's and Sussex's, traceable in the country in 1591 and re-formed at the Rose in 1593) or had perhaps begun in London, as did the conjunction of the Admiral's Men and Strange's Men between 1590 and 1592 that lasted in some form or other until 1594.

Another company that appears to have been formed from a later combination of elements of both these companies, and perhaps of others, secured the Earl of Pembroke's patronage and played for the first half of 1597 under Francis Langley's management at the Swan. They were suppressed after the performance of *The Isle of Dogs* and the company was broken by Langley. We know, at least, that some of the members of the Admiral's company who had thrown in their lot with Langley returned to the Henslowe fold, and, from the litigation that followed between some of their number and the Chamberlain's men, it would appear that the latter had had a substantial share in the enterprise. The Chamberlain's also having re-formed, however, there was still a Pembroke's company able to tour the provinces for some years with every sign of prosperity.

In the early 1590s three Queen's companies appear in the provinces. One was the Children of the Chapel. One was led by Symons and appears to have been the principal acting company. The third was led by the Duttons or Duntons and was a company of acrobats. Attached to one or other of the latter two companies, and possibly at times to either, was a Turkish rope-dancer, who was clearly a crowd-pleaser and usually attracted a high reward. It is not always easy to distinguish these companies, but the record of 1588 at Bath, where a company of Queen's players had already performed on 19 July, probably identifies the Duttons company: 'more given by Mr Mayor to the quenes men that were tumblers ...'. Except when 'the Turk went upon the ropes', when very high rewards might be expected, the usual payment in all country towns for this group is about ten shillings. Symons's group usually doubles or quadruples that amount and is often received and farewelled with ceremony, both before and after 1594.[19]

If the implication of these different rates of reward is accepted, it means that, although divided, and although, as a royal company, they may have been treated with special favour, the Queen's Men, or that section of them that formed the main acting group, do not show at any time signs of the dwindling and struggle that is attributed to them by the conventional account. Although they disappear from London after 1594, and never again appear for the Christmas Court season, their reputation in the country seems to have remained as high as or higher than that of any other company, and their rewards as great or greater.

The 'breaking' of Queen's in 1593–4 has, however, been seen as a significant event in theatrical history. It is recorded in Henslowe's Diary thus:

Lent unto frances henslow the 8 of maye
1593 to laye downe for his share to the Quenes
players when they brocke and went
into the contrey to playe the some of
fyften pownd to be payd vnto me at his
Retorne owt of the contrey I saye lent } xv^{li}

wittnes John Towne
Hew daves &
Richard alleyn[20]

The date of this entry has been taken by Murray, Greg, and Chambers to be an error for 1594, in which case it closely follows the April season when the Queen's Men were acting in combination with Sussex's at the Rose. A combination of these two companies is also found in the country in 1591 at Coventry, Southampton, and Gloucester, and possibly also at Exeter, where the clerk's entry of Essex's is probably an error; but during the intervening years the Queen's Men had travelled independently and appear to have met with their accustomed esteem. After 1594 there is no record of their combination with any other company.

Chambers thought it was a sign of 'defeat' for the company that nine of their plays found their way into the publishers' hands in 1594 and 1595.[21] These were *A Looking Glass for London and England*, *King Leir*, *James IV*, *The Famous Victories*, *The True Tragedy of Richard III*, *Selimus*, *The Old Wive's Tale* and *Valentine and Orson*. *Friar Bacon and Friar Bungay* was also published as theirs, although this possibly belonged to the Henslowe repertory and had been played by others at the Rose. Before this time the only play known to be theirs that had appeared in print was *The Troublesome Reign of King John* (1591), and the only one that appeared subsequently was *Sir Clyomon and Sir Clamydes* (1599). Now, as we have seen, all the plays in the first list, except *The True Tragedy* (*Valentine and Orson* is lost) are sixteen-cast plays, as are *Friar Bacon* and *The Troublesome Reign*. If this was the touring repertory of the Queen's company, it offers little support to the idea that they travelled with a reduced cast. The exception is *Sir Clyomon*, but, stylistically, that belongs to the early 1580s.

There is nothing really against the supposition, however, that the date of Henslowe's record of the Queen's Men's breaking, witnessed by three others, is correct, and that the company's fortunes ran rather differently. We need not take the final-sounding 'went into the contrey to playe' too seriously. The company went into the country every year. Henslowe is clearly expecting them to return, and, as they had one final season at Court in January 1594, it is possible, as the loan to Frances suggests, that they had re-formed as a sixteen-cast company, only to have fallen on evil times after their return to London and to have been forced to combine with Sussex's. Either way, it is not of great importance. The season of the joint companies at the Rose in April 1594 is the last record of the Queen's

Men in London, and the last record of Sussex's altogether. It seems likely, as Chambers surmised, that the former company absorbed the latter. The appearance of their plays on the market may indicate nothing more than a cash-flow crisis during the re-alignment of personnel.

It is not unreasonable to conclude that touring companies normally carried with them a repertory of plays of a certain composition: one that represented the number of players available when the troupe set out. In the Queen's Men's case this would have been sixteen men and between five and eight boys. Plays with smaller cast requirements could, of course, be played by a larger company, merely by allowing greater numbers of attendants, or by easing out the doubling pattern; but if the company were to break, or to fall below its original complement, its stock of plays would be useless. The actors' first recourse would be to restore their numbers by combining with another company. That solution, as we have seen, was frequently adopted. Their next might be to acquire a new stock of plays, and finally, they may, indeed, have hit on the solution, dear to the hearts of textual bibliographers, and eminently reasonable in itself, of re-writing the text. Despite the fact that playbooks of this kind would not carry the authorisation of the Master of the Revels, texts such as *Alcazar* were thought by Greg to be the normal results of orderly abridgment made directly from the authorised prompt-book.

Orlando Furioso, on the other hand, printed in 1594 'as it was plaid before the Queenes Maiestie', and possibly the version said in *A Defence of Cony-Catching* (1592) to have been sold over again by Greene to the Queen's Men for twenty nobles, is described by Greg as such an abridged text as 'could only have taken shape in the course of acting before a low-class audience by a company whose performance was unregulated by any formal prompt-book at all'.[22] For this opinion there can be no other support than the critic's analysis of the internal stigmata of the text itself, and there are strong reasons for disagreement. *Orlando* is, in fact, a rather attractively printed Quarto on which some care seems to have been spent. It is certainly fuller than usual of Greene's characteristic rodomontade, but that is not what worries Greg, who complains of 'the omission of much of the high-flown poetry of the original'. It is a text that would hardly contain more suspect readings than the best examples of dramatic printing of the period, were it not for the fact that we have Alleyn's actor's scroll for Orlando with which to compare sections of it. The scroll does reveal differences in the ending of one of the comic scenes, and it expands Orlando's ravings into absurdities that even Greene might have blushed to own. One may take issue at every point with the readings that Greg judges on bibliographical grounds to be 'superior' in the scroll. But, questions of literary judgment apart, it is sufficient here to observe that, unless both the low-class audience and the actors who re-vamped the script were unable to count, *Orlando* is as firmly a sixteen-cast play as any other in the Queen's repertory.

While it is not unlikely, and cannot be disproved, that from time to time in the course of sixty years scrambled-up texts for reduced companies may have been produced in these ways, such evidence as exists suggests that the texts in a company's possession governed its composition and that once broken by even quite small reductions, it had either to recruit new players, combine with other troupes or cease to function. The histories of Lady Elizabeth's Men and of Pembroke's London company in 1597 are indicative.

In 1615 the Lady Elizabeth's Men drew up Articles of Grievance against Philip Henslowe and Jacob Meade which claim that Henslowe had broken the company and made it up again five times since 1612. His object, in their view, was to keep them perpetually in debt to him so that he could exercise control. One of their complaints was that 'In February last 1614 perceav[ing]e the Companie drewe out of his debt and Called vppon him for his accompts hee brooke the Companie againe, by withdrawinge the hired men from them ... ' It appears, indeed, that it was Henslowe's custom to bind the hired men of the companies he financed to him personally, as he did in 1597 after the break-up of Pembroke's company, no doubt with just such an object in mind, although the wages of the men were paid by the company. As thirteen actors are named as signatories to bonds for the financing of the Lady Elizabeth's troupe, the hired men cannot have been numerous, but their withdrawal appears to have precipitated Lady Elizabeth's into a series of combinations with Prince Charles's and the Queen's Revels troupes, and it was not until 1618 that the company was able to emerge again in its own right in London much changed in personnel. In this instance Henslowe had made their situation doubly impossible by withholding their playbooks, which must have numbered about twenty since they valued them at £200.[23]

Langley appears to have treated Pembroke's company at the Swan in much the same way in 1597, but he compounded the injury by pursuing the five members who had subsequently joined or re-joined the Admiral's Men for the forfeiture of their bonds of £100. Their defence in the Court of Requests was that they had been made unable to meet the conditions of the bonds, first because of the restraint of playing provoked by their performance of *The Isle of Dogs*, and then by Langley's action in returning their indentures to two, or, as they said later, three of the players and thus breaking the company 'so as they Cannott Continewe theire plaie and Exercise as they shoulde'. By the players' account, it appears that, after the restraint was lifted, Pembroke's company had obtained a new licence to play, but Langley had not been able to secure permission to re-open the Swan, and had deliberately broken the company in order to force the forfeiture of the bonds, because the dissident players had not been willing to risk using an unlicensed theatre.

According to Langley, the five members who had joined the Admiral's Men had merely been premature. They might have played in his house, he argued, as others of their fellows had done. He had presumably succeeded at last in getting a licence and in re-forming a company (although he now represents himself merely as a lessor). But this company must have been performing a new repertory, for he complains of the great costs and charges he has disbursed and laid out at and by the appointment of the complainants of the old company, and of his expenses in furnishing himself with 'sundry sorts of rich attire and apparel for them to play withal', for which he has ever since had little use.

Meanwhile, it was the depleted Admiral's company at their regular London house, the Rose, that appears to have adopted an expedient not unlike that proposed by Sir Walter Greg. The Plot of *Frederick and Basilea* shows that they called in the gatherers in the place of the usual attendants. This was a new play in June and may have been specially written for the circumstances in which the Admiral's Men now found themselves. Others that were played in repertory with it were also new since January. They are: *A Woman Hard to Please*, *Alexander and Lodwicke*, *Guido*, *Five Plays in One*, *A French Comedy*, *The Life and Death of Henry I*, *Uther Pendragon*, and possibly *That Will Be Shall Be*. Late in the month came the addition of *The Life and Death of Martin Swart*. About none of these do we know anything. It is perhaps of interest that from 19 May until 28 July, when playing ceased, these plays, with the occasional additions of *Bellendon* (*Belin Dun*?), *Jeronimo*, *The Wiseman of Westchester and The Witch of Islington*, formed the complete repertory. The last may have been a new play; the others had been part of the stock for some years and may have been re-vamped for the occasion. If, however, *Jeronimo* and *The Wiseman of Westchester* are the plays we know as *The Spanish Tragedy* and *John a Kent and John a Cumber*, no sign remains in the extant texts of their having been reduced for performance by a cast of twelve, and it may be that Henslowe quickly re-established his normal complement of players.

It is surely unlikely that a London company on the road would have taken its gatherers along. Some of the names in the Stutville list may be those of gatherers, but the only record of gathering in the provinces I know of is at Ludlow, in 1627, when some town roughs drunkenly abused Richard Errington who was taking money at the door for the Red Bull Revels company, and beat up the sergeant who came to his rescue. Errington was, however, an actor, and one of the leading members of the company. In any case, it has not, as far as I know, been argued that the Henslowe expedient in the case of *Frederick and Basilea* can be traced in the shorter extant printed texts and manuscripts and we need not consider it further.

The large company that finally concerns us is that of the combination of Strange's and the Admiral's Men between 1590 and 1592. As we have seen, this troupe must have been very large indeed, and may, in London, have consisted of as many as thirty-two men, and, on occasion, a number of boys so great as to suggest an amalgamation with a regular boys' company. The chief external evidence for its existence, as Chambers points out, is to be found in the Court records for the Christmas season of 1590, where the Privy Council entries of warrants for payment are made out for the Admiral's company, while the corresponding records of payments in the Chamber Accounts are to Strange's. Off and on, the amalgamation ran in some form until 1594.

This company had begun to play at the Theatre sometime after 1589 and had rapidly become the principal company at Court for the Christmas season, presenting six plays in 1590–1. It has been generally supposed that after their quarrel with James Burbage they transferred to the Rose about May 1591, gaining there the addition of Edward Alleyn, but losing, for the time being, the services of the other great actor of the age, Richard Burbage. The company seems generally to have gone under the name of Strange's Men, but Alleyn never gave up his status as servant of the Lord Admiral, and it is the appearance of his name under this form in the company's travelling passport that is the assurance of the combination. It is also, however, the cause of the confusion of nomenclature, both at Court and in the provincial records. Chambers surmised that in the country, as in the Court records, clerks may have written down the name of either company named in the licence and thus that the provincial records may conceal from us the actual nature of the troupe when it travelled.

Chambers also believed that it was from this great company that three others arose in 1594 – a new Admiral's, a new Pembroke's, and something very like the old Strange's – but its travelling composition has posed something of a problem.[24] If the company had, indeed, taken to the road in 1591, its expenses may well have been as ruinous as it claimed in a petition to the Privy Council:

Forasmuche (righte honorable) oure Companie is greate, and thearbie our chardge intollerable, in travelling the Countrie, and the Contynuaunce thereof wilbe a meane to bringe vs to division and seperacion, whearebie wee shall not onelie be vndone, but alsoe vnreadie to serve her maiestie, when it shall please her highenes to commaund vs... our humble peticion and suite thearefore to your good honnours is, That youe wilbe pleased of your speciall favour to recall this our restrainte, and permitt vs the vse of the said Plaiehowse againe.

The reason for the restraint on the company is unknown. It appears to have been directed at the theatre, the Rose, rather than at Strange's Men themselves, for they had permission to play three days a week at Newington Butts, and other companies appear to have been unaffected. They were supported in their claim by the Thames watermen whose livelihood was threatened, or so they alleged, by the closure of the Rose. Was then the intolerable charge to the company merely the expense of travelling to Newington? It is not, after all, such a long walk. And would not the theatre-going population who lived west of London Bridge have found it as convenient to cross by water to arrive there as to reach the Bankside theatres?

The warrant from the Privy Council for the re-opening of the Rose does suggest that Newington was the problem:

Wheareas not longe since vpon some Consideracions we did restraine the Lorde Straunge his servauntes from playinge at the Rose on the banckside, and enioyned them to plaie three daies at Newington Butts, Now forasmuch as wee are satisfied that by reason of the tediousness of the waie and that of long tyme plaies have not there bene vsed on working daies, And for that a nomber of poore watermen are therby releeved, Youe shall permitt and suffer them or any other there to exercise them selves in suche sorte as they have don heretofore.[25]

I believe, however, that this bureaucratic rehearsal of circumstance does not necessarily imply that the company had played nowhere but at Newington. Chambers argued as follows:

The provincial records show that the company probably travelled during 1592, but not in 1591. If the petition belongs to 1592, it is obvious that the plague intervened [between the end of their season at the Rose in July and the issuing of a travelling licence in May 1593], and I strongly suspect that the company's fears proved justified, and that the re-organization for provincial work did in fact lead to a 'division and separacion', by splitting off some of the combine as Pembroke's men.[26]

Chambers's interpretation of the complex facts is eminently fair and reasonable, and one hesitates to disagree, but I believe that the repertory of Strange's eighteen-week season at the Rose, beginning on 19 February 1592, clearly indicates that the big company had already broken. All the plays we can trace in Henslowe's diary from that season are sixteen-cast plays: *Friar Bacon*, *Orlando*, *A Looking-glass for London and England*, *The Jew of Malta*, *A Knack to Know a Knave*, 'harey the 6' (which seems to me more likely to be one or other part of *The Seven Deadly Sins* than Shakespeare's *1 Henry VI*) and '*mvlomvllucco*'(i.e. 'Muly Molocco'), which cannot be other than *The Battle of Alcazar*. One might add to the list *Jeronymo*, if one could be certain that it is *The Spanish Tragedy*. The piece called 'tittus and vespacia', however, which is commonly taken to be a version or forerunner of *Titus Andronicus*, must surely have been a play about the conquest of Jerusalem (i.e. '*Titus and Vespasian*'), although perhaps not the same play as that which appears in Henslowe's record as 'Q Jerusalem' for 22 March, and can have had no connection with the 'tittus & ondronicus' played by Sussex's Men in January 1594.

Alleyn still travelled with Strange's in 1593 as an Admiral's man,[27] but this sixteen-cast repertory henceforward becomes the basis of those played by all the companies at the Rose either singly or in combination, and was, no doubt, influential in creating a standard for the optimum size of a dramatic company.

If the great company of 1590 did, indeed, take to the road, it probably did not survive for long.[28] If, however, the record at Shrewsbury of Strange's and the Admiral's meeting together in 1593 and playing for a high fee otherwise offered only to the players of the Lord President of Wales can be taken to represent the two complete companies playing in conjunction, it is tempting to believe that the townsfolk were treated to what may have been the first and must have been the last provincial performance of *The Whole Contention of the Honourable Houses of York and Lancaster*.[29]

The idea, and perhaps the actuality, of a company large enough to play the repertory of 1590 must, however, have persisted. The epilogue to *Henry V*, recalling York and Lancaster's long jars 'which oft our stage has shown', must have been spoken in 1599, but would it have been topical in reference to plays ten years old? Plays, moreover, that could not have been performed by any London company in the meantime, except one? Might it not have been given point by a recent revival of the revised *Contention* as the *Henry VI* trilogy, when the same theatrical elements temporarily joined forces again under Pembroke's protection and Langley's management at the Swan? The probability has been obscured by the insistence of textual critics that the *Contention* quartos are memorial corruptions, but it is to this company at the Swan, rather than to that of 1590, that we can positively trace the conjunction of the actors whose names are recorded in the text of the first Folio.

From the puzzling circumstances of the Admiral's Men in the country between 1592 and 1593, it is not unreasonable to assume that they may have been strongly tempted to adapt their repertory, but, as we shall see, a depleted company could not have played *Alcazar*. Reasons for the regular or 'normal' reduction of playbooks are hard to sustain. That does not mean, of course, that it could not and did not happen, or that companies did not suffer calamitous depletions, but the occasional mandatory controls that the Masters placed on the size of companies plainly indicate their desire to limit excessive numbers of actors on the road. By this means they could to some degree assist the corporations in identifying the troupes and in controlling the incidence of masterless men banding together with the licensed companies. It is probable, I believe, that placing a limit on the size of a company was also designed to give the Masters some control over its stock of plays: it was a kind of declaration that the actors were to play the repertory they set out with and to perform whatever feats of activity they were licensed to perform.

There was, of course, a greater danger than in London that players might alter their scripts, introducing obscenities or glancing at living people or matters of state. Certainly, even in London, companies are known to have risked playing unlicensed pieces. Chapman's *Byron* roused the wrath of the French ambassador in 1608 and Sir George Buc was persuaded to suppress it, but when the Court was safely out of London it was brought on again. That resulted in the arrest of three of the actors, although Chapman managed to escape.

The King's Men tried some less innocent politicking in 1624 with Middleton's *A Game at Chess*. This had been properly licensed by Sir Henry Herbert, who, influenced perhaps by the general joy at the return of Prince Charles and Buckingham from the unsuccessful negotiations about the Spanish marriage, at first saw no harm in its rather flimsy allegory. What he presumably did not know was that the actors intended to represent Count Gondomar, the Spanish ambassador, to the life. Staged once again while the Court was out of London, the play ran for an unprecedented nine days and made a huge profit. Popular feeling must have saved the players from the worst effects of the royal anger. They were suppressed for only ten days and put on a bond of £300 for their good behaviour. Encouraged by this success, they then went further and performed an altogether unlicensed play called *The Spanish Viceroy*. We do not know the full consequences of this surprising act of indiscretion, but nine years afterwards, when they were in trouble again over *The Tamer Tamed*, Herbert entered in his Office Book 'as a remembrance against their disorders' the abject apology the master actors had been obliged to sign, freely confessing the Master's power to punish and promising never again to compromise his authority.[30]

Herbert appears to have been stricter and more conscientious than Masters before him – at least that was his own opinion – but the impression that it was a justified opinion is perhaps only the result of our fuller information about his activities. Tilney's conditional licence for the play of *Sir Thomas More* is not alone in enjoining the actors to observe his reformations at their peril, and there is no doubt that the peril was considerable. The Masters had wide powers of arbitrary imprisonment. But life being what it is, and actors being an unruly lot, one might suppose that companies in the provinces could most likely get away with a good deal more than in the metropolis. How far they may have been emboldened in times of crisis to re-write their plays in order to accommodate them to a reduced cast must, however, remain a matter of belief, depending entirely on the internal textual evidence than can be produced. That they could have taken very great liberties with their texts, however, seems to me against the balance of probability and involves the assumption that the Mayors and Headboroughs of towns who attended the performances were as naïve and low-class as it sometimes suited Sir Walter Greg to represent them. Is it not likely that they would have been quite as sensitive to profanity and scurrility as their brethren in the City, and, if politically more naïve, the more troubled in mind about treasonable matter? Being reluctant to welcome the players in the first place, would they not have been the more ready to discover enormities, and to cavil, as indeed they did, at the smallest irregularities?

The second major reason for the revision of texts has been thought to be that of reducing their playing time; but that the conditions of country touring necessitated such treatment, or that country audiences were incapable of an attention-span as great as that of their city cousins, is, once again, a mere *a priori* assumption that is strongly qualified by such evidence as exists. From the corporations come nothing but complaints about performances of excessive duration. We may judge from the time performances ended that country audiences were not given short measure. There are records of playing commencing in the country at one o'clock in the afternoon. In London the starting time for at least one company changed in 1594 from four o'clock to two o'clock, presumably in order to clear the time of evening prayer. Lord Hunsdon wrote in these terms to the Lord Mayor asking leave for his company to play in the city, promising that they would end performances between four and five and that they would use no drums or trumpets for calling the people together.[31] The object of an early start in the country would also, of course, be to avoid disrupting evening service, surely just as sensitive a concern as in the city; so that we may take it that the duration of a performance in the provinces, as in London, fitted Ben Jonson's computation of 'two hours and a half and somewhat more'. The Canterbury Burgmote Books record a resolution of 15 April 1595, forbidding Sunday playing and limiting any company to a maximum visit of two days. Its preamble complains that:

> the contynuance of them so longe tyme as commonly hath byn vsed ys deemed verie inconvenient and hurtefull to the state and good quiet of this Cittie and Impoverishinge thereof especially the same beinge so late as usually they have byn in the nighte time.[32]

Norwich adopted a similar rule in 1599, limiting playing to 9 p.m., and in 1611 forbade the Queen's Men to play at night altogether. Chester followed suit in 1615 as did Worcester sometime before 1622. Late playing was still common, however. At Nottingham in 1603 Richard Jackson, an inn-keeper, was gaoled for 'sufferynge players to sound thyere tru[m]petts and playing in his howse without lycence, and for suffering his guests to be out all night', and the scrimmage at Ludlow in 1627, described above, took place, according to Richard Errington's deposition, while the play was still in progress at ten or eleven o'clock. Puritans like Henry Crosse inveighed against 'these nocturnall and night Playes, at unseasonable and undue times',[33] and, if these examples seem too late to apply to our period, there is Heywood's story, if one cares to believe it, in *An Apology for Actors*, written probably about 1607, of the rout of a surprised party of Spanish raiders at 'Perin' in Cornwall, who fled when a company of actors, playing late in the night, sounded their drums and trumpets. Heywood dates this 'about 12 years ago or less'. However unlikely the actual event, it is witness from an experienced playwright of the occurrence in the 1590s of extended evening performances in quite remote parts of the country. There is nothing much here to indicate that the provinces were regularly treated to maimed and truncated performances. Like so much else in our story, our reading of the evidence can reach little further than the our initial hypotheses, but it is not quite a case of believe as you list.

4

The Plotter at work

We may now gather that the Plot of *Alcazar* was composed at the commencement of a stable period in the history of the Admiral's Men, when a cast of sixteen had been reconstituted after the Langley affair at the Swan. The text, by our method of computation, requires sixteen men to fit its stage-directions, but the Plotter, who has sixteen men, nevertheless behaves as if he needed more. We must now turn to enquire why, and stand our hypothesis on its head.

We have been subjecting the texts to a process that accords with the simplest notion we can form of what the Plotter actually did, but with what we presume to be the reverse intention. We were seeking, from the point of view of a commonsense assumption of authorial competence, the answer he started from – the size of his cast. His purpose, on the other hand, must have been to construct a counting device, starting from his knowledge of the number of actors available, that would enable him to make the final adjustments between the author's script and the resources of the company. We shall see that he had many other concerns as well, but we need be in no doubt that every Plot serves in some way as a method of counting and keeping track of the actors.

The Stage-reviser was no mere flunkey. He would no doubt do his best to respect the playwright's text, but he clearly had ideas of his own about how a scene should go and he was sometimes left with the business of putting together the contributions of a number of collaborating writers, as was Ralph Crane, assisted by the reviser, in preparing the book of *Barnavelt*. Sometimes he directs what is to be re-written by others, as does the reviser of *Sir Thomas More*. Dramatists clearly trusted him to sort out small details and left directions in draft such as 'Enter as many Aldermen as may' (in *More*), 'The Show as you know' (in *John of Bordeaux*), and 'Either strikes him with a staffe or casts a stone' (in *The Captives*).

But what was his actual purpose in making out the Plot? A careful examination of the seven extant Plots leads one to the conclusion that, meticulously edited as they were in *Dramatic Documents from the Elizabethan Playhouses* (1932), Greg's *a priori* assumptions about their function led him to many dubious conclusions. The enthusiastic declaration of John Quincey Adams in 1945 that we now understand 'the exact nature and purpose of the Elizabethan theatrical plot' was certainly over-optimistic.[1]

The extant Plots reproduced in chapter 5 are arranged in probable order of dating. All but two belonged to the Admiral's company and were played at various times between 1592 and 1602. The other two are *The Dead Man's Fortune* (*c.* 1590), played by an unidentified company and containing the names of few actors, and *The Second Part of the Seven Deady Sins* (*c.* 1592), which gives a fairly full account of the cast of Strange's Men. Of the Admiral's Plots, two survive only as fragments: they are the second part of *Fortune's Tennis* (*c.* 1598), prepared in the same hand as that of *The Seven Deadly Sins*, and a Plot whose title is missing but which I shall follow Greg in calling *Troilus and Cressida* (*c.* 1600), although it appears to have taken a much wider sweep through the story of the Trojan War. This was prepared by the same Plotter who made up the more fully preserved *Battle of Alcazar* (*c.* 1598–1601) and probably also *1 Tamar Cam* (*c.* 1602). The remaining Plot, *Frederick and Basilea*, is in a different hand from either of these, and may be dated with precision to June 1597.

It would seem that Adams could hardly have been wrong in describing a Plot as 'an outline' serving 'as a very necessary and practical guide to actors, stage-hands and other employees of the theatre in the smooth performance of the play'. Nevertheless, it appears to me almost certain that this was not the way in which the Plots were used, or the purpose for which they were prepared.

A Plot is without doubt an outline of some kind, and made with a practical end in view. It is a skeleton sketch of the action, but quite different in kind from the synopses, called 'author-plots', that exist for Jonson's *The Sad Shepherd* and the unnamed tragi-comedy that Adams printed in *The Library*. The latter are literary and narrative in character, designed to serve as *aide-memoires* for composition; the theatre Plots are functional and cryptic in character, designed in some way to assist in the preparation of the plays they represent. They are literary only in so far as they may sometimes catch up phrases from the book, or in so far as the Plotter's imagination is strained to convey actions of some complexity in the briefest possible space.

The distinction between functional and literary theatre language, has undoubtedly been made too much of by textual critics. It is often assumed, for example, that directions are literary when in the indicative or optative mood and theatrical in the imperative. This will not hold, even for the Plots. Descriptions of any kind of action may take a variety of forms. When they are descriptive of the manner of the action, it is perhaps reasonable to assume, as critics do, that they have picked up the language of the Book. This may be the case with directions such as 'Enter Porrex sad' (*Sins*, scene viii), and 'Enter orleance musing' (*Fortune's Tennis*, line 15), but such directions of mood and manner are very rare in the play texts, and it may be well to consider whether they have not some practical meaning for the Plotter, and are mistakenly considered 'literary'. A more elaborate example appears in *2 Seven Deadly Sins*:

Enter Arbactus pursuing Sardanapalus and the Ladies
fly. After enter Sarda wth as many Jewels robes and
Gold as he can cary.

It is tempting to imagine that this has picked up some literary flavour from the prompt copy. The first sentence, indeed, may well be the original stage-direction; but the form of the second ('as many ... as he can carry') is not dramatist's language. Conversely, it is not language addressed to the actor, to whom it is not of great use to be told to pick up as much miscellaneous stuff as he can bring back onto the stage. It reads rather more like a note of what the Plotter expects to see, or perhaps to hear, and its practical function is, more likely, to mark an immediate re-entrance that will involve a short pause in the action and a momentary silence on stage. The properties may need noting for future inscription in the Book, but it is also possible that Sardanapalus's last entrance is wordless – but spectacular – as he crosses the stage, laden with treasure, on the road to immolation in his palace.

Likewise, the wording 'on the walls' to direct appearances 'above' is sometimes taken as literary, but it occurs so frequently in play texts, even when no walls are strictly involved, that we have no grounds for supposing it to be other than theatrical and functional. In the Plot of *Troilus* there is, naturally, frequent mention of walls and the direction 'to them on the walls' may well be in the imperative mood, but the final words of that Plot, 'they on the wall descend to them' were certainly not written for the purpose of directing actors and would have been unavailable for consultation by them.

It is not likely that authorial directions are to blame for the delightful 'literary' muddle in which the Plotter of *The Dead Man's Fortune* landed when trying to organise the sequential entrance and exit of three fairies who save his heroes from the axe in the last scene. Writing at speed, as we may suppose, the best he could arrive at was:

then after that the musicke plaies & ther Enters
3 antique faires dancynge on after a nother the
firste takes the sworde from the executioner &
sendes him a waye the other caryes a waie the blocke
& the third sends a waie the offycers & vnbindes
allgeryus & tesephon & as they entred so they departe

Once again, it is hard to see how this could be of practical use to anyone but the Plotter himself. Greg was no doubt right in regarding this Plot as a fairly primitive example of the craft, but if, as he assumed, Plots served as call-sheets, or if, as Adams assumed in consequence, they served as practical guides to actors, stage-hands, and other employees, what are we to make of a direction such as this? For the use of actors, one is conscious only of what it will *not* do. First of all, the words 'then after that' give no indication of what 'that' is. The preceding direction merely says 'to them carynus & prylor', but whether these characters engage in dialogue, or how much action there may be following their entrance will be quite unclear to the musicians. The fairies will presumably enter on the music cue, but, unless they have a clear recollection of rehearsals they may be tempted to enter all at once, and it will not be until they have read to the end of the entry, and worked out the cryptic message of '& *as they entred so they departe*', that they will see that they were intended to enter and exit one by one, by which time it would be rather too late – if it were not, in any case, an impossible feat to accomplish! The language is descriptive rather than imperative and is less technical in tone ('*sendes him a waye*') than the great majority of directions in the printed texts, but are we therefore justified in assuming that this early Plot is a defective and amateurish performance compared with later examples?

In none of the Plots is there evidence of a fully settled and regular way of registering whatever information it is they are intended to register. Only one (*Tamar Cam*) attempts to assign actors' names to all the characters. Not all mark medial or final exits. Some mark in property notes in the margin and others appear to record properties in the general text, but *Frederick and Basilea* does neither. Most note sound cues, but the last-mentioned Plot, again, does not, and in another the evidence is missing. Greg tentatively classified them in order of sophistication from less elaborate to more elaborate, but he observed elements of experiment appearing even in the latest (*Tamar Cam*). It seems likely that in *Troilus*, *Alcazar*, and *Tamar Cam* we do meet an experienced practitioner who had developed a fairly standard technique of notation, but, in the absence of the texts, it is really impossible to be sure that these later Plots are at a higher stage of evolution than their predecessors, although they are fuller of detail.

Greg stated his assumptions with great caution, but his picture of the Plots in use was influenced by the fact that, in all of them, where the paper has not decayed, there are to be observed holes about a third of the way down the page that suggest that the sheets were hung on a nail or peg. This led him to the natural conclusion that they were hung up in some public place, probably the tiring-house, for use either by the cast generally or by the Elizabethan equivalent of a call-boy.

There are several features of the Plots that work against this assumption. In the first place, as Greg himself observes, the 'massing' of entries, although a mark of the sophisticated Plots, would have made rapid consultation very difficult. A massed entry is one that lists character names in order and then follows them with a list of actors' names. But all Plots list the actors incompletely, and some entries, worse still, list them in the reverse order of the character names. Although this may have been less confusing for the actors, who can be supposed to have remembered what roles were assigned to them, than to a scholar attempting to reconstruct the situation in his study, it must still have been confusing enough for a rapidly doubling minor actor when entering in a new role to which he was wrongly assigned. This happens to the boys Nick and Ned in the second section of *The Seven Deadly Sins*, and to Cowley and Robert Pallant in the same Plot. The latter are almost certainly confused at their first entrance as attendant lords belonging to opposing parties, and their appearance of having changed allegiance at their second is illusory. In *Frederick and Basilea* the reversal of actors' names is particularly common in the early scenes, but, as there is almost no doubling required in that Plot, it was perhaps of no great moment and was allowed to stand uncorrected.

Also indicative is the appearance in 'sophisticated' Plots of the use of 'manet' to keep account of actors remaining on stage when others exit. Such a direction is, of course, useless for consultation. An actor cannot leave the stage in order to discover whether he is meant to remain on it. Then, the general descriptions of the minor roles may often have been unsatisfactory for directing the lesser fry, even when no actual change of identity is involved. The usages 'Lords', 'Captaines', 'Guards', 'Soldiers', 'Attendants' tend to shade into each other in the Plots as they do in the texts and the manuscript plays. It can be seen in the study that, when a Plot specifies Attendants, without listing the actors involved, it may well intend the re-entry of the same Lords or Captaines who appeared with a major enterer on the last occasion, but actors would have had no time to ponder the possibilities, and the Plotter himself, as we shall see, sometimes had to check his own listings. The unassigned Soldiers and Attendants in scenes v and viii of *Frederick and Basilea* are probably of this kind, but take some time to sort out, even in the study. In the same Plot the 'gatherers' are brought on to swell the crowd, but as to who they are or by what means they are to be called on stage we remain in the dark.

A similar situation in *1 Tamar Cam* is the most convincing piece of evidence that that Plot, at least, was not used as a call-sheet. In the final scene there occurs what appears to be a procession of conquered races across the stage. It calls on the complete acting cast of sixteen men and four boys, all of whom are known by name, and an additional six persons to represent the Geats, the Nagars, and the Cannibals. They are listed in a numbered order which we may suppose to have had some importance in the spoken text. Some of their names, however, are unknown to the Plotter. One of the boys ('gils his boy') is listed under his master's name, which was common enough practice, and two others are distinguished as 'little Will' and 'little Will Barne'. The Cannibals 'Rester' and 'old Browne' must have been theatre identities, but the listing of one of the Nagars (niggers) as 'the red-faced fellow' could hardly have remained on display in the tiring-house without becoming at best a standing joke, and would have been impossible for use by a call-boy who valued his skin. In the penultimate scene of the Plot appears the nymph Thea, possibly a disguise role, assigned to 'the other little boy'. Even though this lad must have been 'Mr Denygton's (Doughton's) little boy' who entered two scenes earlier as one of Tarmia's sons, it is obvious that the Plot was not written for *his* benefit.

It therefore appears to me most unlikely that the Plots were prepared for use *by* actors or that they could have been of much use to a call-boy, if such a person existed. A call-boy may have been able to sort out the obscurities of a direction as comparatively simple as this from *Alcazar*:

Enter in a Charriott Muly {M}ahamett
& Calipolis : on each side {a} pag{e}
moores attendant Pisano mr Hunt
& w . Cartwright and young Mahamet
Anthony Jeffes : exit mr Sam manet
the rest : to them mr Sam a gaine exeunt

for he might remember that the two littlest boys dressed as blackamoors have to be got on as pages to move Mahamet's chariot, and he might be able to work out that Pisano, a character only once named in the text, and appearing only in this scene, is Sam Rowley, and must be called on at the beginning, although his name is listed only upon his exit.

But when we come upon errors in the Plots, as we do, a call-boy would have been as much at a loss as a scholar. In *Alcazar*, for example, there is an uncorrected entry:

Enter Governor {o}f Tan{ge}r {:} & a
Captaines mr Sha{a H} J{effes e}xeunt

I believe Greg himself failed to interpret this correctly. He supposed that only the named actors were called on stage, that Shaa played the Governor and that 'Captaines' was therefore an error. His impulse was always, of course, to mistrust the text; but the text at this point cannot be fitted by fewer than three actors without falling into total absurdity, and in fact may call for more than three. Its direction reads:

Enter Don de Menysis gouernor of Tangar, with his companie speaking to the Captaine.

It appears to me much more likely that 'a' is the error in the Plot, picked up directly from the textual direction that seems to demand only one other speaking character. When the Plotter then saw that a second had to be found, he was forced, precisely on the principles I have proposed, into the improbable solution of casting the heir-apparent to the throne of Morocco as the other. This strongly suggests, as do other signs of *ad hoc* alterations in *Alcazar* and in other Plots also, that a Plot was a working document prepared in the process of a 'run-through' and that the Plotter had his cast about him, calling them on stage as required and making adjustments as he went.

If, then, the Plots are of uncertain use from the actors' and the stage-keeper's point of view, they appear even more defective as a set of instructions intended for stage functionaries of other kinds. In the matter of properties, their record is very patchy. In one, *Frederick and Basilea*, no properties of any kind are listed, while in only one, *Alcazar*, are properties listed both in the body of the Plot and in the margins. In *The Dead Man's Fortune* and *2 Seven Deadly Sins* it may be that all the properties needed are listed, but there is no notation in the margins. The same may be true of *Tamar Cam*, although it is difficult to believe that the three heads brought on stage in III, iii exhaust the possibilities in a play that appears to be full of magical occurrences. Steevens may have failed to copy the marginal directions in the second column, although it is true that those in the first are exclusively concerned with music and sound effects. In the fragmentary *Troilus* there remains only one direction for a light to be carried on by Cressida's waiting-maid, but marginal listings may also have disappeared, through decay.

Alcazar is thus the only Plot in which marginal notations of properties certainly appear. Even in *Alcazar*, the Plotter fails to repeat directions for props in the margin on at least two occasions, and several times introduces marginal notes where nothing is called for in the scene itself. If we did not have the text of the play we should have no idea why he noted the provision of '3 violls of blood and a sheeps gather' for the third dumb-show, and not much of why he notes 'Chains and boxes for presents' against the fifth scene. But there are spectacular properties called for by the playtext that make no appearance in the Plot. It is very doubtful, then, whether it was a main function of the Plot to make a list of properties. Actors were, perhaps, responsible for getting their own properties on and off stage. The common directions take the form : 'Enter Progne wth the Sampler' and 'to them Philomele wth Itis hed in a dish' in the penultimate scene of *2 Seven Deadly Sins*. The final direction of *The Dead Man's Fortune*: 'Enter the panteloun & causeth the cheste or truncke to be broughte forth' also appears to be a direction to the actor, although it could hardly be vaguer from the point of view of the stage-keeper. These appear to be literary or narrative directions from the Plotter's point of view, directed at what the actors are *doing*, with occasional indications of what they need if they are to do it. In the later Plots actors are appointed to carry large objects: tables, banquets, chairs of estate, and the like, but these properties rarely rate a side-note. Even the Moor's chariot in Alcazar was presumably the responsibility solely of Edward Alleyn and his two black pages and is not listed in the margin.

In communication with the stage crew the Plots apparently played no part. That was the business of the Book. In the manuscript copies readying notes for properties are frequent. For example, in *Woodstock* (or *1 Richard II*) we find 'A bed for Woodstock' preceding its revelation behind the curtains by fifty-four lines. In *The Waspe* a Table and Banquet are readied in the last act, twenty-five lines in advance. In *The Welsh Ambassador* the direction 'sett out a Table' appears twenty-eight lines in advance of its being disclosed with the clown writing at it. In *Believe as You List*, where King Antiochus enters in prison, there is a warning note: 'Gascoine & Hubert below: ready to open the Trap doore for Mr Taylor', and a 'Chime' for the working of magic effects is noted several times in *John of Bordeaux*. In many of the manuscripts smaller properties are also prepared for in the margin of the text. The time allowed before their appearance is usually so long that there seems to be no reason why the Plots should not have been used for the purpose if such had been the intention, although it is obvious that a Plot gives only a faint sense of the time-continuum of the action.

In its rather full notation of properties, *Alcazar* is clearly an exception. It is, I believe, a production piece in which the Plotter himself has revised the spectacle and elaborated the dumb-shows, the second of which (III, Chor.) does not exist in the printed text and the third of which (IV, Chor.) is merely noted in the direction '*Enter to the bloudie banket*'. His marginal annotations are thus *aide-memoires*, made for the purpose of being entered into the Book, which would have needed considerable marking-up for this revival. We cannot, however, press the evidence of the silence of the other Plots too far. Many plays of the period have need of very few properties. It may be that *Frederick and Basilea* is not exceptional in its failure to note any but simply needed none.

Cues for sound present an entirely different picture. In the later Admiral's Plots they are fully and regularly marked. They appear to have more to do with the business of Plotting than does the provision of properties. This I believe to be an illusion, but it is a suggestive one.

There can be no doubt that the governance of the music was always the responsibility of the Book. Music must be cued to dialogue and musicians need to be readied in advance of the moment they are to begin playing. It is not a matter of wonder that manuscripts and many printed texts contain fairly full and precise directions for music and sound effects, including readying notes for singers and musicians when they are to perform in special locations. There is, in theory, no reason whatever for marking music cues on the Plot, for, it must be stressed, the Plot itself can give only a very inexact measure of time.

We find no sound cues at all in *Frederick and Basilea*, nor are there, strictly speaking, any in *The Dead Man's Fortune*, except for the direction we have already noted : 'and then the music plays'. This Plot, however, was at some time provided with entr'acte music in a different hand from that of the original Plotter. The points at which it was to occur are marked very clearly with lines and crosses between the scenes. No other sound effects are marked in. Perhaps none were required in a romance comedy with a domestic alternative plot. *2 Seven Deadly Sins* notes in its text a 'Senitt' to introduce the first dumb-show, and the direction 'Alarum' three times, one of these entries apparently being adjusted to cue it into the scene following, but no directions for sound are entered in the margin. Oddly enough, musicians are called for in the text, two of whom seem to be Sardanapalus's captains in disguise, and one a singing boy, Vincent, but there is no direction for a song and the action is inscrutable without the text of the play. *Fortune's Tennis* is too decayed to provide information, but the remaining three Plots are very fully marked up for sound.

I believe the reason for this is connected with another innovation seen in these Plots. They regularly mark medial and final exits. They also use the term 'manet' to list the characters remaining on stage. This was very puzzling to Greg who calls it 'an apparently useless convention', as, of course, it is, if the Plots were used as call-sheets. It appears to me, on the contrary to be a marked advance in the craft of plotting and I shall discuss its importance in due course. For the moment it is only necessary to observe that the new convention allows, as a minor benefit, a clearer impression of the time sequence of the action and thus makes these Plots at least marginally serviceable for the cueing-in of music and sound effects, as the older convention was not. The point may be quickly seen by editing a scene from one of the later Plots in the earlier style. In the example below the sections in bold type represent the additions of the new convention:

Alarum Enter Assinico & a Persian : Mr Singer
& Parsons : To them Colmogra **Exeunt**
manet Colmogra : To him Tamar Cam
Otanes : 3 nobles : W. Cart : Tho: Marbeck
& W.Parr **: Exit Colmogra** To them
Colmogra & Mango : guard George: parsons.
Sound Exeunt, manet Colmogra : Exit

The initial sound cue might well have appeared in an early Plot, but it is clear that the direction 'Sound', which must accompany the exit of Tamar, could not have been signalled in the old style, nor could the order of events after the last entrance have been anticipated by musicians awaiting their cue.

Precise music cues must always have remained under the control of the prompter and were marked in the Book. Consultation of the much less accurate Plot would merely have been an inconvenience for his purposes. Moreover, it would be quite useless for him to attempt to convey the direction that appears in the margin of the *Troilus* Plot at line 9 : '3. severall Tucketts'. If these mark three separate entrances, as they may do, they would surely need to be cued individually for the musicians. If, however, the trumpets represent a Greek challenge, with pauses between the soundings, the musicians are in a slightly better position, but still have no way of knowing precisely when they are to begin. Once again the notation appears to be merely descriptive from the point of view of the Plotter, but it is at least possible that these Plots, having served their primary purpose, at last found their way to the music room. There they might have been hung up to serve as rough but convenient readying notes, enabling the musicians to prepare for their actual cues with some degree of foreknowledge. The markings for entr'acte music added to *The Dead Man's Fortune* faintly support the possibility that this was a practice adopted in more than one company, but this remains mere speculation.

Returning, then, to the purpose of the Plots, we see that their primary concern is with the management of the acting cast: the fitting of the character roles called for by the text to the cast of available actors. The

Plotter appears to have worked with his cast about him, carefully filling the text's demands for entering actors, keeping check of the doubling of roles as the supply runs low, and occasionally correcting himself when it is found that an actor is unavailable for a part for which he at first seemed free. His apparent errors or changes of intent are perhaps the most revealing clues to his working methods. This is the case with the two Pages who are reduced to one at line 45 of *Alcazar*, and with John Holland, whose deletion from the first scene of *2 Seven Deadly Sins*, presumably because he was needed to play one of the unassigned Sins in the prologue, reduces the number of Warders to one. In *Frederick and Basilea*, Black Dick is deleted as a guard in scene ix, when it is realised that he alone is available to play the Messenger in the same scene.

In some cases there are signs of the text itself having to be adjusted, as is suggested in *Troilus* with the replacement of Antenor by Priam at line 12, this correction clearly having been made after the Plotter had progressed almost to the end of the second column (cf. line 33). In *The Dead Man's Fortune* a scene has been added in the margin immediately before Act V. It is not in the hand of the original Plotter, and may have been written by whoever added the music cues. Its point appears to be to add material preparing for the final entrance of the reconciled lovers with the knowledge that Eschines has shed his disguise as Bellveile; but it may merely have been a scene the Plotter had forgotten, just as he originally forgot the second (comic?) scene of the play and had to start his Plot again on the other side of the sheet. No casting problem arises, for all the actors in both scenes are available to enter. It may be that these Plotters were struggling with a Book that had not quite been consolidated. Such a text exists in *John of Bordeaux*, which can be shown to have been prepared in order to incorporate comic material into the author's incomplete original draft.[2] In *Alcazar*, however thc Plotter had to solve his casting difficulties in a more drastic way by removing a whole scene of the original text.

The Plotter was thus involved both with fitting the play to the company and the company to the play. The logical conclusion is that the Plot was made up before the Book was complete, and must have had, as one of its purposes, the consolidation of the Book itself. The Plot and the Book clearly served different functions, but, their making-up was interdependent, and primarily concerned with the correct ordering of the written records for performance. As we shall see, there were occasions when, for explicable reasons, the Book itself usurped some of the functions of the Plot.

There must have existed, however, a third document on which both depended. That is the cast-list. No complete example of such a list has come down to us, but some record must have been kept in the theatre from which the partial cast-lists attached to many printed plays were prepared. Most of these record only the actors who played the major roles, but two plays list some doubled roles: *The Duchess of Malfi* and *Hannibal and Scipio*. *The Soddered Citizen* also has a fairly complete cast-list with some minimal doubling. We can reconstruct one other complete cast and assign all the doubled roles with some confidence from the manuscript of *Believe as You List*.

The cast-list of *The Duchess of Malfi* (pub. 1623) records a revival of the play by the King's Men sometime about 1619, in which it appears that Lowin re-created his original role of Bosola. For the other three principal roles the original actors are named, as well as those playing in the revival. Richard Burbage was the first Ferdinand, Henry Condell the Cardinal, and William Ostler Antonio. In the revival these roles were played by Joseph Taylor, Richard Robinson, and Robert Benfield. The remainder of the men listed are Nick Underwood (Delio), Thomas Pollard (Silvio), Nicholas Tooley (Forobosco), Robert Pallant (Doctor), and John Rice (Marquess of Pescara). Underwood and Tooley double as madmen. This entry is followed by an '&c.', but no other names are listed. Confusion arises, however, over Pallant's doubling roles. He is bracketed together with Cariola and the court officers. Bentley is almost certainly right in regarding this as an error.[3] If Pallant was the actor who appears in the Plot of *2 Seven Deadly Sins*, he was an old man at the time, and in fact died in 1619. He would hardly have doubled in the role of a waiting-woman. But Greg may be correct in supposing that this Robert Pallant was his son, born in 1605, and thus young enough to have played a woman's role, although hardly old enough for the Doctor. If we suppose this boy to have played both parts it is a sign that the King's Men were hard pressed indeed in these bad years of plague, for *The Duchess of Malfi* can easily be played by a cast of twelve men, which is the limiting number displayed in III, ii, the madmen's scene, while many other actors are available to double as the doctor in V, i.

The appearance of Forobosco, a character only mentioned in the text, is also confusing. A nonce name might be assigned to a stand-in, but Tooley must play a character of some importance and this is perhaps a deliberate revision of the name of Castruchio, to which role no actor is allotted. The other unassigned roles are those of Roderigo, Grisolan, Mallateste, the pilgrims, servants, guards and executioners, the old Lady, and possibly, as we have seen, Cariola. The first three of these, however, are merely original nonce names in the text for glorified attendants.

This list, whatever its origin, is about as elaborate as a cast-list would need to be, although one could wish it clearer in detail. Five actors will play single roles and will not need to be named in the Plot. The minimum requirements of the text have been met when two middle-ranking actors are pre-cast to double as madmen. Seven actors, including Pallant, Rice, and Pollard will double all the servants, pilgrims, officers, executioners, and remaining madmen. Underwood and Tooley are pre-cast to dodge as madmen, because their other roles are of some importance. The others are pre-cast for minor parts and will be named for their doubling roles in the Plot as they are come to scene by scene.

The only scene that might have presented difficulties for a cast of twelve is III, v, the scene of the Cardinal's investiture, which requires an elaborate dumb-show. A troop of guards appears with Bosola immediately afterwards. Although the text is said on the title-page to contain 'diuerse things Printed, that the length of the Play would not beare in the Presentment', the investiture scene is certain to have been played, for Webster disowned the song in it in a textual note. Bosola and his guard are vizarded when they enter, however, and the troop might therefore be made up of almost anyone. Bosola's immediate re-entry un-vizarded in IV, i shows that the action was punctuated by act breaks, but even without a break before IV, i, there is ample time before IV, ii for the positioning of Antonio and the children behind the arras (to appear as their own effigies in waxwork) and for the general change into madmen's attire.

For *Believe as You List* (1631) we can use the negative evidence of the manuscript to reconstruct the original cast-list, with a result markedly similar to that of *The Duchess of Malfi*. We know by chance the names of five principal actors from the list of 'writings' that have to be prepared and carried on stage, and we can thus work out, by comparing the Plotter's annotations with his silences, what the pre-assigned roles must have been. The tortuous method of arriving at this conclusion I have argued elsewhere, but state the conclusions here.[4] *Believe as You List* has a cast of sixteen actors in which, once again, five actors are cast for single roles throughout:

Joseph Taylor (King Antiochus)
Thomas Pollard (the flamen, Berecinthius)
John Lowin (Titus Flaminius)
John Honyman (Merchant)
Curtis Greville (Merchant)

The four boys who play the Queen of Bithynia, a courtesan, Cornelia, and Zanthia, the moorish maidservant, would also have been pre-cast, but we do not know their names. Others would have appeared in the cast-list in the following roles:

William Penn (Merchant)
Eliard Swanston (Chrysalus in I, i and either Metellus or Sempronius after IV, i)
Richard Robinson (Syrus in I, i and either Metellus or Sempronius after IV, i)
Francis Balls (Geta in I, i)
Robert Benfield (Stoic in I, i, Amilcar in II, ii, and Marcellus in V, i)

The remaining roles are left to be filled as they are come to in the script. The actors available are Richard Baxter, William Patrick, William Mago, Rowland Dowle, Nick Underhill, Mr Hobbs, and Francis Balls. These are all doubled to a greater or lesser extent in a variety of roles. They form the lesser members of the Carthaginian Senate, the court of King Prusias of Bithynia, including the King himself, and the soldiers, guards, and attendants on the Roman Legate, Flaminius, and the pro-consul of Sicily, Marcellus. In the greater number of these entrances their names appear in the Book. But they are not quite sufficient for the task. Some of them, Francis Balls and William Patrick in particular, seem scarcely to have achieved the status of speaking actors. When Lentulus, an important emissary from Rome, arrives for a single short scene (III, i) the role is allotted in the Book to a principal actor, Richard Robinson. Likewise, one of the Merchants, William Penn, has to be called on to play the gaoler in IV, ii. This almost certainly leads to the interesting result that the roles of the Merchants, who are merely called 1, 2, and 3, had to be switched, so that John Honeyman is named in IV, iii as the first Merchant, and the others in V, i as the second and third, Penn now being the second and Curtis Greville the third. This, indeed, is how and why we know their names. In the cast-list itself Penn would have appeared as 1 Merchant.

This listing of the Merchants gives us an important clue to interpreting the splitting of roles that is unique in this text. In marking the Book the Plotter is clearly concerned above all with the *speaking* cast. He keeps a check on the silent attendants, but in such a perfunctory manner that it is really only by luck that we have enough information to work out the full cast. When speaking is involved, however, the actors must be named. Now the splitting of roles is between the evil and undifferentiated henchmen of Flaminius, the Roman Legate, the villain of the story. There are three of them, called Calistus, Demetrius, and Titus. Calistus and Demetrius are cast only at their *second* (speaking) appearance in II, i, their first having been silent. At that point Calistus is Baxter and Demetrius is Patrick. When next they appear, in III, i, Calistus is played by Mr Hobbs, and Demetrius by Rowland Dowle, while Titus, who is a new character, is taken on by Baxter. Baxter then remains the sole attendant on Flaminius and is named at every subsequent entrance, because the character he has now assumed, although it might just as well be Titus, was in fact called Demetrius by the playwright. In III, ii indeed, the Plotter bothered to change the speech-headings, but as in IV, iii Baxter appears as an officer of the guard – although once again he is doing a job that might as well have been done by Titus or either of the others – he ceased to bother. All that is important in these roles has been taken over by the character 'Baxter'. Patrick, on the other hand, must have been delighted with his few lines of dialogue in II, i, for in the rest of the play he says not a word and was clearly the second or third lowest in the company hierarchy. Probably he would not even have been allowed that moment of glory, except that Mr Hobbs was for some inscrutable reason not available and had to be 'calld up', while every other member of the cast is either on stage in this scene or preparing to enter in the next.

Hannibal and Scipio (1635) by Thomas Nabbes is a Queen Henrietta's play. It is called 'An Historicall Tragedy', but is a curious, spectacular piece with much dancing and masking. Scenery was employed, each act representing a separate country and the scenes being changed to the accompaniment of the entr'acte music. It is therefore episodic, like *Believe as You List*, and some of the major actors have time to double. The printed text names eleven men and one boy as 'the speaking persons' and lists some of their doubled roles. William Shurlocke plays Maharbell in Act I and King Prusias of Bithynia in Act V; George Stutfield plays a Common Soldier (a character of importance) in Act I and Bostar in Act IV; Hugh Clarke plays the Nuntius who appears twice, dodging the role with Syphax in Act II; Robert Axon plays Bomilcar in Act I and Gisgon in Act IV.

The limiting scenes involve at least fifteen actors and the final scene calls for a large number of mutes. A battle is to be represented during the last entr'acte and the directions read:

The Souldiers led in by their Captaines, distinguist severally by their Armes and Ensignes, to the Musick of the following, put themselves into a figure like a battaglia – the dance expressing a fight

As in *Tamar Cam*, however, there appears to be a limit to the number of mutes available. The military must rapidly leave their balletic warfare at the end of Act IV to seat themselves at the beginning of Act V as the 'full senate' of Bithynia, an effect so odd that King Prusias is moved to declare that his 'Court looks like a Parliament of souldiers'.

From the functional nature of the directions and the fact that a partial cast-list found its way to the printer, one would suppose this play to have been printed from prompt copy. If *Believe as You List* had passed to the printer, he could hardy have avoided picking up some of the prompter's markings. That there are none in *Hannibal and Scipio* suggests that in this play the record of the minor doubling roles would have appeared only on the Plot. That I believe would have been the normal situation. The marking-up of prompt-books with actors' names must be exceptional and indicates some unusual circumstance in their preparation. That is certainly true of *Believe as You List* and *Barnevelt*.

The manuscript of *The Soddered Citizen* (1626–35), a King's Men's play, gives a rather full cast of 'The Persons (And) Actors', including some roles that, although apparently doubled, are in fact only disguises. Richard Sharpe is the *jeune premier* and also speaks the prologue and epilogue; Thomas Pollard plays 'a deboyst young gent'& a Prisoner' (these being the same role) and a disguised role as Birdlyme, a Scrivenor. Nick Underhill as Shackle disguises himself as Brayde, a haberdasher, and Anthony Smith as Clutch disguises himself as Querpo, a decayed gentleman. The limiting scene requires fifteen men, but the directions are uncommonly precise, calling for three servants and seven maskers in IV, i. We may be confident that the cast was exactly sixteen and that the nine adult actors listed in the cast played recognisable roles throughout, even though some are in disguise. The remaining seven actors would then have appeared in II, i as the six Creditors' servants and the 'serving man in blacks'; in IV, i as the seven maskers; and in V, ii as the three Creditors, two Commissioners, the Solicitor, and the re-appearing servant in blacks. Four speaking boys are named, although one is known to the Plotter only as 'Iohn: Shanks Boy', and there are three other boys listed as 'Mute &c.'. The unnamed singing boy probably increases the juvenile cast to eight. The point to be observed is that in a play in which the Plot turns heavily on disguise, the roles that are actually doubled are separated by long intervals and have a kind of thematic (if comic) consistency.

The three genuine cast-lists described above differ very considerably, for each text makes different demands upon its personnel. But they are just such lists as we should expect to supplement the record of the Plots and the manuscripts. The list we can reconstruct from *Believe as You List* tends to confirm their characteristics.

We may conclude, then, that in the normal process of preparing a play for production the Plotter was concerned with three documents: the manuscript or Book, the initial cast-list, or sketching-out of the major roles, and the Plot which it was his business to construct.

The Book was clearly the magisterial document in performance, as the presence of readying notes for actors, musicians, and properties in many of the manuscripts attests. It was the final authority in the hands of the prompter. The Plot can give no clear indication of time-sequence, and, although duplicating much information that also appears in the Book, does not seem to have any particular use in conjunction with it.

The Plot springs to life as a theatre document, however, as soon as it is put together with the actors' parts: those records together would be sufficient to direct an acted run-through. It served, indeed, two essential functions: first, as a means of making out the actors' scrolls correctly, and second as a skeleton or ground plan of the action.

The word itself: 'plot' or 'platt' or 'platform' in Elizabethan usage, of course, means 'ground-plan', and there are obvious reasons for its employment in the theatre. It is clear that companies treasured their prompt-books and duplicated them as little as possible. The safest course for any company was to possess only a single copy of any play. Prompt copies were required by law to carry the signature of the Master of the Revels or his deputy allowing the performance, and such signatures exist on the most perfectly preserved copies we have. The King's Men sought injunctions to prevent other companies performing their plays and finally secured a guarantee that none might be printed without their permission first being obtained. Two versions of a play may sometimes have been kept in the company archives, and copies were sometimes requested by private patrons. The scribe of *Bonduca*, Ralph Crane, preparing such a copy some years after the performance, could not reconstruct the complete stage version and had to confess that the King's Men's prompt-book was lost, and that he had found and copied the author's foul papers. In some cases, however, we know the author provided fair copy. The prompt-book of *Believe as You List* is in Massinger's own hand, although there must have been an antecedent (censored) manuscript from which this was prepared.

If we piece together these suggestions with the evidence of Robert Daborne's letters to Henslowe, we may picture the ordinary process of the

Admiral's Men in preparing a play as follows. First of all, the company (or Henslowe himself) would commission a single dramatist or a group. The topic itself might actually be suggested, for Henslowe sometimes lent his authors books as source material. After a time the author would have sketched out a plan. It may have consisted of a brief scenario, such as Ben Jonson is known to have made. If the dramatist were trusted, this might be deemed sufficient for part-payment to be made and a go-ahead given for further work. Henslowe was sometimes disappointed of a completed play and the scenario was passed to other writers. So we have a record of Chapman being paid for finishing a play according to Benjamin's Plot.[5]

If the writer were more fluent than the laborious Jonson, he might produce a full version of the play at one hit. That is the way Shakespeare is said to have worked. Or he might produce a fairly full version of the play with some descriptive notes for acting and even some suggestions for casting. But there would be unfinished scenes and second thoughts not fully integrated. Versions such as these we may possess in the printed texts of *Timon of Athens*, *All's Well*, and *Troilus and Cressida* (which possibly show more accurately how Shakespeare did work), as well as in Q. 2 *Romeo and Juliet* and the versions of *Much Ado* and *Love's Labours Lost*.

After the composition of the primary material, the play would be heard by the company, or by some of its members appointed for the purpose. The price of £8 paid for *2 Henry Richmond* shows that it was a complete play when Robert Shaa heard it and scribbled the sketch of a Plot. But normally, only a part-payment would be made at this hearing, and the author would return home to complete his final, perfected version. Either on this occasion, or when the script returned to the theatre as a completed play, it was the custom of the company to meet at the Sun Tavern in New Fish street for a preliminary reading. Henslowe's Diary records some of these meetings, because he stood the drinks, or recorded the sum for reimbursement. It may well have been at these meetings that the Plot was made out. If not, it must have been prepared in the theatre very shortly afterwards.

The company would then set about purchasing costumes and collecting properties. Even if the author were dilatory and sent in his perfected copy bit by bit, the Plotter now had enough material to work on and could proceed with confidence to make up the long scrolls of 'every man's part according to the scrip' from the record of the doubled roles in the Plot. From Daborne's letter to Henslowe of 25 June 1613, we learn that the actors' parts for his new play *Machiavel* had already been written out as far as Act III, while he was still engaged in writing out Act V fair. He says that he has made alterations in Act V and there will have to be (consequential?) changes in the actors' scrolls for Act III. When Henslowe is pressing him over another play, Daborne offers, as proof of good faith, the testimony of Henslowe's messenger that the play is actually complete, and that he found him *copying* merely, not composing. He even offers to send the sheet he was copying from.[6]

As soon as the text was complete, it would have to be sent to the Master of the Revels for licensing, and rehearsals would have to carry on in the absence of the Book for some time. Here the Plot once again comes into its own: it is the skeleton key by which the actors' parts can be fitted together in rehearsal, and – in the Plotter's hands – it does in a manner serve as a call-sheet for bringing the cast on stage scene by scene.

If this scenario reconstructs anything like the true picture, it carries the interesting implication that prompt-books produced in the regular way would not have carried notations concerning the actors. Sound cues, readying notes, and notes for the working of the stage machinery would no doubt have been marked in when the copy was returned from the Revels office, but actors' names registering the management of the casting would only have appeared, if they needed to be recorded at all, at the preliminary stage of preparation, that is, at the same time as the Plot was made out. Thus, they would have appeared not on the Book, but on the author's draft or foul papers. This conclusion is supported by some of the extant manuscripts. *The Welsh Ambassador*, for example, is very regularly marked-up with readying notes and music cues, but has no other markings of any kind. The two dramatic manuscripts in Munday's hand, *John a Kent* and *Sir Thomas More*, were also originally very clean texts with no cast markings. The former had presumably served as a prompt-book. The latter may not have done, but when the revisers had finished with it, it was certainly anything but clean. It had, as it were, reverted to the condition of foul papers. Most of the manuscripts that bear signs of arranging the cast can be regarded as authorial foul papers in this sense. Several have been prepared for revivals and thus would need to be plotted over again. Others, like *The Captives* and *Believe as You List*, are holograph manuscripts. Others, like *Barnavelt*, are scribal copies of the author's foul papers, still in need of re-writing and adjustment. The two latter plays, moreover, were produced in exceptional circumstances. Some of the plays in the Beaumont and Fletcher First Folio of 1647 appear to have been printed from marked-up authorial copy of this kind. There are implications for bibliography here, but they are not my concern at present. The point is that printed texts, no less than manuscripts, could be and were treated as primary material for revivals in this way, and it is important to note that (contrary to one of Greg's unstated, but strongly implied premises) the existence of a Plot does not presuppose the existence of fair manuscript prompt copy.

Some revision for a revival may always have been necessary, and desirable even if not necessary. In *The Profession of Dramatist in Shakespeare's Time*, Professor Bentley points to the contemporary popular assumption that 'plays regularly performed would be regularly revised' and concludes from the wealth of evidence he produces that 'the refurbishing of old plays in the repertory seems to have been the universal practice in the London theatres from 1590 to 1642'.[7]

It might be assumed that, for each revival, whether a revision of the old play was undertaken or not, a new Plot would have to be made out if the

1 [T]he plotte of the deade mans fo[r]tune /

Enter the prolouge /

I. i — Enter laertes Eſchines and vrganda

I. ii — Enter peſſcodde to him his father

I. iii — Enter *Teſephon* allgeryus laertes w[th] atendantes : Darlowe : lee : b ſamme : to
7 them allcyane and ſtatyra

I. iv — Enter validore & aſſpida at ſeverall dores to them the panteloun

——x——x——x——x——x——x——x——x——x——

muſ ique

II. i — Enter carynus and p[r]lior to them
11 ſtatyra and allcyane

II. ii — Enter vrganda laertes *Eſchines* : Exit *Eſchines* and Enter fo[r] Bell veile

II. iii — Enter panteloun & his man to them his wife
15 aſſpida to hir validore

II. iv — Enter *Teſephoun* allgerius alcyane & ſtatyra w[th] atendantes to them [to th] carynus & prelyor to them laertes & Bell veile

Dar lee ſam

II. v — Enter valydore & aſſpida cuttynge of ... to them the maide

Muſique

Enter Vrganda Alcione Statira Enter Laertes Eſchines. Enter w[t] out diſguiſe

Enter aſſpida & [valydore] peſcodde to hir — IV. iv
Enters roſe 43

Enter panteloun & peſcodde — IV. v

Enter aſpida & validore diſguiſd like roſe w[th] — IV. vi
a flaſket of clothes to them roſe w[th] a
nother flaſket of clothes to them the pan 47
teloun to them [to them] peſcodde

x x x x x x x x x x x x x

Enter kinge Egereon allgeryus teſephon — V. ii
w[th] lordes the [x] executioner wth[is] his 50
ſworde & blocke & offycers w[th] holberds
to them carynus & p[r]lyor then after that (V. i)
the muſicke plaies & ther Enters 3 an
tique ſaires dancynge on after a nother
the firſte takes the ſworde from the ex 55
ecutioner & ſendes him a wâye the other
caryes a waie the blocke & the third ſends
a waie[s] the offycers & vnbindes allgeryus
& teſephon & as they entred ſo they departe 59

Enter to them vrganda laertes and *Eſchines* leadinge ther laides hand in hand — V. iii

Enter the[n] panteloun & peſcode — V. iv

Enter validore [and aſſpida] — V. v

II. vi Enter panteloun whiles he ſpeakes validore paſſeth ore the ſtage diſguiſde then Enter peſſcode to them aſſpida to
24 them the maide wth peſſcodds apparell

Musique ——×——×——×——×——×——×——×——×——

III. i Enter carynus and p^{r}lyor = here the laydes ſpeake[s] in pryſoun

III. ii Enter laertes & Bell veile to them the Iayler to them the laydes

III. iii Enter *Teſephon* allgerius at ſeverall dores
30 diſguiſd wth meate to them the Iayler

III. iv Enter pateloun & peſſcode = enter aſſpida to hir validore & his man · b · ſamme to them the panteloun & peſcode wth ſpectakles

Musique ——×——×——×——×——×——×——×——×——

IV. i Enter teſephon allgerius wth atendantes Dar & tyre man
35 & others to them Burbage a meſſenger to them Euphrodore = Robart lee & b ſamme

IV. ii Enter carynus & p^{r}lyor to them vrganda wth a lookinge glaſſe acõmpaned wth ſatires plainge on ther Inſtruments

IV. iii Enter carynus madde to him prelyor
41 [d] madde

V. vii Enter the panteloun & cauſeth the cheſte or truncke to be broughte forth

finis 67

Beginning of the Plot as Originally Written on the Reverse and Abandoned as Incorrect

The plotte of the deade mans fortune

Enter the prolouge /

Enter laertes Eſchines and vrganda

Enter *Teſephon* allgerius laertes w^{t}⟨^{h}⟩
atendantes : Darlowe lee & b ſamme to 5
them allcyane and ſtatyra

2 *The Dead Man's Fortune*
(British Museum, MS. Add. 10449, fol. 1)–transcript of Plot

company had changed in membership. This holds true for the methods of the later Plotter of the Admiral's Men, but it is not necessarily so for the earlier method of plotting seen in *The Dead Man's Fortune* where actors' names are rarely used. Clearly the method might vary from play to play, depending on the demands made on the cast by the text. There is, thus, no system of Plotting that can with any certainty be judged more or less sophisticated than any other, but, we may at least have some confidence that we have arrived at a correct estimate of the reasons for the Plotter's activity. Even in the absence of the playtexts, it will now be possible to offer descriptions of the behaviour of individual practitioners and finally to interpret the Plot of *Alcazar*.

5

Interpreting the Plots

'The Plotte of The Deade Mans Fortune'

The earliest Plot names only four actors and thus depends upon a cast-list that must itself have involved some preliminary doubling. A restriction of cast is evident, yet there are characters who appear in early scenes without re-appearing, and other characters who appear only in the last scene, without having any previous history. On the assumption that roles were doubled wherever possible, we still have a situation that may easily be coped with within the numbers required by the limiting scene, which is the last. There, precisely sixteen men are called on stage and eight boys, if we count the Antic Fairies as boys. If the fairies are not boys, they may well be other members of the cast, even possibly senior members, re-entering in disguise. The fable may involve a magical rescue exactly similar to the one that occurs in *John a Kent*, IV, ii. Whether or not that is so, there are still sixteen adult actors required and the company appears to be of a standard composition.

The obscurities, however, are rather great. It might be argued that in the last scene the direction 'kinge Egereon' brings two actors on stage, neither of whom has appeared previously. That would involve a cast of seventeen, but, although I have not discovered a romance in which anyone of this name exists, it seems likely enough that the King's name is Egerion. It is not clear whether Peascod's father and the Pantaloon are the same, but whatever solution we arrive at does not, in this case, alter the acting cast. If we decide that they are not the same, we may follow Chambers in supposing that Peascod takes service with the Pantaloon and enters as his man in II, iii. If they are the same, we may reserve an actor in one place, but must then provide one for the 'man' in another. Another possible solution is that the fable involves Peascod taking service with his own father in disguise. As he must change costume at a later stage, this is not an unlikely twist of the intrigue; but whichever actor we save will be obliged to play King Egerion in the final scene.

None of these difficulties would have existed for the Plotter. He must have worked out the greater part of his cast-list in advance, but the attendants on Tesephon and Allgeryus had to be pondered. They are listed in the text of the third scene as Darlowe, Lee, and b Samme. These were, then, the last three members of the company not otherwise cast. When attendants were called for they were cast on the spot and noted by the Plotter. Their identity was then taken for granted, for in II, iv, when the same principals appear, attendants are mentioned, but remain anonymous in the body of the text. At their third entrance at IV, i, however, a complex situation has arisen and we have the confusing (to us) entry which I give below in what I believe to have been its original form:

Enter tesephon allgerius wth attendantes
& others to them Burbage a messenger
to them Euphrodore = Robart lee

To this has been added in the right margin, and partly overlapping the text: 'Dar & tyre man & b Samme'. The addition appears to be in the same hand as the text, although some letters, notably the 'e's, are formed rather differently, probably because the writing is small and cramped. The words '& b Samme' thus appear to follow 'Robart lee' in the last line and Greg's transcript represents the whole wording 'Robart lee & b Samme' falling within the margin, in small type, as if it were all part of the later addition. A careful examination shows this to be mistaken. The words '& b Samme' are simply written following the addition to the line above in the first available space within the margin. The intention is to list Darlowe, the tire-man, and b Samme as the 'attendantes & others'. The explanation is that some change has been made necessary by the fact that Euphrodore, a previously unassigned character, is now allotted to Robert Lee. It may even be that Euphrodore is a nonce-name given to one of the attendants who has been sent on some special mission and is now re-appearing. No real change of identity need be involved for Robert Lee: it may simply be that he has been chosen out of the three to speak and to perform some special action at this point. In the absence of marked exits, we cannot tell. He may have no more importance here than a messenger, entering in the scene for the first time at this point, but still recognisably an attendant of Tesephon's, as he has always been. All three of the original attendants may have had equally fancy names, and it may simply happen that we never discover the names of the others. The call for 'others' might have been one of Greg's 'odds and ends' accidentally copied from the book, but, as the tire-man is now called in, it appears that the others are for some reason important.

It can be seen that the Plotter was puzzled over this difficulty with attendants. Had it been merely a question of mute officers, he might have altered the text, or supplied one actor where the text calls for at least two. That sometimes happens in tight moments in the manuscript plays and in the other Plots. This Plotter, however, returned to check the previous appearance of the three attendants, and noted in the left margin, opposite II, iv, that the attendants there are, indeed, Darlowe, Lee, and b Samme, just as they were in I, iii. The implication is that at least two speaking parts were involved in IV, i and that he has had to keep track of how the parts are to be made out. Or else he is simply counting the actors available to him to make quite sure that the changes he is now forced to make in IV, i are indeed feasible, the requirements of the text being for attendants who are more numerous than two, and of whom at least two, and possibly Euphrodore in addition, are recognisable.

It is not impossible that this situation is created by the Plotter himself and arises because of his preference for a particular actor in a particular role, for it is not clear, in the absence of the text, that the plotting has reached such a state of crisis that the tire-man *must* be called in. It is also a possibility that the problem arises because of the casting of b Samme as Validore's man in the previous scene in the extended plot, III, iv. It may have appeared at first that he would be blocked from returning to his former role as an attendant in the main plot. Whatever the situation, the dodging of b Samme shows that the Plotter is in a tight corner and that he is not free to call above sixteen men and the tire-man on stage.

There remains the problem of whether 'Burbage a messenger' in IV, i calls on one actor or two. There is little else in the Plot to compare with such an entry. The Plotter's use of '&', however, appears to be consistent elsewhere when two enterers are involved, and the natural conclusion is that the messenger was played by Burbage. Greg's assumptions about this were needlessly complicated. He believed that the story might be made sense of if Burbage played Urganda and entered here in that role as a messenger, the Plotter, by oversight, naming the actor instead of the role. Urganda, however, is an enchantress in *Amadis de Gaul* and in Munday's derivative romances, and although Burbage must have been a young man at the time of this performance, it is hard to believe that he would have played a female role. Moreover it would be unusual for a Plotter to name a boy by his surname. A more likely explanation is that Burbage played Eschines, one of a pair of young lovers (Laertes being the other) who, with the aid of the enchantress Urganda, win the hands of their ladies, against parental opposition and the attempts of rivals, by means of disguise and trickery. Eschines (Burbage) disguises himself as Bellveile in II, ii, and presumably remains in that role thereafter. If, in IV, ii, he is to enter in another disguise as a messenger, possibly to convey some kind of false information to his own and Laertes' fathers, Tesephon and Allgerius, the Plotter will not know what to call him. He cannot write 'Bellveile', or 'Eschines', for either will imply that he is to be recognisable in one or other of those roles, which, presumably, he must not be. The only solution is to name the actor.

These justifications of the Plotter's solutions may appear far-fetched when it is seen that he was capable of making an initial error in the order of his scenes, even though he corrected it almost at once, and that such a serious inattention may well indicate the presence of other errors undiscoverable in the text. As we have seen, however, a possible explanation is that the play was in a somewhat fluid state and would have been consolidated by the creation of the Plot. The account I offer, if correct, has the advantage over Greg's of exonerating the Plotter's final version from error, and showing that it would have been perfectly

The Platt of The Secound Parte of the Seuen Deadlie Sinns

(I) *A tent being plast one the stage for Henry the sixt · he in it A sleepe to him The Leutenãt A purceuaunt R Cowly Jo Duke and i wardere [J Holland] R Pallant : to them Pride · Gluttony Wrath and Couetousnes at one dore · at an other dore Enuie · Sloth and Lechery · The Three put back the foure · and so Exeunt*

(II) *Henry Awaking Enter A Keeper J sincler · to him a seruaunt T Belt · to him Lidgate and the Keeper · Exit then enter againe · Then Enuy passeth ouer the stag · Lidgate speakes*

(III) *A senitt · Dumb show · Enter King Gorboduk wth 2 Counsailers · R Burbadg m^{r} Brian · Th Goodale · The Queene wth ferrex and Porrex and som attendaunts follow · saunder w sly Harry J Duke · Kitt · Ro Pallant · J Holland After Gordbeduk hath Consulted wth his Lords he brings his 2 sonns to to seuerall seates · They enuing on on other ferrex offers to take Porex his Corowne · he draws his weopon The King Queen and Lords step between them They Thrust Them away and menasing [ect] ech other exit · The Queene and L⟨o s⟩ Depart Heuilie · Lidgate speaks*

Lidgat speake (XIII)

Enter Nicanor wth other Captaines R Pall · J sincler · Kitt · J Holland R Cowly · to them Arbactus · m^{r} Pope · to him will foole · J Duke to him Rodopeie · Ned · to her Sardanapalus Like A woman wth Aspatia Rodope Pompeia will foole to them Arbactus and 3 musitions m^{r} Pope J sincler · Vincent R Cowly to them Nicanor and others R P · Kitt

Enter sardanapa · wth the Ladies to them A Messenger · Th Goodale · to him will foole Runing A Larum (XIV)

Enter Arbactus pursuing Sardanapalus and The Ladies fly · After Enter Sarda wth as many Jewels robes and Gold as he ca⟨n⟩ cary · (XV)

A larum

Enter Arbactus Nicanor and The other Captains in triumph · m^{r} Pope · R Pa · Kitt J Holl R Cow · J Sinc (XVI)

Henry speaks and Lidgate Lechery passeth ouer · the stag (XVII)

Enter Tereus Philomele · Julio and ⟨ot.. (XVIII)

(iv) *Enter ferrex Crownd wth Drum and Coulers and ſoldiers*
one way · Harry · Kitt · R Cowly John duke · to them
At a nother dore · Porrex drum and Collors and ſoldie
29 *W ſly · R Pallant · John Sincler · J Holland ·*

(v) *Enter [Gorb] Queene · wth 2 Counſailors · mr Brian*
Tho Goodale · to them ferrex and Porrex ſeuerall waies
wth [his] Drums and Powers · Gorboduk entreing in
The midst between · Henry ſpeaks

A Larum wth Excurtions After
35 *Lidgate ſpeakes*

(vi) *Enter ferrex and Porrex ſeuerally Gorboduke*
still following them · Lucius and Damaſus mr Bry
T Good ·

(vii) *Enter ferrex at one dore · Porrex at an other The*
40 *fight ferrex is ſlayn : to them Videna The Queene*
to hir Damaſus · to him Lucius ·

(viii) *Enter Porrex ſad wth Dordan his man · R P · w ſly :*
to them the Queene and A Ladie Nick ſaunder
44 *And Lords R Cowly mr Brian · to them Lucius Ruñing*

(ix) *Henry and Lidgat ſpeaks Sloth Paſseth ouer*

(x) *Enter Giraldus Phroneſius Aſpatia Pompeia Rodope*
R Cowly Th Goodale · R Go · Ned · Nick ·

(xi) *Enter Sardinapalus Arbactus Nicanor and*
Captaines marching · mr Phillipps mr Pope R Pa
50 *Kit J ſincler · J Holland ·*

(xii) *Enter A Captaine wth Aſpatia and the Ladies Kitt*

Enter Progne Jtis and Lords ſaunder will (xix)
J Duke w ſly Hary. 75

Enter Philomele and Tereus to them Julio (xx)

Enter Progne Panthea Jtis and Lords · ſaunder (xxi)
T Belt will w ſly Hary Th Goodale to them
Tereus wth Lords · R Burbadg · J Duk R Cowly 79

A Dumb ſhow · Lidgate ſpeakes (xxii)
Enter Progne wth the Sampler to her Tereus
from Hunting · wth his Lords to them Philomele
wth Jtis hed in a diſh · Mercury Comes and all
Vaniſh · to him 3 Lords Th Goodale Hary w ſly · 84

Henry ſpeaks to him Leiutenant Purſeuaunt (xxiii)
and warders R Cowly J Duke · J Holland Joh
ſincler · to them Warwick · mr Brian

Lidgate ſpeaks to the (xxiv)
Audiens and ſo
Exitts · 90

finis 91

3 *The Seven Deadly Sins*, Part II (Dulwich College, MS. xix) – transcript of Plot

serviceable, together with the cast-list and the actors' parts, for the purposes we have supposed it was intended to serve.

The Plots are not always free from error, but the mistakes that are of no importance and may be left standing on a call-sheet are of a different kind from those that may stand uncorrected on a rehearsal schedule. On a call-sheet, IV, i could not have failed to confuse the actors, but there is no reason to suppose that it would have confused the Plotter in making out the parts or in directing a rehearsal.

There is one seeming error of a different kind, however, where the scene Greg calls V, i, has been added after the Plot was complete. This appears to introduce the dénouement of the play and was added in a hand other than the original Plotter's. The reason that might be suggested for it is that the undisguising of Eschines had been left out of the text and needed explanation for the audience before the triumphant entrance of the lovers in their proper persons and rightful pairs in V, iii. This is perhaps the strongest of several indications that the text was in a fluid state when the Plot was composed. It should be noted that V, ii and V, iii in fact constitute a single long scene. The entrance of the lovers undisguised would thus have occurred at the end of a complicated untying of the intrigue and needed to be striking. Eschines, as a character, has not been seen since Act II, and it may be that for this unravelling to achieve its greatest effect he needed to be re-identified. The new Plotter's addition of the direction 'Enter w^{t} out disguise' suggests the purpose of the addition of this introductory scene to Act V.

'The platt of the secound parte of The Seven Deadlie Sins'

This Plot is preserved at Dulwich College (Dulwich MS. xix) and has recently been most carefully and beautifully remounted. It contains twenty-four scenes, including the Epilogue spoken by Lydgate, the scenes being grouped into three sections, each bearing on the theme of a single sin. These are Envy (the story of Gorboduc), Sloth (the story of Sardanapalus), and Lechery (the story of Tereus and Philomel), and there are two scenes of introduction and two of conclusion. It is clearly structured as an episodic moral narrative presented by the poet Lydgate to Henry VI, and may have been represented as a dream allegory. Henry remains in bed in his tent on stage throughout the action. This Plot shows a minimum cast of fifteen, or, more probably, sixteen men and seven or eight boys.

Its underlying text has been supposed by Chambers, Greg, and others to be a revision of, or possibly identical with, the *Three Plays in One*, which, together with *Five Plays in One*, was played in 1585 by the Queen's Men: these titles being presumed to represent different slices of *The Seven Deadly Sins*, known to have been written by Richard Tarleton the famous comic actor. The absence from the incompletely listed cast of Edward Alleyn, into whose possession the Plot eventually came, is not evidence that he did not play in it, and, as the cast is recognisable as Strange's company at some time between the years 1590 and 1593, it is possible that the Plot represents a performance of the *Four Plays in One* by Strange's company at the Rose on 6 March 1592, when Alleyn was of their number. If so, this company also played 'Muly Molocco' (*Alcazar*), *Friar Bacon, The Jew of Malta, A Looking Glass for London and England, Henry VI*, and 'Jeronimo' (*The Spanish Tragedy*). One of the members of the cast, however, is Richard Burbage, and it appeared to Greg that he was most unlikely to have appeared in the cast of a play at the Rose after the quarrel of Strange's Men with his father in 1591. He therefore dates the Plot tentatively as played at the Theatre in 1590. Now, as we have seen, the repertory of the combined Strange's and Admiral's companies at the Theatre consisted in all likelihood of plays whose adult cast numbered at least twenty-five, and whose boys numbered at least twelve. The actors representing the Sins are not named in the Plot, and may be underused personnel of the remainder of the company. On the other hand, there are quite sufficient actors in the listed cast to double as the Sins. In fact, the boys alone could do it. At the same time there are clearly restrictions at work on the total number of actors available that force the major actors to double roles, even within single episodes. It therefore seems unlikely that this is a Theatre piece. Moreover, when we see that Shakespeare's *Henry VI* is quite out of place, for reasons of casting, in Strange's repertory at the Rose in 1592, it appears more probable that this Plot passed under the name of *Henry VI* in Henslowe's records than that it was the *Four Plays in One*.

The listing of the cast is very full, but there are puzzles about several roles. We do not know the names of the actors who played Henry VI and Lydgate, or of the actor who played Mercury in the last dumb-show. The action is episodic and almost all the named actors, including the boys, double at least once. The exceptions are Phillips, who plays only Sardanapalus, and Pope, who plays only Arbactus in the 'Sloth' section. Vincent appears only as a musician in scene xiii, and may have been a singing boy, although there is a tenuous possibility that he was the Book-keeper or prompter of the company. Ned plays only Rodope. That exhausts the list, providing we assume that the 'Ro' who plays Philomela in the 'Lechery' section is the same as Robert Gough who plays Aspatia in 'Sloth'.

Despite the obvious limitations at work on the cast, the Plotter does not appear to be particularly hard pressed. Doubling breaks no illusion in a discontinuous episodic action of this kind, and it would appear that the cast could have been worked harder than it is without creating improbabilities; that is, if we allow that the Captains who appear as musicians with Sardanapalus in scene xiii do so for reasons of the fable rather than from necessity. The only appearance of difficulty is in the same scene where Kitt enters alone to represent 'others' (line 60), but as there seems to be no lack of available actors, this may simply be a matter of choice, the role being mute. Perhaps John Holland's name is omitted here in error, for he re-appears with Kitt and the erstwhile musicians in their regular roles as Captains belonging to the forces of Nicanor in scene xvi.

The style of the Plot, like that of *The Dead Man's Fortune*, is predominantly 'literary', and the dumb-shows lend it a generally descriptive flavour: 'Gorboduk entreing in / The midst between'; 'still following them'; 'Enter Porrex sad'; 'Mercury Comes and all Vanish'; 'Henry speaks'; 'Lechery passeth ouer the stag'. Some internal exits are marked, but others are implied, as in the previous Plot, only by the change from plural to singular number ('To them Videna The Queene / to hir Damasus : to him Lucius.'). We cannot be sure that all are accounted for in this way. Final exits are not marked, nor is 'manet' used. We must therefore assume that there is some kind of general exit either just before or just after the entrance of Nicanor at line 60 in scene xiii, otherwise an immediate re-entry of Sardanapalus and the Ladies would occur in scene xiv, contrary to the rules we have proposed. Another example may exist in scene viii, where there occurs the direction 'Enter Lucius running', immediately following the entrance of the Lords played by Cowley and Brian. Brian may have played Lucius, in which case his previous exit is unmarked, but it is probable that Thomas Goodale took that role. One or two other examples may be hidden from us by ignorance of the text.

The confusion over the role of Lucius is not an isolated example. This Plot frequently assigns actors in reverse order. Ferrex and Porrex are reversed at their first entrance. Porrex and Dordan are reversed in scene viii. The actors for Rodope and Pompeia are either reversed at their first entrance, or else Rodope is wrongly entered in scene xiii for Pompeia. The players of the Queen and her Lady are wrongly ascribed in scene viii. It is also possible that Brian and Goodale are reversed as the players of Lucius and Damasus in scene vi.

Here, then, are quite serious errors in a Plot that would have been undoubted causes of confusion. Why were they not corrected or made clearer? The graphic evidence suggests that the making out of the actors' scrolls from the original notation was a problem that did confront the Plotter. To us, the confusions have, indeed, been made to seem worse than they were by his own later annotations when putting things right. Let me attempt a clarification.

The first error of inscription was probably of little importance. Scene iii is a dumb-show and the reversal of the roles of Ferrex and Porrex may be left to stand without correction, because no speaking is involved. Even in rehearsal there would be no confusion. At the next entrance, these two are in their correct order, and their parts may be made out accordingly. The second is more puzzling. In scene vi, the Plot seems originally to have read: 'Lucius and Damasus / T Good'. The words 'mr Bry' are written smaller and appear to have been crammed into the available space immediately after 'Damasus'. Now Lucius and Damasus are the two chief counsellors of Gorboduc and they have appeared twice before, listed on both occasions in the order Brian and Goodale. Their character names may well have appeared at an earlier stage in the spoken text, so that, when first they are listed by them in scene vi, they will appear in the order they have always been addressed. That is, Lucius will have been played by Mr Brian and Damasus by Thomas Goodale. Mr Brian may well have become so strongly identified as first counsellor that 'Lucius' is now sufficient to bring him on stage, and the lesser actor is noted by name as 'T Good'. That will be sufficiently clear for the run-through on stage. But when the Plotter comes to recall it in his study, it will be no more clear to him than it is to us. For, at the next entrance of Brian, in scene viii, he is simply described as a Lord, and to the characters on stage comes 'Lucius Running'. There may well have been an intervening exit in the text of scene viii, as in *Alcazar*, I, ii, and, in its absence, the Plotter cannot tell which of the counsellors is which. He therefore returns to scene vi and corrects it so that the names read in their normal correct order.

It is more likely that we are applying the wrong kind of logic here. It may be that there is no intervening exit in scene viii and that the novel presence on stage of Cowley with Brian as Lords accompanying the Queen means that Goodale is and has always been, Lucius, for otherwise Goodale has mysteriously disappeared. Scene vi might then be explained as having begun with the simple omission of Brian's name following Goodale's at line 38. When the Plotter, writing out the actors' parts, came to rectify the omission, he may have jotted in 'mr Bry' as close as he could to 'Damasus', a solution clear enough for his immediate purposes, but leaving the entry reading in what appears to us to be the wrong order. In either case, he was clearly revising later in order to get the casting straight – but in a way that would be quite confusing for actors, or for anyone but himself.

Pretty clearly this was not his only problem with scene viii. A similar explanation is probable for other apparent confusions. Robert Pallant, who has always been the first of Porrex's party, described once as an attendant and once as a soldier, is now made Porrex's man and given the name Dordan. The original entry thus read, as with the entry of Lucius and Damasus above: 'Enter Porrex sad with Dordan his man. RP.' This is sufficient for a run-through, but when sitting down to make out the parts, the Plotter needed to refresh his memory about the eminently confusable Ferrex and Porrex, and jotted in the space following 'RP' the name of the actor of Porrex – 'w. sly.' The same process was repeated in the following line of scene viii, where Nick appears for the first time as a Lady attendant on the Queen. Once again, the name of the boy who plays the Queen, Saunder, is entered following Nick in what then reads as the wrong order. In the first two of these cases there is little doubt, on close inspection, that the names were added later to the Plot and are more hastily and carelessly written than the rest.

So far we may explain the probable order of events according to our hypotheses about the function of the Plots, but in scene x the Plotter seems to have landed in a total muddle, and has left obvious errors uncorrected. Here he introduces Ned as Pompeia and Nick as Rodope. The two appear again merely as 'the Ladies' in scene xii, but when Rodopeie (*sic*) enters again in scene xiii, she is played by Ned, and, worse still, all the ladies, including herself, are said to enter to her. The only possible explanation for this confusion – intolerable for an actor attempting to follow his cues from the Plot! – is that only two speaking roles were involved: that of Aspatia, played by Robert Gough, and that of Rodope, who was probably to speak only once at her solitary entrance in scene xiii, when her lines are allotted to Ned. In rehearsal the logic of the situation would automatically cancel her subsequent entry to herself (whichever character Ned is supposed to be at that moment), but no-one has bothered to put a pen through the superfluous Lady in the list of those who follow Sardanapalus on stage. Subsequent mention of the Ladies is made corporately: 'Enter Sardanapalus wth the Ladies' and 'the Ladies fly'; so that we may be reasonably sure that such speaking parts as they had came to an end with scene xii.

Two errors of a more informative kind are found in the Plot. The first concerns the entrance of the Warders in scene i. Here the Plot originally read: '2 warderes / J Holland R Pallant'. This was altered to 'i wardere' and Holland's name was deleted. Holland must have been noted in the cast-list as a Warder, for he appears in that role in the last scene with the other officers of the Tower who also appear in scene i, whereas Pallant does not. The only reason I can suggest for his omission here is that he was listed to play one of the four Deadly Sins who are 'put back' by the three.

The second correction is made *currente calamo* and is merely a re-ordering of the action, but it shows that the Plotter's hand is also to some degree a Director's hand. The description of scene v begins conventionally 'Enter Gorb ... ', no doubt following the stage-direction of the text. But before the word is completed, a more elaborate method is adopted to convey the necessary stage positioning: 'Enter [Gorb] Queene . wth 2 Counsailors . mr Brian / Tho Goodale . to them Ferrex and Porrex severall waies / wth [his] Drum and Powers . Gorboduk entreing in / The midst between'. The implication of this re-arranged wording is that a composite entrance involving symbolic positioning of the actors is being set up before any dialogue takes place. It is worth observing here, because it is one of Greg's unstressed assumptions in his criticism of the text of *Alcazar* that when the words 'to them' occur in a Plot they must always have been preceded by dialogue.

A final objection to the notion that the Plots served as call-sheets may be noted. 'Excurtions' are called for at line 34, but no attempt has been made to plot these out in action. The teams prepared for battle are clear enough, but the actual business of the fight must have been established at rehearsals. In *Troilus* the main battle is also represented by the word 'Excursions' in scene B, but there are some incidents in the fight that need separate recording (in scene D) and the Plotter has therefore noted further excursions and a retreat in the margin, to indicate that the general melée continues in between the individual combats. The Plots fail to offer a fuller account of battle scenes than may be gathered from most texts, and their notation of them remains markedly more confused. That is because they cannot give a clear idea of the time-scheme involved, and because it is not their business to mark in the tiny narrative details of the spoken text that often render the battle sequences of the playscripts intelligible to the actor and the reader. Ajax in *Troilus*, will be quite unclear about what he is to do, for, although exits are commonly marked in this Plot, there is none marked for him. In what circumstances, then is he to re-enter, and with whom, if anyone, is he to do battle? No doubt his actor's scroll would have told him, but it is not the business of the Plot to confirm the information. He must work it out from the dialogue. Richard Burbage, likewise, must have been somewhat at a loss as Gorboduc if the only information he had was that he was to enter 'still following' his two sons who are said to enter 'severally'.

Complex business is no more adequately recorded in the Plots than in the texts. In *2 Seven Deadly Sins*, for example, the direction 'Mercury comes and all vanish' is as inexplicit about how the feat is to be performed as are the directions for the witches' disappearances in *Macbeth*. Once again, we are led to the conclusion that the actual behaviour of the actors on stage, and their appreciation of how to enter and leave it, must have been governed far more by their intelligent participation in the dialogue than by any assistance they may have received from consulting the Plot.

'The plott of Frederick & Basilea'

This is the least fully documented of all the Plots. It has no sound or music cues and is not marked up for properties, either in the text or in the margin. It must nevertheless represent the preparation of an actual performance of the play recorded in Henslowe's Diary on 3 June 1597, and four times thereafter, at a time when the company was temporarily depleted by the defection of some of its members to Langley's enterprise at the Swan. It lists a cast of precisely twelve men and four boys, uncommonly small for the Admiral's Men, and was therefore thought by Greg to have been specially commissioned for this period of temporary decline in the fortunes and personnel of the company.[1] While that may be the case, I cannot see why a specially commissioned play should not have been fitted to the acting cast, rather than being deliberately designed to call in the gatherers four and possibly five times. Moreover, there are other signs that the Plotter was in difficulties. He is reduced to allocating a guard by an '&c', and on two other occasions has left a guard and a company of soldiers unassigned. In these cases it is not impossible to find a theoretical solution from the acting cast, but it seems to me probable that

1 # The plott of Frederick & Basilea

2	Enter Prologue : Richard Alleine
Sc. i	Enter Frederick Kinge : Mr Jubie R Allenn To them Basilea seruant Black Dick, Dick .
Sc. ii 6	Enter Gouernor Athanasia Moore : Mr Dunstann . Griffen Charles, To them Heraclius Seruants . Tho : hunt black Dick
Sc. iii 10	Enter Leonora, Sebastian, Theodore, Pedro, Philippo Andreo Mr Allen, will, Mr Martyn . Ed Dutton, ledbeter, Pigg : To them King frederick Basilea Guarde . Mr Juby . R Allen Dick Tho . Hunt, black Dick .
Sc. iv	Enter Myron=hamec, lords . Tho : Towne . Tho Hunt ledbeter To them Heraclius, Thamar, Sam Charles
Sc. v	Enter Gouernor Mr Dunstann, To hym Messenger Th : Hunt To them Heraclius Sam, To them Myranhamec Soliors .
Sc. vi 17	Enter ffrederick, Basilea, R Allen . Dick, To them Kinge Mr ' Jubie To them Messenger Black Dick, To them Sebastian, Heraclius, Theodore, Pedro, Philippo Andreo Thamar . Mr Allen, Sam : Mr Martyn . leadb : Dutton Pigg . To them Leonora, will,
Sc. vii 22	Enter ffrederick Basilea, R Allen : Dick . To them Philippo, Duttonn, To her King ffrederick, Mr Jubie R Allenn :
Sc. viii	Enter, Myron=hamec, Sebastian, Pedroe lords Tho : Towne . Mr Allenn, ledbeter . Attendaunts .
Sc. ix	Enter King Theodore ffrederick, Mr Jubie, Mr Martyn R Allenn . To them Philipo Basilea E Dutton his boye Guard

		leonora Pedroe Andreo . Mr Allen : Tho Towne *will : leadbeter Pigg guard gatherers .*
Sc. x		*Enter ffrederick Basilea To them Pedro confederates* *Rob : leadb : Black Dick Gatherers .*
Sc. xi	 35	*Enter ffrederick Guard . Mr Juby R Allen* *Th : [Tow] Hunt &c' . To them Sebastian [leonora]* *Theodore Myranhamec Guard Mr Allen . Martyn* *To them Pedro Basilea vpon the walls . come doune* *Pedro Basilea . ledb : Dick .*
Sc. xii		*Enter Theodore Andreo . Mr Martyn Pigg To hym* *Thamar Heraclius Sam charles .*
Sc. xiii	 41	*Enter ffrederick, Basilea, ffryer, R Allen : Dick* *Mr Dunstann .*
Sc. xiv	 44	*Enter Heraclius Thamar Andreo, Sam . Charles* *Pigg . To them ffryer . Mr Dunstann, To them* *Theodore Martynn*
Sc. xv		*Enter ffrederick Basilea R Allen . Dick, To them* *ffryer Mr Dunstann, To them Heraclius Sam*
Sc. xvi		*Enter Leonora Myronhamec, Sebastian Soliors* *Will : Mr Towne, Mr Allen . Tho Hunt black Dick*
Sc. xvii		*To the queen Theodore Martynn .*
Sc. xviii	 52	*Enter Heraclius Thamar Sam charles To hym* *Theodore ffryer Dunstan Martynn To them* *Enter King Basilea ffrederick Messenger* *Mr Juby R Allen Dick Black Dick . To them* *Sebastian leonora Myranhamec Thamar Soliors* *Mr Allen will Tho Towne Charles . Tho : Hunt* *Black Dick gatherers .*
	57	*Epilog' R Allenn Finis :/*

4 *Frederick and Basilea* (British Museum, MS. Add. 10449, Fol. 2) – transcript of Plot

the performance gave a poor account of the text as far as the provision of attendants was concerned, and that the play was therefore most likely a sixteen-cast play rather desperately pressed into service. We cannot be certain that any of the lost, or thinly identified, plays that were performed in repertory with it in 1597 were themselves sixteen-cast plays, but most were played in repertory at other times with plays that certainly were.

Nevertheless, there is little doubling in *Frederick and Basilea*: only four actors are required to double, and possibly fewer. Mr Dunstan doubles the roles of Governor and Friar, both presumably speaking roles, but Robert Ledbetter's appearance as a Lord of Myronhamec is not certainly inconsistent with his normal role of Pedro. Thomas Hunt probably spoke only as a Messenger in scene v. All other Messenger speeches would have fallen to Black Dick, who may well have been mute in his other appearances as servant, guard, and soldier. The Plotter's intention appears to have been to achieve a complete listing of the cast with their character names; but that he was not, in this case, particularly concerned about the major roles is shown by his persistent habit of listing them in the wrong order, an order that appears to have more to do with the status of the actors in the company than with the need for careful identification, and by his occasional omission either of the actor's name or of the character's. To order the speaking parts even as vaguely as this, however, it was necessary to run through the whole picture of the casting in the conventional way. In scene ix, for example, the extraction of Black Dick from the guard to play the role of a messenger was clearly made necessary by some inhibition that exists to keep Sam, Charles, and Mr Dunstan off stage. His absence from the guard even perhaps made necessary the first calling in of the gatherers.

The omission of medial and final exits makes it particularly difficult to follow the Plotter's intention. Only when he makes a positive revision, as in the case just mentioned, are we able to see the restrictions at work upon his cast. Two other errors he makes in assigning roles appear to be mere anticipations or mishearings. On one occasion he omits an actor's name, and on another a character name, but these may easily be supplied. The apparent inconsistencies of the final scenes, which result from the omission of exits, call for explanation, and it will be instructive to attempt to follow the Plotter's thought-processes.

Without the recourse of a 'manet', the rapid comings and goings of the dénouement of any play put a strain on the 'primitive' Plot in keeping track of the availability of actors to enter. One solution is to break up the individual entrances into separate scenes in the continental manner, beginning each with phrases such as 'Enter then ...', or 'Enter to them ...', as we have seen in *The Dead Man's Fortune*. It may well be, as Greg suggested, that the last scenes of that Plot gradually fill the stage until all the cast, with the exception of the Antic Fairies, are on. In *Frederick and Basilea* there is a more complex conclusion, with much coming and going, and still some notable absentees at the very end. In attempting to keep track of this, the Plotter adopted the same method as in the earlier Plot, but made rather a botch of it, although it would have been clear enough for his purpose of writing out the actors' parts.

The dénouement begins, I believe, at scene xvi, with the entry of what we may call the Opposition Party in the persons of Leonora (Will), Myronhamec (Mr Towne), and Sebastian (Edward Alleyn). These have consistently appeared as a party, but have been depleted by the loss of Philippo (Ed Dutton), who disappears at scene vii, never to return, and Andreo (Pigg, i.e. John Pyk), who survives five scenes longer. We may be wrong in thinking of them as the Opposition, for Sebastian is played by the star actor of the company, Edward Alleyn, and is perhaps a more important character than the play's title suggests. He may turn out to be the successful suitor for the hand of Basilea. But a party it is, and for the time being under a cloud, probably, even, under arrest, for it is accompanied by Thomas Hunt and Black Dick who, despite undertaking most of the doubling in the play, began life basically identifiable as soldiers of the royal guard. Contrary to Greg's perfectly rational supposition that the name Basilea ought to identify the Queen, I believe Leonora is the Queen. If she is not, we should be faced with an entirely exceptional entry in scene xviii: 'To the queen Theodore'. There is no other example of the entrance of a character merely being implied by the naming of the second enterer in the scene. I imagine, then, that the Plotter's intention was to make his divisions in the continental manner from scene xvi onwards, marking a separate scene for each successive entrance. Martyn's entrance to the Queen thus begins a separate scene, but, as the implied exit from the previous scene has left Leonora on stage, she cannot be said to enter. It is then probable that Leonora and Theodore, having spoken together, leave the stage just as Heraclius and Thamar enter. This technically makes a scene in the English manner, and the Plotter draws a line under it and leaves it there. Despite this, it appears that the action is continuous. Theodore, who is acting as a liaison between Leonora and the two Moors, is stage-managing the whole affair and re-enters almost immediately to Heraclius and Thamar, bringing with him a Friar, who is presumably the repository of some vital information.

The Plotter's next thought was to mark a separate scene for the exit of either Heraclius or Thamar, but, having begun to draw a line under the record of their entrance, he changed his mind and wrote 'To him Theodore ffryer'. The student may well wish that he had followed the same method as he did in dealing with the Queen in scene xvii, for we cannot tell which of the Moors remains on stage. Neither could an actor consulting the Plot have been certain, for both Moors are listed in the last entrance in scene xviii. However that may be, the Plotter returns to his first plan and draws a line across the page to mark the end of this passage of dialogue, because the two Moors must exit after hearing the Friar's revelation, while Theodore and the Friar remain on stage. For the next entrance, although it is a grand one that brings on the King, he now

The ⟨P

(A) b ⟩re headaed Tho ⟨
⟩....] ſomerton⟨
5 ..⟩⟩ A Childe · dic⟨k .... ..
l⟩adies following mut⟨e ..
to⟩ them A ſ⟨

(B) ....o⟩m⟨

(C) ....⟩

(D) ⟩and
11 ..⟩ne
..⟩a⟨..
⟩n ⟨
14 ⟨..⟩

o⟩nd Par⟨t of⟩ Fortu⟨n 1

⟩is · 2

Enter orleaunce muſing to him Co⟨.. (E)
⟩ Mauritius Boniface · m^r^ ſinger Pau⟨y 16

⟩ Enter Boniface wth ſeruingmen Ge⟨o (F)
⟩ [RTai⟨l ⟩r · w · Cartwright.] ⟨

E Ɛ i ⟩^th^ wine preſser⟨.. (G)
m⟩auritius bleed⟨ 20
w⟩right ·

l⟩la like a Pilgrim⟨ (H)
h⟩e wi⟨n⟩e Preſsers ⟨..

.. ⟩his ſonn at one ⟨d (I)
..⟩ ⟨ 25

..⟩mpaine mauritius / · En⟨ (K)

i⟩es Bertram Ɛdwin ⟨.. (L)

⟩ between Lewes and ⟨.. (M)
t⟩ram Ɛdwine Mau⟨r

⟩ A Table brought in ⟨ (N)
⟩tts · Sam and Ch⟨a l 31

5 *Fortune's Tennis*, Part II (British Museum, MS. Add. 10449, Fol. 4) – transcript of Plot

(A) r ⟩a̅t ⟨..
⟨ ⟩reo⟨ ⟩e, ⟨
Vliſſes A⟨ x
dore ⟨He⟩rrauld⟨
⟨Pr⟩iam, Hecto⟨ ⟩eiph⟨
⟨ex⟩eunt [....] ⟨ o⟩med, ⟨..
& ⟨D⟩eiphob⟨ ⟩ the rest &
⟨He ⟩a⟨u⟩lds, to ⟨ m⟩ Menalaus
3· ſeuera⟨ll⟩ ⟨...... ..⟩s & Diomede, to them Hector
⟨T⟩ucketts ⟨D ⟩hobus, to them Caſſandra exit

(B) Alar⟨ũ⟩ Excurſions
excurſions Enter Hector & [Antenor] (Priam: mr Jones) exeunt

(C) exc⟨.... ⟩ Enter A⟨ ⟩

(D) Alarũ ⟨ ⟩ter Antenor purſue⟨d ⟩by Diomede
to them Aiax, to the⟨m⟩ on the
walls Hector Paris ⟨&⟩ D⟨e⟩iphobus
⟨......etr..t⟩ & ⟨m⟩r H⟨u⟩nt exeunt

(E) E⟨nte⟩r Tro⟨y⟩l⟨ s &⟩ Pandarus
to t⟨h⟩em Creſſida & a waight⟨ ng ⟩
maid wth a l⟨ig⟩ht, mr Jones his boy
exit⟨ w⟩ai⟨g⟩htng maid, exeunt manet
⟨ ⟩ Pan⟨da ⟩ to ⟨h⟩im Deiphobus, exit
D⟨ei⟩p⟨h b ⟩to him Helen & Paris
exit Panda⟨r⟩us, exeunt omnes

(F) E⟨n⟩ter Priam, Hect⟨o⟩r, Deiphobus, Paris
H⟨el ⟩ Caſſandra · [to them] exit
De⟨i b⟩us & Enter ⟨ ⟩ Vliſſes and

(G) ⟩E⟨
⟨.... ⟩ D⟨e
Alarũ Enter⟨ ....

(H) Diomede, menalay⟨ ..
& beat Hector in ·

(I) Alarũ Enter Hector and ^[Antenor] (Antenor; Priam mr J⟨o⟩nes) exeun⟨t

(K) Alarũ Enter Diomede to Achil⟨lis Tent⟩
to them Menalay, to them Vliſſes
to them Achillis in his Tent to
them · Aiax wth patroclus on his
⟨ ⟩ back · exeunt

(L) Enter · Creſſida, wth Beggars, pigg
Stephen, mr Jones his boy · & mutes
to them Troylus, ⟨& Deipho⟩bus & proctor
exeunt

(M) Ente⟨r ⟩ Priam · Hector, Paris Hellena
Caſſan⟨d⟩ra Polixina to the⟨m⟩ Antenor

(N) Alarũ Enter D⟨ ⟩med · & Troylus .. to the⟨m⟩
Achillis · ⟨ ⟩o them Hector & Deipho⟨bus⟩
to them on the walls Priam Paris
a re⟨tr....t⟩ Hellen Polixina & Caſſan⟨dra⟩ to the⟨m⟩
vliſſes Aiax Menalay & H⟨e⟩a⟨r ⟩
Priam & they on the wall desce⟨nd to th⟩em

6 *Troilus and Cressida* (British Museum, MS. Add. 10449, Fol. 5) – transcript of Plot

reverts to his earlier method. He crosses out the scene division line and writes 'To them' on the line above. But although four members of his regular cast do not appear in this final scene, all having departed from the story at least a whole scene beforehand, he still calls on gatherers for soldiers. We may suppose either that the identity of the missing characters is too strongly imprinted for them to have doubled as attendants, or that the gatherers have had a recognisable identity as Confederates, as they are called in scene x, and may be appearing in that guise here. Even this last scene is clearly punctuated by unlisted exits. Black Dick may seem to be having trouble with his allegiance, appearing both as a Messenger to the King and, once again, in his intermediate role of leader of the Confederates, but, if this is a scene of surprising revelations and the reconciliation of parties, there is possibly no conflict between his roles.

It would seem that the problem facing the Plotter was not in this case the sorting out of the major speaking roles. That presents little difficulty. It is more concerned with the availability of Thomas Hunt and Black Dick to stand in at each point as servants, guards, messengers, and Confederates. It is upon the rapid doubling of these two on alternate sides that the smooth succession of scenes depends. It is also clear that in the sequence between scene vii and scene xi, where the extras are most liberally called in, no help from the regular cast is available. When the Plotter allots a guard for the king vaguely in scene xi as 'Mr Hunt &c', he does so in the knowledge that Black Dick, the other member of the royal guard in scene iii, has gone over to the Confederates and is unavailable. I think it is unreasonable to suppose that his failure to list the king as an enterer here means that Edward Jubie, whose name is listed, was required to double as a guard on Frederick. The gatherers are also occupied in the previous scene with Black Dick, and that '&c' could never have become more than a hopeful flourish of the pen. Yet all this while there are three actors standing conspicuously idle: Mr Dunstan (Governor), Sam Rowley (Heraclius), and Charles Massey (Thamar). The reason that bars them from entering, revealed in scene ii, is almost certainly that, as in *Alcazar*, they were Moors. Whether or not the Governor with whom they seem to be allied in scenes ii, iv, and v was also a Moor cannot be ascertained, but his prolonged absence before his re-appearance as a Friar makes it probable. Curiously enough, Black Dick seems to have been a dark-haired Caucasian member of the company and does not take part in the 'black' scenes. He is perhaps so called in order to distinguish him from Edward Dutton's boy Dick, who plays Basilea.

'The plots of the second part of Fortune's Tennis and Troilus and Cressida'

These two Plots, the first composed by the Plotter who prepared *2 Seven Deadly Sins* and the second by the Plotter of *Alcazar* and *Tamar Cam*, are too fragmentary to place much reliance upon, but nevertheless prove informative in various ways. Both belonged to the Admiral's Men some time about the turn of the century.

Fortune's Tennis gives an account of fifteen or sixteen men and three or more boys. The count is probably sixteen, for, by sorting out the named actors and characters into mutually exclusive roles we find that, if we may allow doubling actors to have appeared as wine-pressers in scene G, the servant who appears in scene F was most likely neither of them and is probably the sixteenth man. I also assume that, as Sam and Charles are attendants in the last scene, and Tailor and Cartwright were servants in scene F, none of them could have played either Orleans or his son. Clearly there were no more than sixteen men available, for Tailor and Cartwright are removed from their entrance as servingmen in scene F and enough remains of the following scene to show that Cartwright, at least, was transferred to it. This is an exactly parallel case with the cancellation of Black Dick's entry in scene ix of *Frederick and Basilea*.

This Plotter does not mark final or medial exits, but there is one sign that he was unable to manage without some notation that substituted for the more sophisticated 'manet'. His scene K ends with a diagonal stroke and the word 'Enter'. It is probable that the next scene must have begun with some form of 'to them'. This is a unique example of such a notation. Whether it was forced on the Plotter by the need to order a complex dénouement, as in *Frederick and Basilea*, there is no means of telling. Greg's suggestion that the scribe intended to write 'Enter Chorus' to mark the end of an Act has nothing to commend it.[2] There is no space at the beginning of the Plot for either a Chorus or a Prologue.

The Plot contains no evidence of doubling and shows no signs of crisis other than that mentioned above. The pleasant eccentricity of this Plotter is to enter the indications of mood and manner that also appear in *Sins*: 'orleance musing'; 'Mauritius bleeding'; 'ladies following mute.'

Although more remains of the *Troilus* Plot, it offers less certain information. If we may suppose that Thomas Hunt played the Proctor, there is no doubling to be discovered among the adult cast. It is perhaps significant, therefore, that no names of the adult cast are to be found in the original text, apart from that of Hunt whose actual name may have been accidentally substituted for his function-name in scene D. This Plotter, however, is the most methodical practitioner we have met with. In *Tamar Cam* his intention was pretty clearly to identify every character with an actor at its first appearance and not to repeat the names thereafter. Perhaps he would also have done so here. All the characters can be supplied, without doubling, by a cast of sixteen men. But if Professor Bullough is right in reading the last word in the penultimate line as 'Aga{memnon}', where Greg reads 'Hear{olds}', we should have to account for seventeen, unless Patroclus was played by a boy. That there was some minor doubling, however, appears most probable when we see that at least one of the boys is required to double. 'mr Jones his boy' plays a waiting-maid in scene E, and reappears with Cressida as a beggar in scene L, where he is joined by Stephen, Pigg, and some mutes. Whether the mutes are boys or men is not clear. It is often assumed that Stephen is Stephen Magott, the tire-man of the Admiral's company, and Pigg is, of course, John Pyk, who was Alleyn's boy in 1592, but must now have been a man. At any rate, this unique entry of mutes shows that it was not against the rules to use stand-ins, as long as they did not speak.

Alterations were, however, made to the Plot after it was complete, or almost complete. In scene B Antenor was deleted and replaced by Priam, identified as Mr Jones. The actor's name was, no doubt, listed here because changes would have to be made to his scroll. By accident we are able to see that this change was made at a late stage, for the scene that falls beside it in the second column of the Plot (scene I) is almost identical in wording, and the alteration was first made to that scene and then deleted. We can therefore be fairly certain that the alteration to scene B had nothing to do with any restriction the Plotter had found in bringing Antenor on stage, but came about for some other reason, such as a re-writing of the play-text. That such inconveniences occasionally arose from authors revising their texts after the actors' scrolls had been prepared, we have evidence in Daborne's correspondence.

Although mutes are called in for the Cressida scene, it would seem that there is very little doubling in the adult cast and the Plotter is thus sometimes careless about marking exits. In scene M the 'Exeunt' is omitted altogether, and in scene H the literary implication of 'beat Hector in' is sufficient to clear the stage. While doubling over a scene-break is nowhere permitted in the Plots, scene I in *Troilus* shows that certain kinds of immediate re-entrance were tolerated when no change of identity was involved. The clearing of the stage in the progress of the battle scenes is marked by the Plotter, here and in scenes A, B and C. On each occasion there are immediate re-entrances, but these divisions pretty obviously are for convenience and do not constitute scenes in the strict sense. The same may be true of scenes vi, vii, and viii in *2 Seven Deadly Sins*. It is clear from *Frederick and Basilea* that Prologues and Epilogues were also free from this restriction. *Troilus* also exhibits in scene F an immediate re-entry of Paris and Helen in Priam's train. Depending on the sense of place established in the dialogue, this rapid circumnavigation of the tiring-house could be made convincing, and is found in a number of printed plays. Shakespeare makes a point of it with the direction in *Timon of Athens*: 'A great Banquet seru'd in: and then, Enter Lord Timon, the States, the Athenian Lords, Ventigius which Timon redeem'd from prison. Then comes dropping after all Apemantus discontentedly like himselfe.' Apemantus was, of course, the last to leave the stage in the preceding scene. A similar situation arises in *Alcazar* where the Governor of Tangier, having announced his intention of going to greet the arrival of King Sebastian, is made by the Plotter to leave the stage by one door, only to return through it immediately to meet Sebastian entering at the other.

'The plott of the first parte of Tamar Cam'

This Plot contains nineteen scenes and is divided into five acts by a chorus. The Admiral's Men bought the Book of *Tambercam* (whether the first or the second part is not known) from Edward Alleyn on 2 October 1602. On the evidence of the casting, the Plot is likely to have been created shortly afterwards. It would therefore have been played at the Fortune theatre. The play was an old one, Part 1 being marked as 'ne' by Henslowe on 6 May 1596. It is not certain that this cryptic sign used by Henslowe means 'new': the second part, which Henslowe also marked as 'ne' on 11 June 1596, had been played by Strange's on 28 April 1592. It is possible that both parts had been revised, for the first part possibly, but not inevitably, pre-existed the second part played in 1592. These were the only plays revived in 1596 from the repertory of 1592 that were marked as new, except for the old money-spinner *The Jew of Malta*. As this could not by any stretch of the imagination be regarded as new, without revision, the same may apply to the others. *The Jew*, however, brought in the large return typical of new plays on its first two performances on 9 and 29 January.

The original Plot has disappeared, but it is known from the transcript published by Steevens in the so-called *Variorum Shakespeare* (1802). There are signs of some inaccuracies in the second column, and in the centring of the first direction for the Chorus and the spelling of the name Denygton, which, as Greg, observes, is doubtless a transcription of Doughton, the spelling that appears in *Alcazar*, written in an English hand. This probable difference of orthography casts some doubt on the identity of the Plotter. There are other differences in method that distinguish this Plot and *Alcazar* from that of *Troilus*, but, as I have suggested, this may be because *Troilus* involves very little doubling, perhaps none among the major roles, while both *Alcazar* and *Tamar Cam* exhibit a great deal.

Tamar Cam is the only Plot that furnishes a complete list of its adult personnel. It requires sixteen regular acting men, all of whom are named. The count of boys is only slightly less certain. If Parsons played the Nurse in IV, i, four boys are needed before the last scene. If not, there are five boys. We do not discover the name of the actor for the Shah's daughter, Tarmia, although, as neither she nor her two children appear in the last scene, it is tolerably certain that she is among the four boys listed for the 'other races'. Tarmia's children play the Amazons; in which case the choice of an identity for Tarmia is between Giles's boy and little Will Barne, who play the Pigmies. I think it is extremely unlikely that Parsons played the nurse, so that the other one of these two would be the fifth boy, and will have been cast in that role. The name of the actor for Palmeda, Jack Jones, is known to us only by accident, from a scene begun in error and deleted. It is probable, however, that if the Plotter had not entered the name in the deleted scene he would have listed it in its corrected place.

The plott of The First parte of Tamar Cam.

Enter Chorus Dick Jubie.

I. i	Sound Sennet. Sound flourish.	Enter Mango Cham, 3 noblemen : Mr. Denygten 1 w. Cart. 2 & Tho. Marbeck & W. Parr. attendants : Parsons & George : To them Otanes : Tamar : & Colmogra : H. Jeffs : Mr. Allen & Mr. Burne. exit Mango & nobles : manet the rest Exit Tamor & Otanes manet Colmogra Exit.
I. ii	Sound.	Enter the Persian Shaugh : Artaxes : Trebassus : Mr. Towne, Mr. Charles & Dick Jubie attendants : To them a Scowt : W. Parr : Exeunt.
I. iii	Alarum.	Enter Tamor Cam : Otanes : Parsons : Tho: Marbeck : & W. Cart : Exeunt.
I. iv	Alarum. Sound.	Enter Assinico : & a Persian : Mr. Singer & Parsons : To them Colmogra Exeunt. manet Colmogra : To him Tamor Cam Otanes : 3 nobles : W. Cart : Tho: Marbeck : & W. Parr : Exit Colmogra To them Colmogra & Mango : guard George : parsons. Exeunt, manet Colmogra : Exit.
		Enter Chorus Dick Jubie : Exit.
II. i	Thunder.	Enter Otanes : to him a spirritt : Parsons : To him another Spirrit : Pontus : Tho Marbeck : To him another Diaphines : Dick Jubie. To him another : Ascalon : Mr Sam : Exit

Enter Clowne, Ascalon & Diaphines : To them Otanes & Palmeda.	*III. v*
Enter Tarmia & guarde : Thom. Marbeck, Parsons : W. Parr & George : To her the orracle speakes Mr. Towne. Exeunt.	*III. vi*
Enter Chorus.	
[Enter Otanes & Palmeda : Jack Jones to them.] [2 spirrits : Exeunt.]	
Enter Cam : Otanes : attendants : W. Cart : & W. Parr : To them Tarmia the nurss Tho. Parsons wth children. Tho. Marbeck : & George : To them Otanes & Palmida : & 2. spirritts : Exeunt. manet Tamor & 2. spirritts : Exit. manet spirritts. To them Assinico : To them Palmida. Exeunt. manet Palmida. To herr Tamor Cam : To them Tarmia : To them guard : Tho. Marbeck : W. Parr : Parsons : To them the 2. spirritts : To them the Persian attendants : Mr. Charles : Parsons : George & soldiers : To them Colmogra : To them Tarmia & her 2 sonns : Jack grigerie & Mr. Denygtens little boy. Exeunt.	*IV. i*
Enter Chorus.	
Enter Persian : Tarmia nobles : Mr	*V. i*

II. iii		Enter Otanes : to him Spirritts : Afcalon. To him Diaphines : Exeunt.
II. iv		Enter Colmogra : To him 3 nobles & a Drum : To them Affinico Drunk :
37	Sound.	To them Tamor Cam : Otanes : & guard : & George Parfons : To them Diaphines : Dick Jubie : Exeunt. manet clowne. Exit.
II. v	Sound Alarm.	Enter Tamor Cam : Otanes : attendants : W. Cart : W. Parr : & Tho. Marbeck : Parfons & George : To them a Trumpet. Dick
43		Jubie : Exeunt.
		Enter Chorus : exit.
III. i		Enter Colmogra : To him Otanes & Mr. Charles a pledge for Tamor : W. Cart : for the Perfian Tho: Marbeck.
III. ii	Sound.	Enter at one dore Tamor Cam : Otanes : a Trompett : W. Parr : Attendaunts : Parfons : To him at another dore : the Perfian :
50		Mr. Towne attendants Mr. Charles : Dick Jubie.
	Wind horne.	Exeunt. manet Tamor : Otanes & Perfian : To them Colmogra like a poft : Exit Colmogra : To Otanes enter Afcalon :
54		Mr. Sam : exeunt.
III. iii	Sound.	Entér Colmogra : & 3 nobles : W. Cart : Tho: Marbeck & W. Parr : to them a Meffinger : Tho. Parfons : To them an
	Drum a far of.	other Meffinger : Dick Jubie. To them Tamor Cam : King of Perfia : Tarmia his daughter :
60		Otanes : noblemen : Mr. Charles : Dick Jubie : Guard
	Sound.	George & Parfons. Exeunt Otanes & nobles wth the 3 Rebbells : To them Otanes : wth a head. To them Mr. Charles wth an other head To them Dick Jubie wth an other head.
65	Sound.	Exeunt. manet Otanes. Exit.
III. iv		Enter Captaine & guarde. George & Parfons : & W. Parr : Exeunt.

	nymphes, Heron, and Thia : Mr. Jubie, A. Jeffs. Jack Grigorie & the other little boy. To them Captaines : Tho. Marbeck : & W. Cartwright : To them Afcalon & Diaphines : to them	
	Palmida : Exeunt.	100
	Enter Attaxes : & Artabifus : Mr.	*V. iii*
	Charles : Mr. Boorne : attendants : George W. Parr : & Parsons : Drom and Cullers : To them Captaine Tho Marbeck : To	
	them Tamor Cam : & Palmida & Otanes :	105
1.	Enter the Tartars : Mr. Towne, Mr. Denygten.	
2.	Enter the Geates : Gedion & Gibbs.	
3.	Enter the Amozins : Jack Grigorie & little Will. –	
4.	Enter the Nagars : Tho: Rowley : and the red falt fellow.	
5.	Enter the ollive cullord moores : A. Jeffs Mr. Jubie.	110
6.	Enter Canniballs : Relter : old Browne.	
7.	Enter Hermophrodites : Jeames, Parfons.	
8.	Enter the people of Bohare : W. Parr : W. Cart.	
9.	Enter Pigmies : gils his boy & little will Barne.	
10.	Enter the Crymms : Mr. Sam. Ned Browne.	115
11.	Enter Cattaians : Dick Jubie and George.	
12.	Enter the Bactrians : [W. Parr] : Tho. Marbeck.	
	FINIS.	118

7 *Tamar Cam*, Part I – transcript of Plot from Steevens's print ('Variorum' Shakespeare, 1803, vol. III, p. 414)

In the final scene the cast is doubled with unparalleled intensity, and every available gatherer and theatre functionary is called in, to the number of six, to furnish a procession of what we may take to be conquered races. Only five actors maintain their constant roles: Humphrey Jeffes (Otanes), Edward Alleyn (Tamar), Charles Massey (Artaxes), Jack Jones (Palmeda), and Singer (the Clown, Assinico). The latter is the only actor who does not appear at all. Even so, the subject races fall short by a Bactrian. Parr was at first entered in that role, only to be deleted without replacement when it was seen that he had already been cast as a Bohari four entrances previously. We may thus be fairly confident that *Tamar Cam* records every person of any kind who could be respectably exhibited on the stage of the Fortune in 1602, including some who may only just have passed muster.

The curiosity is that, although there appears to be some intense doubling in the earlier scenes also, two of the senior men, Edward Jubie and Anthony Jeffes, are reserved until the penultimate scene where they play only the Satyrs, Pitho and Linus, before doubling in the final scene as the olive-coloured Moors. The major part of the play is thus performed by fourteen men and four boys and we cannot be certain that it made unusual demands on the cast. It may be that the text either directed, or permitted without absurdity, some of the situations that appear to involve critical changes of identity, and it is therefore worth following the careers of the five or six most rapidly doubling actors in some detail.

Dick Jubie is the wonder-boy. He is the Chorus between the Acts and appears first as the Prologue. After a scene's interval he appears as Trebassus, an attendant on the Persian Shah. In II, i he is the Spirit, Diaphanes, and maintains that role in II, iii and II, iv, but in II, v he appears as a 'Trumpet', presumably a messenger of some kind, and immediately re-enters as the Chorus to Act III. In Act III he appears as an Attendant, a Messenger, and a Persian nobleman. It is possible that all these roles are consistent with his identity as Trebassus, for, in the role of a Persian noble in III, iii, he acts as member of the execution squad for the three rebel Lords, and reappears carrying the head of one of them. In III, v, he resumes his role as Diaphanes and retains it through two more entrances in the single long scene that constitutes Act IV, speaking the Chorus in between. He moves straight out of Act IV to speak the Chorus to Act V. He moves directly from that Chorus to appear once again as a Persian noble in V, i, but returns as Diaphanes in V, ii. It was perhaps fortunate that the piece had no Epilogue, for, in the last scene of all, Jubie has become a Cattaian, that is to say, Chinese.

It appears from Dick Jubie's behaviour that, unless the Elizabethan audience was prepared to accept gross improbabilities of identity, his roles must all somehow have been cognate. If this were not so, he would present flagrant examples of immediate re-entrances in doubled roles on three occasions. It is to be supposed that he spoke the Choruses in Persian attire, just as, in *Alcazar*, Richard Alleyn is first described as 'A

Portingall'. He is probably a supporter of the Shah, but that is not certainly true of the other major Spirit, Ascalon, an undoubled role, played by Sam Rowley, or of the minor Spirits in II, i, played by Marbeck and Parsons, who enter most commonly as nobles attached to Tamar's party. If this piece belongs to the genre of rival magician plays, the Spirits may have been in opposition, as they are in *John of Bordeaux*, so that despite the joint appearances of Ascalon and Diaphanes in their last four entrances, which might be taken to indicate that they are on the same side, it is possible that they belong to different factions, and behave rather like the Good and Evil Angels in *Doctor Faustus*. They have a particular interest in Otanes, to whom they all appear for the first time in II, i, and, as it is Otanes whose allegiance swings in the course of the action, it is worth following his career somewhat closely.

Otanes appears first as a henchman of Tamar's, but is perhaps a Persian sympathiser and rebels against him, unsuccessfully. After two meetings with the Spirits and a final blast from Diaphanes' trumpet in II, iv, he effects a reconciliation between Tamar and the Persian, bringing pledges of good faith for each party in III, i, and assisting in III, iii at the execution of the rebel Lords who appear to have broken the truce. After the Oracle has spoken to Tarmia, the daughter of the Persian Shah, perhaps predicting the disinheritance of her children, Otanes is won back to Tamar's party by a promise that he shall wed his daughter, Palmeda. It is at this marriage, celebrated by a mask of Satyrs and Nymphs, that Otanes' allegiance to Tamar is finally confirmed.

Dick Jubie is still a Persian noble in V, i, appearing with Tarmia and the Shah in a scene that must seal their defeat and probable death. The latter pair henceforward disappear from the action, but both Spirits appear at the wedding mask, either in an attempt to interrupt it, or else to add their blessings to it now that the Shah's line is extinct – a probability that is given weight by the appearance in the mask of the two little boys who formerly played Tarmia's children as the Nymphs Heron and Thia. That this outcome is somehow successful for Dick Jubie is suggested by the fact that the only attendants left for Tamar in the final scene are Attaxes (Charles Massey), a constant member of the Persian party throughout, and Artabisus (Mr Bourne), a recent addition to that allegiance, having joined it in V, i, after a long absence from the stage following his role as Colmogra, a seemingly rather eccentric commander of Tamar's party. If this reconstruction has any bearing on the actual story, Dick Jubie's role may have been much simpler than it appears.

The filling of the minor roles, however, faced the Plotter with a number of problems. George we may dispose of at once, for, although his role changes its label several times, he seems to have been a member of Tamar's guard throughout and probably had no speaking part. He is possibly omitted in error from III, ii, where Parsons appears alone as 'Attendants'. The other four actors who double are Cartwright, Marbeck, Parr, and Parsons. They all enter in the first scene, the first three as noblemen associated with Mango Cham. Cartwright and Marbeck are numbered 1 and 2, and presumably were to speak.

Cartwright's history is the simplest of the three. He is one of the Lords who appear with Tamar until the end of Act II, the other two normally being Marbeck and Parr. It may be supposed that the allegiance of these Lords is somehow tampered with in the first scene of the play. Thereafter they hide their disaffection, appearing constantly with Tamar until III, iii, where they are led off to execution and their severed heads are returned to the stage. Cartwright appears, properly, in III, i, as a pledge for Tamar's good faith, a position that he must betray, for his execution appears to be approved by Tamar who is on stage when it is carried out. Attendants are not lightly dispensed with, however, and Cartwright returns to duty, after a decent interval, as an Attendant in Act IV and Captain in Act V.

Marbeck's life-line is closely akin to Cartwright's. He begins in Mango's camp and passes to Tamar's, but is obliged to appear, rather improbably, as a pledge for the Shah's faith in III, i, and has also to make an intermediate entrance as a Spirit named Pontus in II, i. He, too, appears as a guard shortly after his own execution, and finally as a Captain.

Parr appears as the third noble of Mango's faction in I, i, but has to change allegiance almost immediately to enter as a Persian Scout in I, ii. He may, of course, be Tamar's Scout, but as he enters *to* the Persians it is rather difficult to imagine a convincing set of circumstances. He then rejoins Tamar's party and, after one possible entry as a 'Trompett' in III, ii, is beheaded with the rest. The difference in his lot is that he is forced to appear in the following scene as an additional member of the guard that acted as his own execution squad. It is tempting to imagine that the execution is a trick, that the nobles have in fact remained loyal and the severed heads are false witnesses, as in *Measure for Measure*, but that this is more likely a crisis of casting than a twist in the story is suggested by the fact that the lowly George is promoted Captain of the Guard.

Parsons is the junior member of that guard from the first scene onwards, but he, too, is called on to play a Spirit (unnamed) in II, i and a Messenger in III, iii. His appearance as an Hermaphrodite in the final scene suggests that he was a very young man and may conceivably therefore have played the Nurse in IV, i. The ordering of names in IV, i is, however, rather makeshift. It would be as reasonable to suppose from the entry that Marbeck and George played Tarmia's children, which they clearly do not. The Guard that enters later in this scene includes Parsons, as it did in the previous one. I believe the Nurse is certainly the fifth boy, unassigned, just as all the other boys' parts are unassigned in this scene, including Tarmia's, except for the names of the sons which are given at the very end.

The absence of response to the Plotter's call '& soldiers', and his rather vague allocation of attendants on the Shah in IV, i, suggest a crucial situation that is the more striking when we consider that three members of the cast are available to help out but remain idle. They are Mr

Doughton, whose role as Mango Cham came to an end in II, i, and who does not reappear until the final scene in which he plays a Tartar, and Edward Jubie and Anthony Jeffes, who do not appear at all until V, ii, in which they play the two Satyrs. Two conclusions are possible: either that the play-text of *Tamar Cam*, however zany it appears in this skeleton form, was adequately represented by the Plot and placed no great pressure on the cast until the final scene, or that there were hierarchical restrictions upon the casting within the company that made it preferable to double the junior actors almost to the point of absurdity before calling in the sharers and master actors to play minor guards and attendants. The specialisation of the Clown's role tends to suggest that the latter conclusion is the more likely. Singer, as Assinico, makes only four entrances and does not respond at all to the pressure in the final scene, even though the Plotter's spectacle would have been fully satisified by the addition of a single actor. There is undoubtedly much to be known about this aspect of the craft of Plotting that we may never be able to discover.

'The plott of The Battell of Alcazar'

The Plot of *Alcazar* will be considered in more detail in the next chapter, but it will be useful to preface that discussion with a general account of it, such as we have given of the other Plots, and to explain Greg's theory of its relationship with the Quarto text.

This Plot lacks the fifth act completely and is badly decayed in the right-hand column, so that it must be reconstructed from Act III onwards. Enough remains for us to be fairly certain of the wording of IV, ii and V, i, and of the dumb-show for the fourth act, but for three scenes the replacement of the missing parts depends upon the theories of casting we are able to develop from the remainder of the Plot. My own reconstruction of these scenes differs very considerably from Greg's, but I have been encouraged to think it is the more likely one by the fact that a fragment of V, ii, containing traces of five lines for which Greg's reconstruction could find no place, fits naturally into my own when it is moved slightly to the left of the obviously mistaken place where it was pasted by the repairer at some unknown date in the last century.

Alcazar is the most systematic and sophisticated of the Plots. Medial and final exits are marked in without fail, and the Plotter's performance in naming and assigning actors is more assured than in *Tamar Cam*. His practice here is occasionally to split up the massing of entries into sections so that the actors' names follow their character names closely and in the correct order. Actors are assigned to roles at their first entrance and are thereafter listed only by their character names until they double. Unfortunately, the decayed state of the Plot prevents us from knowing whether or not his rule was to name dodging actors again upon their re-entrance in the original character role. From some of the spaces allowed

The Plott of the Battell Of Alcazar

ſound | Enter a Portingall [to him] mʳ Rich : Allen to him
1 Domb ſhew
ſ⟨e⟩nnett | Enter Muly Mahamett mʳ Ed : Allen, his ſonne
Antho : Jeffes : moores attendant : mʳ Sam, mʳ Hunt
& w · Cartwright : ij Pages to attend the moore
mʳ Allens boy, mʳ Townes boy : to them 2 ·
young bretheren : Dab : & Harry : : to them
Abdel⟨m⟩enen w · Kendall : exeunt

ſound | Enter Abdelmelec : mʳ Doughton : Calcepius
baſſa mʳ Jubie : Zareo mʳ Charles attendat
wth ⟨th⟩e Baſſa : w · Kendall : Ro : Tailor &
ſound | Georg⟨e ⟩ them Muly mahamet Xeque
Abdula Rais & Ruben H Jeffes, dick Jubie
ſound | & Jeames : exeunt

ſound | Enter in a Charriott Muly ⟨M⟩ahamett
ſennett | & Calipolis : on each ſide ⟨ ⟩ pag⟨e⟩
moores attendant Piſano mʳ Hunt
& w · Cartwright and young Mahamet
Anthony Jeffes : exit mʳ Sam manet
A⟩larū | the rest : to them mʳ Sam a gaine exeunt

⟩ | E⟨n⟩ter the Preſenter : to him
d⟩ | 2 domb ſhew
t⟩ | En⟨te⟩r aboue Nemeſis, Tho : Dro⟨m ⟩to
them 3 · ghosts w · kendall Dab · ⟨&⟩ines 3 · {..⟩
t⟩o them ⟨l⟩ying behind the Curt⟨a } Ro : T{a⟩
⟩brand & | Furies : Parſons : George &⟨ l⟩or
⟩Chopping | one wth a whipp : a nother wth a ⟨b⟩lody
⟩ knife : | tor⟨ h⟩ : & the 3ᵈ wth a Chop⟨p ⟩kni⟨fe⟩ : exeunt

3 · violls
of blood
& a ſheeps
gather

ſound

ſound

and Robin Tailo⟨ ⟩ to them ⟨ 3 ⟩ diu⟨
mʳ Sam : H Jeffes⟨ .. }
them 3 ghosts⟨:⟩ w·⟨ }
the Furies [Fech] ⟨.. }
& Carrie him out⟨ ..}
Fech in Stukeley⟨ .. }
bring in the Moo⟨r }r

Enter : 2 · bringin⟨g ..}y Tor{ch} {
[mʳ Hunt] : w · Kend⟨all ..
enter at one dore : Seba⟨ ⟩D⟨ e⟩
oj Auero : Stukeley : 1 Pa⟨g ⟩mes
Jonas : & Hercules [th] to ⟨ a⟩t anothe⟨r⟩
dore Embaſſadors of Spai⟨n r⟩ Jones
mʳ Charles : attendants Ge⟨o ge &⟩ w·
Cartwright : exeun⟨ ⟩ manet Stu⟨kel⟩ey
& Duke of Au⟨e ⟩ exeunt

Enter Gouernor ⟨ ⟩f Tan⟨ge⟩r ⟨:⟩ & a
Captains mʳ Sha⟨a H⟩ J⟨eff e⟩xeunt

Enter at one d⟨o .. wi
drom & Cullors : ⟨
Duke of A⟨
Hercules⟨
att anoth⟨
mʳ Shaa⟨
m⟨ʳ⟩ Sam⟨
them mu⟨ l po ⟩is .
in their ⟨ th⟩ moores
o⟨n⟩e on ⟨ n⟩ding young
m⟨a⟩hame⟨t, & w C ⟩right : &

Ch⟩ar[ts]
b x⟩es for
Pre⟨ʃ⟩ents

Calcepius Baʃʃa [Adb] Abd⟨u R⟩ais : &
Ruben : Attendants : m^{r} Hunt ⟨& G⟩eorge
& young ʃonne Dab : exeunt

Enter Diego Lopis : Gouernor of Lisbo⟨ n⟩e
m^{r} Rich : Allen : Stukeley : Jonas
Hercules : & an Jrish Biʃhopp m^{r}
Towne : Ro : Tailor : w kendall & m^{r}
Shaa : exeunt

Enter Mully Mahamet, Calipolis :
young mahamet & 2 moores w · Cartwight
& m^{r} Hunt ex⟨ ⟩ muly mahamet manet
⟩raw the rest : to them muly mahamet a gains
⟩ fleʃh : wth raw fleʃh exeunt manet muly ⟨:⟩ exit

ʃ u d⟩
⟩nett

Enter [2 Pages :] Sebastian : a Page
Jeames ⟨:⟩ Duke of Barcelis : m^{r} Charles
Duke of Auero : m^{r} Jubie luis de
Silua : m^{r} Jones County Vinioʃo
George : Chriʃtoporo de Tauora : Dick
Jubie to them : 2 : moores : embaʃʃadors
m^{r} Sam m^{r} Hunt & 2 . Pages : exit
moores : manet the rest : to them Stukeley
ʃound Jonas, Hercules, & Jrish Biʃhopp exeunt

Enter the Preʃenter : to [them] him
3 · domb ʃhew
Enter Nemeʃis aboue : Tho : Drom
⟨to⟩ her 3 · Furies bringin⟨g⟩ in the⟨
Scales : Georg Somerʃett ⟨ m P⟩arʃ⟨
{ ..}

ʃo⟨u ⟩d

Enter the Preʃenter : to him :
⟨ ⟩ ⟨ ⟩ Domb ʃhew
E⟨n ⟩er a ⟨ a⟩nquett br⟨ou ht ⟩ in by
2. tap⟨ ⟩s m^{r} Hunt & w · Cartwri⟨g ⟩ the ⟨
banqvett enter Sebastian : Muly
Dead mahamet Duke of Auero : & Stukeley
mens heads to them De⟨a⟩th : & ⟨3⟩ F⟨ur ⟩ : m^{r}
& bon⟨es⟩ Sam Ro : Tailor ⟨ G & ⟩ Parʃon⟨s
banquett one wth blood to Dy⟨ .. li⟩ghts : ⟨..
blood ⟨ w⟩th Dead mens head⟨s ⟩ in diʃhes : an⟨o
⟨ ⟩^{h} Dead mens bon⟨ ⟩ to the⟨ ..}ther
⟨ k da⟩ll [D] ⟨.. ⟨..⟩ ..} w{..
⟩Furie ⟨w ⟨..⟩ k}Jub{ie
⟩ ⟨ }exeunt
} {

Ma⟨
att⟨e d {..}
m^{r} [Joe⟨{.. }
Enter⟨ }om & Cu{ll }lls
Seba⟨ }ue . Cel{e
⟨w^{t} }aa : {
& ⟨t } {
the⟨
⟨

} ʃaile :
}keley : & Jonas
..}ors : a guard
}ge, {J }Dick Jubie :
}them { }· kendall : [to]
r}s : m{.. t} : exeunt
o}rg{e h}amet exit

8 *The Battle of Alcazar* – transcript of Plot

in the manuscript we may suppose that such was his intention, but it did not invariably succeed. Only two names are missing from the complete record: those of the actor who played King Sebastian of Portugal, and of the boy who played Calipolis. Probably the drummer-boy is also unnamed, for it would be rash to suppose that his description as 'Tho Drom' is anything but the common soubriquet sometimes to be found even in play-texts.

Despite this seemingly distinguished performance, *Alcazar* would certainly be the most obscure and puzzling of the Plots if we did not possess the text of Peele's play. It is divided into acts by elaborate and mystifying dumb-shows that involve immediate re-entrances in unparalleled number, and it exhibits a pattern of doubling that is more intense than that of any other Plot, and, which, even on its own internal evidence, borders on absurdity. Unlike *2 Seven Deadly Sins*, the play has a continuous narrative line, but, as in the earlier Plot, only four actors remain aloof from the general scrum. The Plotter is pressed beyond any limits we have so far observed, but he does not call in the gatherers, at least in the scenes that remain, but prefers instead to overwork his cast. He must call the boy who plays the Moroccan Queen to double as a Portuguese noble in II, iv. He is forced to dodge four of his major actors. One of them, Richard Alleyn, dodges twice between his roles as Presenter and the Governors of Lisbon and (most probably) Tangier. Another, Charles Massey, dodges in two intermediate roles as a Portuguese noble and a Spanish Ambassador, before returning to his original role of Zareo, the captain of the Barbarian army. Humphrey Jeffes must be extracted from an important role as Muly Mahamet Xeque, heir to the Moroccan throne, for a scene as a Portuguese Captain (Plot III, iii), and Mr Jones must be temporarily relieved of his role as Lewes de Silva, a Portuguese, to enter as the other Spanish Ambassador, before he is doubled again as a Barbarian spy. Nothing comparable happens in any other Plot.

When we compare the Plot with the text of the play, we see that these patterns of doubling are even more curious than they at first appear. In the text, Lewes de Silva is sent off from the Portuguese Court to fetch the Spanish Ambassadors, and returns in the stage direction *with* them. The Plotter, on the other hand, has no option but to bring him back *as* one of the Ambassadors, and to cast another of Sebastian's nobles, the Duke of Barceles, as the other. Moreover, he must give them for attendants yet another of Sebastian's courtiers, the County Vinioso (George), who had earlier been of the Barbarian party, and William Cartwright, who was most recently of the Moorish persuasion and is almost certainly black. In I, ii, as we have seen, Pisano (Sam Rowley) is forced to return to speak (according to the text) a Messenger's speech describing what appears to be his own capture by the enemy, and certainly the loss of the treasure and baggage-train he had been sent to protect.

Finally, the text contains a scene (III, ii) which is completely omitted by the Plotter. This is a scene in the Barbarian camp that intervenes in the text between the scenes marked on the Plot as III, i and III, ii. There can be no doubt that it was an original part of the play, for it is vouched for in detail by the source, in places verbatim.

In *Alcazar and Orlando* Greg naturally looked at this problem from the other end. He admits that the deleted scene must have been an original episode in the play and can find no explanation for its disappearance from the independently derived manuscript he believed the Plotter to be working from. He had not, in fact, discovered the true (English) source of the play, and was working from the French version. But even had he known it, the remarkable closeness of the verbal parallels would not have concerned him. His method was to consider only those cases where the printed text appeared to fall short of the dispositions of the Plot. All deficiencies of the opposite kind were to be explained by the *a priori* assumption of corruption in the text, or by the theory of the ignorant author, traces of whose excessive demands could be supposed to have been accidentally copied by the Stage-reviser responsible for preparing the shortened version. He did not need, therefore, to attempt a theory that might have justified the Plotter's responses to the text as we have it, and was, no doubt, not eager to draw attention to this startling exception to his theory. Nor did his later edition of the Plots give him any confidence that Elizabethan theatre practice might be held to exhibit evidence of regular methods that could stand convincingly against what he took to be the bibliographical facts.

His judgment was based, first, on the brevity of the text – it runs to 1,591 lines in the Malone Society reprint – and then by the appearance of spectacular dumb-shows in the Plot where the Quarto provides alternative directions or none at all for their management on stage. He clearly had in mind not only a general corruption of the Quarto, such as might arise in a reported text, but a reduction that works most forcibly in certain places: in the apparent omission of the dumb-shows. This is surely a very exaggerated account of the matter, when, in every case but one (III, Induction), the Plot's account of the shows would be incomprehensible without the record of the text. Assuming, nevertheless, that these were the points to which the reviser of the 1594 copy had most damagingly directed his attention, Greg observed grounds for a more properly bibliographical argument. There is in the text a mixture of style in the stage-directions, some being in italic and some in roman type. It could be assumed that the roman directions represented the hand of the reviser, and, if textual confusions could also be found in their vicinity, as on occasion they can, the case would be demonstrated.[4] This argument, which he himself admitted only with extreme caution (although he did not trust it the less) would not be tenable without comparison with the Plot. It cannot be consistently maintained on the internal evidence of the text, and even the external evidence fails to support it, for its operation entails that the most drastic revisions have taken place in the vicinity of the dumb-shows. Unfortunately for Greg's position, the directions for the shows and for the scenes immediately preceding and following them, remain stubbornly italic in every case but one, that of II, Induction.

That the Quarto text of *Alcazar* illustrates the 'normal' manner of shortening plays thus remains, as it began, an *a priori* assumption. There are no real means of assailing Greg's argument, for there are no real grounds for proposing it. It could only be maintained by devising a means of *ignoring* the many cases where the Plot fails to meet the demands of the Quarto text. For this purpose there is, ready to hand, the theory of the ignorant author:

If we should find cases in which the quarto suggests the more elaborate setting, we must consider whether it may not retain original features that have been altered in the Plot. This will be particularly likely when we have in the Quarto stage directions of the vaguer sort, such as we may suppose due to the author himself.[5]

We have seen, on the other hand, that the practice of plotting, various though its effects appear to be, had a well understood purpose and was based on principles that can be simply formulated. That purpose was not, as Greg supposed, to direct performances, but to count the actors, to construct a framework for the correct making-out of their acting scrolls, to create a mutual accommodation between the cast and the text, and to direct rehearsals in the absence of the Book.

For these uses the Plot of *Alcazar* is entirely adequate. Like *Tamar Cam*, it is spare and functional, couched uniformly in the imperative mood and lacking the seemingly 'literary' or descriptive embellishments that are to be found in others. The crisis of casting that forces the Plotter to omit a scene of the original, and to create the other apparent anomalies mentioned above, may be explained by his direct operation upon the Quarto text of 1594 according to the principles we have formulated, principles that were equally understood by the playwright and which we have seen – if through a glass darkly – to operate in all the Plots, just as they do in the prompt-books and in the great majority of printed texts.

6

ALCAZAR: The text and the sources

It is now a simple matter to rescue *Alcazar* from the implications of Greg's fanciful reduction of its cast to twelve. When we apply to this text the principles we have applied to others, it appears that there is no foundation at all for the idea. The Plotter calls for seventeen actors, and even if we follow his example by doubling the Queen of Morocco with Christopher de Tavora, and make things a little easier for ourselves by casting the Moor's son as a boy, we cannot reduce the adult cast required by the text below sixteen. Even then we will be in difficulties finding soldiers. The text, as we have seen, contains crucial scenes, and shows itself to be prescient about patterns of doubling that justify our counting the cast as of standard size. But it will not be easily fitted. In the original performance represented by the text, sometime about 1588 or 1589, there must have been a fair complement of boys. At I, ii, 230–3, we are treated to a description of the previous scene in which we are told that Abdilmelec's arrival at Tremissen was greeted by 'many Dames of Fesse in mourning weeds'. They do not appear in stage-directions, except perhaps as 'others' and 'the Ladies', but they are addressed at I, i, 123, and told to wipe their tears away. They must surely have been intended to appear; but there is not a sign of them in the Plot. Then, soldiers are needed for the first scene, to be addressed as 'ye Moors'. With sixteen men we can produce four actors (nos. 10, 11, 15, and 16 in the skeleton cast-plan on p. 244), but only if we had eighteen could we allow any of these to be black, as is their leader Zareo. Once again, the Plotter can provide no Moorish troops at all.

If, according to our rules, the text is in some difficulty, even with a standard cast, what is to be made of Greg's reconstruction? We must pause briefly on this, for his arguments in favour of it have been influential in creating a theory of indiscriminate doubling that is totally at odds with the facts as we have seen them. His cast is really only alleged to be of twelve men and four boys.[1] In fact it demands fifteen players to whom the Plotter in 1598 allots male roles. Greg makes only a small saving by doubling Ruben Arches, the widow of Abdelmunen, with Calipolis, the wife of her sworn enemy. He is not himself quite certain whether four boys are involved, or only two. He thus really allows for an adult cast of fourteen. If that were not so, his Portuguese court would have had a very juvenile appearance, three of Sebastian's four Lords having to be played by boys young enough to play women. Perhaps he felt justified in regarding such a possibility as a fall-back plan, because it is true of two of the five Portuguese Lords cast in the Plot. Attendants for the opposing Moroccan parties he also supplied by allowing two of Sebastian's Lords to alternate in their allegiance and to make immediate re-entrances on opposing sides.

To justify these admitted difficulties, Greg invoked a principle that when a character who is said to enter in the initial direction to a scene is allotted no speaking part, it may be suspected that there was an intention to delete him from the play, or at least from that section of it. The incidence of silent, named characters in good texts of the period is, of course, far too frequent to be any kind of key to corruption, and the wholesale application of Greg's theory would have depopulated the early drama to an alarming extent. Nevertheless, by judicious choice between the silent roles in his Plot of *Alcazar*, it was possible so to arrange the minimum cast as to suggest that the motive for excision in most cases was to eliminate the need for actors to make immediate re-entrances in changed costume in successive scenes.[2] Thus, at the expense of dodging the Presenter and Abdelmelec as the Ambassadors of Muly Mahamet, and dodging the latter as a Spanish Ambassador, he was able to avoid Barceles's change from an attendant Moor between II, iii and II, iv, on the grounds that the text's silent second Moor had been cut. Likewise de Silva must have been excised from III, i, where he does not speak, in order to appear as a Moorish attendant in III, ii.

These arguments are not quite disingenuous. On Greg's principles, there is no crisis for his hypothetical reviser in these scenes. He might have chosen to suppress any of the other non-speaking Lords, especially if, on identical grounds, he had suppressed the silent Muly Mahamet Seth in III, ii and cleared the way to double him as a Portuguese, which is an equally possible solution in other scenes as well. Greg's doubling patterns, therefore, are not truly revealing of limiting or crucial scenes. They are merely convenient possibilities. They cannot be shown to arise of necessity and they admit of too many exceptions to be convincing. They were, indeed, designed to support the proposition that the manuscript from which the text was printed had undergone a process of double revision.

First, Greg posited a reviser whose task was to make a fair copy of the original manuscript in which cuts had been carefully marked, and who wrote his directions in an italic hand. His careful copy would nevertheless have included odds and ends of the original directions that no longer applied. A second Stage-reviser then worked on this revised script, striking out speeches and omitting characters, and sometimes whole scenes, and roughly tidying up passages of dialogue where his cuts had left raw edges. Sometimes, where he had made wholesale revisions, he must have written new directions, but failed to alter the old ones in these scenes to accord with his own changes. Greg then discovered the signs of his activity in the roman stage-directions (both the roman and italic directions, we must assume, having been faithfully followed by the compositor) which he could then regard as more consistent with the revised text than the italic.

On these baseless hypotheses he was able to cast suspicion on the text in quite astonishing ways. For example, the one case that contravenes his observation that when a character is dropped from a scene the directions for his entry are always in italic is the direction for the death of the Duke of Avero in battle (*Malone Society Reprint*, line 1,367). This is easily explained as replacing a whole scene of the original – for at this point there is no parallel offered by the Plot. One is inclined to say with Dr Johnson that he who believes this may believe more. Greg himself saw that a quite different scenario was possible, but, rather than abandon his hypothesis of double revision he was prepared to allow for great inconsistency in the text and to doubt the thoroughness of both his hypothetical Stage-revisers. Thus, he also finds that Calipolis has been cut from an italic direction in which she is not mentioned, although she is addressed in the text and appears in the Plot. His argument for the original Vimioso having been deleted from Sebastian's Lords, in II, iv, is also curiously at odds with the argument that the Stage-reviser's actual intention in this and the subsequent Portuguese scene, III, i, was to remove the silent de Silva, whom he left prominently named, when both Vimioso and the Duke of Barceles have disappeared from the stage-directions without trace.

Suspicion falls on *Alcazar*, then, mainly because of its brevity. This, too, may simply be a matter of false perception. Hart's estimate of the average length of plays of the period as about 2,300 lines, obviously will not hold for plays printed between the opening of the Theatre and 1594, for which the figure is 1,623, just twelve lines longer than the text of our play. We may strongly suspect that *Alcazar*, like *Orlando*, began life as a Queen's play at about the same time as *Locrine*, *1 & 2 The Troublesome Reign of King John*, and *A Looking Glass for London and England*, all of which are sixteen-cast plays and much of a length. It is, perhaps, no accident that the first two share lines in common with *Alcazar* as well as other verbal echoes. It is also true of course that *The True Tragedy of Richard Duke of York* and others of the plays of the Strange's-Admiral's combination also echo *Alcazar*, but Queen's is the more likely company to have furnished the large number of boys Peele anticipates, and a drastic reduction of the men to sixteen from over twenty-five would surely have left gaping wounds. It is probable that either the dramatist himself or the Plotter who prepared the text of the 1594 Quarto did make adjustments to accommodate the text to the available cast, but those that we shall observe affect quite different passages of the text from those that concerned Greg and may be far more simply explained according to our alternative hypothesis. These changes are mainly the result of speeches being re-assigned to other speakers. They do not greatly affect the spoken text and the question of who made them will not be troublesome. As the text is prescient in many places about the casting problems, I propose for the sake of simplicity to speak of it as the dramatist's.

The story and the sources

By the fortunate chance that the source material for the greater part of the play is finite, we may now proceed straightforwardly to give an account of the playwright's strategy in adapting the historical record in sequence to the requirements of his stage and his cast, and thus to justify the text itself from the sources. *Alcazar* may be compared with its sources in a minuteness of detail that can hardly be matched in the case of any but some few of Shakespeare's historical tragedies. It is a highly instructive comparison, for this is a play about contemporary history written by a poet who, if something of a student in handling his historical material, had nothing of the imaginative passion that in Shakespeare transforms the moralised chronicles of Holinshed and Plutarch into the intellectual image of living creation.

Peele did a good job with *Alcazar*. He was writing, probably very rapidly, a popular pot-boiler about the most striking event of the recent past: more portentous in its way than the massacre of St Bartholomew because of its immediate importance for the expansion of Spain and the consequent threat to the precarious destiny of Protestant England. Possibly it had immediate relevance to the expedition of Drake and Norris in support of the pretender Don Antonio, an expedition which, whether the fact was widely known or not in England, had been jointly planned with that very Muly Hamet whose installation as King of Morocco ends the play.[3]

The playwright was clever at turning the historical record into popular spectacle and in giving it some marks of 'classical' prestige. His material itself was not lacking in excitement. It was already instinct with feeling, as the sources themselves indicate, and engaged an incurable bias in the mind of anyone who touched it. This fact is an advantage to the student.

The battle fought at El Ksar Kibir (Alcazar) on Monday, 4 August 1578 was one of the absolutely decisive and therefore forgotten battles of history. Its memory was so painful in Portugal that the true story could not be told. There was scarcely a family that did not mourn the loss of a son, and hardly an estate that had not either lost its heir or been ruined by his ransom. In the catastrophe, the country lost its king, the greater number of its nobility, and its national independence. The kingdom passed, after a brief interregnum, into the heritage of the hated Spaniard. It was not a pretty story for the self-esteem of the proud race of seafarers, the conquerors of the Indies. The nobility who set out from Arzilla on what was, with the Pope's official blessing, the last European Crusade, rolling bravely into Africa in their state coaches, ended it in the midst of a fearful slaughter, cringing under their silken cushions and begging for their lives on any terms. The expedition was in chaos before it sailed, its purpose confused, its leadership disastrous, its strategy incompetent, and its defeat overwhelming. Of the alleged 200,000 Portuguese, only half of them combatants, who made the dismal march to El Ksar Kibir, only some 200 regained the safety of the coastal fortresses.[4] The rest were either massacred or enslaved, a few hundreds of the nobility afterwards being ransomed.

The national reaction was silence and total disbelief, and the official accounts were never published either in Portugal or Spain until the Spanish archives were opened late in the nineteenth century. Philip II's motives in the affair were too much open to question for him to welcome any discussion of it. The Portuguese firmly refused to believe that the last of their Princes was dead, and the ready credence given to every rumour of his whereabouts created the semi-religious cult of the Sebastianists, who were still going strong in the last century, looking for the day when the mystic king should return, like Arthur from Avalon, to restore the national glories.

Accounts of the battle, some of them by eye-witnesses, were nevertheless written and filtered through to the rest of Europe, where they were published in French, Latin, and Italian, and, finally, in English. There are five sources from which Peele could have learnt the story, and it is probable that he knew and used three of them. He could not have known any others, for, before 1594, there quite certainly were none that were not mere transcripts of those already published. Those he had, he followed with such fidelity that there can be little doubt about what he had in front of him as he wrote. We are thus provided with a uniquely accurate check on his text in all the scenes, except the dumb-shows and those dealing with the notorious doings of the adventurer Thomas Stukeley. For the latter he might have drawn on all kinds of material, even including personal acquaintance, but his account of the facts differs so widely from the accepted tradition that it seems more probable that he invented most of it.

Of the 1,590 lines of text, 342 can be traced verbatim in the sources. At least as many more are mere commentary on this material or repetition of it in other ways. We can thus assign just under half the play with literal certainty to the source-materials. This half, moreover, contains the sum total of the information presented on any subject in the text, with the exceptions mentioned above, to which may be added a few incidents that appear to be picturesque inventions: the golden statue of Amurath in I, i, the 'lyones flesh' episode in II, iii, and the scene in which the Moorish ambassadors thrust their hand into a flame in token of good faith. Even some of these can, I believe, be traced to the source-material, at least for the germ of their invention. Ten more lines (lines 512–21) may be vouched for from their parodic misquotation in *Poetaster* (1602), and another six, attributed to Greene, from *England's Parnassus* (1608).

The earliest account to be published was in *Les Voyages et Conquestes des Roys de Portugal* (1578), allegedly the memoirs of a certain Sieur Joachim de Centellas. No such person appears to have existed. The work is almost certainly by Jean d'Ongoys, a Parisian printer and bookseller. His account cannot have been derived from eye-witness reports, for the details are so exceedingly inaccurate that they must simply have been invented, although invented by someone with a considerable knowledge of Portuguese history. Peele probably knew this work, but there is little evidence that he used it, except conceivably for Sebastian's speech to the Moorish ambassadors in II, iv.

The second and most important account for our purposes was written by a brother of the Order of Preaching Friars, Luis Nieto. He had lived some time in Morocco and probably spoke Arabic, for he is very well informed about the history and affairs of the Shareef Kings. In the dedication of his manuscript to Philip II he claims to have been present at the battle itself. His account was never published in Spanish, but a French translation was printed in Paris in 1579 under the title *Histoire véritable des dernières Guerres en Barbarie*. From this also a Latin version was made by Thomas Freigius, *Historia de Bello Africano* (1581), and published at Nuremburg. This, in turn, was translated into English by John Polemon and published in his *Second Booke of Battailes* (1587). It is certain that Peele used the English version and knew the Latin, for he borrows details from the poem prefacing Freigius's translation that was omitted by Polemon. He may also have known the French, for the French and Latin versions are very close and their account of events almost identical. They differ only in their spelling of a few names, in a scattering of mis-translations, and in omissions and additions that reveal their national bias.

The fourth and most authoritative account was published in Genoa in 1585, in a work entitled *Dell' Unione del Regno di Portogallo alla Corona de Castiglia* by Hieronimo Conestaggio, secretary to Cardinal Sforza. Conestaggio's version of the battle is so accurately informed and so critical of the Portuguese that it was immediately suspected of having been provided, if not written in its entirety, by Juan de Silva, the Spanish ambassador to Sebastian's court. Since the opening of the Spanish archives, it has been shown, by the close correspondence of *Dell' Unione* with de Silva's exactly similar but more outspoken despatches to Philip II, that such was almost certainly the case.

De Silva was an eye-witness of the whole train of events. It was he who watched the first levies of Portuguese exercising on the parade ground at Lisbon and wrote cynically back to his master that not one of them could handle a gun, the only instructor to be found being a Friar, who had himself never handled weapons, but had read up the theory from books. It was he who conveyed the frequent messages of dissuasion from Spain, and who understood the utter incompetence of the Portuguese nobility and the insensate chivalry of Sebastian. But Sebastian had his way with de Silva, as he had with most people, and the reluctant ambassador accompanied the expedition and fought valiantly in the king's entourage until the deluded young leader was dead and he himself wounded and forced to beg for his ransom.

The pro-Spanish flavour of Conestaggio's account is unmistakable and could hardly have attracted Peele, who, however, recognised its authoritative tone. On the whole, he used Nieto's account in Polemon's translation and took only the details from Conestaggio that are not vouched for by Nieto, and even then, only when the Spanish bias was not so obvious as to suggest real distortion.

Another account possibly known to Peele was a pamphlet called *A dolorous discourse of a most terrible and bloudy battel, fought in Barbarie* (1578). This is presumably a version of an account written by Don Duarte de Meneses that was known and circulating in London by October 1578. We cannot be certain that this is the exact version he saw, but it may be taken as typical of it. He does not use any of its details, but he may have checked the time-scheme of Nieto and Conestaggio against it, and it may have helped to confirm his imaginative picture of Muly Mahamet, who is called 'the blacke Kinge' throughout. No accounts of the battle other than those deriving from these five appeared in Europe before 1594, nor can the influence of any other accounts be detected in the very few histories or fictions concerning *Alcazar* written in Europe for at least the next hundred years. We may conclude that we have a complete account of all the material on the subject that could have been available to the playwright.

Peele had certainly done his homework, and his careful consideration of the documents is, paradoxically, illustrated by the confused pattern of allegiances his play follows. The sources all tend to be anti-Portuguese and highly favourable to Abdelmelec, the 'enemy'. There are many reasons for this. Muly Molocco was a cultivated ruler, wise, moderate, yet active in the exercise of arms, and proficient in Turkish, Spanish, and Latin. He was thought to be the best poet of his day in Arabic. He had an un-Moslem liking and admiration for Christians, and especially Spaniards, but the austerity of Protestantism attracted him more than the idolatrous worship of Rome. He was in secret correspondence with Queen Elizabeth, whom he much admired. He favoured her envoys, kept English musicians at his court and English dogs for his recreation. The Moroccan traffic with England, vital to the island kingdom as her sole source of saltpetre to furnish gunpowder for the fleet preparing to meet the threat of Spanish invasion, was equally important to Abdelmelec, and the goods that passed south in exchange, under the nose of Philip II, were also materials of war: muskets, firelocks, pikes, lances, heavy artillery, and iron shot. It is one of the major ironies of history that the forces of Portugal, England's oldest ally, were annihilated on the plains of Fez by firearms manufactured in the foundries of Kent and Surrey. It is a minor irony that the deforestation of those counties to feed the furnaces helped to establish the fortunes of Philip Henslowe, and to build the Rose theatre in which our play was performed.

If the personal stature and moderation of Abdelmelec forced Christian Europe to look critically at itself, even in the midst of its struggle with the empire of Suleiman the Magnificent, traditional allegiances were far too strong to represent him as other than an honourable exception to the rule of heathenish superstition and ignorance which it was the unique task of Christianity to confront and overcome. Sebastian's war was a Crusade, even if the Vatican had at first been made to think twice by pressure from

Philip II, whose truce with Amurath, forced on both of them by powerful religious and nationalistic revolutions at home, was endangered by the enterprise of Africa. The Bull for the Holy War had nevertheless arrived in Lisbon as early as 1573, and Philip had shown Sebastian remarkable signs of honour. Cynics might put down Philip's civility to a politic desire to appear attractive in the eyes of the Portuguese, whose king, given the inveterate disinclination of Sebastian to women and the virtually certain disaster of the expedition, he was quite likely to become. But there seems no doubt that he was genuinely fond of the young man. He wanted to stop him making a fool of himself, but was carried away, as everyone was, by the chivalric glamour of his ambitions. Even William of Orange, flattered to be approached with a request for help, allowed some companies of dissident German troops to sail for Lisbon at Sebastian's expense.

Sebastian is cast as the hero of the story: the last chivalric champion of medieval Europe. It is clear that whatever considerations of global strategy or differences in religion may have tempered the offers of practical support from the European princes, and whatever sober reflections about the folly of the expedition may have been provoked after the event by its failure, neither folly nor failure could inhibit the simpler emotional response accorded by everyone, including our playwright, to the ideals it evoked of honourable knight-errantry and the embattled unity of Christendom. It was Sebastian's destiny to live out those ideas, aroused in him by his Jesuit teachers from earliest boyhood, with particular intensity, and to become, only six years after the Spanish axe fell on the neck of the Inca king, Tupac Amaru, their last royal victim.

The villain is, in all accounts, Muly Mahamet. In this luxurious, cowardly, Christian-hating usurper, Sebastian's ally, the wounded sentiments of European chivalry found an apt and perhaps fitting scapegoat. The sources treat Mahamet with reasonable objectivity, commenting on his insignificant stature and indolent nature, but not attributing to him worse vices than might be expected of Moslem rulers. He took his complexion from his mother, who was black-skinned, and this taint was used by Moors and Christians alike to indicate the unreliability of his nature. Even Abdelmelec, his uncle, referred to him contemptuously as 'the negro'. He is thus an appropriate villain for our playwright, who dresses him in more devilish hues than the sources warrant.

This characterisation of Mahamet, however, leads to a conflict of loyalties within the play, because of Peele's peculiarly English preoccupation with the legitimacy of rulers. It does not occur to the writers of the source material to put much emphasis on the tanist method of succession devised by the second of the Shareef Kings, but to the Elizabethan this abrogation of the right of primogeniture becomes a justification of importance for Sebastian's invasion. Mulei Shareef (Mahammed Ech-Cheikh, the *Muli zaref* of line 139 of the text) was the first king to unite Fez and Morocco under a single rule. He declared that the inheritance should always pass to the oldest surviving male member of the Shareef clan. He had thoughtfully put his own brother to death, so that in fact he was followed by his eldest son Abdallas (Abdullah el-Ghalib). Abdallas settled his position by disposing of his remaining cousins, and then, as Peele says, 'reigned his time', but his hand was also against the lives of his own brothers, Abdelmunen (Abd el-Moumen), Abdelmelec (Abd el-Malik), and Muly Mahamet Xeque or Seth (Ahmed el-Mansour) also called Muly Hamet in the play. The mother of two of the boys had taken them to Constantinople where they were brought up in the Turkish court. Abdelmunen had fled to Algiers. Abdallas then made clear his intention of settling the kingdom on his son, Muly Mahamet (Mohammed el-Mesloukh) and duly created him Viceroy of Fez. Abdelmunen was persuaded by promises of goodwill to return as far as Tlemcen (Tremissen) on the borders of Morocco, and there he was slain with an arrow, while at prayer in a mosque, by some followers of his nephew Mahamet.

Upon the death of Abdallas, Abdelmelec immediately begged support from Amurath, and, indeed, from Philip II, and set out for Tangier to assert his right to the crown. This is the point at which the play begins. Having defeated Mahamet in three rapid battles, he invested himself as king, at the same time naming his next brother, Muly Ahmed el-Mansour (Seth), his heir, thus upholding the legal manner of inheritance laid down by his father and ratified, as the play says, 'by voice of all his peers'.

It is a rather complicated story, and all accounts simplify it in one way or another; but all regard Abdelmelec as the rightful king and Mahamet as an usurper. Peele follows the sources in this, and allows Abdelmelec to set forth his claim to the throne in I, i as if the play had no intention of questioning it. At the same time he allows sentiment for the right of primogeniture to colour his emotional picture, and favourably interprets Sebastian's support for Mahamet as consistent with hereditary right 'according to ... our wholesome Christian laws' (III, iv, 1,026). Sebastian's support of a wrongful king would put out all the emotional values of the play, but we are clearly told in the Presenter's first speech (I, Induction) that Mahamet is an usurper, and a murderous one at that, and so we must fall in with Peele's characterisation of him as a vicious and double-dyed hypocrite, without ever quite being able to put our finger on his actual acts of hypocrisy.[5] His offer of the Empire of Morocco to Sebastian is an obvious one, but we should think the less of Sebastian if it were allowed to appear that he had undertaken the expedition solely in hope of gain, and that enticement is rather played down as a motive. Mahamet then remains, like a pocket Iago, a creature of motiveless malignity, and on this rather infirm peg Peele hangs the interpretation of his story. 'Interpretation' is perhaps too positive a word, for he has nothing to say about the events, except for the journalistic comment, that, because of the Nemesis attendant on Mahamet's hypocrisy, so many tall men were 'destinate to dye in Afric here'.

The same confusion is evident in the playwright's treatment of

Stukeley, who speaks the words just quoted. He is allowed to die in Act V as a famous Englishman, and his dying soliloquy is a carefully neutral résumé of the major events of his life. Nothing more is alleged against him than that he was one of those

> that never could endure
> To hear God Mars his drum, but he must march,

and despite his sinister intention of invading Ireland, which brings him in the first place to Lisbon, he is treated throughout as a poor man's Tamburlaine. The typical note of his speeches is:

> Huff it brave mind, and never cease t'aspire
> Until thou raigne sole king of thy desire.

It would be absurd in such a play, where the characters are pasteboard and their motivations automatic, to look for any great subtlety in the handling of the sources, but as we shall see, Peele did criticise his material and tried to get the matter as clear as he could for an audience.

His first problem arose in deciding what to call his characters. This is rather a complex matter, and we had better deal with it at once. The story is to represent four parties: the Portuguese, the English adventurers, and two opposing teams of Moors, one led by Abdelmelec and the other by Muly Mahamet.

The Moroccan story offers four or five characters who have eminently confusable names. First there is 'the Moor', Muly Mahamet (Mahamet el-Mesloukh). In Nieto he is usually called *Muly Mahamet*, *Mahamet*, or *the Moor*, but sometimes the *Xerif*. In *The Dolorous Discourse* he is called *Mulla Sherriffa* or *the Blacke King*, and in Conestaggio, *the Moor*, the *Xariffe* or *Molei Mahamet*. To make things more confusing, Polemon sometimes calls him *Muly Hamet*, which is the commonest name for his youngest uncle.

Then there is the father of Abdelmelec, Mohammed Ech-Cheikh, who needs to be named as the instituter of the law of tanist succession. He is called *Muly Mahamet Xeque* in Nieto and also *Muly Mahamet*. In *The Dolorous Discourse* he is *Mully Hamet Shek*, and in Conestaggio *Molei Mahamet Xariffe*.

The Moor's son (another Mohammed Ech-Cheik) is called *Muly Xeq* (Nieto), *Muly Xeque* (Polemon) and *Moleixeque* (Conestaggio). In Freigius's table he appears merely as *Xequus*.

Abdelmelec's younger brother, Ahmet el-Mansour, who was the reigning king of Morocco at the time the play was written, is called *Muly Hamet* or *Muly Agmet* (Nieto), *Hamet* (Polemon and Conestaggio) and *Mulla Hamet* in *The Dolorous Discourse*.

Finally, there is the progenitor of the whole clan, Mohammed el-Kaim who is called *Xarif* by both Nieto and Conestaggio.

The reader will now be as confused as Peele undoubtedly was. He perhaps did not understand that *Xeque* is the Spanish transliteration of Sheikh, and he may have had no clearer idea than an average modern reader of what a Sheikh and a Mullah really are. He had no means of distinguishing the names of Ahmet (Hamet) and Mahamet from the sources. He appears to have taken the shorter form as a familiar name, much as Harry stands in relation to Henry, and allows that form of address to be used only by members of the family. But he still has three characters to represent with names so similar that they cannot be made clear, and others to mention who are equally confusable. So he begins to distinguish as best he can.

He keeps the title *Xarif* for the first king of Morocco and never uses it elsewhere. It appears as 'our grandsire *Mulizaref*' (I, i, 139). Then he decides to give the Moor's son no name at all in the spoken text. He is called 'boy', 'brave boy', 'my dearest son', 'this young Prince'. Peele *thought* of him as *Muly Mahamet*, however, for that is the form that occurs once in a stage-direction, and also in speech-headings when they vary from 'Moores son' or 'sonne'. He must call the Moor's grandfather *Muly Mahamet Xeque* because he has to be mentioned and there is nothing else to call him. The Moor himself he proposes to call *Muly Mahamet*, and here there will be no confusion, because the grandfather does not appear on stage. But he now has to distinguish Muly Mahamet the Moor from Muly Hamet (or Mahamet) his uncle. His first solution to that was to give the latter the distinguishing name, or title, *Xeque*. At his first entrance he is so called in the stage-direction and in two of his three speech-prefixes, the other being *Muly Mah*. There is no confusion here because the Moor is not on stage, but, as Hamet's grandfather of the same name is mentioned in the spoken text Peele allows the character on stage to remain unidentified, except by Abdelmelec's reference to 'my brother'. At his next appearance, his name has to be mentioned, for he is to be installed as heir to the throne. The dramatist, forced to make a decision and to find a name that can be pronounced (for what English actor could cope with 'Xeque'?), hits on the solution of calling him 'Seth'.

Greg takes this name to be a misreading of *Sech*, Peele's manner of writing the common Elizabethan transliteration *Seich* (Sheikh), but if that were so, we should have to suppose that the compositor misread it five times in an English hand, and once (according to Greg's theory) in an Italian hand. *Seich* is, of course, only one among many English forms for Sheikh. If Peele had wanted an alternative, the spelling *Shek* was available from *The Dolorous Discourse*. That he made a decision about the pronunciation may be guessed from the fact that as soon as Hamet is given that name, all trace of the original *Xeque* disappears from the speech-prefixes. He is listed as *Muly*, *Muly Mah.*, and eventually, after Mahamet is dead, simply as *Mah*. Peele had reason to infer from the sources that *Xeque* was a kind of title for the heir to the throne and he merely transferred it from the usurping family to the rightful tanist heir.[6] In the same way, he seems to have thought of the honorific *Muly* (Mullah) as the equivalent of 'Lord'.

We can now see how he solves the problem of the other Mahamets, distinguishing them quickly as he goes. He knew, as his audience did not, that there was a Muly Mahamet on stage in I, i. When, in I , ii, he is faced with two more, father and son, he calls them simply 'the Moore' and 'his sonne' in the stage-direction and adopts the expedient of using *Moore* for the father's speech-prefixes and *Muly Mah.* for the son's. This serves well enough. In the next scene, where Muly Mahamet Seth is named and speaks, he is now given the form *Muly Mah.* for his speech-prefix, for there can be no confusion with other Muly Mahamets, neither of whom is on stage. In II, iii the Moor enters as *the Moore*, but the son appears as *Muly Mahamet his sonne* and is *Mah.* in his speaking part. Upon the Moor's second entrance (with raw flesh spiked on his sword), *he* is now called *Muly Mahamet* and his first speech-prefix takes the form *Muly Mah.* This is clear enough for Peele's purposes, for the son has nothing more to say in the scene, but it is, of course, confusing for the reader.

In III, iv, where the Moor is addressed in the spoken text as *Muly Mahamet*, *Lord Mahamet*, and *the Arabian Muly Hamet*, the speech-prefix *Muly Mah.* for the son must be abandoned and he is given the elaborate heading *The moores sonne*. In IV, ii, where the son is not on stage, the Moor takes over the forms *Muly Mahamet* and *Muly Mah.*, but in Act V he becomes *Moore* once again. The reason is that in Peele's knowledge the 'boy' who enters with him *is* his son, although the fact that he is hysterically addressed as 'villain' gave Greg the impression that he was merely a servant. Moreover, Greg had been forced to double the son elsewhere in his hypothetical cast and was not disposed to interpret Mahamet's last speeches of neo-Senecan ranting as the work of a responsible dramatist.

After the Moor's speaking part has come to an end, the form *Muly* is taken over by Muly Mahamet Seth. On the report that the Moor is missing, his speech-prefix extends to *Muly Mah.*, and when it is virtually certain that the Moor is dead, he can be allowed the simple form *Mah.*, for he is now the only Mahamet of any shape or form left with a speaking role.

From an editorial point of view this is all totally irregular and, indeed, impossible to standardise, but it provides no grounds for doubting the text. All too often, the theories of textual bibliography can be sustained only by demanding of texts that were prepared for quite other purposes the consistency that is appropriate for the scholar in his study. As soon as we look backwards in this text we are, of course, confused by the haphazard duplication of speech-prefixes, but *au courant* they are clearly functional and explicable. It is very doubtful whether a reviser cutting this play could have maintained such a forward-running consistency. These directions are responsive to the dialogue at every point and must have come from a working dramatist in the act of composition.

One final question of nomenclature remains, that is, the alternative name for Abdelmelec: *Muly Molocco*. It is of some importance to determine whether this play was indeed the *mulomurco* performed by Strange's Men as an old play on 20 February 1592, and thereafter for fourteen performances until 20 January 1593. The name is only twice used of Abdelmelec: at line 15 and at line 418. In both cases it appears to be used as a title with patriotic or thrilling overtones, and there is, of course, no reason at all for it to appear in the Plot. It is not altogether clear from the sources, and may never have dawned on the playwright, that *melec* and *Moluco* are the same. The name occurs in Conestaggio as *Molei Moluco*, and also as *il Moluco*, while Mahamet is called *Molei Mahamet Xariffe* and *il Xariffe Mahamet*. This may well have suggested to Peele that the one had the title *Xariffe* and the other *Moluco*. Greg did not know that the dramatist was following a source in which *Moluco* is the standard form and assumed that the appearance of *Molocco* in the text was some kind of sport, deriving from *The Dolorous Discourse*, which has *Maluca*.[7] For the same reason he failed to grasp the dramatist's intention in Act V, where Abdelmelec's body is set up in a chair on stage 'with cunning props', so that his soul may preside with joy over the defeat of the Christian army. It is Conestaggio's account, alone of the sources, that records the deception practised upon the Moorish army by which the dead Abdelmelec was carried forward against the enemy in his litter as if still alive and directing the operation.[8] Greg supposed that Abdelmelec played only a minor role; but he has the fourth-largest speaking part, and although mute in the fifth act he dominates the stage for the greater part of it. *Muly Molocco* may very well have been the name under which the play passed at the Rose: indeed I think there can be no doubt of its identity, for there could not have been another play about Abdelmelec based on the actual information available that was not exactly like this one.

The doubt Greg cast on the ascription in *Orlando and Alcazar* was provoked by his wish to sustain the roman–italic principle, which, as we have seen, is false. In his edition of Henslowe he had been happy to let the common identification stand, and Chambers followed him without question. But the operation of the roman–italic argument makes it appear that the excised portions of the play must have contained material relating to Sebastian and Stukeley. He was thus inclined to look for the remains of *mulomurco* in *The Famous Historie of Captain Thomas Stukeley*. This play may well have excited the jibe in *Satiromastix* that the Admiral's Men has 'cut a poor Moor in the middle to serve him in twice', for the latter scenes of *The Famous Historie* are a replay of some of the spectacular moments of *Alcazar*. But the name *Molocco* is used only in the Spanish scenes of *Stukeley* and these could not have appeared in the earlier *mulomurco*.

These matters having been disposed of, we may now follow the setting up of the sources in action in somewhat greater comfort.

The sources in action

In the Presenter's first speech, the theme of the action is stated clearly enough: this is to be an account of Portuguese honour and chivalry, caught in the toils of the Nemesis that attends the murderous hypocrisy of Muly Mahamet and his unjust usurpation of the throne from the 'brave Barbarian Lord Muly Molocco'. The actual account of how that usurpation came about is, as we have seen, more than a little difficult to present, and has been further muddled by the attempt of the compositor to rectify his second page. The first part of the speech runs thus:

Honor the spurre that pricks the princely minde,
To follow rule and climbe the stately chaire,
With great desire inflames the Portingall,
An honorable and couragious king,
To vndertake a dangerous dreadfull warre,
And aide with Christian armes the barbarous Moore,
The Negro *Muley Hamet* that with-holds
The kingdome from his vnkle *Abdilmelec*,
Whom proud *Abdallas* wrongd,
And in his throne instals his cruell sonne,
That now vsurps vpon this prince,
This braue Barbarian Lord *Muly Molocco*.
The passage to the crowne by murder made,
Abdallas dies, and deisnes this tyrant king,
Of whom we treate sprong from the Arabian moore
Blacke in his looke, and bloudie in his deeds, 16
And in his shirt staind with a cloud of gore,
Presents himself with naked sword in hand,
Accompanied as now you may behold,
With deuils coted in the shapes of men,
Like those that were by kind of murther mumd.

The punctuation of the text is, of course, nowhere to be trusted, and in the last two lines above I have reversed it in order to make a point. The real confusion arises because of the page division. The last line of this passage, which would otherwise have stood alone at the top of A2^{v}, is printed following the direction for the first dumb-show in which the Moor's young brethren are led to the bed in which they will later be murdered. The reading thus appears to be:

Like those that were by kind of murther mumd,
Sit downe and see what hainous stratagems
These damned wits contriue.

Now the murder of the young brethren has not yet taken place, and the audience can hardly be asked to sit as still as the dead they have just seen murdered when they cannot have seen any such thing. The dumb-shows have clearly been inserted in the first convenient place, simply because there is no exactly right place for them. The shows are almost continuous, but the stage is cleared between them, and the time-continuum of the Presenter's commentary overlaps both, with appropriate pauses. There is no way of rectifying this as a written record, although it is perfectly simple to fit the parts together in performance. The real problem is the line

Like those that were by kind of murther mumd.

One might attempt an emendation of this to read

Like those that were of kind by murther mumd

but I am not sure that this makes any better grammatical sense in Elizabethan speech. The meaning, however, is tolerably clear. The words refer not to the young brethren who are about to suffer, but to their murderers, the 'devils' who accompany Mahamet. These have already been silenced forever because of their nearness to the throne.

The whole passage was troublesome to Greg, because it appeared to him that Abdallas's death is anticipated before the succession is secured. But this is not so. As long as we take 'deisnes' as a finite verb, almost certainly a misprint for the normal Elizabethan usage 'desines' (= nominates, or appoints) the combination of theatrical and historical sense works without obscurity. Peele has merely contracted the order of events for the sake of excitement. He turns at line 16, as it were, from the historical present tense to the theatrical present. *That* is the background to the action; *this* is what we are now to see; but the stage action he has planned causes some overlapping in the narrative.

In Nieto's account, the order of events begins with Abdallas's murder of his kindred, then the installation of Mahamet as heir at an assembly of peers, then Mahamet's murder of Abdelmunen, followed by the death of Abdallas, and finally the fates of the young brothers, one of whom in actuality was killed and the other imprisoned. Peele's intention is to represent the murders of Abdelmunen and the young brothers in his first dumb-shows, although the former event had in fact taken place before Mahamet's accession. These events, however, have nothing to do with 'the passage to the crowne by murther made'. *That* passage was created by the murder of Abdallas's uncle and cousins, and it is their devilish forms who now appear with Mahamet 'coted in the shapes of men'. There are only two of them, perhaps for the reason that two is a good number to carry Abdelmunen in his chair, but rather more probably because the dramatist is already counting his cast. The chair itself – as Greg did not see because it does not appear in the Plot – is an important property. It will later serve as Abdelmelec's litter in which his corpse will be propped up to oversee the battle sequence in Act V, and finally as the throne for Seth's installation.

In the remainder of the Presenter's speech we are returned to chapter IV of Nieto for the briefest possible explanation of Abdelmelec's life among the Turks and the slightly complex fact that the support of Amurath has been offered to him for services rendered to Amurath's predecessor,

Suleiman. We then pass to chapter V of Nieto to witness Abdelmelec's arrival at Algiers and at Tremissen where he meets with Muly Mahamet Xeque. That meeting and the setting out of Abdelmelec's claim to the throne are the principal concerns of I, i.

The characters to be brought on stage are partially drawn from Conestaggio's account, for, as we have seen, the dramatist would have been foolish to burden himself with Moors at this stage if he could have avoided it, and the Plotter could provide none at all. Nieto mentions only that Abdelmelec was given a commission to raise troops in Algiers. That he returned with Moorish troops is recorded only by Conestaggio:

> He obtained three thousand soldiers of the Turke ... [and] with these forces and the Moores that followed him, which wanted not in Africk, he entered his Nephewes kingdom.[9]

Peele takes Conestaggio's word that the Turkish troops had come from the Porte and presumably decided on a name for the leader, Calcepius, before turning the page of Nieto where it is discovered that his name was Rabadan. There can be no doubt that Calcepius is original and was followed by the Plotter. Peele then borrowed Zareo from the later account of the battle, and made him Abdelmelec's chief lieutenant. He is called *Argerd* Zareo, but it is not necessary to think that this suggests some connection with Algiers. I should be tempted to suppose that the word in Peele's copy was *Vizeroie*, carelessly written in an English hand (Zareo is given that title in Polemon). A printing-house reviser, checking from the description of this scene offered in I, ii might have discovered the meeting to have taken place 'Neere to Argier' and invented the curious adjective. But I am reluctant to compete with the speculations of the bibliographers. What is certain is that Zareo is described as a Moor, but his soldiers are not certainly of the same complexion. Indeed, the singling out of Zareo in the stage-direction may suggest that they could not be. As I have said, there is no possibility of these soldiers being blackamoors in a sixteen-cast play, and the Plotter, once again, provides none at all.

The soldiers' welcome will inevitably be rather thin, but Polemon records that Abdelmelec was 'honourably received' at Tremissen. If this is to be represented on stage, it can only be by means of the boys. They appear only as 'others' in the stage-direction, entering with Muly Mahamet Xeque and the royal ladies at line 105, but they are vividly described in the following scene (I, ii):

> Rubyn our vnkles wife that wrings her hands
> For Abdilmunens death, accompanied
> By many dames of Fesse in mourning weeds,
> Neere to Argier encountred Abdilmelec.

As he cannot make a convincing military entrance, the playwright has turned the spectacle into a family occasion, dressing the Dames in black and possibly allowing Ruben to sing a dirge or 'tragicke song'. If so, it has not been preserved, just as songs in many printed texts and manuscripts are missing, but Abdelmelec's rather dry-sounding comment is presumably a response to it:

> Rubin these rights to Abdelmunens ghost
> Haue pearst by this to Plutos graue below.

The rest of the information in this scene is vouched for by the sources; but, as the Plot is seriously in default here, and, by the application of Greg's logic, the text has therefore been suspected, it may be worthwhile to defend two brief passages against the charge of corruption. One concerns the possibility of dropped lines following line 123. Here Abdelmelec addresses the boys on stage as:

> Distressed ladies and yee dames of Fesse,
> Sprong from the true Arabian *Muly Xarif*
> The loadstarre and the honor of our line.

The playwright can hardly have thought this to be literally true. If a line or two is not missing, we must take 'sprong' rather loosely, but that is not at all inconsistent with the strong team spirit that characterises each party in the play. 'Arabian' is, for the Moors, a word of approval. It recalls the direct descent of the royal family from the Prophet Mahamet. Even the black Mahamet is 'sprong from the Arabian moore' (line 18), but Abdelmelec and the dames spring from the 'true Arabian'. I believe that Peele intends to imply that the royal ladies and the dames of Fez are all 'on our side' and are all white. He may possibly have been undecided about whether the Shareef was, indeed, the progenitor of the whole race, or merely the first king, for there is a possible ambiguity in the lines

> And of the Moores that now with vs do wend,
> Our grandsire *Mulizaref* was the first,

but I believe this is to be read as a grammatical inversion and that the name is correctly used as a title by Peele, both here and in the quotation above.

The second suspect passage, lines 111–117, throws some light on the style of the verse. Muly Mahamet Xeque is speaking as one who has arrived at Tremissen having just passed by the camp of the Turkish Janissaries:

> Our Moores haue seen the siluer moons to wane,*
> In banners brauely spreading ouer the plaine,
> And in this semicircles haue descride
> All in a golden field a starre to rise,
> A glorious comet that begins to blase,
> Promising happie sorting to vs all.
> [*sc. waue]

This metaphor, which fits together literal pieces of information and a violent conceit is very offensive to the taste of modern critics. It is, however, typical of the style of the play (cf. lines 125, 257–60, 267–72, 512–22, 550–1, 565–7, 574–5, 578–81, 584–609 – this, a gloriously inverted example, parodied by Shakespeare – 752–5, 806–7, 817–18, 836–7, 888–93, 968–70, 973–5, 1,014–18, 1,021–2, 1,045–9, 1,406–9). The trick was perfected by Marlowe and is natural to the early drama that imitates him. Greg regarded the passage as corrupt because of the breakdown of rhyme after 'plaine / wane'. Yoklavitch correctly pointed out the turned letter in 'wane', but still attempted to support Greg's diagnosis of corruption by observing that the Ottoman flag did not bear a star within the crescent in the sixteenth century. That does not seem to have been recognised by Elizabethan illustrators and Portuguese mapmakers, or by the designer of the Turkish banner captured at the Battle of Lepanto and now in the Doge's Palace in Venice, but even if it were officially so, it is not necessarily relevant to the passage.

Peele is attempting to move from the Moors' observation of the presence of Turkish soldiers, which is literally true and demonstrated by the presence of some few of them on stage, to the abstract joy of the beholders at seeing them. To do so, he fixes on the waving banners of the Janissaries, which, it is the point of the metaphor to say, have put new heart into the Moorish nation. The crescent banners are then transferred, as it were in long-shot, to the (offstage) formation of the main body of the army as it spreads over the plain. Nieto mentions that typical 'demi-circulaire' disposition of a Turkish force, and Polemon translates it as 'new Moon'. De Silva (Conestaggio) well remembered the 'corni della luna' in which Abedelmelec drew up his army at Alcazar and which threw the Christian army into confusion and cut off its retreat. The golden field is, of course, the field of promised success, but also the heraldic field of the crescent banners. The star or comet is an omen of success, but it is also an actual comet that might have been seen rising above the army spread on the plain. This comet appeared in 1577, the year in which Peele took his B.A. at Oxford, and he may well have remembered it as a matter of personal experience. If not, he could not have missed it either in the Latin poem prefixed to Freigius's account, or in the amusing description in Conestaggio of its appearance over Lisbon on 9 November. I do not pretend it is a skilfully managed metaphor, but it is perfectly intelligible when one observes the elements of Peele's reading that went into it.

The dumb-shows, indeed, also spring from the same trick of sub-poetic thought, whereby a verbal allegory is merely made into a literal spectacle. If Mahamet is 'bloody', he appears in a shirt sprinkled with gore; if war is a 'fatal banquet', waited on by weapons, blood and death, a table appears, furnished with dishes of bones and severed heads, and attended by three garçons bearing symbolic properties; if kingdoms are falling, as in Act V, crowns are hung on a tree and persuaded one by one to drop off.

This innocent poetry of make-believe strikes critics as childish, as no doubt it is. The implication of the commentary on these passages is either that Peele could not have written them, or else that they are all corrupt. They are, of course, easily corrupted, for they are close to nonsense as they stand, and one compositorial error throws them into complete confusion.

They naturally excite editorial impatience, because they strain concepts of syntax and are almost totally resistant to modern punctuation.

One other semblance of confusion in this scene might be taken to indicate the omission of some previous action. Calcepius declares that he has come to make Abdelmelec Emperor (lines 99–101) and will say later that he is 'calld for by the Gods / To sit vpon the throne of Barbary', as if that is still to happen in the future. On the other hand, Muly Mahamet Xeque refers to Abdelmelec as 'your anointed king' (line 197). But nothing is missing. There can have been no coronation scene, nor is any suggestion of it included in the description of this scene that is offered in the next. There is, indeed, no mention of any ceremony of installation in the sources. What is involved here is simply the difficulty of keeping the time-sequence straight in a play where the choruses anticipate the action. We have been told in I, Induction that it is Abdelmelec who suffers the wrong of Mahamet's usurpation. We have seen an anonymous uncle strangled in his chair and are now told that Abdelmelec is fighting to revenge 'my deepe wrongs, and my deare brothers death'. The account we have been given, in between, of the tanist laws of inheritance, makes it clear that the man we saw strangled *was* Abdelmunen, the next legitimate heir, whose claim has now passed to Abdelmelec. Abdelmelec's 'anointing' may thus pass as a pardonable exaggeration, indicating merely that he is truly legitimate.

In I, ii we come to the first of the all-black scenes. The Moor appears in his celebrated chariot, counter-marching none too bravely against Abdelmelec's forces, who, we are told, are already encamped near Fez. Muly Mahamet's concern is to get his treasure safely past the enemy lines, but precisely where it is going cannot be made out. Peele routes it through Scyras, a place-name that has no equivalent in the sources, or in any map of North Africa that I have found. I believe it is merely a tag name, invented to serve the moment's need.[10] The treasure is to be captured and a report will arrive that the whole country is turning to Abdelmelec. At the end of the scene the Moor and his company are to leave the stage in flight.

All the sources agree about Mahamet's understanding of the importance of money in warfare. The subject of the treasure (it appears in the stage-direction) is therefore a useful device for the dramatist, for material is already running short and a great part of this scene is taken up with a description of the preceding one. Moreover, there can be no battle, for there are no troops. The dramatist envisages seven black actors, in all, but only three of them are available as soldiers, and two will presumably be necessary to move Mahamet's chariot. If pages were used for the purpose, as in the Plot, they are not mentioned. The other actors available as soldiers have all appeared in the preceding scene on Abdelmelec's side, and, except for Zareo, must all have been 'white'. Thus, the battle of Er-Roken in which Mahamet's treasure was captured, must be represented by a messenger, while Mahamet, his wife, his son and his two attendants remain on stage. It is rather absurd to suppose, as Greg does, that the treasure was a mere flourish of the dramatist's that could not have appeared (because there are no properties listed in the Plot). The treasure is the whole *raison d'être* of this scene and there is no reason why Pisano should not, if necessary, have carried it himself. I suspect that Greg may have assumed that it would need to be carried in the chariot, and, as the chariot does not leave the stage, this must have been another example of truncated spectacle. It is probably Greg, not the dramatist, who is confused here. Pisano is ordered to take a cornet of horse and other forces,

And with our carriage march awaie before.

The impression is thus created that some form of vehicular transport has departed with Pisano, but a carriage is, of course, a sixteenth-century baggage-train, not a chariot.

The appearance of Mahamet's chariot is amusingly justified by the French translation. Mahamet was not personally courageous. He is said in the manuscript to have watched the battle from a *cerro*, or little hill. A copyist or translator mistook the word for *carro*, which Freigius renders as *carrui* [*insistans*], and Polemon as *wagon*. But the French version has *char*. It seems likely that Peele was happy to take the grander of the possible meanings of the French word, but it may also have been attractive because he knew Tamburlaine's chariot was available in the properties' store.

Nevertheless, this scene shows clear evidence of the dramatist's having been in difficulties. The absence of Calipolis from the stage-direction need not detain us, although it is made much of by Greg. There is no reason for cutting her from the scene. A more probable explanation is that she has been added to it. This was probably by the dramatist himself when he came to introduce her first as originally planned in II, iii. There he wrote the elaborate and probably initial direction: *with Calipolis his wife*. Then he realised that she might be called to appear to swell the numbers in the earlier treasure scene and introduced her there simply by adding an extra-metrical word of address to one line (line 221):

Madame, gold is the glue, sinewes and strength of war.

Calipolis simply completes the tally of the six negro Moors who may be called to enter in this scene, but there are signs soon afterwards that the text did need revision because of a shortage of cast and that an impression of numbers was needful.

After the exit of Pisano (which is unmarked), the verse certainly goes to pieces for five lines, while we move into the speech of Young Mahamet's recapitulation of the events of I, i:

(*Moore.*) Now boy whats the newes?
Muly Mah. The newes my Lord is warre, warre and reuenge.
And if I shall declare the circumstance,
Tis thus.
Rubyn our vnkles wife that wrings her hands
For Abdilmunens death, accompanied

With many dames of Fesse in mourning weeds,
Neere to Argier encountred Abdilmelec,
That bends his force puft vp with Amuraths aide
Against your holds and castles of defence.
The yonger brother Muly Mahamet Seth,
Greets the great Bassa, that the king of Turkes
Sends to inuade your right and royall realme,
And basely beg reuenge, arch-rebels all,
To be inflict vpon our progenie.

It teases us out of thought to know how the son came to have learned all this. Moreover, it seems that his reluctance to speak is an admission that he has no business to know it. The speech is really in Messenger language. It is inappropriate for the boy to refer to one of his great-uncles as 'our uncle', and to the other as 'the younger brother', and even more inappropriate for him to speak of '*our* progenie', for, while Peele sometimes uses that term in its widest application to refer to ancestors as well as descendants, the only surviving progeny of the Moor and his son in any sense are the arch-rebels themselves! The most natural conclusion is that the speech originally belonged to a Messenger. When re-allocated to the son, two changes of pronoun have been made. The original would have read: 'Rubyn *your* vncles wife' and 'To be inflict vpon *your* progenie'. The Messenger has more to say, but the boy at this point appears to react in fear, as if he were the progeny intended, and Mahamet's next speech is comforting:

Why boy, is Amurath's Bassa such a bug,
That he is markt to do this doubtie deed?

The son, nevertheless, continues with the Messenger's speech until interrupted by Mahamet with a line that might more appropriately have been addressed to the original Messenger, the change to the son being rectified by the addition of two extra-metrical addresses ('Why boy' and 'Boy') to the following lines :

Moore. Awaie, and let me heare no more of this,
Why boy, are we successours to the great Abdilmelec,
Descended from the Arabian Muly Zarif,
And shall we be afraide of Bassas and of bugs,
Rawe head and bloudie bone?
Boy, seest here this semitarie by my side,
Sith they begin to bath in blond, (sc. bloud)
Bloud be the theame whereon our time shall tread.

'Abdilmelec' is, of course, an error for 'Abdallas'. This may suggest that the patching here was the work of a reviser, but the regularity of the speech-headings is more indicative of the author himself. A reviser is unlikely to have changed an original Messenger's speech-prefixes to *Muly Mah.* for the son in a scene where the father is the more prominent character. But patching there has probably been, and at least one line has dropped out of the text after line 258.

These signs of revision point to the excision of a first Messenger in the scene, and reveal that the playwright had given some thought to the identity of the second Messenger who is now to enter to report the loss of the baggage-train. There seems, on reflection, no reason why the three Moorish attendants should not have left the stage with the treasure, two of them returning subsequently as the two Messengers. The dramatist, however, did not arrange things this way. The speech of the second Messenger implies that more actors remain on stage than Mahamet's immediate family. He cries:

> *Mes.* Flie king of Fesse, king of Moroccus flie,
> Flie with they friends Emperour of Barbary

and, if this is so, there is no-one to enter but Pisano, unless the playwright had been prepared to use a white actor. The dialogue makes that most improbable, for the Messenger gives Mahamet his three royal titles, which no white Moor would do. Thus, it would appear that the dramatist wanted Mahamet to remain attended by his guard, and was even prepared to revise his text in order to permit it, roughly ironing out the rather gross improbability of characterisation in transferring these speeches to the son. There is probably a more compelling reason, concerning the status of the actors, that is hidden from us. When we plot out the roles of these attendants it appears that one is always mute and the other allotted only a very few lines. They are not of sufficient dignity to be allowed to speak these speeches. The Plotter of 1598 adopted precisely the same solution, using the mute William Cartwright as one attendant and Mr Hunt, who can have spoken at most ten lines, as the other, and returning Pisano (Sam Rowley) to the stage to report the loss of the baggage he was sent to guard.

There is no inkling in the remaining part of the scene that the original speech of the second Messenger has been tampered with. The verse is perfectly regular. It is merely perverse of Greg to argue (this being a crucial test of the roman–italic theory) that Pisano was originally recognisable as the El-Dogali of the sources, the captain whose defection at the battle of Er-Roken lost the day for Mahamet.[11] Greg's reason for this is that Pisano's speech implies that treachery has been at work in the surrender of the garrisons – and that is simply not true. The dramatist must also have envisaged the second Messenger as Pisano, just as the Plotter does, for he now had only one more black actor to call on – Zareo! – who is blocked here by having to enter in the next scene. The lack of another must certainly have caused the excision of the first Messenger from the scene. It is fairly clear that the playwright's understanding of the situation was identical with the Plotter's, although, as he was prepared to double Zareo in the Moor's party in a later scene, he may have had that alternative in mind here. The Plotter could not have followed him, for his Zareo is white.

In the Induction to the second Act there is no independent direction for a dumb-show, but one cannot believe that the Presenter's speech was unaccompanied by performance. The verbal cues: *Hearke Lords ... And now start vp ... Thus ... is a councell held*, imply that something is intended to take place. The pantomime is, indeed, essential to the dramatist's theme. The ghosts of the murdered brethren and Abdelmunen are heard crying for revenge, 'as in a hollow place a farre'. Their cries arouse Nemesis, who appears beating on her 'doubling drum'. A drum is not a conventional property of Nemesis, but the drummer-boy of the company is to be pressed into service, and his noise arouses the Furies, who appear with symbolic properties listed in the text. All this is followed to the letter by the Plotter. Despite Greg's suspicions of excisions here, it is difficult to see what could have been omitted. The verse is in need of little emendation, as long as we read the obvious *Dimme Architect*, for *Diuine Architect* at line 312.

The remainder of the Presenter's speech will be cause for comment in some later scenes, for, like I, Induction, it appears to muddle the order of events and to omit the Stukeley scenes altogether. This might give grounds for suspicion, were it not for the fact that lines 340–59 are a précis of chapter VI of Nieto and keep closely to the order of events there recounted. The only thing that is not in Nieto is the description of the ceremony of Calcepius's departure. The Plot contains no mention of the playwright's spectacular invention and it is worth noting:

> The dames of Fesse and ladies of the land,
> In honor of the sonne of Soliman,
> Erect a statue made of beaten gold,
> And sing to Amurath songs of lasting praise.

The scene in which this is enacted immediately follows. There is, admittedly, no mention of the golden statue in the stage-directions, and the Dames of Fesse are called on stage only by their generic name, 'the Ladies'. This is a common term for 'all the boys' and occurs twice, as we have seen, in *2 Seven Deadly Sins*. There may have been a distinction in the playwright's mind between 'the Ladies' who are Dames of Fesse, and enter at the beginning of the scene, and 'the noblest ladies of the land' to whom attention is drawn later in the scene, and who may have been intended to enter at that point, bearing gifts for Calcepius. If that is so, it was not grasped by the Plotter. He brings on all the ladies at the beginning, just as the stage-directions seem to require. From the text, we may picture this strange attempt at an oriental ceremony, in which, to the sounding of trumpets, incense and obeisance are offered to a golden statue of Amurath. This cannot have been another of Greg's vague gestures of the dramatist, for some of the lines will sound very odd without it. The Queen, for example, declares:

> As Rubin giues her sonne, so we ourselues
> To Amurath giue, and fall before his face.

Abdelmelec's payment of his 'due and duties' to Amurath must also be accompanied by some offering or gesture of a like kind.

All this is an attempt by Peele to represent three events of importance recorded in Nieto, chapter VI: the sending away of the Turkish Janissaries, the growing love towards Abdelmelec of all his subjects, who 'with liberall and bountifull mindes brought him verie great, rich, and honourable gifts and presents', and the swearing of 'all the peeres of the kingdom unto his brother Muley Hamet', followed by 'incredible feasts and triumphs'.

One further casting problem for the dramatist in this scene must be observed. We have seen that he had to introduce two white Moors in the very first scene, and might have introduced four if he had wished. It is perhaps more likely that he thought of four Janissaries and two Moors. In the present scene (II, i), he calls once again for Moors and Janissaries, and one might expect that this direction would bring on the same attendants who had appeared previously. But that can no longer be. A new set of characters altogether is to appear in the following scene (II, ii) – Diego Lopez, Governor of Lisbon, the English Captains, Stukeley, Jonas and Hercules, and an Irish Bishop. All but the Governor must have appeared either as Moors or Janissaries in I, i. Thus, in II, i, four of the original supporters of Abdelmelec are blocked from entering and only two actors can appear as Janissaries. They are the actors who will later be needed for the Dukes of Avero and Barceles, but they still have an intervening scene in which to change costume. If Sebastian himself did not double as a Janissary, there is no help for it but to call in the Presenter as the Governor of Lisbon, just as the Plotter does in 1598. The Presenter will, in any case, be needed in some capacity or other, for the only remaining members of cast who can swell this scene are black. The stage-direction for II, i reads:

Alarum within, and then enter Abdilmelec, Muley Mahamet Seth, Calsepius Bassa, with Moores and Ianizaries, and the Ladies.

The text, once again, shows the dramatist to have calculated the situation. We do not know precisely how many Moors he expected to appear. As this scene is imagined to be an entrance from battle, any number of the black cast may be brought on, but, whoever they are, apart from Zareo, they must be of Mahamet's party, and they will at least equal and probably outnumber the Janissaries. Greg, of course, was right in sensing some awkwardness here, but his suspicion that a speech of Abdelmelec's and other speeches of Zareo's had been excised was needless. To have included a victory speech by Zareo would have been insensitive, for he would have to speak as a black Moor who had triumphed over others of his race, whereas the given of the scene is that the victory has been won by the Janissaries. Abdelmelec himself speaks in diplomatic confusion of:

this fight happie and fortunate
Wherein our Moores have lost the day

for the black Moors are still *his* subjects, even if in defeat, and, as the scene must be filled, they are politicly addressed as *our* Moores and *Lords of Barbarie* (line 378).

The second business of the scene is to install Muley Mahamet Seth as heir to the throne. The dramatist could see from Nieto, chapter VI that this involved Abdelmelec's re-affirmation of the tanist law, and the confirmation of it by an oath of the nobility. But it is a little awkward to have a troop of defeated peers swearing allegiance to a man who has so recently been their enemy. Abdelmelec therefore does not ask for their franchise, but appeals to a higher power:

> Ye Gods of Heaven gratulate this deed,
> That men on earth may therewith stand content.

Here, as elsewhere, we can see the playwright giving the best account he can of the source-material with his available cast. He was probably also aware that Calcepius's generous words:

> This chosen gard of Amurath's Ienizaries
> I leaue to honor and attend on thee

would ring very hollow, for neither of the soldiers offered to the new king will ever be able to appear with him again. The story told in Conestaggio, however, has to be kept faith with.

Peele leaves aside the fortunes of Mahamet (described in Nieto, chapter IV) until the next scene, and skips forward to Chapter VII to introduce a scene in Portugal not accounted for in the Presenter's Induction – the arrival of Stukeley and his company at Lisbon. Stukeley's name is not given accurately in any of the sources. Nieto calls him both Count and Marquess of Ireland and Conestaggio corrupts his name to Esternulie, but Peele obviously knew something of his history by common report, and was able to make use of Conestaggio's fuller account, which he follows in general outline.

Conestaggio represents Stukeley as furnished with troops by the Pope at the instigation of Philip II, who, irritated at Elizabeth's secret help to the Netherlands, determined to follow her methods and secretly to abet the plots of the Earl of Desmond and the Catholic faction in Rome against Ireland. The party having been wrecked by a storm in the bay of Lisbon, however, their ship became subject under Portuguese law to the disposal of the crown, and Sebastian lost no time in persuading them to accompany him to Africa in return for promised help on their return. To this Philip could offer no public objection, for he wished his hand in the matter to remain secret, and the Pope was too far away for news of the detour to reach him until the army was already in Africa.

Nieto furnishes Stukeley with 600 Italian troops and three men of war, but he gives no reason for the expedition. Conestaggio gives him only one ship, but confirms the 600 troops, and this figure appears to be correct, for it is also confirmed by the deposition to Burghley of English merchants in Rome. The dramatist has multiplied it tenfold, for effect (line 723), and worked out that an army of 6,000 would need seven tall ships and two pinnaces for its transport.

Greg's feeling that the play once had much more to do with Stukeley stands on very frail ground. Any unbiased reader must admit that the existing Stukeley material is already spread extremely thin. There is much material from which the dramatist might have gathered information about the man, but scant evidence that he used any of it.[12] Stukeley's own speeches are mostly the padded-out hyperboles of a wide-boy who has recently been reading his *Tamburlaine*, and the facts of his life, as given in his dying soliloquy, are few and inaccurate. There is no evidence that he originally appeared in any of the dumb-shows where the Plotter has introduced him.

Once Stukeley is dead, no further mention is made of him and we cannot suppose that he ever had a more prominent part in the finale. The sources are impressed by the spectacle of three kings dead in a day, or, as one says, 'three kings *in re* and one *in spe*', and although Peele seems to have prepared the ground for Stukeley to seek reputation by spilling his blood in the company of kings, the idea is not carried through. The author of *The Famous History* was fully and accurately informed about Stukeley's early life, but when he comes to the affair of Alcazar he, too, goes directly and independently to Polemon for the main details. Peele is able to eke out a little more for Stukeley to say from Conestaggio, and he did know two odd things that he could not have derived from any published source that I have discovered. One is that the Bishop accompanying Stukeley's expedition is made, apparently for the sake of a silly pun, the Bishop of St Asaphs ('asses'). In fact, Bishop Cornelius Goldwell, with whom Stukeley is known to have been associated when in Rome, was Bishop of St Asaphs,[13] and a Bishop Cornelius was reported on the expedition.[14] The other is that the play gives the point of departure from Italy as Ostia ('Austria', line 487), which, according to the reports of the English merchants to Burghley, is more correct than the sources that give it as Civita Vecchia.[15] Stukeley's murder by the Italian forces he commanded is mentioned in both plays and in the ballad tradition, but there appears to be no reliable source for the story.

In II, iii we return to Mahamet fleeing with his party into the mountains. He is without his chariot, but since there are no details of any intervening happening and his opening speech indicates that he is still in flight from the battle, we must suppose that the scene is virtually continuous in time with I, ii. The Presenter has already given us the programme:

> By this imagine was this barbarous Moore
> Chased from his dignitie and his diademe,
> And liues forlorne among the mountaine shrubs,
> And makes his food the flesh of sauage beasts.

'The mountain shrubs' happily translates the French *aux plus espais et touffus lieux de la montagne*, but although Nieto dwells on the hardships of life amidst cold, snow, and perpetual fear, he does not suggest hunger or wild beasts. Peele may have invented the idea of Mahamet's forcing the lioness from her prey and returning with 'lyons flesh vpon his sworde', but he may have found the germ of the idea in various ways. In Conestaggio there is a description of Sebastian's training for war: 'The king gave himself inordinately to the chase, and was never more elated than when he met with the savagest of animals in single combat.'[16] The lions of Barbary were also perhaps known from Drake's account of his voyage round the world, where the English sailors, standing off the Barbary coast near the ruins of the ancient city of Tit at the precise moment of the battle of Er-Roken, saw them to be inhabited by the beasts and could plainly hear their roaring from the sea. This may have given Peele the idea that lions might rend 'The breeding vaultes / Of proudest sauages'[17] (lines 593–4).

This notorious scene was much parodied, and there can be little doubt that it was played in 1598 in the form represented by the text. Pistol misquotes its refrain – 'Then feed and be fat (my faire *Calipolis*)' – in *2 Henry IV*, among much other fustian from play-ends, and, in Jonson's *Poetaster*, two theatre boys, riding one on the other's shoulders, stride round the stage in mimicry of Edward Alleyn's tall frame spouting seven of the ridiculous first ten lines.[18]

The elaborate identification of Calipolis is evidence enough that she was originally introduced here for the first time, in order to provide a motive for Mahamet's hunting. She is named six times in the scene and referred to by the son as 'mother' and possibly as 'my father's wife' (wise?). One may compare with this the case of Calsepius who is named twice on his first appearance and not at all on his second. Even Stukeley, who has a habit of repeating his own name, does so only three times in the first scene in which he appears.

The text, however, creates a mild suspicion that something has been left out, by having jumped ahead in the Act II Induction to give us the programme for the following scene as well:

> Now at last when sober thoughts renude,
> Care of his kingdome and desired crowne,
> The aide that once was offered and refusde
> By messengers, he furiously imployes,
> Sebastians aide braue king of Portugall.

We are told in II, iii that Mahamet has sent ambassadors to Sebastian, as we had previously been told by the Presenter, but the Presenter's list of events, although derived directly from the sources, does not accurately forecast what we are in fact to see. In this matter, as Greg pointedly observes, the text appears to depart from the sources: it should have read 'the aide that *twice* was offered and refusde'. But this is mere obfuscation. The dramatist knew from Conestaggio, as Greg did not, that these negotiations were protracted through many more stages than two. Peele obviously did not want to go into long explanations of how it occurred to Mahamet to seek aid from Portugal, or to probe deeper into Sebastian's motives than that he was 'forward in all armes and chiualrie'. To have done so would have thrown out all the emotional values of the play.

The ordering of the scenes, nevertheless, creates a casting problem. Two of the black actors must appear in II, iv as Mahamet's Ambassadors, and they are therefore precluded from appearing in this scene. Peele thus writes the direction for II, iii precisely:

Enter the Moore, with Calipolis his wife, Muly Mahamet his sonne, and two others.

One of these others has the speech-prefix '*Zareo*', and that is perfectly logical. One of the three black attendants is always mute. Pisano and the first 'devil' will therefore appear as Ambassadors and Zareo must be called in to speak in this scene. It may be that he was initially described as a Moor with this very purpose in mind, for even had Peele contemplated using Mahamet's Moors in two immediate re-entrances in the first three scenes (as Greg's reconstruction does), he would still not have been able to provide four black Moors for Mahamet's party in II, iii and II, iv, and would have had to call in a white actor; or else he would have been forced to what is almost an immediate re-entry for 'Zareo' as the Ambassador in the following scene. The latter solution is, in fact, adopted by the Plotter, who has fewer Moors to call on. His casting could not, of course, allow Zareo to appear in II, iii, because he is the wrong colour.

Re-ordering these scenes would not have solved the playwright's problem. There can be no doubt that by 'two others' he intended two black actors, for even Mahamet calls them negroes. Thus, the Ambassadors cannot be *sent*, physically, because the actors who will play them cannot be allowed to enter. Peele simply has to write his way out of it. The news that the embassy is on its way must first be given under colour of comfort for Calipolis who is fainting from weariness and hunger, and it is to Zareo that the speech falls.

In the Plot, Zareo's lines will fall to Thomas Hunt, who does appear immediately as one of the Ambassadors. To allow him to do so with some show of credibility, the Plotter's solution was to keep Mahamet on stage at the end of the scene with a 'manet muly'. There is no direction for this in the text, and as there is no obvious soliloquy for Mahamet to speak, Greg's suspicions are naturally aroused. The direction for the general exit at the end of this scene is also missing, and Greg fixes his attention on this as positive evidence of revision, even though the direction for the following scene is italic. Mahamet's scenes do tend to end up with rather pointless monologues, and although there appears to be nothing left for him to say in this scene, which is largely filled with his ranting, it does appear that something might be missing.

From the dramatist's point of view, we have seen that, even if there had been a soliloquy positioned here for Mahamet, it would make no difference to the casting. What Zareo speaks is the programme for the following scene, II, iv, and as the implication is that these scenes are concurrent in actual time, he could scarcely appear in it with any credibility, even if he were allowed space to do so. That Mahamet may have been intended to remain on stage briefly at the end of the scene, is, however, consistent with the text, if the reasons that can be offered for it are somewhat bizarre.

The psychology of the scene (if such a term may be applied properly to it) is not a little difficult to interpret. Calipolis appears to oppose Mahamet's cursing of their misfortune with a counsel of patience, submission, and the need for practical action. She is faint and weak, but she does not actually say (though she seems to imply it) that she is dying of hunger. Mahamet's response is to rail against patience and to seek some desperate and glorious action to restore their state. But he agrees, even in this elevated mood, to search for some food worthy of his mettle, and, indeed, to overcome Famine itself. He goes out to hunt lions. The son then also gently rebukes his mother, saying that thoughts of patience are unworthy of the hopes of happiness and ease that princes ought to cherish, and, to comfort her, he and 'Zareo' reveal the hypocritical plan that has been formed for engaging Sebastian's support. Calipolis's 'unhearty soule' fears that this will bring upon them the judgment of heaven. The Moor then returns with an appropriately grand meal of raw flesh that he has forced from a lioness, and offers it to Calipolis as

Meate of a princesse, for a princesse meate,

and continues to press the grisly offering on her to the refrain, parodied by Shakespeare,

Feede then and faint not faire Calipolis.

She replies, with thanks, that the virtue of her mind will prevent her from starving, and the Moor's final speech runs:

Into the shades then faire Calypolis,
And make thy sonne and Negros here good cheere,
Feede and be fat that we may meete the foe
With strength and terror to reuenge our wrong.

There is no happy way of reading these lines. The Moor may be understood to say that, if Calipolis cannot eat the meat herself, she had better take it into the shrubbery and cook it for the others. Clearly a direction to move off stage is implied. But does Calipolis actually take the meat from Mahamet? If she does, 'feede and be fat' must be addressed to the others, for she has declined to eat it. If she does not, then 'make good cheere' will read a little oddly. I believe that her thanks are to be interpreted as a polite refusal and that Mahamet keeps possession of the larder, such as it is. If that is so, his final soliloquy is not far to seek: it consists of the last two lines of the speech quoted above, which can logically be addressed to no-one but himself. If he remains on stage longer it is not to speak, but to eat – to demonstrate his beastly and self-indulgent feeding to the audience. The others will, no doubt, have to content themselves with Shakespeare's reflection that 'small cheer and great welcome maketh a merry feast'. But there is still an uncomfortable feeling that Mahamet's use of the royal plural here is out of key with the rest of his speeches in the scene.

The next scene, II, iv, ushers in the whole Portuguese Court and is imagined as taking place in Lisbon. The two events to be represented are the reception of the Moorish Ambassadors and the arrival of Stukeley and his party. By the end of the scene the whole of the 'white' cast, with the exception of Abdelmelec and Muly Mahamet Seth will be on stage. If the playwright thought of Christophero de Tavora as a man, even Seth would have been forced to appear here as a Portuguese. The other Portuguese lords will all have been Janissaries or white Moors in a previous incarnation. They cannot have been actors of much account, for they are virtually all mute. The Duke of Avero is later given eight lines to speak in IV, ii, and in the present scene eight lines are allotted to an unspecified attendant (the Plotter assigns these to Avero also) and one line to Christophero. No speeches fall to any others of these actors in their Portuguese roles, and as this scene is already the longest in the play, there is no likelihood that they ever had more to say.

Even as it stands, the scene is quite alarmingly short of matter. To make any show of its content, Sebastian is compelled to speak a long and quite improbable panegyric about Queen Elizabeth, which even Stukeley recognises to be somewhat irrelevant. Lines appear to have dropped out in several places from the longer speeches, but, apart from a double set of commands addressed to the Duke of Avero, which may be perfectly innocent, there is no sign that these concerned a revision of the cast. The Plotter here introduces an additional lord, the County Vinioso (properly Vimioso), who might have existed in the prompt-book, but is probably, as we shall see, a convenient addition made possible by the Plotter's white Zareo. It is of little significance either way, for all the Portuguese lords except Avero are merely attendants in fancy dress. There is, moreover, good reason for keeping them silent, for one of them will certainly have to speak as a Spanish Ambassador in the next act.

It is worth pausing at this stage to enquire how Peele derived the names of his Portuguese nobility. The tasks allotted to the lords are in every case unhistorical, except for that of Lewes de Silva, who actually was Sebastian's Ambassador in Madrid. Strangely enough, this fact could not have been gathered from any of the sources, and appears to be contradicted by Conestaggio, who correctly relates that the Ambassador sent to arrange the specific meeting at Guadalupe was Pietro d'Alcasova. The playwright's cast of attendants for Sebastian consists of the Dukes of Avero and Barcellos, Lewes de Silva and Christophero de Tavora. Conestaggio lists the names of four colonels who were charged with mustering the Portuguese troops, but only one of these appears in the play (Diego Lopez de Siqueira), and his name Peele had borrowed for the Governor of Lisbon. Nieto lists no lords until the battle, in which he records Alvares Peres de Tavora, Ludovicke Caesar, Duartes Meneses the governor of Tangier, the Duke of Avero, Don Antonio (later the pretender supported by the English), Christophero de Tavora, and the Bishops of Coimbra and Portua. Conestaggio records a number of other names in the battle and elsewhere, and Peele has pretty clearly chosen from among these those who were closest to the king. These are Luigi di Silva (*uno di piu favoriti del Re*), Cristofforo di Tavora (*suo cameriero e cavallerizo maggiore ch'egli amava oltre modo*), and the Duke of Barcellos, who, despite the fact that he was only about twelve years old and is called by Conestaggio a *giovanetto*, actually did fight beside Sebastian's standard at Alcazar. Apart from Avero he is the highest-ranking noble mentioned in the sources (the style belongs to the eldest son of the Duke of Braganza) and may be given a task worthy of his ancestors of raising soldiers in Antwerp, even if it may seem beyond the capacity of what Peele calls his 'forward youth'. Avero is made Sebastian's principal supporter, for it was his charge in the early stages of the battle that almost secured a Portuguese victory, and his death in the ensuing retreat that sealed their defeat.

Describing the dispositions for the battle, Peele will list, apart from these, Alvaro Peres de Tavora and Lodeuco (Lodovico – Conestaggio's form) Caesar. There is also a Lord Lodowicke addressed in the text in III, iv, who should, by rights be this man, but he does not speak and must have been played in the text, as in the Plot, by Lewes de Silva. His name is a useful combination of the two roles. The playwright will keep Don Duarte de Menysis as Governor of Tangier, although he is not identified in the spoken text. Peele knew, of course that de Menesses was the Master of the Camp, or Commander-in-Chief, but it is more convenient to cede that role to Avero. The case of Vinioso will be more conveniently considered in the discussion of the Plot in the next chapter. It is sufficient to say, here, that there are no Portuguese commanders at Peele's battle who are not vouched for by Conestaggio.

Returning to our scene (II, iv), we recall that the Moorish Ambassadors who appear at the beginning must have been played by Pisano and one of the former 'devils'. Their hypocritical purpose, as explained in the previous scene, is to offer Sebastian the Empire of Morocco. In demonstration of their good faith, they call for fire, and thrust their hands into the flame.[19]

This pantomime allows us to interpret the seemingly corrupt lines spoken by 'Zareo' in the previous scene (lines 562–7):

> His maiestie hath sent Sebastian
> The good and harmelesse king of Portugall,
> A promise to resigne the roialtie
> And kingdome of Marocco to his hands,
> But when this haughtie offer takes effect
> And workes affiance in Sebastian,
> My gracious Lord warnd wisely to aduise,
> I doubt not but will watch occasion,
> And take her fore-top by the slenderest haire,
> To rid vs of this miserable life.

They may be paraphrased: 'And when this high offer works as we intend, and Sebastian begins to show such signs of trust as my lord has wisely given intructions to observe (and encourage), I have no doubt that he will seize any opportunity of improving our wretched situation.'[20] Peele does not take Sebastian for a complete fool. He is shown to be suspicious of Mahamet's motives, but is instantly convinced by the charming classical parallel, when the Ambassadors, like twin Scaevolae, hold their hands to the fire.

The English party are called on stage only by the direction, 'Enter Stukley and the rest'. As they have all been seen before and they all speak, there is no doubt about their identity.

We now come to the Presenter's speech at the beginning of the third act. There is no evidence in the text of the elaborate dumb-show that accompanies this in the Plot, other than the first three lines:

> Lo thus into a lake of bloud and gore
> The braue couragious king of Portugal
> Hath drencht himself.

The unusual form of the preceding direction: *Enter the Presenter and speaks*, does not necessarily suggest a show, and may simply refer to Sebastian's decision at the end of the previous scene to leave immediately for Africa. The purpose of the Induction is to give a brief account of the meeting between Sebastian and Philip II at the monastery of Guadalupea (Polemon's spelling, corrupted in the printing house to 'Sucor da Tupea'). The theme of the whole is the poisonous hypocrisy of Spain which is to contribute to Sebastian's disaster. The rather tortuous expression is brought about, not by excisions, as Greg supposed, but by the dramatist's critical appraisal of his sources. Greg, as I have said, did not know Conestaggio, and was puzzled by the lines referring to Philip II in the Presenter's speech:

> And now doth Spaine promise with holy face,
> As favouring the honor of his cause,
> His aide of armes, and leuies men apace,
> But nothing lesse than king Sebastians good
> He means, yet at Sucor de Tupea,
> He met some saie in person with the Portugall,
> And treateth of a marriage with the king,
> But ware ambitious wiles and poisned eies,
> There was nor aide of armes nor marriage,
> For on his waie without those Spaniardes king Sebastian went.

It may, of course, seem puzzling to the literal-minded that, when the Presenter has declared the Spanish promises to be lies, the next scene should represent the Ambassadors promising those very things. There is no real contradiction. Act III, scene ii is a scene played out 'with holy face', a scene of bitter irony that will end with a shrewd comment from Stukeley about the purpose of the Spanish levies:

> The Spaniard ready to embark himself
> Here gathers to a head, but all too sure,
> Flanders I fear shall feele the force of Spaine.

Both sources record the meeting at Guadalupe, but when the accounts of Nieto and Conestaggio are put together there are strong grounds for suspecting Philip of such hypocrisy that it is hard to imagine a personal meeting at which he could have made such patently false promises. The dramatist is, of course, eager, as a patriotic Englishman, to make the Spanish promises sound a little falser than they were. Both the French translation and Polemon suggest that Philip's concern for Sebastian was genuine, but in the fuller, vehemently pro-Philip, account in Conestaggio, Peele found cause for suspicion. Juan de Silva's account, based on his personal involvement in the negotiations, is concerned to justify Spanish policy and to lay to rest the scandalous imputation that Philip had failed the young king deliberately and sent him to his death. Peele naturally regarded this account with suspicion. He thought of it, with Protestant scepticism, as a 'Catholic case', and was also growing impatient with the usage 'the Catholic king', which is, of course, Conestaggio's ordinary way of referring to Philip II. He will cause Stukeley to say 'Philip whome some call the catholicke king' (line 876), possibly because Nieto does not use the Papal honorific and Polemon does not translate the words 'comme prince vrayement chrestien' that appear in the French.

Conestaggio's defence of Spanish policy, moreover, does leave a very strong smell of fish. The conditions Philip attached to his offer of aid were almost impossible of fulfilment. When the Portuguese inevitably failed to meet them, he did not, according to Conestaggio, allow a single regular soldier to leave Spain, except for the last-minute dispatch of Francesco d'Aldana as a military adviser. In the matter of the marriage, he offered Sebastian one of the Infantas, but did not say which. As both were below marriageable age, this contract too, appeared more likely to be honoured in the breach than the observance. Philip's temporising policy was no doubt intended by de Silva to appear as statesmanlike caution moderated by affability, but it is not surprising that Peele read it as rankest hypocrisy – and on that he builds his scene. He even takes the detail of Don John of Austria's appeal for reinforcements in the Netherlands, which de Silva wishes to represent as a necessary limitation on Philip's ability to engage himself in Africa, as evidence of his real intention in permitting military levies. Nevertheless, both sources record that Spanish troops finally did fight at Alcazar and Peele has simply skewed the account here and in two other places to omit them. In III, iii he will keep Sebastian fifteen days at Cadiz, waiting for Spanish reinforcements that fail to arrive, and in Act V he suppresses all mention of Spanish forces and allows their commander, Alonzo di Aguilar, to take charge of the German troops on the left wing.

There is possibly also a practical reason for misrepresenting the Spanish attitude. Peele cannot bring on the king of Spain, because he does not have an actor to play him. Even the Spanish ambassadors create a problem, although possibly a less acute one than appears in the Plot. The direction that introduces III, i reads :

Enter the king of Portugall and his Lordes, Lewes de Silua, and the Embassadors of Spaine.

Lewes de Silva was dispatched with letters to Spain at the end of II, iv, and it is naturally he who returns with the Ambassadors here, creating a sense of continuity with the earlier scene. It will be a purely visual impression, for in the former scene he is identified only by one word of address, and in this scene he is not identified at all in the spoken text. He shares this anonymity with all the other Lords, but the prominent appearance of his name in the stage-direction must surely indicate that he is important for some reason. The dramatist is showing no sign of strain here.[21] He can still write 'and his Lordes', just as he brings Stukeley on with 'the rest', and he can allot speeches to 'another' without calculating too precisely. For him, there can be several others who might serve the purpose. For the Plotter the other must be the Duke of Avero, because he is the only Portuguese Lord remaining. This shortage of white cast is, oddly enough, the mathematical result of changing Zareo's colour, and it is the Plotter, not the dramatist, who has to pay a heavy penalty. He will be forced to omit the next scene altogether.

The dramatist is much better off. He might have kept all Sebastian's Lords on stage by using Hercules and Jonas as the Spanish Ambassadors. He might even have used the Irish Bishop. He will have had to sacrifice one of the lords, but might seem to have one other recourse that is not open to the Plotter: he might have called in the Presenter as a replacement. The Presenter, as we have seen, probably played Diego Lopez in II, ii, as he does in the Plot. He might therefore have entered at II, iv, 701, conducting the English party, whom he is the first to meet, to Sebastian's court. But there is no sign of him there, and the direction that follows II, iv: *Enter the presenter and speakes*, indicates that he did not. His function in the play has begun to define itself otherwise.

It is the Presenter's task throughout to keep us in mind of the destiny of King Sebastian, and the very first words he speaks in the play establish that intention. But the playwright is following the order of events related in his sources. These all deal with the affairs of Barbary, before turning to the intervention of the Portuguese. Sebastian therefore does not appear in person until II, iv. It is perhaps as much for this reason as for the audience's advance knowledge of the failure of the expedition that the Inductions have been cast ironically. All the action preceding Sebastian's arrival at Tangier is interpreted as the gathering of the forces that will bring the Portuguese innocently to destruction. The irony is embodied neither in the action nor in character, but applied externally, as it were, through the words of the Presenter and the pantomimes of Devils and Furies roused by the drums of Nemesis.

The first appearances of Nemesis are connected with the hypocrisy of Muly Mahamet. In II, Induction, it is his appeal to Sebastian for help, and the hypocritical offer of the throne of Morocco that begins 'Sebastians tragedie in the tragicke warre', but other strands of irony are also at work.

The chance arrival of the English at Lisbon is the third. In this the Presenter himself will play a part as Diego Lopez, welcoming the reinforcements that encourage Sebastian's resolution. When the latter two events are in position, Sebastian will cry:

> Follow me Lords, Sebastian leads the way
> To plant the christian fa[i]th in Africa.

His words are immediately ironised once again by the Presenter in III, Induction:

> Lo thus into a lake of bloud and gore
> The brave courageous king of Portugall
> Hath drenched himself.

The fourth string of the fatal events is now to be shown: the failure of the Spanish promises of aid and the hypocrisy of Philip II. Act III, scene i is thus, in itself a pantomime. All the information in it is known to be false before it is played. There is thus no reason why the Presenter himself might not take part in it, acting out the ironies it has been his function to interpret. It is perhaps for this very reason that he warns the audience to beware 'ambitious wiles and poisned eies', before moving into the scene as one of the Spanish Ambassadors himself. The contrary situation will almost certainly occur at the end of III, iv, where the Presenter, now appearing as the Governor of Tangier, will have to move straight out of that scene to speak the Induction to Act IV. It is suggestive that whereas in every other instance the Presenter is said to 'Enter', in Act IV there appear only the words *The presenter speaketh*.

In III, i, then, we may suppose the dramatist meant all his European cast to be on stage. The natural consequence, of course, is that one of the Moorish parties must enter next, and, as there is nothing that can be told of Mahamet, who is merely waiting at or near Tangier for Sebastian's arrival, the following scene, III, ii, brings on Abdelmelec. The material is mostly taken from Polemon with some additions from Conestaggio, relating the secret negotiations between Abdelmelec and Philip II, which offer further proof of Spanish perfidy.

The Plotter, as we have seen, could not play this scene at all, and there is probably also a mild problem for the dramatist about who is to accompany Abdelmelec. The directions call for Muly Mahamet Seth, Zareo '*and their Traine*'. The train may be composed once again of Ladies, for there is nothing much to indicate a military scene. The Janissaries and white Moors have all been absorbed into the European party, so that unless Stukeley's dialogue with 'another' was long enough to allow a change of costume, Abdelmelec can have only black Moors and boys at this point. We may infer from the Plotter's behaviour that the twenty-one lines of dialogue were insufficient in 1598 to allow Zareo to dodge over this scene break, and thus the time was likely to have been too short in the dramatist's estimation for the European Lords to reappear as Abdelmelec's soldiers.[22]

The reference in the text to 'Zareo and ye manly moores' does probably mean that the three or four black actors who appeared with Abdelmelec in II, i are on stage again. 'Manly', like 'Arabian' is a white's term of approval for a blackamoor. It is used twice by Sebastian's captains of Muly Mahamet in the following scene and stands in contrast to 'Negro moore' which always implies contempt. Abdelmelec will later be able to recover one actor who appeared with him as a white Moor in I, i, but for the present that actor is blocked by having to appear as a Portuguese Captain in the next scene. There is no help for the embarrassment that may be caused to the black cast at hearing one of their own colour contemptuously referred to as a Negro.

At this point we can foresee dimly what the dramatist must always have known: that the battle of Alcazar will have to be fought and won for Muly Mahamet Seth almost wholly by troops of the opposing Moorish faction. The text of the battle scenes will divide the forces without any confusion into Christians and Moors.

Act III, scene iii presents no problems. There are only three actors who can possibly enter in it, for all the cast, with the exception of the three principals of the last scene – Abdelmelec, Muley Mahamet Seth, and Zareo – are to be on stage in III, iv, and the time-scheme is continuous. Peele has taken from Conestaggio the story of Sebastian's refusal to disembark at Lisbon once he had gone aboard, but he transfers the incident to Cadiz in order to underline the double-dealing of the Spaniards, whose expected troops do not arrive. The Governor of Tangier must be played by the Presenter whose long speech seems to have been written with just that situation in mind. It is pure narration material of the expedition's sailing, purporting to have arrived by letter, and narrowly saved from improbability (for where could such information have been sent *from*, and when?) only by the arrival of the fleet on the heels of the message itself. There is also a quite ingenious suggestion in the metaphor of Achilles cursing for want of wind in Aulis that the main fleet is late because it was becalmed. The subterfuge of putting this speech in the Governor's mouth is helped out by our knowledge that he is in fact the Presenter. This may also account for the rather perfunctory dramatisation of the remainder.

It is of some small consequence to note that Peele may have pondered the time-scheme of the voyage, which is not easy to gather from the sources, and that he produces an original version, once again emphasising the effect of the false promises of Spain. Sebastian certainly left Lisbon on 26 June 1578, but Peele keeps the ships at sea for twelve days on the short passage to Cadiz. He must have mistaken the date of the departure from Cadiz (8 July) for the date of the fleet's arrival. He then keeps Sebastian at Cadiz for fifteen days, in accord with Nieto, and thus appears almost to square the date of its departure with that given in *The Dolorous Discourse* (22 July). This is the only evidence I have found that Peele may have consulted the latter work, on which Greg places great reliance, and it is rather slight.[23]

Act III, scene iv, being very largely the playwright's own invention, is a formal reprise of information we already know. Peele turns the meeting of Sebastian and Mahamet into a discussion of hereditary right and allows Mahamet to speak his own condemnation with unconscious irony. The business, so far as it advances the story, is the offering of Young Mahamet to Sebastian as a hostage and his dispatch to Mazagan. Both sources describe the event, Conestaggio recording that the young prince was placed under the conduct of Martin Correa de Silva. Peele gives the task jointly to the Duke of Avero and 'Lord Lodowicke'. There can be no-one on stage for whom that name is fitting except Lewes de Silva, and thus my picture of the dramatist's casting plan gains some fragile support. If it is supposed that the lightly identified de Silva is the Lodovico Caesar who is mentioned in Act V it will not matter, and it is doubtful whether any audience would pick up the detail. If the Presenter is on stage, as I believe he is, he cannot be Lord Lodowicke, for Peele thinks of him, correctly, as Don Duarte de Meneses, and, in any case, he must remain on stage to speak the Induction to Act IV.

The Induction to Act IV adds nothing to our knowledge of events, but contains the direction *Enter to the bloudie banket*. If we may judge by the Plotter's response, this was to be a pantomime allegory based on the verbal cue (lines 1,063–4):

> And warre and weapons now, and bloud and death
> Wait on the counsels of this cursed king.

Although the Presenter's speech is brief, we may imagine that the show took some little time, for one actor at least must double into the role of Celybin.

The action now begins to move forward to the battle and Peele takes survey of the forces in IV, i. He has no option, of course, according to the conventional workings of the stage, but to do so through the eyes of Abdelmelec. In the historical record, the next action is the mustering of the Portuguese army before the walls of Arzilla, and this is therefore reported to Abdelmelec by the spy, Celybin, whose name, borrowed either from *Tamburlaine*, or from the account of the battle of Lepanto in Polemon, suggests that he is thought of as a revived Janissary. If he is a white actor, he can be doubled only with one of the Captains of Tangier, or with Lewes de Silva. The material is all taken from chapter IX of Nieto, but there is no doubt that Peele was here following Polemon's translation. He takes over Polemon's account verbatim for the first twenty lines and uses the figure of 1,500 wagons for the baggage-train that appears in no other source.

Having used the muster at Arzilla to get his scene going, Peele now skips on to the actual disposition of the forces on the day of the battle in Polemon's version of Nieto, chapter XI. To anyone following the sources, he gives the impression of having moved Sebastian to Alcazar in twenty-four lines, thus anticipating the following scene, but that, of course, is not the audience's case. The only change he makes in the battle positions is in placing Mahamet in the centre instead of the right wing, and surrounding him with 'twice three thousand needless armed pikes', instead of Polemon's 600 spears. The intention is, of course, to emphasise Mahamet's cowardice. For his troops, Peele has simply multiplied Polemon's figures by ten, as he did earlier with Stukeley's Italians. As for the personnel of the scene itself, the stage-directions call simply for '*Abdilmelec and his traine*'. This must be intended to call on those who appeared with him in III, ii, who, apart from such boys as there may have been, must have been Moors. With the addition of Celybin, however, he is now able, once again, to speak of his 'trustie gard / Of Ianizaries, fortunate in warre'.

We now pass in IV, ii to the Portuguese camp on the eve of battle. The programme is taken from Polemon (Nieto, chapter IX). Abdelmelec's letters mentioned in III, ii have now reached Sebastian, and his Council agrees that prudence demands avoiding a pitched battle, but Sebastian, being eager to test himself in personal combat, pays no heed. The Portuguese are momentarily dismayed by the huge numbers arrayed against them, until Mahamet arrives with the persuasive, but false, information that Abdelmelec's army is ready to desert to him. Sebastian and his Lords leave the stage as if to commence the fight and Mahamet remains to soliloquise in the hysterical vein of a triumphant Senecan villain.

This is the last scene contained in the Plot. It is of some importance to us, because of the questions raised by the decay of the paper as to who ought and who ought not to be on stage. The dramatist even seems to be mildly uncertain here, and brings on Sebastian, Avero, Stukely, *and others*. Hercules turns out to be one of the others, so that we may suppose Jonas also to be on stage. The other actors available are Lewes de Silva and one of the Portuguese Captains, but they have nothing to say. Peele must have known that the Portuguese who appeared in III, i are still, roughly speaking, available, with some subtractions, but he will not know precisely what name to give any of them at this stage. Even from the decayed fragments of the Plot, it is clear that the Plotter also treated this scene rather freely and had trouble in reconstituting Sebastian's powers, for he had doubled Celybin with Lewes de Silva and his Barceles had reverted to his original role as Zareo, while his Vinioso had been demoted to the status of a guard.

This last point is of some importance, for had Greg known that Vimioso played a role of some prominence in Conestaggio's account of the first Council at Arzilla, he would have had even greater confidence in supposing this scene to have been heavily cut. Peele is here paraphrasing and running together the end of Nieto, chapter IX and the beginning of chapter X, which make no mention of Vimioso, but, as the dramatist includes details of the Council at Arzilla in the account of the Council before the battle, it will be necessary to trace out the events in a little detail.

On meeting with Muly Mahamet at Tangier, Sebastian sent the major part of the fleet southward to Arzilla. His intention was to rejoin the ships there and to sail on to Alarache (Larissa), a Portuguese 'hold' that would be a convenient base for operations against Fez. The soldiers who left the ships at Arzilla, however, proved more willing to face the perils of the land than those of the sea and refused to re-embark. They were now in hostile territory, supplies were running low, and it was vital to press on to Larissa where arrangements had been made for provisioning them by sea. The question was, how to get there. To march southward along the coast presented great danger, for the route lay over marshy tidal flats and across difficult river mouths. To march on a detour inland to the east and far south would bring them to a convenient ford over the river Loukkos (Lixus), but near that ford, not far from the town of El Ksar Kibir, the main body of Abdelmelec's army was encamped. This was, nevertheless, the plan decided upon.

It was known at the Council at Arzilla that Abdelmelec was willing to avoid an engagement if the Portuguese would only return quietly to their ships and go home. Even when they arrived at Alcazar, he contrived to let them know that he would not attack if they would turn towards the sea. Both Councils, then, debated the question of whether to march back to Alarache, or to seek out the enemy and give battle, but at the time of the second Council the Portuguese were trapped in a fork of the river, with the Wadi-el-Mekhazen behind them. To march on to the ford over the Lixus would expose their flank dangerously, should Abdelmelec change his mind.

The dramatist sets his scene at this point. He follows Nieto in representing Mahamet as eager to encourage battle, lest the Portuguese should give over the enterprise and leave him to the mercy of his uncle's vastly superior forces. Mahamet therefore urges, untruthfully, that the great mass of Abdelmelec's troops will desert to him and fight for the Portuguese. This is for Nieto, and for Peele, the final proof of his murderous hypocrisy. Mahamet's advice, according to Nieto, was given on the Saturday evening. There may therefore be some justification for placing here a fragment of the Plot containing what appears to be a mention of torchlight ('y Tor'), on the assumption that the scene takes place at night. The Council itself, at which the lords advised retreat and Sebastian was adamant for battle, also took place, according to Nieto, at night on Sunday, although the other sources place it on Sunday morning. In the play, the Portuguese leave the stage as if to give immediate battle, but that may be mere theatrical enthusiasm: we still have to wait for the Presenter's description of the preliminaries and the dumb-show in the Induction to Act V.

The question of whether there might once have been additional material in this scene, derived from Conestaggio's account of the Council at Arzilla cannot, then, be solved, by reference to the sources. Vimioso might still have been original to the play, even though he was disgraced at Arzilla for the failure of the commissariat. The internal evidence of the argument, however, suggests that no further material could have been admitted. The dramatist is always unwilling to allow dishonourable behaviour in any of the European party. A debate in which some of the Lords must have appeared as cowards would not have been to his taste, nor could he have allowed any of the motives of favour and false flattery that Conestaggio attributes to Vimioso to appear.

There is, indeed, a dislocation in the text as it stands, directly attributable to this desire to keep European honour bright. Hercules has pretty clearly been thrust in as a speaker to take over half of the lines of the Duke of Avero counselling moderation. After Sebastian's declaration of berserk valour, Avero's speech would originally have run:

> So well become these words a kingly mouth
> That are of force to make a coward fight,
> But when aduice and prudent fore-sight,
> Is joynd with such magnanimitie,
> Troupes of victorie and kingly spoiles
> Adorn his crowne, his kingdome, and his fame.
> We haue descride vpon the mountaine tops
> A hugie companie of inuading Moores,
> And they my lord, as thicke as winters haile,
> Will fall vpon our heads at vnawares,
> Best then betimes t'auoide this gloomie storme,
> It is in vaine to striue with such a streame.

That is, Avero is arguing that advice and prudent foresight consists in recognising when you are outnumbered and when the enemy has the initiative and the advantage. Mahamet then enters with his false assurance of victory, and Avero is forced to recant even this eminently reasonable point of view:

> Shame be his share that flies when kings do fight,
> Auero laies his life before your feet.

Peele obviously disliked, on second thoughts, the faint imputation of cowardice in the first speech, and divided it, giving the last six lines to Hercules. He was presumably untroubled by the penalty (at least to a cynical, modern mind) that Avero is then left with the foolish appearance of praising Sebastian's berserk valour as prudent foresight. It is hard to believe that the scene ever ventured on a debate of more complex issues, when even this mild criticism of Sebastian's actions calls for such ignominious repentance. The interpolation of Hercules, of course, also cancels the sense of recantation from Avero's second speech quoted above, and allows it to read as hysterical enthusiasm. The Plotter was perhaps as puzzled as a modern critic by this curious arrangement of speeches, and decided to introduce Hercules as a kind of messenger, bursting on to the stage with his news, and thus to create an impression of 'dastard flight' more vividly than anything the dramatist appears to have had in mind.

The Plot now deserts us, but Act V follows chapter XII of Nieto so closely that there can be no doubt of the playwright's intention. He simplifies the battle, of course, and slightly changes the order of events for theatrical reasons, but he is so close to Polemon's narrative that he frequently reproduces phrases from it. We are thus able to supply with ease the missing material at the two or three places where lines have dropped out of the text.

The hiatus on either side of line 1,313, in the following passage, for example, is clearly to be supplied from within the passage of Polemon that is quoted below it:

Peele

My Lord, when with our ordenance fierce we sent
Our Moores with smaller shot as thick as haile   l. 1,313
Follows apace to charge the Portugall,
The valiant Duke the deuill of Auero,
The bane of Barbary, fraughted full of ire
Breakes through the rankes, and with fiue hundred horsse
Assaults the middle wing ...

Polemon

the Moores did first begin to shoote off their great ordenance against the Christians, but they had not shot off three, but that the Christians answered them with theirs. And straight waie the harquebusiers on foote on both sides discharged as thick as haile, with such a horrible, furious and terrible tempest, that the cracking and roaring of the Gunnes did make the earth so tremble, as though it would have sunk downe to hell, and the element seemed to burn with the fire, flames, lightning and thunder of the Gunnes. After that the storme of the shot was past five hundreth men of armes of the first battaile, whom the Duke *de Avero* lead, gave a charge on the left wing of the Moores, and brake and scattered them ...[24]

A second example, at line 1,585, reads:

Peele

His skin we will be parted from his flesh,
And being stifned out and stuft with strawe,
So to deterre and feare the lookers on,
From any such foule fact or bad attempt

Polemon

But as for the bodye of *Muley Mahamet*, the newe king his uncle commaunded the skinne to be pulled off (because he had beene the author of so many slaughters) and to bee salted, and then stuffed with strawe, and to be carried thorough out all the provinces of his kingdom, for to deterre all other for attempting the like at anie time after.[25]

It is clear that omissions of this kind do not result from theatrical cutting, for no attempt is made to tidy up the sense. They are simply the accidental omissions of a careless compositor and arise from the casual omission of one or two lines. Similar lacunae occur between lines 258–9, 395–6, 492–3, 717–18, 747–8 and 1,025–1,026. Three other passages that appear to dislocate the sense in the same way are probably in need only of literal emendation.

For some of the details of the spectacle, Peele drew on the Latin poem attached to Freigius's account. First, there is the dumb-show, a particularly elaborate affair involving lightning and thunder, the appearance of a tree and the descent of Fame to hang three crowns on it, the setting off of a huge Catherine-wheel representing the comet, and the falling of the three kingdoms, represented by the crowns. The passage from Freigius's poem is as follows:

> Lapsa trium quoque cernis humi diademata Regum.
> Quisnam magnanimo regi persuasit, ut ipse
> Insidos Mauros ferro tentarit inerti?
> Quam pia cura Deum? non hanc praenuncia cladem
> Signa e sublime (si mens non laeva fuisset)
> Dixerunt specula? an cauda candente Cometes
> Falsus erat vates splendenti extensus in aula
> Caelestis regni?[26]

Perhaps the most astonishing omission in Greg's account of the text is his failure to account for the existence of this dumb-show. To regard it as one of the 'odds and ends' accidentally copied by the reviser from the original Book is to stretch credulity to its limits. Would this not have been the first thing to go in preparation for a country tour? Admittedly it makes no great demands on the cast. Only the Presenter and one of the boys appear on stage, but the Presenter's Induction is essential to allow time for the re-grouping of forces that are immediately to appear in battle, and his lines would hardly make sense without the displays of stage-machinery that accompany them.

The cast is now divided simply into 'Christians', among whom Muly Mahamet and his son will be included, and 'Moors', that is to say, all the rest, including the former black troops of Mahamet who are now fighting on the side of Abdelmelec. The text represents the new alignment clearly. All the troops on Muly Mahamet Seth's side now become 'our Moores', while Stukely will complain of 'These barbarous Moores'. Hercules will murder him for having tied their fortunes to 'the ruthless furie of our heathen foe', while even Muly Mahamet and his son now fly in fear of 'these ruthlesse Moores' pursuing them at the heels. If this were not so, the installation of Muly Mahamet Seth as the new king could hardly have been attended by anyone but Zareo, and even being so, his train will be small, for two Portuguese and two Moors must be off stage, searching for the bodies of Mahamet and Sebastian with which they enter later in the scene. It is no doubt for this reason that Stukeley is given a long biographical soliloquy:

> Harke friends, and with the story of my life
> Let me beguile the torment of my death

and so on – for forty-nine lines! This must be spoken in order to give

Jonas and Hercules, and probably others of the slain Portuguese, time to change into Moorish attire for the impressive final exit with reversed arms bearing off the bodies of Sebastian and Abdelmelec. One cannot, of course, be certain that extras were not called in for the finale, but it is unlikely that they would have been called in for the battle itself. I have found in plotting through the texts that there is a tendency to level the numbers of opposing sides in battle scenes, and here there will be approximately eight 'Christians' (including Mahamet) and eight 'Moors' (including Abdelmelec) available.

The death of Muley Mahamet by drowning is mentioned in all the sources, but Peele appears to have taken the details from Freigius's Introduction (A4, A4^{v}):

Mulejus Mahametus, autor tot tantorumque malorum prostratis unique copiis fugae sese mandans, dum fluvium Mazagam trajicere conatur, ab equo ex caeno eluctante excussus, in lutulento aquae gurgite submersus periit.[27]

It is from this introduction that he must have gathered the odd (and false) information that the Moors commonly embalmed their dead with salt. But the reference to embalming was perhaps suggestive of a dramatic way of representing the battle scene. Greg failed to understand what Peele was up to here, for he did not grasp the significance of the direction at line 1,302 : 'Skirmish still, then enter Abdilmelec in his chaire.' This chair is undoubtedly the same chair as that in which Abdelmunen was brought in to be strangled (I, Induction), and it is the best the theatre can manage for the litter in which his brother Abdelmelec travelled from Morocco to the battle, and in which he died. The litter is mentioned in Nieto, but its full significance becomes apparent only in the account of Conestaggio.

Abdelmelec died at the crucial moment of the battle, from the accumulated effects of arsenical poisoning administered by his Turkish captains who feared he would send them back to Constantinople. He was taken from his horse and placed in his litter, but his death was dissembled and the litter was carried forward against the enemy as if Abdelmelec's commands still issued from it. Peele naturally could not represent him on his horse, but he invents a famous *coup de théâtre* by having him die calling for it; and he brings Hamet back from the fight a little earlier than in the sources so that Abdelmelec may be set up in his chair 'with cunning props', in his 'apparel as he dyed':

That our Barbarians may beholde their King
And think he doth repose him in his Tent.

The detail of the king's sumptuous apparel is taken from the general conclusion to Nieto's account. There can be no question that Peele intended the battle to sway to and fro on stage under the gaze of the glittering figure of the dead Abdelmelec whose 'soule', as Hamet says, is joyfully to 'sit and see the sight'.

When Mahamet Seth returns in victory and is to be proclaimed king, the chair in which Abdelmelec sits now represents the throne, in its usual central position under the hangings. In order to be installed, Hamet has, of course, to get Abdelmelec out of it, and he commands that his brother be taken down and laid upon the earth 'till further for his funeralls / We provide'. Hamet is then crowned by Zareo, Elizabethan-fashion, with the diadem that Moroccan kings did not wear.

Stukeley's part in the battle is not mentioned in any of the sources, but as, in the play, it is he who in reality has been the principal member of Sebastian's party throughout, his presence allows the reporting of the major incidents of the deaths of Avero and Sebastian. The latter report accounts, as it were, for the passage which, in Polemon and in the play, immediately precedes Mahamet Seth's installation. There is no basis for Greg's suggestion that Stukeley's soliloquy was added to replace a scene in which Sebastian was killed. *That* is better left as a mystery. All the sources point to Sebastian being sought for among the dead after the battle, and the playwright must have wished to follow them, in order to enhance the pathos of the later scene in which he is carried in, 'done to death with many a mortall wound' and wrapped in his country's colours. A precise dramatisation of Sebastian's death would certainly spoil this effect. That no such scene was intended is suggested by the fact that the manner of his death is not certainly known to the Moors (lines 1,526–7), who believe that he has been treacherously killed by his captors.

No conclusions about the reliability of the text can be of the highest degree of certainty, but I believe two things appear very clearly from the evidence presented in this chapter. The first is that the playwright is prescient and consistent in the calls he makes for actors and appears to have a clear casting scheme in mind. We have seen him carefully adjusting his text, and the very manner and order of telling his story, to the cast he knows to be available at each point. The second is that, in every case where Greg suspects some large excision, Peele is most often following his sources with fidelity and has used all the available material. On the occasions when we can see that there is more in the sources that might have been used, there are reasons of casting that can be advanced to show why it was not. It would, indeed, be astonishing, if a play that had originally contained a good deal of incidental matter, had been cut down, in all the relevant sections, in a way that accidentally brought it into such close and literal conformity with its sources as is the case with *Alcazar*.

What, then, was the nature of the copy for the text of *Alcazar*? There are signs, particularly in the spelling of unfamiliar names, that it was difficult to decipher. Almost certainly its punctuation was deficient or marked simply by slashes which the compositor has not often interpreted with insight. Rather a large number of its corruptions appear to arise from dictation ('Austria' for 'Ostia'; 'Aldest gulfe' for 'Aulis gulfe') rather than from copying by eye, although others that appeared corrupt to Greg (Efestian for Hephaestion) are common spellings found in other play-texts. Turned letters and minim errors are frequent, and passages of one or more lines have dropped out in several places, leaving gaps in the sense.

There may, of course, be other examples of all three kinds of error that we cannot detect, when the text makes reasonable sense.

Whether these stigmata may or may not be regarded as typical of a compositor's handling of an author's manuscript in the Elizabethan printing-house is a matter far from being settled by bibliographical analysis. *Alcazar*, in its printed form, is an infinitely superior text to the manuscript of *John of Bordeaux*, or to any edited version so far produced of the manuscript of *Sir Thomas More*, which Greg took as his exemplar. If we were to assume that the copy had been prepared by a scribe who worked with about the same degee of accuracy as the scribe of *John of Bordeaux*, we should have to allow for a very great deal of regularisation and tidying up in the printing-house, whatever we might guess of the competence of the compositor. If, on the other hand, we assume that the copy handed to the printer was as good as that of the manuscript of *John a Kent and John a Cumber*, we might suppose that he could have made a very good fist of it.

The record of Elizabethan compositors on play-texts is not wholly encouraging, however, even on good copy. Pollard himself pointed out that the reprint of *Richard II* is about three times as incorrect as Q. 1, and concluded: 'It is not possible to say in the case of the average first Quarto, duly entered ... that the blunders in it cannot all be due to the printers. The proved inaccuracy of the printers suffices to account for all the faults.'[28]

Alcazar was not duly entered, but that is not now thought to be automatically a ground for suspicion. The play was never reprinted, and collation reveals very few variants, so that it is difficult to form any opinion about the accuracy of the press-work from internal evidence. I believe I have provided good reason for concluding that, errors of carelessness in the transmission apart, the text represents with reasonable accuracy the copy as it left Peele's hands. Greg was, of course, committed to regarding the printer's copy as a prompt-book, whatever its treatment in the press, so that, whether the play was or was not cut down for a travelling company, his argument must allow for at least one stage of copying, with its consequential accumulation of error, before it reached the printing-house. The possibility that the prompt copy for the 1598 performance differed in many minor respects from the printed play cannot, of course, be ruled out. Such unimportant differences exist between the autograph version and the printed edition of Daborne's *The Poor Man's Comfort*. That the prompt-book of *Alcazar* may have differed in major respects is difficult to maintain in the light of the theatrical consistency of the printed text.

The only real ground on which the suspicion of wholesale shortening of *Alcazar* rests is its brevity, and even this, when compared with the majority of other plays of the 1580,s is not exceptional. If, then, we may assume that the Plotter was working from this very text, or something so close to it that it may, for all practical purposes, be regarded as identical,

The Plott of the Battell Of Alcazar

I. Cho.

Enter a Portingall [to him.] mʳ Rich: Allen to him
1 Domb shew *(sound / s⟨e⟩nnett)*
Enter Muly Mahamett mʳ Ed: Allen, his sonne
Antho: Jeffes: moores attendant: mʳ Sam, mʳ Hunt
& w · Cartwright: ij Pages to attend the moore
mʳ Allens boy, mʳ Townes boy: to them 2 ·
young bretheren: Dab: & Harry:: to them
Abdel⟨m⟩enen w · Kendall : exeunt

I. i *(sound)*

Enter Abdelmelec : mʳ Doughton : Calcepius
bassa mʳ Jubie : Zareo mʳ Charles attendat
wth ⟨th⟩e Bassa : w · Kendall : Ro : Tailor &
Georg⟨e : to⟩ them Muly mahamet Xeque *(sound)*
Abdula Rais & Ruben H Jeffes, dick Jubie
& Jeames : exeunt *(sound)*

I. ii *(sound / sennett)*

Enter in a Charriott Muly ⟨M⟩ahamett
& Calipolis : on each side ⟨a⟩ pag⟨e⟩
moores attendant Pisano mʳ Hunt
& w · Cartwright and young Mahamet
Anthony Jeffes : exit mʳ Sam manet
the rest : to them mʳ Sam a gaine exeunt *(⟨A⟩larū)*

II. Cho.

E⟨n⟩ter the Presenter : to him
2 domb shew *(⟨sound⟩ / ⟨sennett⟩)*
En⟨te⟩r aboue Nemesis, Tho : Dro⟨m⟩to
them 3 · ghosts w· kendall Dab · ⟨& Harry :⟩
⟨t⟩o them ⟨l⟩ying behind the Curt⟨a⟩ines 3 · *(⟨a whipp⟩ / brand & / Chopping / knife :)*
Furies : Parsons : George & Ro : T⟨ail⟩or
one wth a whipp : a nother wth a ⟨b⟩lody
tor⟨ch⟩ : & the 3ᵈ wth a Chop⟨ping⟩kni⟨fe⟩ : exeunt

and Robin Tailo⟨r :⟩ to them ⟨3 ·⟩ diu⟨e⟩lls
mʳ Sam : H Jeffes⟨ & Antho : Jeffes to⟩
them 3 ghosts ⟨:⟩ w · ⟨ kendall Dab & Harry⟩ *(3 · violls of blood & a sheeps gather)*
the Furies [Fech] ⟨First Fech in Sebastian⟩
& Carrie him out⟨ again, which done they⟩
Fech in Stukeley⟨ & Carrie him out, then⟩
bring in the Moo⟨re & Carrie him out : exeunt⟩

III. i *(sound)*

Enter : 2 · bringin⟨g in a chair of state⟩
[mʳ Hunt] : w · Kend⟨all Dab & Harry⟩
enter at one dore : Seba⟨stian : ⟩D⟨uke⟩
of Auero : Stukeley : 1 Pa⟨ge[s] Jea⟩mes
Jonas : & Hercules [th] to ⟨them a⟩t anothe⟨r⟩
dore Embassadors of Spai⟨ne mʳ⟩ Jones
mʳ Charles : attendants Ge⟨orge &⟩ w ·
Cartwright : exeun⟨t ⟩ manet Stu⟨kel⟩ey
& Duke of Au⟨ero : ⟩ exeunt

III. ii

Enter Gouernor ⟨o⟩f Tan⟨ge⟩r ⟨:⟩ & a
Captains mʳ Sha⟨a H⟩ J⟨effes : e⟩xeunt

III. iii *(sound)*

Enter at one d⟨ore the Portingall army with⟩
drom & Cullors : ⟨ Sebastian Christoporo⟩
Duke of A⟨uero : Stukeley Jonas &⟩
H e r c u l e s⟨ : Lodouico Caesar mʳ Jones :⟩
att anoth⟨er dore Gouernor of Tanger⟩
mʳ Shaa⟨ & 2 Captains H Jeffes &⟩
m⟨ʳ⟩ Sam ⟨ from behind the Curtaines to⟩
them mu⟨ly mahamet & Calipol⟩is .
in their ⟨Charriott with⟩ moores
o⟨n⟩e on ⟨each side & atten⟩ding young
m⟨a⟩h a m e⟨t, & w · Cartw⟩right : &
George : exeu⟨n⟩t

II. i	ſound	Enter Abdelmelec, mahamet ⟨Xeq⟩ue, Zare⟨o⟩
	⟨Ch⟩ai^{rs}	Calcepius Baſſa [Adb] Abd⟨ula R⟩ais : &
	⟨box⟩es for	Ruben : Attendants : m^{r} Hunt ⟨& G⟩eorge
	Pre⟨ſ⟩ents	& young ſonne Dab : exeunt
II. ii		Enter Diego Lopis : Gouernor of Lisbo⟨rn⟩e
		m^{r} Rich : Allen : Stukeley : Jonas
		Hercules : & an Jrish Biſhopp m^{r}
		Towne : Ro : Tailor : w kendall & m^{r}
		Shaa : exeunt
II. iii		Enter Mully Mahamet, Calipolis :
		young mahamet & 2 moores w · Cartwight
		& m^{r} Hunt ex⟨it⟩ muly mahamet manet
	raw	the rest : to them muly mahamet a gains
	fleſh :	wth raw fleſh exeunt manet muly ⟨:⟩ exit
II. iv	⟨ſound⟩	Enter [2 Pages :] Sebastian : a Page
	⟨ſen⟩nett	Jeames ⟨:⟩ Duke of Barcelis : m Charles
		Duke of Auero : m^{r} Jubie luis de
		Silua : m^{r} Jones County Vinioſo
		George : Chriſtoporo de Tauora : Dick
		Jubie to them : 2 : moores : embaſſadors
		m^{r} Sam m^{r} Hunt & 2 . Pages : exit
		moores : manet the rest : to them Stukeley
	ſound	Jonas, Hercules, & Jrish Biſhopp exeunt
III. Cho.		Enter the Preſenter : to [them] him
		3 · domb ſhew
		Enter Nemeſis aboue : Tho : Drom
		⟨to⟩ her 3 · Furies bringin⟨g⟩ in the⟨
		Scales : Georg Somerſett ⟨Tom P⟩arſ⟨ons

		Enter the Preſenter : to him :
	ſo⟨un⟩d	⟨ ⟩ ⟨4⟩ Domb ſhew
		E⟨nt⟩er a ⟨ ba⟩nquett br⟨ought ⟩ in by
	2. tap⟨er⟩s	m^{r} Hunt & w · Cartwri⟨ght : to⟩ the
		banqvett enter Sebastian : Muly
	Dead	mahamet Duke of Auero : & Stukeley
	mens heads	to them De⟨a⟩th : & ⟨3⟩ F⟨uries⟩ : m^{r}·
	& bon⟨es⟩	Sam Ro : Tailor ⟨ George & ⟩ Parſon⟨s ⟩
	banquett	one wth blood to Dy⟨ppe li⟩ghts : ⟨one⟩
	blood	⟨w⟩th Dead mens head⟨s ⟩ in diſhes : an⟨o⟩ther
		⟨w^{t}⟩^{h} Dead mens bon⟨es ⟩ to the⟨m} w{ar⟩
		⟨w · kenda⟩ll · [D] ⟨weapons dick} Jub{ie⟩
		⟨& a ⟩Furie ⟨wth bloody clothes }exeunt
		⟨ ⟩ ⟨ } · { } { ⟩
IV. i		⟨Enter with dr}om & Cu{llors Abdelmelec⟩
		Ma⟨hamet Xeq}ue . Cel{ebin Zareo &⟩
		att⟨endants m^{r} Sh}aa : {m^{r} Charles m^{r} Hunt⟩
		m^{r} [Joe⟨s⟩] Jones} {exeunt ⟩
IV. ii		Enter⟨ b}y Tor ch light to coun} ſaile :
		Seba⟨stian Duke of Auero Stu}keley : & Jonas
		⟨wth attendants & soldi}ors : a guard
		& ⟨to them Chriſtoporo }Dick Jubie :
		the⟨ Gouernor of Tanger : & w} · kendall : [to]
		⟨to them muly mahamet} : exeunt
		⟨manet muly mah}amet exit

9 *The Battle of Alcazar* – transcript of Plot with fragments re-arranged and conjectured restorations

we shall see that the result he achieves, although appearing to Greg to differ drastically from the intentions of the dramatist, actually arises from the very same logic we have seen to be at work in the text. In the consideration of the Plot, to which we now turn, we shall see that the Plotter's logic, like the dramatist's, is governed by principles identical with at least four of the five propositions from which we began.

7

The Plotter under pressure

If we have now gained some degree of confidence in the text of 1595 as a functional document of theatre, it is possible to give a virtually complete account of the Plotter's behaviour in reponse to it, according to the principles of stagecraft we have seen to operate. The craft of Plotting, as we have seen, involves a process of mutual adjustment between the Book and the cast available. We have reason to believe that the text itself foresaw some of the casting problems, and that adjustments had already been made to prepare it for a cast of standard size. We cannot entirely rule out the possibility that those adjustments were themselves the work of a Stage-reviser, reducing a play originally written for a much larger cast, but I have given reasons for believing that they were, in all likelihood, the work of the author himself, performed in the act of composition for a company whose membership he knew. That company certainly had more boys available than did the Admiral's Men in 1598.

Were it not for the bibliographical premises of Greg's argument that allow him to ignore, as authorial extravagances, demands of the text that exceed the Plotter's resources, we might have seen that it is often the Plot rather than the text that is seriously in default. The text of *Alcazar* contains a number of obscurities that we might not have been able to interpret without the help of the Plotter's response, particularly in the occasional slight disjunctions between the stage-directions and the spoken text, such as are often found in later and more sophisticated manuscripts. The revival at the turn of the century, however, must have merited the ridicule it received from the *literati*. The style of the play itself was dated almost beyond recovery and the ambition of the Plotter to turn it into a bloody extravaganza, largely by elaborating the dumb-shows, forced him into solutions that can be perfectly well understood according to the rules of his theatre, but which must have seemed bizarre, even to his contemporaries.

The casting of the Plot is illustrated in diagrammatic form on p. 246, but, for the sake of clarity, I have made one departure from the normal method: I have expanded simultaneous entrances in order to make the team allegiances clearer to the eye. The diagrammatic casting of the text on p. 244 has also been arranged, for convenience, to enable the closest possible comparison with the Plot. We cannot always tell precisely which doubling patterns the dramatist may have chosen. In some scenes his choices would have been freer than the Plotter's, but, as he would almost always have had to double one actor or another where the Plotter has been forced to do so, I have represented him, wherever possible, as having made the same choice. I shall explain the alternative possibilities as we progress. It will also be most convenient to discuss the reconstruction of scenes in the decayed second column of the Plot as we come to them. My own solutions are, I believe, more strictly in accordance with the observed behaviour of the Plotter than Greg's, and better suited to the blank spaces available to be filled. In IV, ii, they correspond convincingly with five lines of a fragment that could not be used in Greg's reconstruction, and they provide an explanation of the team allegiances that satisfies a theatrical logic common to the text and the Plot, but which produces strikingly different results in some scenes. The cause, as we have seen, is a seemingly small and unimportant decision to change the colour of a single actor.

The cast-list

In *Alcazar*, as in other Plots, a certain number of actors are treated as if more value attaches to their presence than to that of others. They are kept off stage in any but the single role they play. These may or may not include the 'stars' of the company, but they play the characters who must remain recognisable in order that the story may be clearly told. They will not double, even in situations of great stress. Our Plotter therefore keeps the following actors off stage in any but their single character role:

Edward Alleyn	Muly Mahamet, the Moore
Unknown	Sebastian, King of Portugal
Thomas Downton	Abdelmelec (Muly Molocco)
Thomas Towne	Captain Thomas Stukeley

The part of Sebastian is unallocated. It may have been taken by William Birde or Bourne who was one of the sharers in the Admiral's company at about this time. John Singer may also have been available, but Singer is supposed to have played clowns' roles, and, as there is no clown in the play, he may be absent from the cast for that reason. He is known to have left the Admiral's company by 1601, but he appears in *Tamar Cam*. I have not found compelling evidence that the clown was as specialised a performer as he is often taken to be. If, however, one major member of the company is entirely unoccupied in this performance, we may well understand why the Plotter is forced to the unusual course of employing at least one of his boys as men.

To the list above we should perhaps add Anthony Jeffes who plays Young Mahamet. It is certain that Anthony Jeffes never appears in another named speaking role, but he may have been cast as a Devil in the Induction to Act III. The space into which Greg introduces him there should be filled by William Cartwright, but I believe Humphrey's initial ('H Jeffes'), which certainly appears just before that space, has been entered in error for Anthony's.

There are, in addition, some minor actors who do not double, probably because they were boys, too young and inexperienced to be cast in any but the role for which they had been coached. These are:

Unknown	Calipolis
Thomas Parsons	A Fury
Mr Alleyn's boy	Page to Mahamet
Mr Towne's boy	Page to Mahamet
Harry	Young Brother
Tho. Drom	Nemesis

One of these may, however, have played Fame in the Induction to Act V. Apart from Calipolis they are all mutes. Harry and his companion Dab, who play the Moor's Young Brethren, appear in the later dumb-shows as their own ghosts, and in that role they are allowed a cry of 'Vindicta' as they lie behind the curtains, but they are otherwise silent. Dab doubles as Ruben's Young Son, but that, too, is a mute role.

The Plotter's cast thus consists of sixteen or seventeen actors who appear only in adult male roles, and ten boys. I have counted Young Mahamet as the leading boy of the company in order to allow a strict comparison with the text. He is called 'boy', 'young Prince' and 'forward youth'. Anthony Jeffes was clearly ready to take on adult parts.[1] Two boys double male and female roles. Jeames (possibly James Bristow, Henslowe's boy) plays Ruben Archis, the widow of Abdelmunen, and afterwards appears as a Portuguese Page. There is not much doubt about his youth. The other, our old acquaintance, Dick Jubie, doubles the roles of Abdula Rais (Abdelmelec's Queen) and Christophero de Tavora (King Sebastian's favourite).

Even in the cast represented by the text, which we have assumed to be of standard composition, there is no possibility that the Portuguese Lords could have been fully represented by men, unless the Presenter had been called in, and even then with difficulty. It appears that either or both of the roles of Barceles or de Tavora must have been designed for a boy to play. Barceles, who in historical fact was little more than twelve years old, is the most obvious candidate. The Plotter, however, failed to take that hint and doubles Charles Massey in the part, but he must have been happy to take Sebastian's address to de Tavora as his Hephaestion and bedfellow (line 699), rather more enthusiastically than was, perhaps, intended, and to allot the role to a handsome youth.[2] Greg believed that Jeames and Dick Jubie appeared as men in the battle scenes in Act V, because he could find no place in the last scene of the Plot for the misplaced fragment of paper that retains traces of their names. We shall see, however, that this fragment is not far from its correct place, and that, after their brief, enforced moments of glory, both boys in their male roles are described as Pages.

The other twelve actors are all called on to double roles, some of them more than once, and, ignoring for the moment the heavy traffic of the dumb-shows, three actors are required to dodge in principal, speaking roles. Why then, is the Plotter of *Alcazar* hard pressed beyond the limits we have observed in any other Plot?

The general answer is that he probably had little more specialised knowledge of the demands of this play when he began than would a modern reader or director. If the stage-directions appear inexplicit to us, they probably appeared to him almost equally so, and some, especially those implied in the dialogue, he must have dealt with, either by cutting the references from the text, or simply by allowing meaningless dialogue to stand, unsupported either by action or spectacle. The latter custom is so common among modern directors of our classical repertory that it need cause no surprise.[3]

The particular reason is that, correctly following the general mode of the text, he had determined to interpret it as an allegorical spectacle, but, in concentrating on the spectacular element, he decided to make one change for which he had to pay heavy and probably unexpected penalties. He decided to underline the team allegiances in the early part of the play by separating his principal cast into all-black and all-white. This could be done by the seemingly simple method of changing the colour of the dramatist's black Zareo.

The effects of this change are such that he is unable in eight or nine and perhaps even more cases to meet the demands of the text, and is forced to reveal his predicament in a number of crucial scenes. We have seen that the text is also prescient at points where actors appear to be running short. These are not always the same points as in the Plot, so that we cannot simply accuse one or other of our documents of consistent error or failure. There is an elasticity in their relationship as far as the casting is concerned, and we must therefore consider all those points at which informative discrepancies arise.

References to the text in the following account are to the Presenter's Inductions and the act and scene divisions in the Malone Society reprint. The text itself carries notations only for the second act ('*Actus secunda, Scaena prima*') and the fourth ('*Actus 4.*'). It was clearly Peele's intention to divide the play into five acts by the Presenter's Inductions, but less certainly to accompany each with a dumb-show. The dumb-shows are numbered 'first' and 'second' (both occur within the first Induction) and 'last' (beginning the fifth act). Shows are pretty clearly involved at the beginning of Acts I, II, IV and V, but less certainly at Act III. After III, i, the numbering of the scenes differs in the text and the Plot, because the Plot omits the text's III, ii. I have therefore followed the text's numbering of the latter scenes. My own reconstruction of the second column, is to be found on pp. 192–3 in parallel with Greg's.

Act I, scene i

Sound Drummes and trumpets, and enter Abdelmelec with Calsepius Bassa and his gard, and Zareo a Moore with souldiers.

Enter Abdelmelec : mr Doughton : Calcepius bassa mr Jubie : Zareo mr Charles attendants wth {th}e Bassa : w. kendall : Ro : Tailor & Georg{e}:

The first example of a restriction at work in the Plot appears in the first stage-direction after the introductory dumb-shows. The Plotter can manage to provide three actors for Calcepius's guard, but for the Moorish attendants on Zareo there is no-one. Yet, as we have seen, these Moors, meeting with Abdelmelec at Tremissen, are addressed in the first line of the spoken text.

Calcepius's soldiers, of course, are the crack Turkish Janissaries lent to Abdelmelec by Sultan Amurath and identified as such several times during the early scenes. Eight lines further on, Abdelmelec compares them to Achilles' Myrmidons, and Young Mahamet will describe them (lines 255–6) as

> that braue guard of sturdie Ianizaries
> That Amurath to Abdilmelec gave,
> And bad him boldly be to them as safe
> As if he slept within a walled town.

They must make a brave show, for they are to be rememberd as a spectacle, but they will never be able to appear again in strength. On their next appearance in the Plot, two of them will have disappeared, leaving only George. After that, they disappear completely until IV, i, when Abdelmelec will speak of them again as if they are represented in some way on stage. The Janissaries of the text must have evaporated in precisely the same way, the only difference being that in IV, i Abdelmelec could have been provided with one actor who actually had been a Janissary. In the Plot even that is not feasible. Yet it seems as though it might have been, for Shaa and Jones, who both do appear with Abdelmelec in the later scene, are also available to appear with him in I, i, but they are not called on.

The Plotter here appears to be obeying a law of company organisation that we could not have inferred as an *a priori* principle of Plotting. That is, he does not call on speaking actors to play attendants, except in situations of great stress. Such a situation does exist, as we shall see, in IV, i, where Jones appears as an attendant. He is mute in the text, but might easily have been allotted some of the spoken lines of that scene. Shaa speaks in each of his three roles, and is presumably senior in the organisation to Jones, who is also mute in his main role as Lewis de Silva. If not allowed a speaking part in IV, i, Jones will have spoken only as the Spanish Ambassador.

If such a law operates, as it appears to do in the remainder of the Plot, a crisis is already apparent in I, i. For, if more than two Janissaries are to be provided, Kendall, who has just been murdered in the first dumb-show as Abdelmunen, and will later speak in his main role as Hercules, has to make a rapid re-entrance. He is in appropriate costume and will not need to change. Of the other two Janissaries, Tailor and George Somerset, Tailor speaks nine lines in his role as Jonas, but George is always mute. These three, together with Cartwright, are presumably the hired men. None are given the honorific 'Mr'.

It may be for the same reason that Zareo appears alone doing duty for his whole contingent. The Plotter's attendant Moors – the actors in black make-up – are Mr Sam (Rowley), Mr Hunt, and William Cartwright. They have all appeared in the first dumb-show, and if Kendall can move into the next scene, after twenty-seven lines of the Presenter's speech, there seems nothing to bar them from doing likewise. Sam and Hunt certainly have speaking parts and Cartwright probably. They are also barred here, however, by the fact that if they appeared they would all have to make immediate re-entrances in the scene that follows (I, ii). Now it is possible that the dramatist may have been less concerned about that situation, because his Zareo is black. Two of his black soldiers might be inconspicuous as Mahamet's mute attendants in I, ii, provided that the speaking attendant, Pisano, had not been on stage in I, i. But the Plotter has lavishly brought on three black 'murderers' with the Moor in the first dumb-shows (where the dramatist calls for only two), so that his problems of identification are the more difficult to conceal. The Zareo of the Plot, moreover, is white. The Plotter has pretty clearly envisaged a striking colour alternation in the first three scenes, and will keep his Moors off stage in I,i, where the text clearly anticipated using them. Whether he deleted the reference to Moors in the first line of his prompt-book we cannot, of course, tell.

At the medial entrance in I, i, the Plot is clearly in default. At line 104 there is the direction:

Enter Muly Mahamet Xeque, Rubin Arches, Abdil
Rayes, with others.

to} them Muly Mahamet Xeque
Abdula Rais & Ruben H Jeffes, dick Jubie
& Jeames : exeunt.

The 'others' of the text are the Dames of Fesse. They are addressed at I, i, 123, and described in their mourning weeds at I, ii, 231. In the Induction to Act II they again figure prominently in a preview of what is to happen in II, i:

The Dames of Fesse and ladies of the land,
In honour of the sonne of Soliman,
Erect a statue made of beaten gold,
And sing to Amurath songs of lasting praise.

There can be no question that the Dames of Fesse are an original part of the play and provide with spectacular visual effect the impression given in the sources of the inhabitants of Morocco greeting Abdelmelec with rich presents. There is not the slightest sign of them in the Plot. The actors above are named in the correct order of their character roles. The Plotter has ten boys, about the same number as appear in *Tamar Cam*, and not many fewer than are called for in plays such as *Locrine*, *Edward I*, *A Looking Glass for London and England*, and *Alphonsus*, *Emperor of Germany*, which are all early plays by Peele or associated with him. His problem is once again one of colour. Three of his boys are already on stage in named roles; another is the drummer boy who has presumably remained on stage as Nemesis in the dumb-show and is blocked by a costume change; four of the remaining six are black, and two of these (Young Mahamet and Calipolis) would in any case be highly inappropriate as enterers in Abdelmelec's party. One can only suppose that he despaired of fielding Thomas Parsons and Harry convincingly as 'many Dames of Fesse'. Perhaps they were very little boys, for they play only small, single, mute roles.

Act I, scene ii

Enter the Moore in his Chariot, attended with his sonne.
Pisano his captaine with his gard and treasure.

Enter in a Charriott Muly {M}a hamett
& Calipolis : on each side {a} pag{e
moores attendant Pisano mr Hunt
& w . Cartwright and young Mahamet
Anthony Jeffes : exit mr Sam manet
the rest : to them mr Sam a gaine exeunt

This entry is not as clear as the Plotter's usual style. Comparison with the text shows us that Pisano was played by Sam Rowley, but that is derived only from the order of exits and entrances. The text gives the lines that Sam speaks on his re-entrance to an unnamed 'Messenger'. I have given reasons in the previous chapter for supposing that the first Messenger's speeches in this scene had already been transferred to Young Mahamet. The diagram of the dramatist's cast clearly shows the reason: he can have had no *Moorish* Messenger to enter. The Plotter is in precisely the same fix and makes no attempt to restore the first Messenger.

It is difficult to give a precise reason for his failure to restore the second Messenger in place of Mr Sam. It seems to be theoretically possible for the attendants to leave the stage with Pisano and for either of them to return to report the loss of the baggage and treasure. It may be that in the dramatist's arrangement they were the means of propulsion for Mahamet's chariot, for there is no mention of Pages in the text. The chariot is accompanied in the Plot on both its appearances by the two black Pages who may have been its motive force, but, on the other hand, it is possible that the Pages are merely decorative, for two small boys may be hard put to it to drag a chariot in which two people are standing. Nevertheless, it would have been feasible for a returning messenger to help wheel the Moor off stage at the end of the scene. Most probably we are once again involved with questions of company status. If there is any speaking to be allotted when Sam, Hunt and Cartwright are together on stage, the lines will fall first to Mr Sam if at all possible, just as, when the dramatist later brings on two Moors in II, iii, one of whom is Zareo, it is he who speaks, despite the possibility that he will be recognised as a henchman of Abdelmelec's.

Pisano's re-entry as the Messenger really creates no greater difficulty than the slightly odd effect of putting messenger language into the mouth of a trusted captain of horse. There is nothing positively contradictory to his function in the substance of his speech. Greg's suggestion that 'in the original Pisano was still recognisable as El Dogali', was prompted by the observation that the direction for this entrance is in Roman. That is really doubly illogical when it is considered that the second Messenger's lines were in all probability not written for that character, whichever name he may be imagined to have gone under. The fact that the Messenger makes no charge against himself for the loss of the treasure and the defection of the towns to Abdelmelec can hardly be taken as evidence of corruption or revision in the text! The treacherous El Dogali of the sources did not come back at all. If he had been intended to re-enter in the play, he would hardly have been such a ninny as to accuse himself of the disaster he reports.

In his later discussion of the Plot, Greg saw the force of this argument (although he unnecessarily supposed that the messenger reports the capture of El Dogali), and felt himself to be on the brink of an admission that would seriously have undermined his whole position: that is, that here was a case where the text had anticipated two actors where the Plotter could provide only one. Fortunately, Dover Wilson was at hand to bridge the abyss with the vague suggestion that 'there is a tendency in Elizabethan plays to double parts within the scene if possible'. For this very exaggerated claim, there is scarcely a shred of evidence (what sort of evidence, in any case, could establish a 'tendency'?). In the Plot of *Alcazar*, the reason for its occurrence is the careful and uncalled-for segregation of the black cast.[4]

This scene, then, is a grand entrancc of all the Moors. The Plotter does not miss the presence of Calipolis, who appears to have been an afterthought of the playwright, and places her in the chariot with Mahamet. The Pages are nowhere mentioned in the text, but have been introduced to swell the spectacle and possibly as crew to provide the motive power of the chariot.

Act II, scene i

Alarum within, and then enter Abdilmelec, Muly Mahamet Seth, Calsepius Bassa, with Moores and Ianizaries, and the Ladies.

Enter Abdelmelec, mahamet {Xe}que, Zare{o}
Calcepius Bassa [Adb] Abd{ula R}ais : &
Ruben : Attendants : mr Hunt {& G}eorge
& young sonne Dab : exeunt

In this complex scene we have already noted the failure of the Plotter to provide adequately for the 'Ladies' who have been described in the Presenter's Induction as 'The dames of Fesse and ladies of the land'. The latter phrase obviously indicates the royal ladies who are once again described at line 392 as 'the noblest ladies of the land'. The term 'Ladies' in the stage-direction is, of course, simply the generic name for the theatre's boys. But of the Dames of Fesse there is no sign.

The directions of the text also call for at least two more men than the Plotter provides. His Janissaries and Moors are represented by George Somerset, who is the one possible remaining Janissary, and Mr Hunt, who is, of course, a Moor. The Plotter thus composes his scene of four white soldiers and one black. His ambition was perhaps to stick to his racial segregation for as long as he could, in order to illustrate Abdelmelec's description of his victory as:

> this fight happy and fortunate,
> Wherein our Moores haue lost the day.

His dispositions will just cover Abdelmelec's address to the 'Lords of Barbary', for the presence of Mr Hunt and Zareo permits the plural address, but the text is prescient of the probability that the Moors will equal or outnumber the Janissaries in this scene, and of that the Plotter takes no advantage. There is not a strict prohibition on the appearance of Sam and Cartwright, for no immediate re-entrance would be involved on either side, and none of the Moors speak. Clearly another kind of logic is influencing his allocation of cast. The working of that logic has to do with the recognisability of the characters, and the sense of time and place in relation to the narrative. No-one, I believe, would suppose that Muly Mahamet and his son could reasonably appear among the conquered Moors in this scene, for their absence is demanded by the story. The lesser characters also have life-histories that need to be kept as consistent as possible. Mr Sam will not appear again until he plays one of the Moorish Ambassadors. He is strongly identified as Mahamet's lieutenant and has recently been seen fleeing from the battle with his master. Two Moors must appear with Mahamet seeking refuge among the mountain shrubs in the next scene but one (II. iii), and they must be Hunt and Cartwright. Thus, even to allow one Moor to appear as a representative of the defeated party in II, i is probably a reluctant concession on the Plotter's part. We may assume that Hunt's appearance here debars him from speaking in II, iii, for whoever speaks the lines in II, iii would be out of place as an Ambassador in II, iv for reasons of the story, and the other Ambassador with Sam is Hunt. It is pretty clearly Cartwright who will be the 'recognisable', speaking, Moor in II, iii, and for that reason he is not permitted on stage in II, i. The playwright, who had an additional Moor, is in a much better case, but, working on the same logic, even he could have allowed only two Moors to appear in II, i. Moreover, his speaking Moor in II, iii is Zareo, and it is highly probable that the same logic applies, for Zareo, despite Greg's opinion that he must originally have appeared in II, i as the triumphant leader of Abdelmelec's forces, is not mentioned in the initial direction to that scene, and was most probably kept off stage. The whole business of the scene is, of course, to reward the triumphant general – who is not Zareo (as Greg supposed) but Calcepius Bassa.

The dramatist's black Zareo will thus have spoken first in his dodged role as an attendant of Mahamet, and has a space of two scenes and a dumb-show before re-appearing as a speaking member of Abdelmelec's party, in III, ii. The white Zareo of the Plot speaks first in his dodged role as a Spanish Ambassador in III, i, but as he has insufficient time to change costume in the twenty-one lines following his exit, the Plotter's drastic solution was to cut III, ii altogether. Like some modern directors of Ibsen, he was in love with his own invention, and was not prepared to re-calculate the disastrous effects of his small disobedience to the precise directions of the dramatist. It may be noted, however, that dramatist and Plotter appear to agree on the need to maintain as far as possible a naturalistic life-line for each character, and that the doubling of roles is by no means as arbitrary as in the Morality drama.

For the Janissaries, however, Peele would have been in no better case than the Plotter, unless he could have allowed his actor no. 15 (Lewes de Silva in the Plot) to have appeared in that capacity. All other white actors except King Sebastian are blocked by their entrance into the next scene.

The Young Son's appearance in the Plot creates no likelihood of the text having been tampered with. Greg focuses his suspicion on his absence from the stage-directions, but he is as solidly present in the text as one could desire. He does not speak, but he is offered by his mother as a 'sacrifice' to Amurath and presumably leaves the stage with Calcepius on his way to Constantinople. The entrances of boys are very often omitted or vaguely registered, both in the manuscripts and printed texts. Indeed we have seen examples in the Plots themselves. But the cutting of the Young Son would indeed be desirable for the maintenance of Greg's argument, for his presence points to yet another default in the Plot.

We have been told by the Presenter that the Dames of Fesse have erected a golden statue of Amurath and the text insists that oriental honours of incense and obeisance are paid to it, to the sounding of trumpets. Abdelmelec's first speech clearly implies some such action on his part (lines 371–4):

> Here find we time to breath, and now begin
> To paie thy due and duties thou doest owe,
> To heauen and earth, to Gods and Amurath
> Sound Trumpets
> And now draw neere ...

What he is doing here is perhaps indicated in Ruben's speech presenting her son to Calcepius (lines 397–401):

> To Amurath the God of earthly kings,
> Doth Rubin giue and sacrifice her sonne,
> Not with sweet smoake of fire, or sweet perfume,
> But with his fathers sword, his mothers thankes
> Doth Rubin giue her sonne to Amurath.

To this Abdil Rayes replies:

> As Rubin giues her sonne, so we our selues
> To Amurath giue, and fall before his face.

There is no sign in the Plot of the golden statue or of the double sounding of trumpets, or of a sword for Ruben to carry, or of fire or incense. Is it necessary to believe that the Plotter was content to allow these things to remain in the text as mere figures of speech, without representation? There is certainly one line that will have been uncomfortable for him, when Calcepius departs with a wave at poor, solitary George, saying:

> This chosen gard of Amuraths Ienizaries
> I leaue to honor and attend on thee,

and without a statue of Amurath the queen's speech will sound embarrassingly like hysterical raving. Certainly, much of the rhetoric of the play is so overblown that even this might pass muster, but we have seen that Plotters do not invariably note properties, and even in this Plot, where they are very fully recorded, especially for the dumb-shows, there must be at least one other missing for a torch or brazier in II, iv, where the Moorish Ambassadors thrust their hands into the flame in token of their good faith. It is strange, but possible, that the greater significance of the scene had been overlooked in favour of the rewarding of the Bassa. The marginal note shows that the 'noblest ladies of the land' did bring on 'presents', possibly in boxes, and something that may read as '{Ch}aires', but either is or ought to have been '{Ch}aines'. These are offered to Calcepius to wear so that he will 'glister like the pallace of the Sunne' with the gold of Barbary. The absence of the less noble dames, however, perhaps indicates that these golden gifts had to suffice for the spectacle in the Plot.

Even supposing that the statue had appeared in 1598, this scene is very poorly provided for. The playwright has planned a great spectacle for which the Plotter can provide only a skeleton cast. Why cannot the boys be used? Hunt and George may be the only men available, but if George, who played a Fury in the preceding dumb-show can enter, Parsons can; and if Dab, who played his own ghost, can come on at the beginning of the scene, Harry can. The Moorish Pages are perhaps too strongly identified with Mahamet to appear, but they are available at a pinch. Even if Harry and Parsons cannot be brought on as Dames, because of the difficult and time-consuming business of donning Elizabethan women's clothing, they might have been brought on to fill the military parade. That they are not is interesting incidental support for the proposition that boys are not normally called on to appear as men. More important are the conclusions that may be drawn from the Plotter's treatment of this scene. First that the cast of boys anticipated by the text is much larger than that available to the Plotter. Second, that although there are some grounds for thinking that the text demands a larger cast of men, it could certainly not be satisfied with fewer.

Act II, scene ii

Enter Diego Lopis gouernor of Lisborne, the Irish Bishop, Stukley, Ionas, and Hercules.

Enter Diego Lopis : Governor of Lisbo{rn}e
mr Rich : Allen : Stukeley : Jonas
Hercules : & and Irish Bishopp mr
Towne : Ro : Tailor : w kendall & mr
Shaa : exeunt

There would be little to detain us in this scene, except for the far-reaching effects of the Plotter's calling in the Presenter to double as the Governor of Lisbon. The Presenter is costumed as a 'Portingall' in the Plot, and there is no reason why he cannot appear. Kendall and Tailor are now doubling in their new roles as English Captains, having had a whole scene to change costume, and Shaa and Towne have been reserved from the beginning to enter as the Irish Bishop and Stukeley.

I have given reasons for believing that the playwright's Presenter would also have appeared as Don Duarte de Meneses, the Governor of Tangier, and probably again as one of the Spanish Ambassadors. The Plotter does not call him as a Spanish Ambassador, but he names him as Governor of Lisbon. Act IV, scene ii, in which the Governor of Tangier appears, and which calls for three actors, is supplied in the Plot with only two. The Plotter has certainly left an error standing, but *which* error is not clear from the graphic evidence. He has either left one character unnamed, or cut an actor from the cast. Greg is, of course, always eager to show that the text has been reduced, and, as the stage-direction there brings on the Governor '*with his companie speaking to the Captaine*', he is happy to believe that the 'company' is an irresponsible flourish of the dramatist's, accidentally copied from the Book, and that only one Captain can have appeared. Moreover, in his reconstruction of the Plot's III, iii (Text, III, iv) his picture of the team allegiances leads him to the conclusion that Shaa must have played the Governor. With the support, once again, of Dover Wilson's not wholly untenable opinion that in Elizabethan plays it is a case of 'once a Governor always a Governor', Greg is therefore mildly inclined to doubt even the Plotter's accuracy in introducing Richard Allen in the present scene as the Governor of Lisbon.

For this role, the Plotter has a choice of two actors: Allen and Mr Jones. Greg believed that Sam Rowley might have stood in, but he, of course, is the wrong colour. Jones has been kept rather pointlessly idle all this time to play the mute and thinly identified role of Lewes de Silva. De Silva appears from the stage-directions to be marginally more important than the other Portuguese Lords, which was perhaps the reason why the Plotter chose to double Avero (Mr Jubie) with Calcepius Bassa, when either might have served. De Silva is thus free, if the Plotter had so wished, to appear as the Governor of Lisbon. The Governor is not identified by name in the spoken text and the audience would not have been aware of any dislocation if he had appeared as de Silva in II, iv, for he promises to conduct the English party to the king (line 485) and might have appeared in the later scene as if having achieved that object.

These *post hoc facto* considerations are appropriate only for the study. We can see, after very long reflection, what the Plotter might have done, if he had been prepared to treat the text with rather greater freedom. What he does do is to make a rapid decision about the only choice he has at this stage to distinguish the characters and to furnish the demands of the text *in sequence, as the dramatist has written it*. He reserves Jones, doubles Allen as the Governor, and sets out on a road towards an unforeseen disaster, the effects of which will force him, whether he will or no, to use Allen again as Governor of Tangier.

Act II, scene iii

Enter the Moore, with Calipolis his wife, Muly Mahamet
his sonne, and two others.

…

Enter Muly Mahamet with lyons flesh vpon
his sworde

Enter Mully Mahamet, Calipolis :
young mahamet & 2 moores w. Cartwright
& mr Hunt ex{it} muly mahamet manet
the rest : to them muly mahamet a gains
wth raw flesh exeunt manet muly exit

The Plotter here follows the direction of the text with strict accuracy, introducing precisely two Moors, Hunt and Cartwright. The directions are all in italic, so that no question arises for Greg about the early part of the scene, some of which is vouched for by Ben Jonson's parody in *Poetaster*. There is, however, as we know, no indication in the text of how the exits are to be managed, and Greg supposes that a final soliloquy has disappeared, possibly involving other excisions as well. He thus makes a quite gratuitous case for the reviser's intention to suppress the second Moor, partly on the grounds that he does not speak, but then on the wholly illogical grounds that, in his fanciful reconstruction of the minimum cast, the Moor was needed to double with Lewes de Silva. Mahamet's soliloquy would thus originally have existed in order to give this Moor time to change before the following scene, but was cut out when he was suppressed and it became unnecessary!

The Plotter's actual problem, like the dramatist's, is how to manage this scene together with the next, where the Moorish Ambassadors appear in Lisbon. The time scheme suggests that the two scenes are contemporaneous, or nearly so. At any rate we are told (line 560) that Mahamet has already sent the Ambassadors, with wise instructions about how they are to behave. It will seem decidedly odd if the actors in this scene appear as the Ambassadors in the next. For Peele a solution was possible, because he had one more black actor than the Plotter. He therefore avoids one kind of improbability by creating a lesser one: he calls in Zareo to play one of the two Moors. He can then bring on as Ambassadors actors who have not been seen for at least the space of two scenes, and probably for as much as three scenes and a dumb-show. The Plotter, however, is now beginning to pay the penalty for keeping Zareo white, for his Zareo, who has not appeared for two scenes, has been changing costume to play the Duke of Barceles in the next. But he can still finesse. One Ambassador can be Pisano, who has not been on stage since I, ii, and only one Ambassador needs to speak. The other, he decides, will be Mr Hunt. Hunt will therefore have to make what is in effect an immediate re-entrance within the space of four lines of dialogue. The time is strung out a little by the ceremonial entrance of the Portuguese Court, but the more time Hunt has, the better. It may well be that keeping Mahamet on stage is an invention of the Plotter, and that his recourse was either, as I have suggested, to show Mahamet *eating* the 'raw flesh' he has brought back on his sword point, or to write in a soliloquy. That must have been quite within his own capabilities, for Mahamet's lines do not ordinarily make much sense.

Once again, we have a kind of control that suggests the Plotter has some conscience on the point. The Moor, on his two previous appearances, has been accompanied by his two black Pages, and they will also be with him on his next. If the Plotter were happy to move actors indiscriminately across a scene break, he might have brought the Pages in here as well, but we find that Mahamet has kindly lent them to the Ambassadors for II, iv, and they do not appear. On the other hand, it may be that they are normally necessary to manage the chariot, and are freed in this scene where it has temporarily gone missing. The Pages themselves, of course, are inventions of the Plotter and have no part in the text. I have assumed that, in order to conceal Mr Hunt's identity in this scene as far as possible, the Plotter would have allotted the speaking part to Cartwright, for Hunt had lately appeared in Abdelmelec's victory celebrations. The protocol of seniority may, however, have outweighed the preference for anonymity. If Hunt did not speak here, he cannot have spoken at all in any part of the play represented by the Plot.

Act II, scene iv

Enter Sebastian king of Portugall, the Duke of Auero
the duke of Barceles, Leues de Silua, Christophero de Tauera

Enter [2 Pages :] Sebastian : a Page
Jeames {:} Duke of Barcelis : m Charles
Duke of Auero : mr Jubie luis de
Silua : mr Jones County Vinioso
George : Christopero de Tavora : Dick
Jubie to them : 2 : moores : embassadors
mr Sam mr Hunt & 2 . Pages : exit
moores : manet the rest : to them Stukeley
Jonas, Hercules, & Irish Bishopp exeunt

There is no entrance marked in the text for the Moorish Ambassadors, except for a direction '*Exit one*' in the right margin after the second line of the scene when Sebastian commands them to be fetched. They are addressed immediately afterwards. Stukeley's party is clearly identified from II, ii, and needs only the direction : 'Enter Stukley and the rest.' Zareo (Charles Massey) is now doubling as Barceles, and Dick Jubie has changed in the space of two scenes from Abdelmelec's Queen to Christophero de Tavora. George Somerset, who has been seen as the last surviving Janissary, and as a Fury in the Act II dumb-show, is now a Portuguese lord who has no equivalent in the text.

For the dramatist, this is a limiting scene, and possibly a crucial one. All the adult cast who can be on stage are on stage at one time or another. If he was not prepared to call in the Presenter as a Portuguese noble, he would have had to call in a boy to play either Christophero or Barceles, just as the Plotter does, and there is some suggestion in the dialogue that he planned at least to use a youthful Barceles. It is of interest that he writes the initial direction rather precisely, in a way that suggests calculation. There are no general calls for 'attendants' or 'lords'. He names just those characters he expects to see.

The Plotter now appears to reap the advantage of having kept Zareo white, for he is able to introduce a character who does not exist in the text – the County Vinioso. Vinioso's 'disappearance' from the text seems to confirm Greg's argument. Here is a character who must have appeared in the original and has been so completely excised that no trace of him would remain if the evidence of the Plot were lacking. Further, his disappearance explains a textual peculiarity. In Sebastian's speech allotting various duties to his nobles (lines 675–700), he first commands Avero to call in the Englishmen, but before Avero has time to cross the stage he is given another commission to 'take the muster of the Portugals'. The direction for Stukeley's entrance, as it happens, is in roman, and does not mention Avero's return. What more natural conclusion, then, that one of these jobs originally fell to the County Vinioso, whose name is a perfectly acceptable metrical substitute for Avero? Probably that job was to call in the English, who, when he was cut, were forced to enter unattended.

Moreover, in the account of the battle given by the historian Luis de Oxeda, to which Greg makes reference, Vinioso (or Vimioso, to give his name its correct spelling) plays an important part. It is a mere quibble to reply that the playwright could not have known Oxeda's account, which remained in manuscript in the Spanish archives, for, although Greg did not know it, Vimioso also has a part of some importance in Conestaggio's account. It is also quibbling to suggest that all the other names of Portuguese are equally good metrical substitutes for Avero, or that, if the playwright did not mean what he wrote, he could equally well have called in the Presenter as Diego Lopez, or Duarte de Meneses. It is less of a quibble to observe that at this stage in the progress of the story, which we have seen the dramatist to follow with fidelity, Vimioso is mentioned as a participant only by Conestaggio, who recalls, in a retrospective passage, that he was disgraced for the failure of the commissariat.

A far simpler explanation is that Zareo's white skin is a bonus for the Plotter in this scene. He will want the Portuguese entrance to look as lavish as possible. Muly Mahamet has been able to appear with seven adherents, Abdelmelec with eight. Can he be content to furnish the king of Portugal, the hero of our story, with a bare four?

Clearly that is the problem he sets his mind to, and we can almost see him counting the cast. First, he makes an uncharacteristic entry of attendants before the principals. He writes 'Enter 2 Pages', and immediately deletes it, writing in the expected 'Sebastian'. That this is not merely an error of order is shown by the entry that follows: 'a Page Jeames'. He has had to reduce the number of Pages by one. We shall see in the reconstruction of the second column of the Plot that his natural inclination is to show Sebastian attended by two Pages, one of whom is always Jeames. The other eventually turns out to be Dick Jubie. Having decided that the text of this scene allows him to represent de Tavora as a youth, he casts Dick for that role. The other available boys, Dab, Harry, and Parsons, whose use appears always to be restricted, are not called on, but there is now one spare member of cast – George Somerset. George has hitherto played a Janissary and Fury, but he is white, and, thanks to Zareo having undertaken the role of Barceles, he can be introduced here as a Portuguese. He may, indeed, be introduced precisely to solve the problem presented in the text of the two commands given to Avero. George is given a resplendent costume and pushed on stage to make a sixth attendant on Sebastian. He never has anything to say, and, unless the Plotter wrote his name into the text, his role in the Plot here is as a ghost, like many another named, mute role discoverable in the printed texts. The practice was commonly understood. Queen Margaret in *Richard III* employs it naturally as a metaphor when she calls Elizabeth 'A queen in jest, only to fill the scene.'

Vimioso's title may have been chosen by the Plotter more or less at random from the nearest source. This happened to be Conestaggio, or, rather, was necessarily Conestaggio, for Nieto's account does not mention Vimioso at all. Nor do *The Dolorous Discourse* or any others of the sources known to Greg that the Plotter could have consulted. But in *Dell'Unione* the list of commanders slain in the battle is headed by Alfonso di Portogallo, Conte di Vimioso. The English transliteration of the Italian title as 'County' strongly suggests that this was the origin of the name, but it may have been well known in England. Vimioso's son had been received by Elizabeth at court and took part in the expedition of Drake and Norris in support of the pretender Don Antonio.

George's moment in the sun is brief. On his next appearance he is downgraded again to be an anonymous attendant on the Spanish Ambassadors, and, in a later scene (IV, ii), where he might have been useful as Vimioso, he appears only as a Guard, probably carrying the colours. There is certainly no room for the listing of his title, and Greg, who had perhaps overlooked the importance for his argument of

Vimioso's re-appearance at the Council at Arzilla, made no attempt to amend him into existence.

The speaking part of the Moorish Ambassador will have fallen to Sam Rowley, although it is possible that the two lines of his second speech may have been allotted to Hunt. If Cartwright spoke as the first Moor in II, iii, these are the only lines that Hunt could have spoken before Act V. There is thus the possibility that either Hunt or Cartwright was completely silent, unless they shared between them the speeches of the Moors who bring in Mahamet's body in the final scene. That action must have fallen to these two, and the speech-prefixes simply allot the speeches to 'One'.

It may be, however, that Hunt's seniority in the company designated him as the speaker in II, iii, and it is this probability, joined with the ambiguity of the time-scheme, that excited Greg's suspicions of great textual excisions hereabouts. There ought to have been a scene, he felt, in which Mahamet was shown dispatching the Ambassadors with sage and statesmanly counsel, and, as there is no other place for it in the Plot, it must originally have formed part of II, iii. In the Induction to Act II, the Presenter offers the following forecast of events that are to take place immediately after the scene of Abdelmelec's victory (lines 350–6):

Muly Mahamet's furie ouer-rulde,
His crueltie controld, and pride rebukt,
Now at last when sober thoughts renude,
Care of his kingdome and desired crowne,
The aide that once was offered and refusde
By messengers, he furiously imployes,
Sebastians aide braue king of Portugall.

The puzzle, if there is one, is really only that of the grammatical tenses in a prospective chorus. The Presenter has already given us the programme for II, iii (lines 340–3):

By this imagine was this barbarous Moore
Chased from his dignitie and his diademe,
And liues forlorne among the mountaine shrubs,
And makes his food the flesh of sauage beasts.

What then has become of the sending of Ambassadors, for which there is neither time nor psychological plausibility? The answer is, of course, that it must be imagined to have happened in between the Moor's appearances. But, as we have seen, II, iii is represented as virtually continuous in time with I, ii. The Presenter seems to have proposed an action that cannot take place until after the scene in which it is already reported to have happened. Shakespeare made rather a bad fist of an exactly similar problem with the second Chorus of *Henry V*. The playwright clearly never had any intention of allowing his ranting villain to engage in an episode of sage and statesmanly advice, but his henchmen may be allowed to interpret, and to report as such, a scene that could not credibly have been played.

3 · violls of blood & a sheeps gather	and Robin Tailo⟨r :⟩ to them ⟨3 ·⟩ diu⟨e⟩lls m^r^ Sam : H Jeffes⟨ & Antho : Jeffes to⟩ them 3 ghosts ⟨:⟩ w · ⟨ kendall Dab & Harry⟩ the Furies [Fech] ⟨First Fech in Sebastian⟩ & Carrie him out⟨ again, which done they⟩ Fech in Stukeley⟨ & Carrie him out, then⟩ bring in the Moo⟨re & Carrie him out : exeunt⟩		59 60 65
found	Enter : 2 · bringin⟨g in a chair of state⟩ [m^r^ Hunt] : w · Kend⟨all Dab & Harry⟩ enter at one dore : Seba⟨stian : ⟩D⟨uke⟩ of Auero : Stukeley : 1 Pa⟨ge[s] Jea⟩mes Jonas : & Hercules [th] to ⟨them a⟩t anothe⟨r⟩ dore Embassadors of Spai⟨ne m^r^⟩ Jones m^r^ Charles : attendants Ge⟨orge &⟩ w · Cartwright : exeun⟨t ⟩ manet Stu⟨kel⟩ey & Duke of Au⟨ero : ⟩ exeunt	Enter : 2 · bringin⟨g in the S t a t e : mr. Sam⟩ [mr Hunt] : w · Kend⟨all & Ro : Tailor : then⟩ enter at one dore : Seba⟨stian :⟩ D⟨uke⟩ of Avero : Stukeley : [2] 1 Pa⟨ge : Jea⟩mes Jonas : & Hercules [th] to ⟨them a⟩ t anothe⟨r⟩ dore Embassadors of Spai⟨ne mr.⟩ Jones mr Charles : attendants Ge⟨orge : &⟩ w · Cartwright : exeun⟨t⟩ manet Stu⟨kel⟩ey & Duke of Au⟨ero :⟩ exeunt	III. i 70 74
	Enter Gouernor ⟨o⟩f Tan⟨ge⟩r ⟨:⟩ & a Captains m^r^ Sha⟨a H⟩ J⟨effes : e⟩xeunt	Enter Governor ⟨o⟩f Tan⟨ge⟩r ⟨:⟩ & a Captains mr Sha⟨a : H⟩ J⟨effes : e⟩xeunt	III. ii
found	Enter at one d⟨ore the Portingall army with⟩ drom & Cullors : ⟨ Sebastian Christoporo⟩ Duke of A⟨uero : Stukeley Jonas &⟩ H e r c u l e s⟨ : Lodouico Caesar m^r^ Jones :⟩ att anoth⟨er dore Gouernor of Tanger⟩ m^r^ Shaa⟨ & 2 Captains H Jeffes &⟩ m⟨^r^⟩ Sam ⟨ from behind the Curtaines to⟩ them mu⟨ly mahamet & Calipol⟩is . in their ⟨Charriott with⟩ moores o⟨n⟩e on ⟨ each side & atten⟩ding young m ⟨ a ⟩ h a m e⟨t, & w · Cartw⟩right : & George : exeu⟨n⟩t	Enter at one d⟨ore the Portingalls wth drom & Cullors :⟨ Sebastian : luis de Silua Duke of A⟨uero : Stukeley : Jonas &⟩ Hercules ⟨ : 2 pages : Jeames : Dick Jubie⟩ att anoth⟨er dore : Governor of Tanger :⟩ mr Shaa ⟨: H. Jeffes : to them 2 moores⟩ m⟨r⟩ Sam ⟨: mr Hunt : & young M ahamet : to⟩ them mu⟨ly M ahamett & Calipol⟩is . in their ⟨chariott wth ii Pages :⟩ moores o⟨n⟩e on ⟨each side : atten⟩ding young m⟨a⟩hame⟨t : & w. Cartw⟩right : & George : exeunt	III. iii 80 85

	Enter the Preſenter : to him :		IV.
ſo⟨un⟩d	⟨ ⟩ ⟨4⟩ Domb ſhew		
	E⟨nt⟩er a ⟨ ba⟩nquett br⟨ought ⟩ in by		
2. tap⟨er⟩s	mr Hunt & w · Cartwri⟨ght : to⟩ the		
	banqvett enter Sebastian : Muly		
Dead	mahamet Duke of Auero : & Stukeley		
mens heads	to them De⟨a⟩th : & ⟨3⟩ F⟨uries⟩ : mr		
& bon⟨es⟩	Sam Ro : Tailor ⟨ George & ⟩ Parſon⟨s ⟩		
banquett	one wth blood to Dy⟨ppe li⟩ghts : ⟨one⟩		
blood ·	⟨w⟩th Dead mens head⟨s ⟩ in diſhes : an⟨o⟩ther		
	⟨w'⟩h Dead mens bon⟨es ⟩ to the⟨m⟩ w{ar⟩		
	⟨w · kenda⟩ll [D] ⟨weapons dick} Jub{ie⟩		
	⟨& a ⟩Furie ⟨wth bloody clothes }exeunt		
	⟨ ⟩ ⟨ } { · } { ⟩		
	⟨Enter with dr}om & Cu{llors Abdelmelec⟩	⟨Enter with dr}om & Cull{ors : Abdelmelec : Muly⟩	IV. i
	Ma⟨hamet Xeq}ue . Cel{ebin Zareo &⟩	M a⟨hamet Xeq}ue . Cel}ebin : Zareo : & an⟩	
	att⟨endants mr Sh}aa : {mr Charles mr Hunt⟩	att⟨endant : mr Sh}aa : { mr Charles : &⟩	
	mr [Joe⟨s] Jones} {exeunt ⟩	mr [Joe⟨s] Jones :} { exeunt⟩	
	Enter⟨ b}y Tor ch light to coun} ſaile :	Enter {at one dore to Coun}saile :	IV. ii
	Seba⟨stian Duke of Auero Stu}keley : & Jonas	Seba{stian : Auero : Stu}keiey : & Jonas	
	⟨wth attendants & soldi}ors : a guard	⟨at another dore wth drom & Cull}ors : a guard	
	& ⟨to them Chriſtoporo }Dick Jubie :	& t{wo Pages : Geor}ge : H{eames : } Dick Jubie	
	the⟨ Gouernor of Tanger : & w} · kendall : [to]	the{n enter to} them {w:} kendall :[too]	
	⟨to them muly mahamet} : exeunt	⟨ 2 : moores :} mr ⟨Sa ⟩m {: mr Hun}t : exeunt	
	⟨manet muly mah}amet exit	⟨ w. kendall & Geo}rge {: manet the rest :⟩	
		⟨to them Mully Mahamet :} ex{eunt⟩	
		⟨manet Mully Maha} met : exit	

10 Comparative reconstruction of the Second Column

That is precisely what the dramatist's Zareo and either the Plotter's Hunt or Cartwright does in II, iii. The information is allowed to pass, as we have seen, under cover of comfort to Calipolis, and as a means of giving the programme for III, iv. That will be the game of seizing whatever opportunity offers of raising Sebastian's confidence in the offer of the crown of Morocco. If one of the actors in that game is recognised as having been on stage in the previous scene, the incongruity will be obscured by the audience's recognising the accuracy of the prediction of events. They will simply assume that a little more time has elapsed than they were originally led to believe. It is not inconceivable that the playwright wrote the 'programme' speech in the oblique manner in which it exists to provide for the same eventuality. The fact that he allows the Portuguese Court to form before the Ambassadors are called in is also suggestive of that possibility, although, as far as we can see, neither of *his* Moors would have been forced into an immediate re-entrance.

8

Reconstructing the second column

We are now in a position to reconstruct the second column of the Plot by following the team allegiances we have observed. In this chapter, my solutions are, I believe, more strictly in accordance with the observed behaviour of the Plotter than Greg's, and better suited to the blank spaces available to be filled. In IV, ii, they correspond convincingly with five lines of a fragment that could not be used in Greg's reconstruction, and they satisfy a theatrical logic common to the text and the Plot, which now, as a result of seemingly small and unimportant changes, produce strikingly different results in some scenes. The cause, as we have seen, is the decision to change the colour of a single actor.

Act III, scene i

Enter the king of Portugal and his Lordes, Lewes de Syl-
ua, and the Embassadors of Spaine.

Enter : 2 . bringin{
[mr Hunt] : w. Kend{
enter at one dore : Seba{stian :} D{uke}
of Avero : Stukeley : [2] 1 Pa{ge : Jea}mes
Jonas : & Hercules [th] to { }t anothe{r}
dore Embassadors of Spai{ne : mr} Jones
mr Charles : attendants Ge{orge } w.
Cartwright : exeun{t} manet Stu{kel}ey
& Duke of Av{ero} exeunt

(I have included everything in this corrupt section of the Plot that can be read or supplied with certainty. Square brackets indicate deletions. Mr Hunt has been deleted in line 2, the Pages have been reduced from two to one in line 4, and in line 5 the Plotter has deleted 'th', which may have been an anticipation of 'to them', or perhaps the beginning of 'then'.)

Even the fragmentary condition of this scene leaves us in no doubt that the Plotter is now in a desperate fix. He is forced to bring back Lewes de Silva and the erstwhile Duke of Barceles from their diplomatic missions, not *with* the Ambassadors of Spain, but *as* the Ambassadors.

The dramatist has a variety of recourses for filling this scene. He might, for example, have used Hercules and Jonas as the Ambassadors, for there is no sign of them in the text, unless the direction 'Lordes' that certainly brings on Stukeley, must be supposed to have brought on all the original contingent from II, iv. He might have called on the Presenter or his actor no. 13, the Irish Bishop, who takes no further part in the play.

The Plotter, on the other hand, shows that he is worried about a number of matters. Someone has to bring something on stage, possibly a Chair of State, and it will take two to carry it. Mr Hunt is first thought suitable and then deleted. The task falls to Kendall and someone else, unknown. Now Kendall is Hercules, and it is clear that Hercules re-enters immediately in Sebastian's train. As that direction says 'enter', and is unlikely to have been preceded by 'to them', the Plotter's intention must have been to have two actors place something on stage and then to begin the scene with Sebastian's arrival. For these 'two' Greg supplies Kendall, Dab, and Harry. That looks uncommonly like three, but Greg is working on the plausible idea that the Plotter will have chosen a regular group of characters, and these three have appeared together twice as ghosts in the dumb-shows. Dab and Harry are, of course, available, but if they are to enter at all, why cannot they carry out the task by themselves? If a symmetrical pair is to be found with Kendall, it will be Tailor, who plays his inseparable companion and re-enters with him later in the scene.

Hunt and Kendall will not have been thought of as a pair, for Hunt is black and Kendall is white. It is, then, likely that Hunt was named second of an original pair, and that we should seek in the blank space of the first line for the name of his companion. It must be either Sam or Cartwright, and, as Cartwright would not be listed before Hunt, we arrive, by a process of elimination, at Sam. The Plotter's first thought must have been to use the Moorish Ambassadors as a decorative pair to carry on the throne, but he then changed his mind and used the slightly less improbable English Captains, in order to keep his scene as 'white' as possible, even though they would have to make an immediate re-entrance in Sebastian's train. Re-enter they certainly must, for there can be no Portuguese lords in this scene other than Avero. George, who is certainly present, may be entering in his role as Vimioso, standing in, as it were, for the unavoidably absent Lewes de Silva, but it is more likely that he is, as the Plot calls him, an attendant on the Spaniards, for Cartwright, his fellow attendant, is a newcomer to the scenes of the Portuguese court, and is still almost certainly black.

Once again, the Plotter seems to have intended two Pages for Sebastian. The other, in all likelihood, would have been Dick Jubie, but there is no room for his name. Dick, therefore, fails to appear altogether, and that is distinctly odd. He was addressed in II, iv in terms that ought to have made him the king's inseparable companion:

> Christopher de Tavera, next vnto my selfe
> My good Efestian, and my bedfellow,
> Thy cares and mine shall be alike in this,
> And thou and I will liue and die together.

Looking back, we see that the Plotter was by no means as comfortable in that scene as he appeared. George, as Vinioso, may have seemed a luxury, but the strain of providing a show of nobles for Sebastian, and of using George to solve the problem of the double command given to Avero (if that was his motive) is apparent in the casting of the boy, Dick, in a man's role. For the historical de Tavora *was* Sebastian's bedfellow, and would therefore have been about the same age as the king. As soon as the English Captains are available to take over as the royal attendants, Dick is not merely demoted, like George, but forgotten. Perhaps, indeed, he is excluded from appearing in this scene: on the one hand, because he is too small among eight substantial men, and, on the other hand, because he is too recognisable as Chistophero to resume his proper role as a Page, and would make the Plotter's former predicament apparent to the audience. Even as things stand that predicament is only saved from looking like an international incident by the fact that neither Charles nor Jones has yet *spoken* in any other role. If this is, indeed, the reason for Dick's temporary disappearance, it is strong confirmation that boys were doubled as men only in situations of extreme difficulty.

At the end of the scene, after the others have left, there is a dialogue between Stukeley and 'another'. The speech-prefixes also distribute the speeches to 'The other'. In the Plot, this must of course be Avero, for he is the only one there is. Despite the absence of Dick Jubie, then, this is obviously a crucial scene for the Plotter, who is now about to pay the full penalty for keeping his Zareo white.

Act III, scene ii

Enter Abdelmelec, Muly Mahamet Seth, Zareo and their Traine.

(This scene is not to be found in the Plot.)

The purpose of this scene is to demonstrate the moderation of Abdelmelec and to report the information that he has been in correspondence both with Sebastian and with Philip II of Spain. The latter's hypocrisy is stressed once again, and is derived by the dramatist from Conestaggio's account. There is no doubt that the scene was original, as Greg attests. It presents no textual problems at all and was unquestioned throughout by Dyce and Bullen. Any explanation of the relationship of the text and the Plot that fails to account for the excision of this scene can hardly be trusted, and, in all fairness to Greg, he frankly admits this weakness in his argument.

The playwright himself would have been hard put to it to provide Abdelmelec's train from his white actors, but he shows no signs of having wished to do so. The usage of both the text and the Plot is consistent in using the word 'Moor' to mean a black man, and, as the playwright's Zareo is black, there is no problem for him in making use of the black cast as attendants. Although there might be slight embarrassment for the black troops in Abdelmelec's references to his nephew as 'this Negro moore' (lines 902, 921), he cheers *them* on as 'ye manly moores'.

If the Plotter could have retained this scene, he would have had no option but to follow suit, but he is saved from the necessity of breaking his colour division quite yet by having a more compelling reason for omitting it. His Zareo has just appeared as a Spanish Ambassador and clearly has insufficient time to change in the twenty-one lines of dialogue following his exit in that role.

This is a more complex predicament than at first appears, for, if Zareo is blocked, all the actors in the scene are blocked. Even had the Plotter chosen the bolder expedient of altering the text to eliminate Zareo from III, ii, by reallocating his lines to Mahamet Seth, he would then find Seth blocked from entering into the text's III, iii (Plot, III, ii) where he will still be vitally necessary as a Captain. Moreover, if a more ingenious solution had been found for the Spanish Ambassadors, and III, ii had been played, it would have had the consequence of depriving the grand entrance of Sebastian into III, iv of his two remaining Portuguese Lords, for the Captaines in III, iii must then have been supplied from among the Lords appearing in III, i.

It is primarily, however, Zareo's doubling in the Portuguese scenes that creates the blockage, and prevents III, ii from being played. Nothing else would call for our attention here, were it not for the egregious – it is the only word for it – conclusion arrived at in *Alcazar and Orlando*. Mahamet Seth is mute in the scene, and Greg, this time in the teeth of the roman-italic principle, supposes him to have been cut from the text. This suggestion is made bizarre by the reason proffered for it: namely, that in the reduced-cast version Seth must have doubled with Sebastian, thus prefiguring the conclusion that the kings' bodies carried on the the final scene were represented by dummies. But Greg did not, finally, enshrine his conclusion about the doubling of Seth and Sebastian in his plan for the minimum cast, where, working on the principle of unlimited doubling, he found there was, after all, no need of it. Anyonc less intent on arriving at a pre-ordained conclusion might have checked at this damaging inconsistency.

Act III, scene iii

Enter Don de Menysis governor of Tangar, with his companie speaking to the Captaine.

(Plot: Act III, scene ii)

Enter Governor {o}f Tan{ga}r {:} & a
Captains mr Sha{a H} J{effes : e}xeunt

The Plotter is now slightly more comfortable, but he leaves an error standing and presents us with a problem about who is called on stage. He cannot bring on a company of more than two, but he brings on the two actors who are free. One of them, Humphrey Jeffes, has been freed from his role as Mahamet Seth by the suppression of the previous scene, and now has plenty of time to change on either side. The other is Mr Shaa, last seen as the Irish Bishop. He has been kept out of III, i, where he might logically have appeared to help out the shortage of lords, for the express purpose of filling this scene.

The question is whether the Governor is Mr Shaa, or whether there is a third actor on stage. If there is, it can be no-one but the Presenter. The text appears to call for only one Captain in the initial direction, but it envisages a second speaker in the 'company' and allots him some lines. We see that the dramatist must have had at his disposal a precisely equal number of personnel. His call for the Governor and his company could be answered by no more than three actors, one of whom must also have been the Presenter.

Greg naturally thought the text shows signs of having wanted to reduce the Captains to one, and proposed that the Plotter helped the process along a little and did so. But it is not hard to see what has happened. This is an informative scene. Its information is all vouched for by the sources and there is no suspicion of corruption or reduction in the text itself; but its dramatic interest is rather slight. It is planned largely as a monologue, punctuated by loyal and enthusiastic exclamations from the Portuguese captains of the Tangier garrison, who speak one after the other. Peele's style is echolalically repetitive, but there is really too much adjectival duplication in these speeches to allot them to a single speaker, unless he were understood to be temporarily hysterical from sunstroke.

The Governor's address (lines 955–75), which is otherwise taken verbatim from Polemon, begins with the line

Captaines, he cometh hitherward amaine,

and there seems little doubt that at least two Captains were originally intended; but in the first line of the scene, the singular address 'Captaine' is extrametrical, as is the word 'Madame' addressed to Calipolis in I, ii, which we supposed to have been added to the scene. I imagine that Peele merely made a slight alteration as he was composing, in order to vary the formal pattern of entrances that are commonly completed in other scenes before the speeches begin. In this most formal oration scene, he has attempted to introduce a little life by allowing the Governor to enter in conversation. To make it immediately clear who his auditor is, he has simply added the tag 'Captaine', and written in the direction 'speaking to the Captaine', not because he had only one, but to mark the manner of the scene's opening.

I do not believe the Plotter is in default here, except that he has omitted to note that the Governor is, once again, Richard Allen. Greg wanted to believe that the Presenter was not called in and that the second Captain (whom he supposed to have been Sam Rowley) had somehow been omitted from the entry. The reason is that the association of Shaa, Jeffes, and Sam will make sense of lines 5 and 6 of his reconstruction of the succeeding scene in the Plot. It would not, of course, be a total absurdity to allow one black Moroccan as a member of the Portuguese garrison of Tangier, but Sam is too strongly identified as Mahamet's leading supporter for his appearance here to be feasible.

The reason for the probability of Allen's appearance is, once again, connected with Zareo's white skin. We have seen some cause to suspect that, in the dramatist's doubling pattern, the Presenter may have appeared as one of the Spanish Ambassadors. Had the Plotter used him in that way, however, he would, indeed, have had no-one to appear as the second Captain except a black actor, or George, or Abdelmelec, or Dick Jubie himself. As Dick is not even used as a Portuguese to overcome the absurdity of doubling the Spanish Ambassadors, it would seem that none of these solutions was attractive and that the Presenter was called in because he was the only actor other than Shaa and Jeffes who was suitable and not positively blocked. It may indeed have seemed to the Plotter that the most obvious way of dealing with the problem of III, ii, was to reserve Allen for this appearance, and *then* to calculate how to deal with the Ambassadors. It is not likely that Allen would have been kept idle for two scenes where the Plot is in default by his absence. I believe we may be confident that he did appear as the Governor of Tangier. The Plotter has, once again, managed to keep his team identification clear.

It also appears to me likely that the Plotter would have recognised the clues in the speeches of the Governor that suggest his original identity as the Presenter. The material is a rather carefully selected and slanted précis of the descriptions of Sebastian's sailing from Lisbon, and it completes the story of Spanish duplicity, first broached by the Presenter in III, Induction and then poured out by Stukeley to Avero at the end of II, i. It is pure narration material, more appropriate in the Presenter's mouth than the Governor's, or, to put it the other way round, the thin subterfuge of putting it in the Governor's mouth is helped out by the knowledge that he is, in fact, the Presenter. This, no doubt, also accounts for the rather perfunctory dramatisation of the material, whose hasty composition shows in its many verbal echoes of the last scene but one.

Act III, scene iii

The Trumpets sound, the chambers are dischargde. Then enter the king of Portugall and the Moore, with all theyr traine.

(Plot: Act III, scene ii)

Enter at one d{
drom & Cullers :{
Duke of A{
Hercules{
att anoth{
mr Shaa{
them mu{ }is.
in their{ }moores
o{ }e on }ding young
m{ }hame{ }right : &
George : exeu{ }t

There is no suspicion of default in this scene: the directions call every available person on stage and the Plotter probably responds. Only Mr

Downton who plays Abdelmelec certainly ignores the call. Even Downton, if he were needed, has plenty of time to climb in and out of a disguise, but when we play with the various possibilities of what the Plotter may have written in this very decayed entry, there never appears to be space for him. It is not likely that Zareo is involved either, but the other members of Abdelmelec's party are on stage: Mahamet Seth (Humphrey Jeffes) is disguised as a Portuguese Captain, as is his companion, Mr Shaa, who will later play Celybin.

I have purposely omitted every conjectural reading from the fragments of the Plot, for it is important to base our arguments first on the natural results of our enquiry, and then to justify them by reference to Greg's conjectural readings. Any solution must remain to a great degree tentative, but I believe we are in a stronger position than Greg to understand the Plotter's behaviour.

First, there is a conventional entry to be expected: 'at one dore ... and att another'. There is little doubt about who will enter through the doors. Sebastian's party will come from one side and the Tangier garrison from the other, for Mr Shaa follows soon after and the Governor has just spoken the programme (ll. 971–5):

> And hetherward he comes, and lookes to meete
> This manly Moore, whose case he vndertakes,
> Therefore go we to welcome and rescue,
> With canon shot, and shouts of yong and olde,
> This fleet of Portugals and troupe of Moores.

Our reconstruction of the first four lines must begin from Hercules. He is never without Jonas, and on the other three occasions on which they appear Jonas is listed first. Line 3, then, will conclude 'Jonas &'. There are then four spaces to fill. Into these must be fitted Sebastian, Stukeley and at least the two Lords who are addressed in the text: Avero and 'Lord Lodowicke'. Avero is clearly in place at the beginning of line 3. He is usually listed before Stukeley, and it is most likely that Stukeley will follow here again, preceding the other members of the English party.

Who the other lord may be is something of a puzzle. He may be Lodovico Caesar, mentioned at IV, i, 1,114 as the leader of the fourth legion of Portuguese, or he may be Lewes de Silva. It is not a matter of great importance. He may be addressed in either case as 'Lord Lodowicke', and whoever he is taken to be, he must be played by Mr Jones, for there is no-one else. The only question is how much space there is for the listing of the role. If he is thought of as Lodovico Caesar, he is a new character, and, as Greg observes, the actor would then most likely be named. The only line on which there is space enough for that is line 4, where Greg places him. But if he is thought of as de Silva, it is possible that he will be listed by that name alone, even though he has appeared in the dodged role of the Spanish Ambassador. A comparable case is that of Humphrey Jeffes who is listed on his return from the role of Portuguese Captain only as

Mahamet Xeque. The name 'luis de Silua' might then appear following Sebastian in line 2.

My own reconstruction of these lines does not differ so greatly from Greg's as it may appear. The same actors are brought on stage, except that my reconstruction allows space for the habitual provision of Sebastian's page, Jeames. He has appeared in both the preceding scenes at the Portuguese Court and there is no reason why he should not have journeyed to Africa. It will now, I believe, be possible for the Plotter to satisfy the frustrated itch he has shown on previous occasions to furnish Sebastian with two pages. The other will then be Dick Jubie. We shall see that these two will re-appear as Sebastian's pages in IV, ii. The advantage of this suggestion is that the space is exactly right for their two names, and avoids Greg's awkward and uncharacteristic listing of de Tavora as 'Christopero'. If he had been so familiarly important in the Plotter's scheme of things, he would surely have been introduced into III, i. All possible members of the Portuguese party are thus accounted for.

We may now make a guess that the first line includes only general directions for the entrance, since it cannot contain character names. I have no great faith in my wording of this line. I have chosen it only to suggest that Greg's 'army' is not inevitable, and is, indeed, uncharacteristic of Elizabethan theatrical language.

The last eight lines present no difficulty about personnel, for we know the team allegiances. The only problem is about the disposition of the characters on stage and the order of entrances. Mr Shaa's name, beginning line 6, makes it clear that the garrison which left the stage at the end of the last scene now re-enters immediately, the immediate re-entrance being prepared for in the dialogue, and the short interval filled with discharge of cannon and general noise. The whole Portuguese party will then have gathered, without a word spoken, before the entrancc of the Moors. Thus, the space in line 5 will contain the words 'Governor of Tangar', although it might equally well read 'Governor & 2: captaines', and line 6 will be partially filled by the name of the other Captain, 'H. Jeffes'. Greg, who believed that the Governor *was* Mr Shaa, now has an opportunity to fill the beginning of line 6 with 'and 2 Captaines', thus accounting for 'Mr Sam' on line 7, who must, he thinks, have been accidentally omitted from IV, ii. But Mr Sam cannot have been a Tangier Captain.

What then is Mr Sam doing at the beginning of line 7, in a position preceding the entrance of the Moors? The answer, I believe, is that there is not a single Moorish entrance, but two, and for that there is good reason. The main business of the scene, after the simple matter of arrival and welcome, is the handing over of Young Mahamet to the Portuguese as a hostage for the Moor's good faith. He will be the centre of interest in the scene, yet there is no space in Greg's reconstruction in which his entrance can be recorded. It would be highly unusual to imply the appearance of a character by listing his attendants. I believe he will have been ushered onto the stage. At lines 10–11 the fragments pretty clearly must have read 'attending young mahamet', but this is rather far distant from Mr Sam. What must happen is that two black characters are first appointed to conduct the young prince in. They will be the most important members of the Moorish party, Mr Sam and Mr Hunt. Line 7 will thus read: 'mr Sam : mr Hunt : & young mahamet'. There is nothing odd in the masters being listed before the boy. It happens at their second appearance together in I, ii.

The Plotter now turns to the entrance of the Moor and Calipolis, and it is natural to complete the phrase at line 9 beginning 'in their' by 'charriott'. In that case we shall expect the reappearance of the two Moorish Pages, especially as the phrase 'one on' in line 10 is conveniently completed by 'each side'. On their last appearance with the chariot, the Pages were also described as 'on each side'. It is, however, only the appearance of that expression that suggests the presence of Pages, and it is only the suggestion that the Pages are present that implies the appearance of the chariot. Mahamet was last seen pining with hunger among the mountain shrubs without it, and as four separate entrances are implied in this scene it may be that a more appropriate wording would be 'in their Tent', just as Achilles enters 'in his Tent' in the Plot of *Troilus and Cressida*. There is more space in this line than Greg's reconstruction uses, but I am not quite sure that there is enough to list both the chariot and the Pages. The chariot was a well-remembered property, however. In the equivalent of this scene in *The Famous History of Captain Thomas Stukeley* it is produced again, and Sebastian is graciously offered a ride round the stage in it. I think we may pass its probable appearance here, and if we allow the chariot, there is little doubt about the Pages.

Greg's wording implies that George and Cartwright are doing double duty as attendants on both the chariot and Young Mahamet, and that George is a Moor, which is not the case, although Cartwright is. There are two problems here. One is that before the word 'moores' on line 9 there are two letters, difficult to decipher, that Greg reads as 'th' (the last letters of 'with'), but which appear to me to be 'ck'. The slope of the first letter is quite uncharacteristic of the Plotter's 't'. I suppose that the Plotter wrote '2 : pages black moores / one on each side', perhaps because he was distinguishing them mentally from the two white Pages already on stage. The other puzzle is that there are clear signs of the tail of an '&' that must have stood in line 10, just above the beginning of Cartwright's name in line 11. The Plotter must have written: 'one on each side & attending young / mahamet & w. Cartwright : & / George'. This might imply that it is the Pages who are doing double duty as attendants. Cartwright and George, who last appeared as attendants on the Spanish Ambassadors, are, of course, simply the other available members of the cast. As they do not make a symmetrical pair and no longer have any clear affiliation with either party, they are left until last. The least inappropriate way of bringing them on stage is, perhaps, to attach them *post hoc facto* to the attendants on Young Mahamet, who is to be the centre of interest in the scene. That is what I believe the Plotter intended, but, once again, he presumably left standing an error of little importance for his purposes. With the addition of these two, the complete cast is on stage except for Downton (Abdelmelec), Charles (Zareo), Dab, Harry, and Parsons.

All this would appear very strange to Greg, but, oddly enough, it is perfectly in accord with the sources. In both major accounts it is recorded that Young Mahamet was the first to meet with Sebastian, and actually sailed some distance from the coast to join him at sea. Thus it would not be surprising if he entered *with* Sebastian, but the dramatist does not suggest it, and the Plotter avoids colour confusions of that kind if he can help it. It may be that the Plotter himself, as we have seen reason to suspect, knew at least one of the sources, and has chosen to organise his most crowded entrance in a way that he knew to be consistent with the story. But it seems to me more likely that he simply chose to add a little emphasis to a perfectly intelligible reading of the text.

Act IV, scene i

Enter Abdilmelec and his traine.

{	}om & Cull{
Ma{	}ue . Cel{
att{	}aa : {
mr [Joe{	

The right-hand fragment of this section was wrongly pasted a scene too low in the re-mounting and is here restored, as in Greg's reconstruction, to its rightful place. There is little doubt about whom we should find in the first three lines. This is a scene of preparation for battle, and the first line will almost certainly read: 'Enter with drom and Cullors'. Abdelmelec will be listed first, and there are clear enough signs of Muly Mahamet Xeque on the second line, although he has no speaking part in the text. Celybin is addressed in the first line of the text and has the major speaking part. Zareo is also on stage and speaks, so his character name will follow Celybin's. Then there is either an attendant or some attendants, and the appearance of part of Mr Shaa's name. As Mr Jones appears misspelt (and presumably deleted and re-written correctly) on the last line, followed by a blank space, we must suppose that he is the attendant, or at least the last of them. We shall see, however, that the remainder of the white cast and all the black cast, except Cartwright, are on stage in the next scene. Cartwright's name is probably too long for the space available here, and is unlikely to have been listed before Mr Jones; so even if Cartwright has somehow managed to change colour, we have in fact completed the list of the people who may enter in this scene. The reading must therefore be not 'attendants', but 'an attendant', and we may assume from the space allowed that the Plotter named Mr Charles returning to his dodged role as Zareo, although he did not name Humphrey Jeffes re-appearing as Xeque. Jones, as Lewes de Silva, has now been extracted from Sebastian's party, as he must also have been from the playwright's cast, and there is no further mention of de Silva in the text or the Plot.

Act IV, scene ii

Enter Sebastian king of Portugall, the Duke of Avero,
Stukley, and others.

...

Enter Muly Mahamet.

...

Manet Muly Mahamet.

Enter{ }aile :
Seba{ }keley : & Jonas
at{ ..}ors : a guard
& t{ }ge, J{}Dick Jubie :
the{ }them { } kendall : [too]
}s : m{.. t} : exeunt
o}rg{e }ex{
h}amet exit

The above is as nearly as I can represent in typescript the last scene preserved in the Plot. The left-hand section is firmly attached to the paper of the left-hand column of the Plot and cannot be shifted. The other fragments, however, have been treated somewhat roughly in the mounting and are all in the wrong place, the bottom line having been placed about two inches too low. There has also pretty clearly been some stretching while the paper was wet, and some damage to the surface. The right-hand fragment of IV, i, with which we have already dealt, was pasted against the left-hand fragment of this scene, and has been removed in the reproduction above for purposes of clarity. The right-hand section consists of three fragments that are shown by the slight mis-alignment of the writing to be all out of place. The paste-up represents 'rge' as sitting level with 'exeunt', but the 'exeunt' is itself made up of two separate pieces of paper, divided horizontally, which must have contained two recensions of the same word (i.e. 'exeunt') that are now crammed awkwardly together.

We are reduced to playing a jigsaw puzzle with these remaining pieces of the Plot, and we cannot achieve the firmest assurance of the Plotter's intention, apart from the justifications of probability that can be made for one placement of the pieces against another. For the battle, the Plotter deserts us altogether. But we could not leave our investigation of his methods without asking how he will fare when he brings the main subject of his play onto the stage. If we should be forced to conclude that he could not have represented the battle as the text reports it, or, conversely, that he had many more actors than the text requires, we could have no confidence in our arguments so far.

Sir Walter Greg, too, now deserts us, for in the absence of the Plot his arguments against the text evaporate, except for two observations: that the death of Avero probably replaces a scene of the original, and that the reduced cast could have managed the last scene only by requiring the kings to help carry on their own dead bodies in the form of dummies. He was impressed by 'the Mores limmes' in Henslowe's inventory, perhaps because the idea of using dummies to represent dismembered corpses has some relevance to the arguments for the primacy of the B text of *Doctor Faustus*, but afterwards came to see that these limbs are costumes, not properties. They were presumably stockings and long gloves, and explain simply why the black cast cannot double with the white. To change colour for an Elizabethan actor was not just a matter of an actor's washing his face. He would have had to strip to the skin. The solution of the kings carrying their own bodies would have provided an hilarious finale, and I do not think it need be taken seriously, but, as we shall see, the cast of 1598 is often so hard pressed that the Plotter must have wished he could have adopted Greg's proposal.

Before the trumpets sound, then, we must discover the composition of the forces they are to summon, and the solution of IV, ii will be of some importance. Once the battle begins, there will be no time for changing sides, for, with the constant presence of the figure of the dead Abdelmelec on stage, the action is undoubtedly continuous and the pressure of traffic in the tiring-house will be as great as the traffic on stage. We must try, therefore, to ascertain which lords command which followers so that we can follow the Plotter's progress. The general lines of division are already clear, but there are two actors whose allegiance is unknown, or uncertain – Mr Jones and George.

George has been a Janissary, a Fury, County Vinioso, an attendant on the Spanish Ambassadors and finally an attendant on Young Mahamet. He has perhaps had time to change costume and colour, although he may logically have appeared in the latter role as a Portuguese. Jones has played Lewes de Silva in his own right, and in his transformation into a Spanish Ambassador, but, following that entrance, he disappears from Sebastian's party, both in the text and, as far as we can see, in the Plot. His role as de Silva appears to have been 'written out' by the dramatist for precisely the same reason.

The evidence for this is stronger than mere supposition, for the results of our conjectures enable us to reconstruct the last scene of the Plot in a manner more consistent than Greg's with the Plotter's normal methods, and to make use of the larger floating fragment for which Greg could find no place. This fragment needs ony to be moved about an inch to the left and slightly downwards to provide us with the clue to the interpretation of the scene.

Having moved up the right-hand fragments so that the letters 'saile' are level with 'Enter', as in the reconstruction above, our attention can focus on the second line in which Stukeley clearly appears with Jonas. One would then expect Hercules to follow on line 3, but the letters that appear there are quite inconsistent with that possibility. Greg read them as 'wth', but the traces that remain are perfectly compatible with the way the Plotter writes 'at'. It thus occurred to me to try the regular formulation, 'Enter at one dore ... and at another', having, at first, very little idea of who was likely to enter at the other. The letters 'ors' in line 3, followed by 'a guard' are hardly likely to be the end of 'soldiors', for 'soldiers : a guard' would be pleonastic in theatrical usage, so that whoever enters probably does so with 'drom and cullors', in the conventional way. That may be compared with the usage in the Plot's III, iii and IV, i. Moreover, we see that this scene in the text is really a companion piece with the preceding one: each party is seen preparing for the fight, and each will leave the stage as if to engage in immediate battle. Even though the scene appears to begin as a Council (for the letters '... saile' must surely be echoing the 'Counsell' of the text) there will be drums and colours somewhere in the offing.

Now the second line begins with 'Sebastian'. We shall therefore not expect to find any actors' names in the first line, but only general directions for the entrance. The second line must then read: 'Sebastian : Duke of Avero : Stukeley and Jonas', and the third is most likely to read: 'at another dore wth drom and Cullors : a guard'. This seems at least to be a more consistent reading that Greg's unallocated 'attendants and soldiers', which would be quite uncharacteristic of this Plot. The only problem is that, despite the running-on of the line over the margin, there appears to be not quite enough room for the words 'Duke of', and it is possible that Avero is listed for the first time without his title. As he must be on stage, however, room must be found for him in that line. We should expect the names of the guard, and whoever follows the '&', to appear on the fourth line, and we see that that line ends with 'Dick Jubie'.

Dick has not appeared as Christophero de Tavora since II, iv, and we have reason to believe that he may have appeared with Jeames as a Page in III, iii, even if only in our own reconstruction. The remaining members of the Portuguese party who could possibly appear in this scene are, then, Kendall, who is certainly on stage later, George Somerset, Jeames the Page, and Mr Jones. Now the fourth line begins with '&', followed by a crossed letter that might be a 't', but might equally well be a rather decayed 'p'. Whatever else we may infer, it is clear that some further description of this entering party is involved. Greg's suggestion of '& to them ...' cannot be paralleled in this Plot or in others. We may suppose that the Plotter has continued to regard Jeames and Dick as Pages to Sebastian, and to represent them here entering with drum and colours. He might have written either '& two ...', or '& pages ... ' The first of these usages would be uncharacteristic, plurals elsewhere being given in numerals, but not impossible. As a 'p', the slope of the letter and its positioning in relation to the Plotter's characteristic '&' may be compared with the entry of the Moorish Pages in II, iv. Whichever alternative we suppose the Plotter to have used, it is likely that the words will bring on the same characters, for the only Portuguese remaining who make a pair are the Pages. Kendall appears to enter or re-enter later in the scene, and Mr Jones is our least likely starter, so we may perhaps try George as the guard. Our fourth line will then read: '& Pages : George : Jeames & Dick Jubie'.

It may now be seen that the larger fragment on the right-hand side, when moved to its correct position, confirms this reading. Its top line contains a '... ge,' followed by a 'J...', so that whether or not Jeames and Dick Jubie are listed as 'two pages', the order of names is correct, and there is certainly not space for the grander titles they once enjoyed. What happens next is, however, unexpected. With the fragment now in its place we can see that the next line will read:

the{ } them { } kendall :[too]

which might plausibly be completed as :

the{n to} them { w :} kendall :[too]

That is to say, Hercules comes on to the stage. In the sixth line we see that someone appears to enter with him, and, at the end of this fifth line, there is a deletion, not of 'to' as in Greg's reconstruction, but of 'too', which suggests that the Plotter meant to write 'two', rather than 'to them'. That may then appear corrected on the next line as '2', but whether that is so or not, it appears that the someone who enters with Kendall may be plural. Whoever it is, it cannot yet be Muly Mahamet, for the entry of his name is blocked by the remaining lines of the fragment. The enterers may, indeed, be 'Moores', for Greg read the faint and partially obliterated letter in the third line of the fragment, before what appears to be an 's', as an 'e', and on this ground supposed it to have something to do with the stage-direction for the battle in Act V where two Moors 'set vpon Stukley, and he driveth them in' (lines 1,384–5). The reading 'Moores' is certainly not incompatible with the evidence.

This sixth line is, however, the most difficult to decipher. The remaining traces appear to be:

{ }es m{ }t : exeunt.

The centrally placed letters are those that can be deciphered in the fragment, although the first two might not be 'es', and only part of the 'e' is visible. There are vestiges of a tall letter before 'exeunt' that is almost certainly a 't', but insufficient room between the 'm' and the 't' for the entry of 'Mahamet'. The Plotter, in any case, always favours Muly Mahamet with capitals, and there is no place for the other Mahamets in this scene. At the beginning of the line, too, there is not a great deal of room, so that '2 : Moores' would just about fill the space available.

I believe the first readable letters in the line (those appearing on the fragment) are not 'es' but the end of the curious usage of the Plotter in writing 'mr', and may be compared with the deleted entry of Jones immediately above. The following 'm' will be the last letter of 'Sam', the intervening letters, of which there are faint traces, having been smudged out in the mounting. The spaces available are exactly right to be filled with the conjectural reading:

{2 : moores :}mr{Sa}m{ : mr Hun}t : exeunt.

This reconstruction may be compared with a line where the writing is of approximately the same size in I, i.

There is now a seventh line of the entry, for which we have no information, except that George's name is on it. This is indicated by the letters 'rge' on the bottom line of the displaced fragment. The line is preceded by an exeunt, and it is a reasonable guess that at some time after the entrance of Kendall and the two Moors, George and another (or some others) leave the stage.

We may now be pretty certain that in addition to this almost vanished line, there is another completely missing from the entry, except for the bottom curls of the 'x' in exeunt. These curls are on a separate fragment, but have been pushed up against the top half of the word 'exeunt' which has been partially split by the decay of the paper. Thus, what looks like one rather blurred 'exeunt' is in fact made out of two that must have been written almost exactly underneath each other, but were originally separated by an intervening line of text. There is not much doubt that that line must have recorded the entrance of Muly Mahamet, and that what follows will be in accord with the directions of the Quarto. That is, the Portuguese party leave the stage to take up their battle positions, while the Moor remains to soliloquise. Apart from the conjectural information in the first line, then, the complete entry might have read:

Enter at one dore to Counsaile
Sebastian : Auero : Stukeley : & Jonas
at another door wth drom & Cullors : a guard
& Pages : George, Jeames : Dick Jubie :
then enter to them : w. kendall : [too]
2 : moores : mr Sam: mr Hunt : exeunt
w. kendall : George : manet the rest :
to them Muly Mahamett : exeunt
manet Mully Mahamet: exit.

The only totally unsupported element in the above is the assumption that Kendall will exit with George. The space of Kendall's name might equally well be filled with 'Pages' or 'Moores'. However that may be, there is an obvious departure in this scene from the directions of the text. I believe it can be explained quite simply.

The Plotter was presumably as puzzled as the modern reader by the curious dislocation of the speeches we observed in the previous chapter, where an original speech of Avero's appears to have been re-distributed between Avero and Hercules. His solution was to create an additional entrance and to bring Hercules on stage, hotfoot, with the news of the sighting of the Moorish troops. The surprise is the appearance with him of black Captains who may look very like the 'inuading Moores' whose appearance has stricken him with terror. These Captains, are, however, recognisable as Mahamet's chief henchmen, and, if they remain on stage to welcome their king, we may interpret their entrance as an attempt by the Plotter to give some credibility to Mahamet's claim, when he finally enters, that Abdelmelec's army is ready to desert:

> For now is all the armie resolute,
> To leaue the traitor helplesse in the fight,
> And flie to me as to their rightfull prince,
> Some horse-men haue already lead the waie,
> And vow the like for their companions.

It seems to me equally likely, however, that the Plotter may have been as anxious as Peele to keep Portuguese – and English – honour bright, and was embarrassed by the need to provide a small pageant of soldiers fleeing from the stage in terror. The dramatist has written no direction for it, and perhaps meant the suggestion to be purely verbal, but the text clearly implies some action, either on stage or off, that justifies Mahamet's entering protest:

> Beholde thrice noble Lorde, vncalde I come,
> To counsell where necessitie commands,
> And honor of vndoubted victorie,
> Makes me exclime [*sic*] vpon this dastard flight.

Clearly the Plotter calls on George to run, and, as George is most likely the standard-bearer, that will make a good show as the colours sweep across the stage. It may be that he will take with him the Pages who were his original companions. I have assumed that Kendall (Hercules) who has entered in terror, will be his partner in flight, but it is possible that the Moors are introduced for this very purpose, and that the intention was to ironise Mahamet's words before he speaks them. The space available in the Plot will admit of either possibility, and I can only leave the question to the reader's racial sensibilities. It will be as well for our casting problem if we accept the latter possibility, for, as actors, Sam and Hunt will hereafter have no option but to desert to Abdelmelec.

The remaining question of what should appear in the first line of the scene is a little troublesome, for Greg was convinced this was a night scene and that the small fragment reading 'y Tor', misplaced near the top of the column at the beginning of III, i, should be introduced here. Its only possible expansions would appear to be 'by Torchlight', or 'with smoky Torches' and the line above it shows that it must fit into the initial directions for a scene. I believe the writing is too markedly out of proportion to introduce it here. There are other places in Act V where it might have been appropriate. One is at the beginning of the Act V dumb-show itself, where thunder and lightning are called for together with a display of fireworks. It is possible that the Presenter himself carried a smoking torch. Another is shortly after Mahamet Seth's entry at l. 1504, which would have begun a new scene in the Plot, where he speaks the lines:

> Pay thankes to heauen with sacrificing fire,
> Alcazar and ye townes of Barbarie.

This entrance at the end of the day of battle may well have called for torches. The fragment, then, almost certainly belongs to the back of the sheet, where Act V would have appeared. There is, however, no sign of writing on the reverse of the surviving parts of the second column. The Plot of *Alcazar* probably disintegrated when an attempt was made to split the sheet in order to mount each side separately, as was done successfully in the case of *The Dead Man's Fortune*. This may not be the only fragment that survives from the reverse side, but it is the only one bearing anything intelligible that cannot positively be fitted into our reconstruction.

Act five and the battle

We have seen that, with the forces at his disposal, Peele gives a faithful account of the battle of Alcazar, representing its strategy and the succession of its notable events as vividly as the limitations of the stage and of the cast allow. The text shows itself clearly aware of those limitations and its solutions richly engage the modern reader's sense of the absurd, but the effect it achieves is not without ingenuity.

The three-part division of the cast now has to be abandoned, for, if Abdelmelec is to have any show of winning this battle he must be provided with a force that looks numerically capable of doing so. The dramatist therefore arranges his account of the battle round two symmetrical stage directions: 'Enter to the battell, and the Moores flie' (line 1,301), and 'Enter to the battaile, and the christians flie' (lines 1,365–6). He had probably introduced these dispositions earlier by calling in his black Moors as members of Abdelmelec's party in IV, i. The Plotter does not do so, but appears to bring on Sam and Hunt in IV, ii. If they are still intended as staunch adherents of Mahamet, this is certainly the last time they will be able to appear with him. It is, perhaps, more probable that they and not Kendall flee from the stage with George and are imagined to desert to Abdelmelec.

The battle thus begins with about eight men on each side. Sebastian will be supported by Edward Alleyn, Kendall, Jubie, Tailor, George, Charles, and Mr Towne. Abdelmelec will have Sam, Hunt, Cartwright, Humphrey Jeffes, Mr Shaa, and Mr Jones.

Immediately after Stukeley has been murdered by Hercules and Jonas – suddenly transformed into Italian Captains – there is the entry of the triumphant army:

> Enter Muly Mahamet Seth and his traine,
> with Drums and Trumpets.

Brave words. But what has become of the company? Abdelemelec is dead. Sebastian, Stukeley, and Avero, too, have fallen. Mahamet is missing, presumed killed, and his drowned body will later be brought on stage. Hercules and Jonas could perhaps re-enter, for Stukeley's dying soliloquy of forty-nine lines allows time enough for a rapid change of costume. It may be there for the precise purpose of allowing this pair, Mr Jubie (Avero) and George to re-appear in a Moorish incarnation, but, even so, two of these four are required elsewhere. The Moor and Sebastian have to be fetched, each by two men, who, when they enter, are clearly shown not to have been on stage earlier in the scene. Mahamet Seth can thus have as the minimum train for his installation: Charles to present the crown, and Sam, George, Shaa, and Jones to cheer. If the Presenter and Avero are called in he can have a maximum of seven. It is easy to see that questions of identity might make this a rather foreign-looking occasion, and that some of these possible attendants may have been deemed unsuitable. There was, then, clear theatrical advantage in moving Jones to Abdelmelec's party as early as it could be managed.

Sebastian's body is now brought on by two 'Portugals'. I have suggested that this task may have fallen to Jonas and Hercules in the Plot, but they have been both English and Italian Captains and may not have been thought of by the dramatist as feasible Portugals. Whichever actors are allocated to this task must be subtracted from Mahamet Seth's train, but, of course, the others may then be added. The Moor's body will be brought on by Hunt and Cartwright.

There is now the pageant of Sebastian's funeral to be enacted and we cannot be quite certain how many other bodies there may be on stage. Mahamet Seth's final order is a little ambiguous:

My Lord Zareo, let it be your charge,
To see the souldiers tread a solempne march,
Trailing their pikes and Ensignes on the ground,
So to perform the princes funeralls.

It may be that the bodies are four in number. All the sources comment on the notable sight of three dead kings, or, with Stukeley, of four kings – 'three *in re* and one *in spe*' – gathered together in Abdelmelec's tent at the close of the day. This is the eternal cell, indeed, but can it be managed with anything like the dignity the occasion demands? Bodies cannot walk off the Elizabethan stage, and to carry four with any decency takes sixteen bearers. That number the Plotter certainly has not, for, if he could have brought on extras, he would surely have done so in earlier scenes. Equally, it is unlikely that the playwright could have had a greater number. But both will have between nine and eleven. Mahamet Seth's speech indicates that he will not be a bearer, but the Presenter may perhaps be called in. The problem is partly solved by the removal of Mahamet's body on the extra-metrical line 'Awaie with him' (line 1,586), and we may suppose that the bearers return to the stage, although there is not a direction for their re-entrance in the text. It is still possible that there are four bodies to be dealt with, and fewer porters, for Avero may still be on stage. That would leave us with an outside total of ten men to carry four bodies, and would leave no provision for the soldiers who are to follow the cortege with reversed arms.

A possible solution is that the command that brings the standards and pike-blades down to the floor, and the movement in of the bearers to hoist Sebastian onto their shoulders, provided cover for the working of the trap. It is doubtful, however, if a trap-door, even at the Rose or the Fortune, could have carried three bodies, or even two.

It seems probable that Abdelmelec's body remains on stage, for, first, in order to be installed in the very chair in which his brother died, Muly Hamet has to give the command to remove him (lines 1,519–20):

> Now haue him hence, that roially he may
> Be buried and imbalmd, as is meete.

This is not quite the end of the matter, however. The un-propping of Abdelmelec appears to take some time, for Mahamet Seth again commands (lines 1,534–5):

> on this earth bestow
> This princely coarse, till further for his funerals
> We provide.

The 'ground' or 'earth' is also the technical cover-word in the theatre for the trap-door, but there is no actual indication of its employment here. Avero's body is most probably not on stage, for, even though the stage-direction says: 'The Duke of Auero slaine', the dialogue strongly implies that his actual demise is not displayed to the audience (lines 1,370–5):

> *Sebast.* Seest thou not Stukley, O Stukley sees thou not
> The great dishonour done to Christendome?
> Our cheerful onset crost in springing hope,
> The braue and mighty prince, Duke of Auero
> Slaine in my sight, now joy betide his ghost,
> For like a lion did he beare himself.

Likewise, Stukeley's death probably takes place off stage. His dying soliloquy, functional and necessary although it is, is already reminiscent of amateur pantomime, and is probably the object of the parodic dying soliloquy of Ralph in *The Knight of the Burning Pestle*, even though the verbal satire in that speech is of the chorus of *The Spanish Tragedy*. An audience that can take with any seriousness Stukeley's appeal (lines 1,456–7):

> Harke friendes, and with the story of my life
> Let me beguile the torment of my death,

may easily suspend its belief in his imminent mortality long enough to allow him to leave the stage at the end of his tale (lines 1,501–2):

> Now goe, and in that bed of honour dye
> Where braue Sebastians breathles Course doth lie,

even though the stage direction plainly says 'He dyeth'.

At any rate, no mention is made of the presence of either Avero or Stukeley in the remainder of the text. We have thus a choice of imagining one of three possibilities. Either the text intended that Abdelmelec is to be carried off at the end with Sebastian; or that the trap-door was used to conceal the body of Abdelmelec; or that gatherers were called in.

To these alternatives there are corollaries. If the first suggestion is correct, the consequence is that the funeral rites will be maimed, with at most three soldiers to 'tread a solempne march'. The Plotter cannot, then, have had a cast larger than that envisaged by the dramatist. If either of the other suggestions apply, the text must clearly have been designed for a London theatre. These conditions are extremely unlikely to have been envisaged in a performance truncated for country touring with a reduced cast. Even if it be allowed that trap-doors could somehow be rigged up in country halls and market-places, and that small travelling companies took along their gatherers, the hypothesis that a reviser could accidentally have copied so many inoperative odds and ends from a fuller version, in the process of producing a text as functional and prescient as this one, is impossible to maintain. The battle sequences lead us once again to the conclusion that the Plotter and the dramatist were working with casts of very similar size, except for the number of boys, and that apart from small differences in their exercise of theatrical ingenuity, their understanding of the rules of the game was identical.

We can also see that the Plotter, having made certain decisions about his spectacle that lead to awkward consequences, followed the stage-directions and the internal suggestions of the playwright's text as faithfully as he could. He is forced, *in extremis*, to omit a whole scene, but, in the very few cases where he appears to be changing or elaborating the dramatist's plan, we can follow his logic without great difficulty. In the body of the play he is simply concerned with fitting the text with the cast available, according to the principles we have inferred, and to some others in addition that are probably concerned with the status of particular actors and the prestige of speaking roles. In the introductory dumb-shows, however, he has allowed his imagination more freedom, and I have therefore left the discussion of them until last. It was, of course, from the Plotter's response to the dumb-shows in particular that Greg's notion of the reduction of the text derived.

9

The dumb-shows

It is not easy to find a comparison with the Presenter's Inductions in *Alcazar*. If we were to regard them simply as speeches without accompanying action, they are perhaps closest in technique to the prospective narrative style of the Choruses in *Henry V*. They provide temporal continuity, predict selective parts of the action that is to follow, appeal to the audience's patience and to its inward perception of events, introduce entering characters, and set the mood for each act.

Peele adopts as the key to the understanding of his action the idea of the Nemesis attendant on wrongful ambition. As I have said earlier, this idea is not implicit in the action itself, but *applied* to it by the Presenter as an interpretation. The effect is to infuse an historical melodrama with a kind of irony that might be called tragic, if it were not so solemnly portentous and therefore, to a cynical modern mind, absurdly funny. The more typical chorus of early English tragedy is spoken by Ate, a fury or a ghost. Peele was, as far as I know, the first dramatist of the popular theatre to hit on the idea of Nemesis, although she appears in the Morality *Respublica*, and the example was later followed by the author of *The Tragedy of Nero* (1603).

There is very little in the Presenter's speeches that might not stand on its own without accompanying representation, even in those parts of the Inductions to Act I and Act V that were certainly written to be paralleled by dumb-shows. At these points, the shows are written in and described as the 'first', 'second', and 'last', the first and second both occurring within the Act I Induction. The Induction to Act I invokes, in addition, the sound effect of a drum by which Nemesis is figured arousing the Furies and the god of war. A drum is not a normal property or emblem of Nemesis,[1] and it is therefore reasonable to assume that the thundering noise was intended as an actual accompaniment of the prologue, but there is little indication that the Furies were intended to appear at this stage, nor does the Plotter introduce them.

The Induction to Act II, for which the same sound effect is implied, may well, however, have been intended as a more elaborate performance. The drum is now accompanied by the voices of the ghosts of Mahamet's murdered victims crying 'Vindicta', and an actual entrance of Furies is suggested in the lines (lines 331–2):

And now start vp these torments of the world
Wakt with the thunder of Ramusians (sc. Rhamnusias) drum ...
Thus Muly Mahamet is a counsell held,
To wreake the wrongs and murthers thou hast done.[2]

The allegory of the Furies conferring together might merely be a figure of rhetoric, but the noise of the drum appears again to be actual, and the circumstantial detail of this hellish council, with appropriate properties, which the Plotter follows precisely, is so fully described that there was probably no need for an independent stage-direction.

The Induction to Act III, has no direction for a show. The only indication of performance it carries is the traditional interpretative language of the opening (lines 798–9):

Lo thus into a lake of blood and gore
The braue courageous king of Portugall
Hath drencht himself,

but in this case the words might well apply to the immediately preceding declaration of Sebastian, urged by the offer of the crown of Morocco, and fortified by the arrival of the English party (lines. 791–2):

Follow me Lords, Sebastian leades the way
To plant the christian fa[i]th in Affrica.

On the other hand, the Induction to Act IV carries the direction '*Enter to the bloudy banket*', but there is no description of the intended mime.

It is easy to assume, then, that the playwright had a consistent plan in mind that is imperfectly represented by the text, and that he intended to introduce each of his five acts by an Induction spoken by the Presenter and accompanied by a dumb-show. It is upon this assumption of regularity, as we have seen, that Greg's major argument for the reduction and revision of the text rests. Once again, however, we are on very thin ice in assuming such a purposeful symmetry of composition.

The originality of Elizabethan playwrights is seen nowhere so clearly as in the ingenious variety of the framing devices with which they surround their actions, and the methods they adopt for telling their stories by hook or by crook: telescoping the time-sequence of the action by choruses; enlarging it by direct narration from all kinds of characters; sometimes allowing dumb-shows to serve simply in place of narration; sometimes employing shows to parallel the action with thematic *exempla* from history, or with allegories that serve in various ways as guessing games to concentrate attention on the themes. The characters who appear in the shows may be allegorical figures, they may be historical personages quite separate from the story to be told, or they may include, as in the case of *Alcazar*, characters of the play itself, mixed with figures of allegory and supernatural beings.

Certainly Peele's Inductions divide the action into five parts and two of these are marked as acts: the second by the elaborate 'Actus secunda.

Scaena prima', and the fourth as 'Actus 4.' There is, however, very little normative evidence on which we can base an assumption of his intention to accompany them all with shows. Only five earlier extant plays are regularly equipped in that way – *Gorboduc* (1562), *Jocasta* (1566), *The Rare Triumphs of Love and Fortune* (1582), *The Misfortunes of Arthur* (1588), and *Locrine* (1594) – and only three of a later date: *The Whore of Babylon* (1606) and two of Heywood's *Ages* plays, *The Golden Age* (1610) and *The Silver Age* (1611).

The regular division of the action into five parts by choruses is itself the exception rather than the rule in the plays of the public theatre, and does not appear to have been an internalised artistic convention in the mind of dramatists. The Folio text of *Henry V*, like *Alcazar*, introduces each act with a chorus, but it has an Epilogue, which *Alcazar* lacks. *Pericles* has seven choruses and an epilogue, and accompanies three of them with dumb-shows. In this, it parallels the Plot of *2 Seven Deadly Sins*. *Romeo and Juliet* has only two choruses, and Peele's own *David and Bethsabe* has a Prologue and two choruses, although the second chorus, which was perhaps intended to introduce the fifth act of the undivided and imperfect text, is labelled '5. Chorus.' Choric figures appear in a great variety of guises, and choric functions may very often be taken over by messengers, and even by major characters themselves, just as dumb-shows may appear at any point in the story and are not confined to the beginnings or ends of acts.

The variousness in the presentation of dumb-shows, likewise, is too great to allow its formulation as a settled convention. The shows in *Gorboduc*, for example, are emblematic of the action that follows, which they moralise, but they are presented as guessing games, and interpreted only at the end of each act. Their composition, with explications for the printed version, was apparently regarded as a literary exercise in the Middle Temple where the play was performed, and distributed among various authors. Those in *Locrine* are of the same kind, but are interpreted immediately following their presentation. *The Downfall of Robert, Earl of Huntingdon* presents the introductory dumb-show as a mysterious mimed summary of the story thus far, and then replays it in sections with a choric exposition; but this may have been elaborated for publication. The frame Inductions of the five acts of Greene's *James IV* introduce simple divertissements of dance and song into the commentary by Oberon and the wild man Bohun, but the Quarto of 1598 is furnished with an 'appendix' of three dumb-shows, following the first chorus, representing the vanity of worldly pomp in historical episodes. These appear to be alternative Inductions, but it is not certain how or where they are to be fitted into the play. In many other plays dumb-shows serve, in a variety of ways, merely as summarising devices for parts of the story that might often have been represented, without loss of time, as part of the spoken text. Even in manuscripts that have served as prompt-books, or as something closely approximating to prompt copy, there may be directions quite as vague as 'Enter to the bloudy banket'. *John of Bordeaux* has a direction for 'The show as you know', and another for 'The scene of the wiper', which may or may not have been a mime. Printed texts, likewise, very often have the sketchiest directions for the shows that are intended.

The Plot of *2 Seven Deadly Sins* itself is instructive. Only one of its seven choruses is accompanied by a fully described dumb-show. Its very first scene, in which the Sins contest for priority on the stage, may have been a mime. If so, it does not appear to have had a choric accompaniment. The story of Gorboduc (scene iii) is introduced with a narrative show in action, serving as exposition and presumably interpreted by Lydgate. A further chorus within that story follows the direction 'Alarum wth Excurtions', which suggests that a battle itself might be treated as a dumb-show. We have seen a much later example in *Hannibal and Scipio*. The Inductions to the stories of Sloth and Lechery are accompanied only by the passage across the stage of the figure of the Sin to be represented. But there is a show called for within the story of Tereus and Philomel (Lechery, scene xxii) that is accompanied by a speech from Lydgate but remains undescribed in the Plot. It is unlikely that scene xxii could have been a show of the kind that introduces the Gorboduc story. It would appear that Philomela is in prison in scene xx, and Itys is still alive in scene xxi. In scene xxii, Progne has the tapestry ('sampler' in the Plot) in which Philomela has woven the story of her rape, and Philomela enters 'wth Itis hed in a dish.' The dumb-show, then, must surely have represented one or other, or perhaps both, of the two intervening incidents in the *Metamorphoses*: the rescue of Philomela by Procne in the course of a Bacchic festival, or the murder of Itys.[3]

These few observations suffice to show that no reliance can be placed on the appearance or non-appearance of directions for dumb-shows in the play-texts of the period. Dr Mehl's full investigation of the situation in *The Elizabethan Dumbshow* (1965) reveals that the commonest number of shows recorded as accompanying choric Inductions, in the few texts that contain them, is three. This happens to be the number recorded in the text of *Alcazar*, but the fact is without significance. The mere absence of stage-directions in Elizabethan texts is, of course, no evidence in itself of an intention to omit the action, especially when the text describes or strongly implies what is to take place, and it is noteworthy that the Plotter's interpretation of the implied pantomime in *Alcazar*, in every case where we can follow it with reasonable certainty, bears a close relationship to the text.

We cannot divine the playwright's intention, but it is certain that the Plotter aimed to accompany each of the Inductions with a dumb-show, and, as his cast was limited in various ways, because he had fewer boys and partly because he had made other small alterations that led to the surprisingly severe restrictions we have observed, he had simply to regard these shows as – in football parlance – 'time out'. That is to say, while preserving the common rules of cast-management that operate in the narrative episodes of the play, he is forced to break them in minor ways in representing the moral allegories of the Inductions.

For the second of these (II, Induction) he needed little imagination. There is no direction in the text, except for the crying of the ghosts, but the Plotter has taken his programme from the Presenter's speech more or less as it stands. He introduces on the upper stage the drummer-boy of the company as Nemesis, omitting the emblematic property of a 'bloudie whip' which the dramatist's figure of speech had inconveniently thrust into her drum hand. He brings on stage the revengeful ghosts, whose actual appearance seems to be denied by the text, and follows them, more plausibly, with the Furies, bearing their traditional properties, as described. He thus creates slight problems of identity for Kendall, George and Dab. Kendall is appearing here as Abdelmunen's ghost, having played an unidentified Janissary in the mean time. Probably no change of costume is involved. George, too, has been a Janissary, and now appears as a Fury. He must also appear in the following scene in his Janissary's role. Dab appears as his own ghost, but will double into the next scene as Ruben's Young Son. The remaining twenty-three lines of the Presenter's speech allow time for these changes to be physically possible.

For the 'bloudie banket' of the Act IV Induction, the Plotter had perhaps to exercise his inventive powers more actively. The text offers him the skeletal programme:

> Now hardned is this haplesse heathen prince,
> And strengthned by the armes of Portugall,
> And warre and weapons now, and bloud and death
> Wait on the counsels of this cursed king:
> And to a bloudie banket he inuites
> The braue Sebastian and his noble peeres.
> *Enter to the bloudie banket.*

Enough remains of the Plot to show that the Plotter took these directions as simple allegory. A banquet was to be brought in attended by sinister figures representing War, Weapons, and Death, and possibly also a Fury with bloody clothes. The three Furies – Tailor, George, and Parsons – can be employed once again as waiters to carry on the repast of blood, dead men's heads and dead men's bones, and the whole scene introduced by the three black characters, or 'devils': Hunt and Cartwright, who carry the table, and Sam who appears as Death. The guest-list, however, is rather meagre, there being only four diners: Mahamet, Sebastian, Stukeley, and Avero. Sebastian's other 'noble peers' are unavoidably absent, for, as we have seen, the only surviving members of his party are Tailor (Jonas), who is occupied as a Fury, Kendall (Hercules), who is impersonating War, and Dick Jubie (Christophero de Tavora), who is certainly on stage in another role, probably Weapons.

No suspicion falls on the text at this point, and, as an appropriate menu for a bloody banquet is not far to seek, it would appear that the Plotter's 'original' text, if he had one, might not have differed in essentials from the record remaining in the Quarto. My suspicion is that, in attempting to give an account of the text we have, and being obliged to make do with the cast at his disposal, the Plotter was forced into the kind of primitive pantomime that the professional Elizabethan stage had outgrown. All the characters who appear in this show, with the exception of Parsons and Dick Jubie, had been on stage in the previous scene. They have a mere seven lines of the Presenter's speech to change, and must therefore have appeared recognisably in their own persons, transformed into allegorical mode only by the symbolic properties they were able to snatch up in a hurry. Two of the Furies may have been in considerable trouble – the third, Parsons, plays no other role – but perhaps the snaky head-dresses and bloody drapes that were the traditional garb of these emanations of the underworld could be put on and off in seconds. The dramatist may, of course, have had similar problems, except that there is no indication in the text that his Furies appeared more than once. His boys may well have been able to stand in here where the Plotter is forced to use men for attendants.

Of a show for the Act III Induction, there is no sign in the text apart from the opening words:

> Lo thus into a lake of bloud and gore,
> The braue couragious king of Portugall
> Hath drencht himselfe.

It is prefaced only by the direction:

Enter the presenter and speakes.

In comparison with other initial directions, the natural way of reading this is that no show was intended. For the second act, prefaced as it is with an elaborate act and scene heading, there is the direction (unfortunately for Greg's theory, in roman type): 'Alarum. And then the presenter speaketh'. The show of the Furies later enters to him. Moreover, after the shows in the Induction to Act I, occur the forms *And then the presenter speaketh* and *And then the Presenter saith*. For the unmarked fifth act, the direction reads: *Enter the Presenter before the last dumbe show, and speaketh.* His first five lines are a commentary on the preceding scene, just as the words opening Act III, quoted above, appear to be. Thus, apart from the absence of an act heading, there is no natural reason to suppose that directions for a dumb-show preceding his entrance in Act III have disappeared.

It seems to me most likely that the playwright intended this metaphor of a lake of blood and gore as no more than a poetic confirmation of the thematic imagery of blood that informs the early scenes of the play. The action is explicitly introduced as 'a modern matter full of bloud and ruth' and several hyperbolic passages reiterate the theme. In I, i, Ruben Arches frames her tragic songs 'Of death, of bloud, of wreake, and deepe reuenge'. Young Mahamet reports in I, ii the sight of the opposition party taking up their weapons and 'threatning reuenge. / Bloudie reuenge, bloudie reuengefull warre', and Mahamet elaborates the theme (lines 266–72):

Boy, seest here this semitarie by my side,
Sith they begin to bath in blond [sc. bloud],
Bloud be the theame whereon our time shall tread,
Such slaughter with my weapon shall I make,
As through the streame and bloudye chanels deepe,
Our Moores shall saile in ships and pinnaces,
From Tanger shore vnto the gates of Fesse.

The dumb-show introduced in the Plot would appear to add little except a crude literalness to this verbal preparation for the effects of the toils of Mahamet's hypocrisy in which Sebastian is seen gradually to enmesh himself. Sebastian, Stukeley, and Mahamet are carried severally on to the stage while some bloody pantomime is enacted with the properties that are noted in the margin as '3. violls of blood and a sheeps gather'. One thing, however, is added, of which there is no suggestion in the text. Some scales are brought on stage, and we may guess that the fates of all three protagonists are predicted as they are weighed in the balance.[4] No Elizabethan Plotter with fresh memories of *Locrine* or the Mask of Hymen in *The Spanish Tragedy* would have been greatly exercised to restore such a show, if it had been lost. The only question is – did it ever exist in the mind of the playwright?[5]

The Plotter, at any rate, was interested in producing a symmetry of effect that did not necessarily exist in the original concept. He proposes once again to bring on Nemesis, followed by the Furies to carry the scales, and to supplement them with the ghosts and devils, for there are problems of porterage in carrying three grown men rapidly on and off stage. But to do so lands him in trouble of one kind or another. Precisely what kind of trouble can only be gucssed at, for this is the most problematical scene of the whole Plot. As nearly as it can be deciphered, it ran thus:

Enter the Presenter : to [them] him
3. domb shew
Enter Nemesis aboue : Tho : Drom
{to} her 3. Furies bringin{g} in th{
Scales : Georg Somersett { }m Pars{

---

and Robin Tailo{ } to them { } deu{
mr Sam : H Jeffes{
them 3 ghosts {:} w.{
the Furies [Fech]{
& Carrie him out{
Fech in Stukeley{
bring in the Moo{r

There are fragments of paper in the right-hand side of the second column, aligned with the right margin. The marginal line appears to run over the backing sheet, which suggests that there has been some touching up in the mounting, but whether that is so or not, the fragments appear to be in the wrong place. One, on which the final letter 'r' appears, together with indecipherable remains above and below it, should almost certainly be shifted to the space three scenes lower, where it would exactly fit the short line produced by the entry of the Governor of Tangier. We thus have no control for the length of the last six lines above.

The word 'deuills' at the top of the second column certainly ran over the margin. The end of it is, in fact, preserved on a fragment mounted five scenes lower. The number of devils remains in doubt, but as it is probably to the devils that the porterage must fall, because at least one member of each of the other groups is a boy, there may well be four of them. The third was almost certainly William Cartwright, for there is a trace of a tall letter, doubtless a 't', under the 'e' of 'them' in the top line. If there was a fourth, his identity is certain. He would be Mr Hunt. The order of names might then be interchangeable, for his name would also fit the space exactly, leaving Cartwright to run slightly over the margin.

There seems no reason why Hunt may not enter here, for if Sam can, he can. The puzzle is in the introduction of Humphrey Jeffes among the devils. Their original complement in the first dumb-show consisted of Sam, Hunt, and Cartwright, who all appear again in the fourth. Greg logically supposed that the third devil was in fact Anthony Jeffes, but the space is too great for the placement of the 't' in his name. Perhaps he was not technically a devil, since those who are so-called in the first Induction are imagined to be reincarnations of the victims of Abdallas. He is, however, black, as Humphrey is not, and I believe the entry of 'H Jeffes' is, in fact, an error for Anthony. It is not an error that calls for immediate correction, for there are no parts to be made out for a dumb-show and the black characters will, of course, know who they are. Humphrey is certainly available, but the likelihood is that the Plotter intended an entrance of the four black characters other than Mahamet. The Furies are listed in their ordinary roles, and the ghosts will also, of course, be played by the same actors as before: the beginning of Kendall's name is clearly visible.

The action of the show, however, and the disposition of the entrances, bears no relation to anything in the text, apart from the exhibition of blood and gore. The Presenter enters at the beginning in his normal way. But if there were, indeed, no additional lines for him to speak, he would have either to remain mute while the show is in progress, or to speak only the first two and a half lines before the entrance of Nemesis. It is possible that the show may have been introduced at the end of the first ten lines, or at some intermediate stage. There appear to be a number of possible cues, but each will have anticipated matter that is irrelevant to the action. The whole passage runs thus:

> Lo thus into a lake of bloud and gore,
> The braue couragious king of Portugall
> Hath drencht himself, and now prepares amaine

With sailes and oares to crosse the swelling seas,
With men and ships, courage and canon shot,
To plant this cursed Moore in fatall houre,
And in this Catholike case the king of Spaine
Is cald vpon by sweet Sebastian.
Who surfetting in prime time of his youth,
Vpon ambitious poison dies thereon.

The customary form 'Lo thus ... ' may imply that additional matter did exist here, either in the original prompt-book, or written in for the performance of 1598, but it is hard to imagine a form it could have taken that would not render the explicatory language of the lines above pleonastic.

Even if the Presenter had a great deal more to say both before and after the show, the Plotter is in difficuties. Very rapid changes of identity are involved. If the show did exist in some precedent version, there was every reason for cutting it. The Plotter is forced once again to treat his spectacle as 'time out', for all the actors we have supposed to be on stage, with the exception of Dab, Harry, Parsons, and Cartwright, were on stage in the previous scene, and all except the boys and Anthony Jeffes will appear again in the next. As in the fourth dumb-show, the shift into the mode of allegory must largely have been achieved by the manner of action, perhaps by exaggerated and off-beat gesturing, and could have involved only minimal changes of costume. Much must have depended on the audience's willing co-operation. George's quick change into a Fury will hardly conceal the fact that he has just appeared as the County Vinioso and will be on stage again shortly with the Spanish Ambassadors. Robin Tailor must by now be clearly recognisable as Jonas with snaky locks, and his companion Kendall has for the second time to dodge unconvincingly between the roles of Hercules and the ghost of Abdelmunen, without having time for better disguise than 'an old foul sheet'. The devils, of course, like the major characters, are free to make immediate re-entrances, without changing costume, and simply play themselves, being taken indifferently for Moors or devils as the occasion demands.

It is worth reminding ourselves at this point that there is no evidence that the playwright created or anticipated any of the exigencies with which the Plotter struggles in the dumb-shows. A show extending the time of the Act IV Induction, where he has written the direction for the 'bloody banket', would certainly have been of use to him. One of his cast, just as in the Plot, would need to have undergone a major change of identity from a Portuguese Captain to the spy or janissary, Celebin. The 'bloody banket', whatever it may have consisted of, will have helped this transformation, for there are only thirteen lines of the Presenter's speech in which to make the change. No such necessity exists for him at the point of the Act III Induction.

The Plotter, however, has a triple problem in Act III. He has kept Zareo white and thus has to omit III, ii. As a consequence he brings III, iii up against III, i and has to provide for two Portuguese Captains and the

Governor of Tangier only twenty-one lines after the exit of the Spanish Ambassadors, whom he has been forced to double with the Portuguese Lords. His white Zareo enables him to employ George as a Portuguese Lord in II, iv, but George will also be needed to appear as a Spanish attendant in III, i. Thus the Plotter has every incentive to create as great a time-lapse as possible between the two scenes in Portugal that flank the Induction.

The playwright, on the other hand, can fill his own stage-directions in III, i à *la lettre*. He can still play III, ii, and has at least two practical choices for Ambassadors, without depriving Sebastian of any Lords at all. His interest is in moving on as quickly as possible from Sebastian's decision to embark for Africa to the duplicitous offers of Spanish aid, thus to complete the symmetry of his plan to get the Portuguese story moving by the appearance of two *false* embassies, punctuated by the chance arrival of the English party, with its assurance of *true* support. The bloody results of Sebastian's trust in hypocritical promises have been so strongly emphasised in the heavy ironies of the text that there is hardly need at this juncture for a dumb-show to underline them. Moreover, the show proposed for Act IV is clearly a very similar representation of the lake of blood and gore that the Plotter provides for Act III, but at the later point in the play it will serve the purpose of ironising the scenes of enthusiastic preparation for battle that precede it. To the dramatist, the ironising of the narrative is important.

The Plotter was willing to forgo some part of the narrative insistence of the text, some of its more complex political ironies, and, indeed, some of the actual narrative itself, in order to play up the theme of Nemesis in allegory. In her figure, in those of the ghosts of Abdelmunen and the young brethren, and in the appearances of the 'devils', the chain of blood vengeance descending from Mahamet's murderous usurpation is duplicated and kept in the audience's mind more insistently than the playwright appears to have intended. Admittedly, the Induction to Act V of the text still maintains:

> Bloud will have bloud, foul murther scape no scourge,

but by this time the play has also developed a vestigial notion of a more complex fate that leads Stukeley to cry:

> Ah sweet Sebastian, hadst thou been well aduisde
> Thou mightst haue manag'd armes sucsessfully.
> But from our Cradles we were marked all
> And destinate to dye in Affric heere.

The different emphasis placed by the text and the Plot of the idea of Nemesis throws some light on the difficulties editors have found with the dumb-shows in I, Induction. It is in these shows alone that a strict comparison with the Plot is possible and we are able to see how the Plotter deals with actual directions. At first appearance there is considerable divergence between the two accounts, and neither is quite consistent with the text. They run as follows:

The first dumbe shew.
Enter Muly Mahamet and his sonne, and his two young brethren, the Moore sheweth them the bed, and then takes his leaue of them, and they betake them to their rest. And then the presenter speaketh.

The second dumbe shew.
Enter the Moore and two murdrers bringing in his vnkle Abdelmunen, then they draw the curtains and smoother the yong princes in the bed. Which done, in sight of the uncle they strangle him in his chaire, and then goe forth. And then the Presenter saith.

I Domb shew
Enter Muly Mahamet mr Ed: Allen, his sonne
Antho: Jeffes : moores attendant : mr Sam, mr Hunt
& w. Cartwright : ii Pages to attend the moore
mr Allens boy, mr Townes boy : to them 2.
young bretheren : Dab : & Harry: : to them
Abdelmenen w. Kendall : exeunt

The Plotter has taken his cue from the text itself rather than from the printed descriptions of the show. From the first, he brings on Mahamet and his son, as the text implies, with attendants:

Accompanied as now you may behold
With deuils coted in the shapes of men,
Like those that were by kind of murther mumd.

I have already discussed the probable re-arrangement of the text that should be made to this passage, and the lines above represent what I believe to be the true reading. It is, as the Plotter correctly divined, Mahamet's henchmen who are the devils. They appear dressed as men, but they are to be taken as emanations from hell, 'damned wits', the victims of Abdallas's settlement of the succession, murdered because of their nearness 'by kind' to the throne.

The playwright's directions for the first show do not mention the attendants. It must be that the intention was to present a passage of the Moor and the devils across the stage 'with naked sword in hand' (their appearance governed by spoken text), and then to allow Mahamet and his son to re-enter leading in the young brethren. Whichever way one reads the lines above, it is clear from the context that the 'devils' are not the young brethren. *Their* murder has not yet taken place. That is to happen further on:

And lo alas
How lyke poore lambs prepard for sacrifice,
This traitor king hales to their longest home,
These tender Lords his yonger brethren both.

The dumb-shows, then, although called the first and second, are in reality the second and third. The three segments are continuous and are only separated for convenience. The lines above would be more correctly placed immediately before the 'first'. Then, as Mahamet and the murderers re-enter with Abdelmunen, the Presenter would speak the lines below:

His brethren thus in fatall bed behearst,
His fathers brother of too light beleefe,
This Negro puts to death by proud command.

The second dumb-show will then follow and everything is in order.

The Plotter simplifies the arrangement considerably. He brings on all the murderers at the beginning and, as far as we can see, allows the young brethren and Abdelmunen to walk innocently on to the stage of their own accord. In the case of Abdelmunen, that has dramatic point in interpreting the words 'of too light belief' (i.e. of too trusting a nature), but we cannot be sure that the victims are not fetched in. The recording of action within the shows is, as we have seen, quite sketchy, and the same is sometimes true of exits and re-entrances within a scene. In II, iv, for example, no-one leaves the stage to fetch the Moorish Ambassadors, although the quarto has a marginal direction *Exit one*, and, in the same scene, our puzzle over the double command given to Avero may appear quite pointless when we observe that the Plotter dispenses with conductors and simply marks in the entrance of the English party with the direction 'exit moores : manet the rest : to them Stukeley.' It may well be that brief exits and re-entrances of a ceremonial kind go unrecorded in the Plots, and the same may be true of the internal action of this dumb-show.

There is certainly one omission and one addition, however. The Plotter makes no provision for the chair in which Abdelmunen is strangled. Perhaps, like Greg, he missed its meaning. There is no reason in the historical record why Abdelmunen should have been carried in a chair. He was, in fact, slain by an arrow while at prayer in a mosque. But, for the dramatist, as we have seen, it almost certainly makes a connection with the chair, representing the famous litter, in which Abdelmelec is carried in Act V, and in which his corpse is set up with cunning props. That chair will also be put to use as Muly Hamet's throne, and, in this first scene, is perhaps a symbol of Abdelmunen's legitimacy for the dramatist, even if its meaning may not be immediately apparent to the audience. The addition the Plotter makes is of the two black pages who accompany Mahamet, and these are introduced for no necessary reason, but simply because the boys were available and presumably too young to play any other roles. They help to make this first entrance an impressive show of all the 'devils'.

The black characters in the play, as the Plotter recognised, are thus allegorised at their first entrance. They may appear to be men, but they are in some sense, unrecognised by Mahamet, the simulacra of his and his father's victims: vengeful agents of the nemesis that pursues wrongful ambition. Like devils, they helpfully cooperate in leading the Moor to deeper villainies in order to seal his fate. Their victims, in turn, become their associates. It may not be too fanciful to propose that the Plotter's changing of Zareo's colour was not a wholly arbitrary decision, but a consequence of his 'reading' of the play.

The dramatist, however, moves into a more heroic mode after the introduction of Sebastian's story in Act II. By Act V, if somewhat confusedly, he will have replaced the figure of Nemesis with the figure of Fame. Sebastian's ambition we must think of as honourable. No nemesis attends *it*, and his 'tragedie in this tragicke warre' is the result of the deep hypocrisy of his pretended allies. In this, the black contingent, other than Mahamet, play no further part. The playwright, as we have seen, mixes his black and white troops and thus could not easily have maintained the repeated allegorical shift that is to be found in the Plot. His Zareo is a trusty leader of the legitimate forces, and presumably not one of the two murderers introduced in the first scene. His Young Mahamet becomes temporarily a hero to the Portuguese, and, if, as I believe, he is the boy who finds a horse for Mahamet in his flight from the battle, he also shows a fine streak of self-sacrifice. We hear nothing of his ultimate fate, but certainly he neither merits nor earns the ill will of anyone, and appears to be innocent of his father's duplicity. The rest of the blackamoors fight as honest soldiers, no doubt deserving of the epithet 'manly' from their commanders, and are only 'cursed', 'ruthless' and 'barbarous' to their adversaries – whoever, at any given moment their adversaries may happen to be!

In a masterly article on the two texts of *Doctor Faustus*, Michael J. Warren observes that bibliography, at least as it is practised in the elucidation of Elizabethan play-texts, 'is not a relatively accurate scientific activity, but rather a subjective art in which at all times interpretation precedes analysis and deduction'. In the case of the A text of *Doctor Faustus*, he argues, 'once one disabuses one's mind of a 'reported text', one finds merely differences of meaning'.[6] One of the chief aims of textual bibliography was, of course, to put itself at the service of the recovery of the perfect, original text as it left the author's hands. One of its chief effects has been to magnify by accumulation what may be very small and chance differences into large theories of textual corruption. In the case of *Alcazar*, the dumb-shows that introduce Acts III and IV in the Plot, from which such heavy inferences of the existence of a fuller original text have been drawn, prove, on an alternative theatrical hypothesis, to be nothing other than the product of the Plotter's interpretative hand. It is he who simply chooses to maintain a strict colour differentiation between his black and white scenes. Despite the difficulties of identity he thus creates, he is enabled to reconstruct and repeat the allegory of Nemesis with her attendant ghosts, furies and devils in places where there is no sign of them in the text, and where they would, indeed, have been an embarrassment to the dramatist. In so doing, he undoubtedly reveals a perceptive reading of the playwright's intention in the Induction to Act I. It is ironic that his simplified responses to the stage-directions for the shows in that Induction itself have served even further to convince critics and editors of the unsoundness of the text.

Appendix

Cast-lists of public theatre plays from 1497 to 1625

Summary

	Number of plays	Eight cast	Twelve cast	Sixteen cast	Sixteen +cast	Oddball	% Sixteen cast
Derby's	2	1	1	—	—	—	0
Sussex's	2	—	—	2	—	—	100
Queen's	14	2	2	9	1	—	64.2
Admiral's / Prince's	46	—	5	35	5	1	76
Worcester's / Queen Anne's	23	—	1	15	6	1	65
Strange's / Chamberlain's / King's	124	—	26	84	9	5	67
Pembroke's	3	—	—	—	3	—	0
Oxford's	1	—	—	1	—	—	100
Lady Elizabeth's	18	—	8	10	—	—	55
Revels Companies	9	—	—	3	4	2	33
Queen Henrietta's	2	—	—	2	—	—	100
Unknown	21	3	2	10	2	4	48
	265	6	45	171	30	13	64

The earliest notice of a play is often that of its entry in the Stationer's Register. In the following play-tables the dates of entry are given in the third column. I have given no date for the plays that first appeared in the Shakespeare Folio of 1623 or the Beaumont and Fletcher Folio of 1647. These may be assumed to have remained in manuscript in the King's Men's possession until the publication of the Folios, although some few had passed in transcripts to private patrons. Where plays were printed without formal entry they are marked 'N.E.'

For typographical reasons it has not been possible to register the presence of unusual, non-speaking extras. There appear, for example, choristers in no. 12; an uncertain number of devils in nos. 64 and 112; a dog in no. 68; a puppet-show in no. 82; a horse in no. 118; twelve satyrs in no. 174; and Morris dancers in no. 233.

Cast-lists of public theatre plays from 1497 to 1625

Date and author	Play	Date in Stationers' Register	Date of earliest publication	Company	Minimum	Maximum	Probable	Boys	No. of lines
1497 MEDWELL, Henry	**1** *1 & 2 Fulgens and Lucrece*	—	*c. 1512*	Morton's House?	4	5	5	0/2	2,451
1538 BALE, John	**2** *1 & 2 King John*	—	MS. (1560–3)	St Stephens, Canterbury	5	5	5	0	3,360
1555 Anon.	**3** *Jack Juggler*	1562	*c.* 1562–3	Offered for acting (5)	5	5	5	0	1,177
1559 PHILLIP, John	**4** *Patient and Meek Grissil*	1565–6	1566?	Offered for acting (8)	8	8	8	0	2,120
1559 WAGER, W.	**5** *The Longer Thou Livest the More Fool Thou Art*	1568–9	*c.* 1569	Offered for acting (4)	4	4	4	—	1,972
1560 WAGER, W.	**6** *Enough Is as Good as a Feast*	N.E.	*c.* 1565–70	Offered for acting (7)	4	4	4+?	—	1,726
1561 PRESTON, Thomas	**7** *Cambises*	1569–70	*c.* 1569	At Court (?) Offered for acting (8)	6	8	8	4	1,391
1564 B[OWER], R[ichard?]	**8** *Appius and Virginia*	1567–8	1575	Westminster Boys?	5	5+	5+?	2/3	1,502
1567 PICKERING, John	**9** *Horestes*	1567	1567	Rich's or boys at Court? Offered for acting (6)	6+	8+	8	—	1,306
1567 WAGER, W.?	**10** *The Trial of Treasure*	N.E.	1567	Offered for acting (5)	5	5	5	0	1,162
1568 FULWELL, Ulpian	**11** *Like Will to Like*	1568–9	1568	Offered for acting (5)	5	5	5	0	1,274
1568 Anon.	**12** *The Marriage of Wit and Science*	1569–70	*c.* 1569	At Court? Paul's?	6	8	7+	—	1,092
1569 GARTER, Thomas	**13** *The Most Virtuous and Godly Susanna*	1563–9	1578	Offered for acting (8)	7/8	8	7/8	0/1	1,455
1570 Anon. (Preston, T.)	**14** *Clyomon and Clamydes*	N.E.	1599	Queen's	8	9	8+	4	1,254
1572 WOODES, Nathaniel	**15** *The Conflict of Conscience*	N.E.	1581	Offered for acting (5)	5	5	5	0	2,090
1576 WAPULL, George	**16** *The Tide Tarrieth No Man*	22 Oct. 1576	1576	Offered for acting (4)	4	4	4	0	1,940
1577 LUPTON, Thomas	**17** *All for Money*	25 Nov. 1577	1578	Unknown	5	5	5	—	1,471
1579 MERBURY, Francis	**18** *A Marriage between Wit and Wisdom*	N.E.	1579	Offered for acting (6)	4	6	4/6	2/0	1,104
1582 WILSON, Robert	**19** *The Three Ladies of London*	N.E.	1584	Unknown	8	10?	8	3	2,200
1582 Anon. (Munday, A.?)	**20** *The Rare Triumphs of Love and Fortune*	N.E.	1589	Derby's at Court?	8	12	12?	3/10	1,223
1584 Anon. (Munday, A.?)	**21** *Fedele and Fortunio (Two Italian Gentlemen)*	1584	1585	At Court	7	8	6	5	1,807
1585 Anon. (Tarlton, R.)	**22** *2 The Seven Deadly Sins [Henry VI?]*	N.E.	MS., 'Plot' *c.* 1590	Queen's at Court? Strange's	15	16	16	6/7	—
1586 Anon. (Tarlton, R.? Rowley, S.?)	**23** *The Famous Victories of Henry V*	15 May 1594	1598	Queen's at Bull Inn	12	16	16	3	1,712

Cast-lists of public theatre plays from 1497 to 1625 (*cont.*)

Date and author	Play	Date in Stationers' Register	Date of earliest publication	Company	Mini-mum	Maxi-mum	Prob-able	Boys	No. of lines
1587 GREENE, Robert	**24** *Alphonsus, King of Aragon*	N.E.	1599	Unknown	15	16+	16	12	2,174
1587 KYD, T. (revised by Jonson, B.)	**25** *The Spanish Tragedy*	6 Oct. 1592	*c.* 1592	Strange's by 1592	14+	16+	14+	5/8	2,736
		—	1602	(Admiral's in 1597)	14+	16+	16+	6/8	3,021
1587 MARLOWE, Christopher	**26** *1 Tamburlaine the Great*	14 Aug. 1590	1590	Admiral's	14+	16	16	4/6	2,508
1587 PEELE, George	**27** *The Love of King David and Fair Bethsabe*	14 May 1594	1599	Unknown	14	16	?14+	2/4	2,062
1588 LODGE, Thomas	**28** *The Wounds of Civil War*	24 May 1594	1594	Admiral's	24+	25+	25+	2	2,674
1588 MARLOWE, C.	**29** *2 Tamburlaine the Great*	14 Aug. 1590	1590	Admiral's	14	16	16	5+	2,532
1588 PORTER, Henry	**30** *1 The Two Angry Women of Abingdon*	N.E.	1599	Admiral's	11	12	12	4/5	3,097
1588 WILSON, Robert	**31** *The Three Lords and Three Ladies of London*	31 July 1590	1590	Queen's?	16+	19+	19+	10+	2,392
1588 Anon.	**32** *1 Tamar Cam*	—	Copy of MS. Plot 1602	Admiral's	16	16+	16	6	—
1588 Anon. (Peele, G.?)	**33** *1 & 2 The Troublesome Reign of King John*	N.E.	1591	Queen's	14	17	16	8	3,085
1589 GREENE, Robert	**34** *Friar Bacon & Friar Bungay*	14 May 1594	1594	Strange's	15	15+	16	5/6	2,155
1589 MARLOWE C. (revised by Heywood, T.)	**35** *The Jew of Malta*	17 May 1594	1633	Strange's by 1592	15	16	16	4	2,495
1588 MUNDAY, A.	**36** *John a Kent and John a Cumber*	—	Huntingdon MS. 500 1596	Admiral's? Strange's	15	16+	16+	5	1,707
1589 PEELE, George	**37** *The Battle of Alcazar*	N.E.	1594 (text)	Admiral's by 1594	16	16	16	14+	1,591
		—	1598 (Plot)	Admiral's	17	18	17	9	
1589 Anon. (Poss. Shakespeare, W.)	**38** *The Taming of A Shrew*	2 May 1594	1594	Queen's? Pembroke's T/P	10+	12	12	5	1,564
1590 GREENE, Robert	**39** *The Scottish History of James IV*	14 May 1594	1598	Queen's	15+	16−	16	8+	2,593
1590 GREENE, Robert?	**40** *George a Greene, the Pinner of Wakefield*	1 April 1595	1599	Sussex's by 1593	15	17	16	3	1,163
1590 GREENE, R. LODGE, T.	**41** *A Looking Glass for London & England*	5 Mar. 1594	1594 Q4 rev.	Queen's? Strange's	16	16	16	8+	2,376
1590 PEELE, George	**42** *The Old Wive's Tale*	16 Apr. 1595	1595	Queen's	16	16+	16	5/6?	1,190

Cast-lists of public theatre plays from 1497 to 1625 (*cont.*)

Date and author	Play	Date in Stationers' Register	Date of earliest publication	Company	Mini-mum	Maxi-mum	Prob-able	Boys	No. of lines
1590 WILSON, Robert	**43** *The Cobbler's Prophecy*	8 June 1594	1594	At Court?	8	10+	8	4	1,753
1590 Anon.	**44** *The Dead Man's Fortune*	—	1591 (Plot)	Admiral's	15	17	16	7/8	—
1590 Anon (Shakespeare in part)	**45** *Edward III*	1 Dec. 1595	1596	Chamberlain's?	20	21+	21+	4/5	2,654
1590 Anon. (Wilson, R.?)	**46** *Fair Em, the Miller's Daughter*	N.E.	1593?	Strange's	16	16	16	4	1,624
1590 Anon.	**47** *King Leir*	14 May 1594	1605	Queen's & Sussex's	13+	16	16	5/6	2,650
1590 Anon.	**48** *Mucedorus*	—	1598	Queen's? (Later King's 1610)	8	8	8	2/3	1,450
			1606	Offered for acting (8)					
		—	1610		12	12+?	12	8	1,756
1590 Anon. (Kyd, T.?)	**49** *Soliman and Perseda*	20 Nov. 1592	*c.* 1592	Unknown	16	16+	16	6/10	2,405
1591 GREENE, R.	**50** *Orlando Furioso*	7 Dec. 1593	1594	Queen's at Court Strange's	16	16	16	3/5+	1,693
1591 PEELE, George	**51** *Edward I*	8 Oct. 1593	1593	Queen's? Admiral's (1595)	19+	27+	27+	15/16	3,077
1591 W.S. (Peele, G.? Green, R.?)	**52** *Locrine*	29 July 1594	1595	Unknown	16	16	16	10/14	2,280
1591 SHAKESPEARE, William	**53** *2 Henry VI*	12 Mar. 1594	Q. 1594	Pembroke's?	24+	29+	24+	4	2,233
	(*1 Contention betwixt the Two Famous Houses of York & Lancaster*)	—	F. 1623	Chamberlain's?	22	22	22	4	3,466
1591 SHAKESPEARE, William	**54** (*3 Henry VI The True Tragedy of Richard Duke of York*)	19 Apr. 1602	Q. 1595	Pembroke's	22	22	22	8/9	2,114
		—	F. 1623	Pembroke's Chamberlain's?	17	18+	18	8·9	3,246
1591 Anon. (Kyd, T.?)	**55** *Arden of Feversham*	3 Apr. 1592	1591	Unknown	11	12	12	2	2,579
1591 Anon.	**56** *Jack Straw*	3 Oct. 1593	1593	Unknown	14	14+	14+	2	1,175
1591 Anon.	**57** *The True Tragedy of Richard III*	19 June 1594	1594	Queen's	12	12+	12	8	2,243
1592 GREENE, Robert	**58** *1 Selimus* (second part unknown)	N.E.	1594	Queen's	16	16+	16	9	2,572
1592 GREENE, R.? CHETTLE, H.	**59** *John of Bordeaux* or *The Second Part of Friar Bacon*	—	MS. 1592? Alnwick	Strange's?	14+	16	16	5	1,720
1592 MARLOWE, C. (& Rowley, S.?)	**60** *Doctor Faustus*	15 Dec. 1592	1604	Admiral's (by 1594)	12	12+	12+	3	1,514
		—	1616	—	16	16	16	2	2,121

Cast-lists of public theatre plays from 1497 to 1625 (*cont.*)

Date and author	Play	Date in Stationers' Register	Date of earliest publication	Company	Mini-mum	Maxi-mum	Prob-able	Boys	No. of lines
1592 MARLOWE, Christopher	**61** *Edward II*	6 July 1593	1594	Pembroke's 1592–3	20	20+	20+	5	2,839
1592 SHAKESPEARE, William	**62** *The Comedy of Errors*	—	1623	Strange's	15+	16?	16	5	1,946
1592 SHAKESPEARE, William	**63** *1 Henry VI*	—	1623	Strange's?	23	25+	25+	4+	2,984
1592 Anon. (Kempe? Peele? Wilson?)	**64** *A Knack to Know a Knave*	7 Jan. 1594	1594	Ed. Allen & his company + Kemp	12	12	12	2+	1,952
1592 Anon.	**65** *1 Richard II* or *Thomas of Woodstock*	—	*c.* 1592? BM. Egerton 1994	Unknown	16	16	16	5	2,989
1592 MARLOWE, Christopher	**66** *The Massacre at Paris*	N.E.	1594? & MS. frag.	Admiral's Strange's?	13+	16	16	5/6	1,637
1592 SHAKESPEARE, William	**67** *Richard III*	20 Oct. 1597	Q. 1597	Chamberlain's	12	12	12	8	3,481
		—	—	King's	15	16	16	8	4,003
1593 SHAKESPEARE, William	**68** *The Two Gentlemen of Verona*	—	1623	Unknown	8	10	8	3/4	2,324
1593 Anon. (B.J. on T.P.)	**69** *Guy Earl of Warwick*	1620	1661	II Derby's	8	8	8	6/7	1,628
1594 SHAKESPEARE, William	**70** *The Taming of The Shrew*	—	1623	Sussex's? Chamberlain's?	15	17	16	3	2,769
1594 SHAKESPEARE, William	**71** *Titus Andronicus*	6 Feb. 1594	Q. 1594	Derby's Pembroke's Sussex's	16	16+	16	3	1,722
—		—	F. 1623	—	16	16	16	3	2,561
1594 YARRINGTON, Robert	**72** *Two Lamentable Tragedies*	N.E.	1601	Admiral's	14	16	16	5	2,709
1594 Anon. (Geo. Peele?)	**73** *Alphonsus, Emperor of Germany*	9 Sep. 1653	1654	Unknown later King's	16	16	16	10+	2,660
1594 Anon. (Munday? Heywood?)	**74** *A Knack to Know an Honest Man*	26 Nov. 1595	1596	Admiral's	16	16	16	5	1,800
1595 Munday, Dekker, Chettle? Heywood, Shakespeare?	**75** *Sir Thomas More*	—	Original	Unknown	20+	24+	24+	7	*c.* 2,309
		—	Revised MS. BM. Harl. 7368	—	16+	18+	18	7	*c.* 2,333
1595 SHAKESPEARE, William	**76** *Love's Labour's Lost*	N.E.	1598	Chamberlain's	12	12	12	6	2,779

Cast-lists of public theatre plays from 1497 to 1625 (*cont.*)

Date and author	**Play**	Date in Stationers' Register	Date of earliest publication	Company	Mini-mum	Maxi-mum	Prob-able	Boys	No. of lines
1595 SHAKESPEARE, William	**77** *A Midsummer Night's Dream*	8 Oct. 1600	Q. 1600	Chamberlain's	16	16	16	6	2,079
1595 SHAKESPEARE, William	**78** *Richard II*	29 Aug. 1597	1597	Chamberlain's	16	16	16	6	2,858
1595 SHAKESPEARE, William	**79** *Romeo and Juliet*	N.E.	Q.1 1597	Chamberlain's (Hunsdon's)	12	12	12	6/8+	2,270
		—	Q.2 1599		15	16	16	6/7	3,147
1595 Anon. (Shakespeare, W.)	**80** *Edmund Ironside*	—	MS. BM. Egerton 1994	Unknown	16	16+	16+	4/5	1,900
1596 CHAPMAN, George	**81** *The Blind Beggar of Alexandria*	15 Aug. 1598	1598	Admiral's	12	14?	12	8	1,648
1596 JONSON, Ben	**82** *A Tale of a Tub*	7 May 1633	1640	Admiral's?	14	16	16	10	2,732
1596 SHAKESPEARE, William	**83** *King John*	—	1623	Chamberlain's	12	12+	12+	6	2,737
1596 SHAKESPEARE, William	**84** *The Merchant of Venice*	22 July 1598	Q. 1600	Chamberlain's	12	12+	12+	4/5	2,670
		—	F. 1623	King's	16	16	16	5	2,779
1596 Anon. (Heywood, T. in part?)	**85** *Captain Thomas Stukeley*	11 Apr. 1600	1605	Admiral's	16	17	16	4/5	2,985
1597 CHAPMAN, George	**86** *An Humorous Day's Mirth* (*The Comedy of Humours*)	N.E.	1599	Admiral's	16	16	16	6	2,013
1597 JONSON, Ben	**87** *The Case is Altered*	26 Jan. 1609	1609	Unknown. Later Children of Blackfriars and Queen's Revels	15+	16	16	5/6	2,072
1597 SHAKESPEARE, William	**88** *1 Henry IV*	26 Feb. 1598	Q. 1598	Chamberlain's	12	12	12	4	2,858
1597 SHAKESPEARE, William	**89** *2 Henry IV*	23 Aug. 1600	Q. 1600	Chamberlain's (T/P)	16	16	16	6	2,920
		—	F. 1623	—	16	16	16	4/7	3,356
1597 Anon.	**90** *Frederick and Basilea*	—	Plot 1597	Admiral's	12+	12+	12+	4	—
1598 CHETTLE, H. MUNDAY, A.	**91** *The Downfall of Robert, Earl of Huntingdon*	1 Dec. 1600	1601	Admiral's	15	20	17+	4	3,079
1598 CHETTLE H. MUNDAY, A.	**92** *The Death of Robert, Earl of Huntingdon*	1 Dec. 1600	1601	Admiral's	16	16	16	4	2,851
1598 HAUGHTON, William	**93** *Englishmen for My Money*	3 Aug. 1601	1616	Admiral's	15	16+	16	3	2,724
1598 JONSON, Ben	**94** *Every Man in His Humour*	14 Aug. 1600	1601	Chamberlain's	15	16	16	3	3,097
1598 SHAKESPEARE, William	**95** *Much Ado About Nothing*	4 Aug. 1600	Q. 1600	Chamberlain's	16	16	16	5+	2,481

Cast-lists of public theatre plays from 1497 to 1625 (*cont.*)

Date and author	**Play**	Date in Stationers' Register	Date of earliest publication	Company	Mini-mum	Maxi-mum	Prob-able	Boys	No. of lines
1598 CHETTLE, H. DEKKER, T.	**96** *Troilus and Cressida*	—	Plot 1599	Admiral's	15	16	16	?	—
1599 DEKKER, Thomas	**97** *Old Fortunatus*	20 Feb. 1600	1600	Admiral's	12	14+	12*	10+	2,906
1599 DEKKER, Thomas	**98** *The Shoemaker's Holiday*	19 Apr. 1610	1600	Admiral's	16	16	16	5	2,514
1599 DRAYTON, HATHWAY, MUNDAY, WILSON	**99** *1 Sir John Oldcastle*	11 Aug. 1600	1600	Admiral's	16?	?18+	?17	4+?	2,706
1599 HEYWOOD, T.? and others?	**100** *1 & 2 Edward IV* (*1 The Siege of London & The Tanner of Tamworth;*	28 Aug. 1599	1599	Admiral's	15+	16	16	6	2,913
	2 Civil Wars in France?)	—	—	Admiral's	16	16	16	4	3,240
1599 JONSON, Ben	**101** *Every Man out of His Humour*	—	1600	Chamberlain's	15	16	16	5/6	4,555
1598 SHAKESPEARE, William	**102** *As You Like It*	—	1623	Chamberlain's	15	16	16	6	2,841
1599 SHAKESPEARE, William	**103** *Henry V*	4 Aug. 1600	Q. 1600	Chamberlain's	16	16	16	3/5	1,741
					13	13	13	—	(Taylor)
		—	1623	King's	16	16	16	3	3,387
1599 SHAKESPEARE, William	**104** *Julius Caesar*	—	1623	Chamberlain's	15	16	16	3	2,716
1599 WILSON, Robert	**105** *2 Henry Richmond*	—	Plot fragment	Admiral's	16	16	16	4/6	—
1599 Anon.	**106** *Alarum for London* or *The Siege of Antwerp*	27 May 1600	1602	Chamberlain's	16+	16+	16	4	1,734
1599 Anon.	**107** *Look about You*	N.E.	1600	Admiral's	16	16	16	6	3,224
1599 Anon.	**108** *The Thracian Wonder*	29 Nov. 1653	1661	Unknown. Probable boys' play	19	21+	21+	7/8	1,924
1599 Anon.	**109** *A Warning for Fair Women*	17 Nov. 1599	1599	Chamberlain's	16	16+	16	4/6	2,703
1600 CHETTLE, DAY, HEYWOOD	**110** *1 The Blind Beggar of Bednal Green*	14 Sep. 1657	1659	Admiral's	16	16	16	4	2,747
1600 CHETTLE, DEKKER, HAUGHTON	**111** *Patient Grissil*	28 Mar. 1600	1603	Admiral's	14	16	16	5	2,962
1600 HAUGHTON, William	**112** *The Devil and his Dam* or *Grim the Collier of Croydon*	N.E.	1662	Admiral's	12	16	12	4+	2,664
1600 HEYWOOD, Thomas	**113** *The Four Prentices of London*	19 June 1594	1615	Admiral's, Strange's, Queen's at Red Bull	16	16	16	3	2,814
1600 SHAKESPEARE, William	**114** *The Merry Wives of Windsor*	1602	Q. 1602	Chamberlain's	14	16	16	7	1,660
		—	F. 1623	—	16	16	16	7+	2,723
1600 SHAKESPEARE, William	**115** *Twelfth Night* or *What you Will*	—	1623	Chamberlain's	14	14+	14	3/4	2,594

Cast-lists of public theatre plays from 1497 to 1625 (*cont.*)

Date and author	**Play**	Date in Stationers' Register	Date of earliest publication	Company	Mini- mum	Maxi- mum	Prob- able	Boys	No. of lines
1600 Anon. (poss. Chapman, G.)	**116** *Charlemagne* or *The Distracted Emperor*	—	MS. BM. Egerton 1994	Unknown	16?	16?	16?	4	3,360
1600 Anon.	**117** *Lust's Dominion*	N.E.	1657	Admiral's	16	16+?	16	5/7	3,366
1600 Anon.	**118** *Thomas Lord Cromwell*	11 Aug. 1602	1602	Chamberlain's	16	16+?	16	1/2	1,809
1600 Anon. (Dekker, T. in part?)	**119** *The Weakest Goeth to the Wall*	23 Oct. 1600	1600	Oxford's	16	16+?	16	3	2,233
1600 Dekker, T. (Marston, J.?)	**120** *Satiromastix*, or *The Untrussing of the Humorous Poet*	11 Nov. 1601	1602	Paul's and Chamberlain's	15	16	16?	7/8	2,796
1601 Shakespeare, William	**121** *Hamlet*	26 July 1602	Q. 1603	Chamberlain's	12	12	12	3	2,176
		—	Q. 1604	King's	15	16	16	3	3,737
		—	F. 1623		16	16	16	3	3,922
1601 Anon. (Chettle? Heywood?)	**122** *The Trial of Chivalry*	4 Dec. 1604	1605	Derby's, Admiral's?	16	16	16	3/5	2,598
1602 Chettle, Henry	**123** *Hoffman* or *A Revenge for a Father*	26 Feb. 1630	1631	Admiral's	12	16?	16	1/2	2,703
1602 Heywood, T	**124** *How a Man May Choose a Good Wife from a Bad*	N.E.	1602	Worcester's	11	13	12	5/6	2,664
1602 Heywood, T.	**125** *The Royal King and the Loyal Subject*	25 Mar. 1637	1637	Queen Henrietta's in 1637	16	16	16	7	2,553
1602 Shakespeare, William	**126** *All's Well That Ends Well*	—	1623	Chamberlain's	12	12	12	6/8	3,065
1602 Shakespeare, William	**127** *Troilus and Cressida*	7 Feb. 1603	1609	Chamberlain's?	16	18+	16+	5	3,330
1602 Anon. (Heywood, T.?)	**128** *The Fair Maid of the Exchange*	24 Apr. 1607	1607	Unknown, Offered for acting (11)	12	12	12	3	2,571
1602 Anon.	**129** *2 Fortune's Tennis*	—	Plot fragment	Admiral's	15	16	16	4	Plot
1602 Anon. (poss. Dekker, T.)	**130** *The Merry Devil of Edmonton*	22 Oct. 1607	1608	Chamberlain's	12	12+	12+	5	1,563
1603 Heywood, Thomas	**131** *A Woman Killed with Kindness*	N.E.	Q. 1607	Worcester's	14	14	14	6	2,510
		—	Q. 1617	Queen Anne's	15+	16	16	6	2,510
1603 Jonson, Ben	**132** *Sejanus his Fall*	2 Nov. 1604	1605	King's (revised by Johnson)	20+	23+	23+	3/7	3,447
1604 Dekker, T.	**133** *1 The Honest Whore*	9 Nov. 1604	1604	Prince Henry's	16	16	16	4	2,695
1604 Dekker, Webster (and others?)	**134** *Sir Thomas Wyatt*	N.E.	1607	Queen Anne's	16	16	16	3	1,606

Cast-lists of public theatre plays from 1497 to 1625 (*cont.*)

Date and author	Play	Date in Stationers' Register	Date of earliest publication	Company	Minimum	Maximum	Probable	Boys	No. of lines
1604 HEYWOOD, Thomas	**135** *1 If You Know Not Me You Know Nobody* or *The Troubles of Queen Elizabeth* (see part 2 no. 145)	5 July 1605	1606	Queen Anne's	16	24	16+	5	1,850
1604 HEYWOOD, Thomas	**136** *The Wise Woman of Hogsdon*	12 Mar. 1638	1638	Queen Anne's	15	16	16?	6	2,345
1604 MARSTON, J. (add. by Webster)	**137** *The Malcontent*	5 July 1604	1604	Queen's Revels rev. King's	16	16	16	5	1,840 2,505
1604 ROWLEY, Samuel	**138** *When You See Me You Know Me*	12 Feb. 1605	1605	Prince Henry's	15	16+?	16	5/8	3,116
1604 SHAKESPEARE, William	**139** *Measure for Measure*	—	1623	King's	15	16	16	6	2,936
1604 SHAKESPEARE, William	**140** *Othello*	6 Oct. 1621	1622	King's	16−	16−	16?	3	3,259
1604 Anon.	**141** *The Fair Maid of Bristow*	8 Feb. 1605	1605	King's	11	16	12+	4	1,496
1604 Anon.	**142** *1 Jeronimo with The Wars of Portugal*	N.E.	1605	King's? Admiral's	14+	14+	14+	2/4	1,203
1604 Anon. (G. Wilkins?)	**143** *The London Prodigal*	N.E.	1605	King's	14	14+	14+	4	2,035
1605 DEKKER, Thomas	**144** *2 The Honest Whore*	9 June 1630	1630	Prince Henry's	16	16	16	9	3,046
1605 HEYWOOD, Thomas	**145** *2 If You Know Not Me You Know Nobody*	14 Sep. 1605	1606	Queen Anne's	16	16	16	4/5	2,700
1605 SHAKESPEARE, William	**146** *King Lear*	26 Nov. 1607	Q. 1608	King's	16	16	16	3/5	2,900
		—	F. 1623	King's	16	16	16	3/5	3,339
1605 Anon.	**147** *Nobody and Somebody*	8 Jan. 1606	1606	Queen Anne's	16	16	16	4/6	2,275
1606 FLETCHER, John	**148** *The Woman Hater*	20 May 1607	1607	Paul's King's	15	16	16	7/8	2,701
1606 DEKKER, Thomas	**149** *The Whore of Babylon*	20 Apr. 1607	1607	Prince Henry's	16	16+	16+	7/8	2,758
1606 JONSON, Ben	**150** *Volpone* or *The Fox*	N.E.	1607	King's	13	17	16	3/6	3,831
1606 MIDDLETON, Thomas	**151** *A Mad World My Masters*	4 Oct. 1608	1608 1640	Paul's Q. Henrietta's	14+	16	16	4/5	2,277
1606 SHAKESPEARE, William	**152** *Macbeth*	—	1623	King's	16	16	16	4/8	2,563
1606 WILKINS, George	**153** *The Miseries of Enforced Marriage*	31 July 1607	1607	King's	15	16	16−	4/8	2,812
1606 Anon. (Tourneur? Middleton?)	**154** *The Revenger's Tragedy*	7 Oct. 1607	1607/8	King's	16	16	16	3/4	2,653

Cast-lists of public theatre plays from 1497 to 1625 (*cont.*)

Date and author	Play	Date in Stationers' Register	Date of earliest publication	Company	Mini-mum	Maxi-mum	Prob-able	Boys	No. of lines
1606 Anon. (Shakespeare, W., Wilkins, G.?)	**155** *A Yorkshire Tragedy*	2 May 1608	1608	King's	13	16	16?	4	(3,000) est.
1607 Barnes, Barnabe	**156** *The Devils Charter*	16 Oct. 1607	1607	King's	16?	16+?	16	6+	3,231
1607 Day, Rowley, Wilkins	**157** *The Travels of Three English Brothers*	29 June 1607	1607	Queen Anne's at Curtain	16	16+	16+	4/5	2,294
1607 Heywood, Thomas	**158** *The Rape of Lucrece*	3 June 1608	1608	Queen Anne's at Red Bull	15+	16	16	5	2,629
1607 Shakespeare, William	**159** *Antony and Cleopatra*	—	1623	King's	16	16	16	4	3,683
1607 Shakespeare, William	**160** *Timon of Athens*	—	1623	Unacted?	13	16	16−	6	2,621
1608 Dekker, T. Middleton, T.	**161** *The Roaring Girl* or *Moll Cutpurse*	N.E.	1611	Prince Henry's	16	16	16	6	3,170
1608 Shakespeare, William	**162** *Coriolanus*	—	1623	King's	16	16	16	4/6	3,832
1608 Shakespeare, William	**163** *Pericles*	20 May 1608	1609	King's	14+	16	16	4/5	2,447
1609 Fletcher, John with Beaumont, F.	**164** *The Coxcomb*	—	1647	Queen's Revels, later Lady Elizabeth's	12	12	12	8	2,652
1609 Beaumont, F. with Fletcher, J.	**165** *Philaster* or *Love Lies a-Bleeding*	10 Jan. 1620	1620	King's	12	12+	12	5	2,760
1609 Heywood and Rowley	**166** *Fortune by Land and Sea*	20 June 1655	1655	Queen Anne's	16	16+	16	4/5	1,840
1609 Shakespeare, William	**167** *Cymbeline*	—	1623	King's	12+	15+	16	4	4,026
1609 Tourneur, Cyril	**168** *The Atheist's Tragedy*	14 Sep. 1611	1611	King's?	16	16	16	4/5	2,812
1609 Beaumont, F. with Fletcher, J.	**169** *The Maid's Tragedy*	28 Apr. 1619	1619	King's	14	16?	16?	8	2,997
1609 Daborne, Robert	**170** *A Christian Turned Turk*	1 Feb. 1612	1612	King's (?) Queen's Revels	16+	17+	17+?	5	2,368
1609 Heywood, Thomas	**171** *The Fair Maid of the West*	16 June 1631	1631	Queen Anne's	14	14	14	5	2,268
1610 Heywood, Thomas	**172** *The Golden Age*	14 Oct. 1611	1611	Queen Anne's at the Red Bull	16+	16+	16+	8/10	2,431
1610 Jonson, Ben	**173** *The Alchemist*	3 Oct. 1610	1612	King's	12	16	16−	2	3,063
1610 Shakespeare, William	**174** *The Winter's Tale*	—	1623	King's	12	12+	12+	6	3,432
1611 Beaumont F. Fletcher, J.	**175** *A King and No King*	7 Aug. 1618	1619 1625	King's	12 12+	12+ 14	12 14	7/8 7/8	3,382 3,382

Cast-lists of public theatre plays from 1497 to 1625 (*cont.*)

Date and author	**Play**	Date in Stationers' Register	Date of earliest publication	Company	Mini-mum	Maxi-mum	Prob-able	Boys	No. of lines
1611 COOKE, John	**176** *Greene's Tu Quoque*	N.E.	1614	Queen Anne's	15	16+	16	8	3,060
1611 DEKKER, Thomas	**177** *Match Me in London*	8 Nov. 1630	1631	Queen Anne's	14+	14+	16	5	2,497
1611 DEKKER, Thomas	**178** *If It Be Not Good, the Devil Is in It*	N.E.	1612	Queen Anne's at the Red Bull	18+	18+	18+	7+	2,808
1611 FLETCHER, John	**179** *The Woman's Prize* or *The Tamer Tamed*	4 Sep. 1646	1647	Unknown (King's in 1633)	14	14+	14+	8	3,480
1611 HEYWOOD, Thomas	**180** *The Brazen Age*	N.E.	1613	Queen Anne's and King's	16+	16+	16+	10/12	2,552
1611 HEYWOOD, Thomas	**181** *The Silver Age*	N.E.	1613	Queen Anne's and King's	16+	16+	16+	10+	2,793
1611 JONSON, Ben	**182** *Catiline His Conspiracy*	N.E.	1616	King's	20+	20+	20+	5	3,570
1611 MIDDLETON, Thomas	**183** *A Chaste Maid in Cheapside*	8 Apr. 1630	1630	Lady Elizabeth's	11+	12	12+	10	2,317
1611 SHAKESPEARE, William	**184** *The Tempest*	—	1623	King's	13+	15	16	6/7	2,382
1611 Anon. (Middleton, T.?)	**185** *The Second Maiden's Tragedy*	9 Sep. 1653	MS. BM. Lansdowne 807	King's	10	12	12	3/4	2,365
1612 R.A. (Armin, R.?)	**186** *The Valiant Welshman*	21 Feb. 1615	1615	Prince's	16	16	16	4	1,986
1612 FLETCHER, J. (with BEAUMONT, F.?)	**187** *The Captain*	—	1647	King's	12	12+	12	7	3,536
1612 HEYWOOD, T.	**188** *1 The Iron Age*	N.E.	1632	King's and Queen's	20+	20+	20+	12+	2,808
1612 WEBSTER, John	**189** *The White Devil*	N.E.	1612	Queen Anne's	15+	16+	16	8	3,006
1613 FLETCHER, John	**190** *Bonduca*	—	1648 and BM. MS. Add. 36758	King's	16	17−	16	5	2,989
1613 BEAUMONT, F. and FLETCHER, J.	**191** *The Scornful Lady*	19 Mar. 1616	1616	Queen's Revels	12	12	12	8/9	2,866
1613 FLETCHER, John	**192** *The Honest Man's Fortune*	—	1647	Lady Elizabeth's	12	13	12+	5	2,807
		—	MS. Dyce 9	King's	16	16	16	7	*c.* 2,607
1613 MIDDLETON, Thomas	**193** *No Wit, No Help Like a Woman's*	9 Sep. 1653	1657	Lady Elizabeth's?	16	16	16	6	3,960
1613 FLETCHER, John (& Shakespeare, W.?)	**194** *Henry VIII*	—	1623	King's	21+	21+	21+	7/8	3,310
1613 FLETCHER, John (& Shakespeare, W.)	**195** *The Two Noble Kinsmen*	8 Apr. 1634	1634	King's	14	16	16	10	3,256
1614 FLETCHER, John	**196** *Valentinian*	—	1647	King's	16	16	16	6	3,411

Cast-lists of public theatre plays from 1497 to 1625 (*cont.*)

Date and author	**Play**	Date in Stationers' Register	Date of earliest publication	Company	Mini-mum	Maxi-mum	Prob-able	Boys	No. of lines
1614 FLETCHER, John	**197** *Wit Without Money*	25 Apr. 1639	1639	Lady Elizabeth's? Queen Henrietta's	12	12	12	4/5	2,204
1614 JONSON, Ben	**198** *Bartholomew Fair*	N.E.	1631	Lady Elizabeth's	16+	16+	16+	6	3,619
1614 WEBSTER, John	**199** *The Duchess of Malfi*	N.E.	1623	King's	12	12	12	7	3,580
1614 FLETCHER, John	**200** *The Faithful Friends*	—	MS. Dyce 10	Unknown	16	16+	16	5/6	2,859
1615 MIDDLETON, T.	**201** *The Witch*	—	MS. Malone 12	King's	16	16−	16	5/6	2,189
1615 FLETCHER, John	**202** *Love's Pilgrimage*	—	1647	King's	16	16	7	6	3,502
1615 FLETCHER, John	**203** *The Nice Valour* or *The Passionate Mad-man*	—	1647	Unknown	14	14	14	8	2,100
1616 JONSON, Ben	**204** *The Devil is an Ass*	N.E.	1631	King's	15+	18−	16?	5	3,586
1616 MIDDLETON, Tho.	**205** *The Widow*	12 Apr. 1652	1652	King's	15	16	16	3	2,625
1617 DABORNE, R.	**206** *The Poor Man's Comfort*	20 June 1655	1655 MS. BM. Egerton 1994	Queen Anne's	16	16	16	4	2,276
1617 FLETCHER, John	**207** *The Mad Lover*	—	1647	King's	16	16+	16	8	2,370
1617 FLETCHER, John	**208** *The Queen of Corinth*	—	1647	King's	16	16	16	8	2,850
1617 FLETCHER, John	**209** *Thierry and Theodoret*	N.E.	1621	King's	16	16	16	4	2,664
1617 MIDDLETON, T. and ROWLEY, W.	**210** *A Fair Quarrel*	N.E.	1617	Prince's	13+	17−	16	6	2,713
1617 WEBSTER, John	**211** *The Devil's Law Case*	N.E.	1623	Queen Anne's	15	16	16	4	3,116
1618 FLETCHER, John	**212** *The Loyal Subject*	—	1647	King's	16	16	16	6	3,500
1618 FLETCHER, FIELD, MASSINGER	**213** *The Knight of Malta*	—	1647	King's	16	16	16	6/7	2,850
1618 MIDDLETON, T.	**214** *Hengist King of Kent* or *The Mayor of Queenborough*	4 Sep. 1646	1661 MS. Duke of Portland Welbeck Abbey	Unknown King's in 1641	20+	25+	25+	5	2,627
1618 MIDDLETON, T.	**215** *The Old Law*	—	1656	Unknown	16	16	16	7	2,865
1618 SHIRLEY, H.	**216** *The Martyred Soldier*	15 Feb. 1637/8	1638	Queen Anne's?	16+	16	16	5/6	2,375
1618 Anon.	**217** *Swetnam the Woman Hater*	17 Oct. 1619	1620	Queen Anne's	15	16	16	7/8	2,988

Cast-lists of public theatre plays from 1497 to 1625 (*cont.*)

Date and author	Play	Date in Stationers' Register	Date of earliest publication	Company	Mini-mum	Maxi-mum	Prob-able	Boys	No. of lines
1618 'I.C.'	**218** *The Two Merry Milkmaids*	22 May 1620	1620	Red Bull Revels	16	16	16	5	3,543
1619 Field, N.	**219** *The Fatal Dowry*	16 Mar. 1632	1652	King's	15	20	16+	4	2,923
1619 Fletcher, John	**220** *The Humorous Lieutenant (Demetrius and Enanthe)*	—	1647 MS. BM. Harlech	King's	18+	21+	21+	8	3,328
1619 Fletcher, John	**221** *The Bloody Brother*	4 Oct. 1639	1639	King's	16	16	16	6	2,964
1619 Fletcher, John	**222** *The Little French Lawyer*	—	1647	King's	15	16	16	5	2,800
1619 Fletcher, J and Massinger, P.	**223** *Sir John van Olden Barnavelt*	—	MS. BM. 18653	King's	16	16+	16?	4+	3,003
1619 Fletcher, John (or Ford, J.)	**224** *The Laws of Candy*	—	1647	King's	16	16	16	4	2,310
1619 Rowley, William	**225** *All's Lost by Lust*	27 Sep. 1632	1633	Lady Elizabeth's Queen Henrietta's	16	16	16	6	2,442
1620 Dekker, T.	**226** *The Virgin Martyr*	7 Dec. 1621	1622	Red Bull Revel's?	15	16	16	5	2,840
1620 Fletcher, John	**227** *Women Pleased*	—	1647	King's	12	12+	12	9	2,567
1620 Fletcher, John	**228** *The Custom of the Country*	—	1647	King's	16	16	16	6	3,172
1620 Fletcher, John	**229** *The Double Marriage*	—	1647	King's	18	18+	18+	6	3,273
1620 Fletcher, John	**230** *The False One*	—	1647	King's	12	12	12	5	2,752
1620 May, Thomas	**231** *The Heir*	N.E.	1622	Red Bull Revels	21	24+	24+	3	2,109
1620 Anon.	**232** *The Costly Whore*	2 Nov. 1632	1633	Red Bull Revels?	14	14+	14+	5	2,174
1620 Dekker, Ford, Rowley	**233** *The Witch of Edmonton*	7 Apr. 1621	1658	Prince's	15	16+	16+	6	2,248
1621 Fletcher, John	**234** *The Island Princess*	—	1647	King's	16+	16+	16+	6	2,800
1621 Fletcher, John	**235** *The Pilgrim*	—	1647	King's	15	16	16	4/6	2,680
1621 Fletcher, John	**236** *The Wild Goose Chase*	4 Sep. 1646	1652	King's	12	12	12	7/8	2,368
1621 Massinger, Philip	**237** *The Duke of Milan*	20 July 1622/3	1623	King's	11−	12	12	5	2,499
1621 Massinger, Philip	**238** *The Maid of Honour*	16 Jan. 1631/2	1632	Lady Elizabeth's?	16	16+	16	4	2,637
1621 Massinger, Philip	**239** *A New Way to Pay Old Debts*	10 Nov. 1632	1633	Lady Elizabeth's?	12	12	12	6	3,040

Cast-lists of public theatre plays from 1497 to 1625 (*cont.*)

Date and author	Play	Date in Stationers' Register	Date of earliest publication	Company	Mini-mum	Maxi-mum	Prob-able	Boys	No. of lines
1621 MIDDLETON, T.	**240** *Anything for a Quiet Life*	N.E.	1662	King's	15	16	16	8	2,014
1621 MIDDLETON, T.	**241** *Women Beware Women*	9 Sep. 1653	1657	King's?	14	19	14	10	3,583
1622 CHAPMAN, George, revised Shirley, J.	**242** *Chabot, Admiral of France*	24 Oct. 1638	1639	Lady Elizabeth's	16	16+	16	2	2,646
1622 FLETCHER, John	**243** *Beggars' Bush*	—	1647 MS. Folger Shakespeare Library J.B.5.	King's	16	16	16	5	2,790
1622 FLETCHER, John	**244** *The Prophetess*	—	1647	King's	16	16	16	6	2,800
1622 FLETCHER, John	**245** *The Sea Voyage*	—	1647	King's	16	16	16	6	2,500
1622 FLETCHER, John	**246** *The Spanish Curate*	—	1647	King's	15	16	16	5	3,168
1622 MARKHAM, E.	**247** *Herod and Antipater*	22 Feb. 1621/2	1622	Red Bull Revels	28	30	30+	7/10	2,946
1622 MIDDLETON, T.	**248** *The Changeling*	19 Oct. 1652	1653	Lady Elizabeth's	12	12	12	5	2,926
1622 ROWLEY, W.	**249** *A Match at Midnight*	15 Jan. 1633	1633	Red Bull Revels (T/P Children of the Revels)	14−	14	14	6	2,225
1622 Anon.	**250** *The Two Noble Ladies*	—	MS. BM. Egerton 1994	Red Bull Revels	13+	16?	16	3	2,110
1623 DEKKER, T.	**251** *The Welsh Ambassador*	—	MS. Cardiff Pub. Lib. 8719	Lady Elizabeth's?	11	12	12	3	2,310
1623 FLETCHER, John	**252** *The Wandering Lovers (The Lovers' Progress)*	—	1647	King's	16	18	16+	4	2,910
1623 FLETCHER, John	**253** *The Maid in the Mill*	—	1647	King's	16	16+	16	6/8	2,905
1623 MASSINGER, P.	**254** *The Bondman*	12 Mar. 1623/4	1624	Lady Elizabeth's	15	16	16	5	3,040
1623 MIDDLETON, T., ROWLEY, W.	**255** *The Spanish Gypsy*	28 Jan. 1624	1653	Lady Elizabeth's	12+	12	12+	6	2,418
1624 DAVENPORT, R.	**256** *The City Nightcap*	N.E.	1661	Lady Elizabeth's	16	17	16	5	2,337
1624 FLETCHER, John	**257** *Rule a Wife and Have a Wife*	Lic. 19 Oct. 1624	1640	King's	12	12	12	9	2,517
1624 FLETCHER, John	**258** *A Wife for a Month*	—	1647	King's	16	16	16	8	2,800
1624 HEYWOOD, T.	**259** *The Captives*, or *The Lost Recovered*	—	MS. BM. Egerton 1994	Lady Elizabeth's	15+	16	16	4/5	3,125 (reduced to 2,912)

Cast-lists of public theatre plays from 1497 to 1625 (*cont.*)

Date and author	Play	Date in Stationers' Register	Date of earliest publication	Company	Mini-mum	Maxi-mum	Prob-able	Boys	No. of lines
1624 MASSINGER, P.	**260** *The Renegado*	22 Mar. 1629/30	1630	Lady Elizabeth's	15	16	16	3	2,988
1624 MASSINGER, P.	**261** *The Parliament of Love*	29 June 1660	MS. Dyce 39	Lady Elizabeth's	16	16	16	5/6	2,496
1624 MIDDLETON, T.	**262** *A Game at Chess*	N.E.	1625? and MSS.	King's	14	16	16	4/5	2,498
1624 WEBSTER, J.	**263** *Appius and Virginia*	13 May 1654	1654	King's and Queen's Young Company	21	22+	22+	4	2,591
1624 Anon.	**264** *Nero*	Lic. 15 May 1624	1624 and MS. BM. Egerton 1994	Unknown	16	16	16	3	2,356
1624 DAVENPORT, R.	**265** *A New Trick to Cheat the Devil*	28 Mar. 1639	1639	Queen Henrietta's	16	16	16	8	2,669
1624 FLETCHER, John	**266** *The Chances*	—	1647	King's	12	12	12	6/9	2,640
1625 FLETCHER, John	**267** *The Elder Brother*	24 Mar. 1636/6	1637 MS. BM. Egerton 1994	King's	12	12+	12	5/6	2,150
1625 HEYWOOD, Thomas	**268** *The English Traveller*	15 July 1633	1633	Queen Henrietta's	16	16	16	8	2,747
1625 MASSINGER P.	**269** *Love's Cure* or *The Martial Maid*	—	1647	King's	16	16	16	6	2,886
1625 SHIRLEY, J.	**270** *The School of Compliment* (Love Tricks)	25 Feb. 1630/1	1631	Lady Elizabeth's	16	16	16	7/9	2,886
1626 DEKKER, T.	**271** *The Noble Spanish Soldier* (see *The Welsh Ambassador*)	16 May 1631	1634	Admiral's	15	17	16	4	2,516
1626 FLETCHER, John	**272** *The Noble Gentleman*	Lic. 3 Feb. 1626	1647	King's	12	12	12	5	2,554
1626 FLETCHER, John	**273** *The Fair Maid of the Inn*	—	1647	King's	16	16	16	9	2,784
1626 JONSON, Ben	**274** *The Staple of News*	14 Apr. 1626	1631	King's	16+	18	16+	10	3,776
1626 MASSINGER, P.	**275** *The Roman Actor*	Lic. 11 Oct. 1626	1629	King's	15	16	16	5	2,318
1626 MASSINGER, P.	**276** *The Unnatural Combat*	14 Feb. 1638/9	1639	King's	15	16	16	7	2,664
1626 MAY, Thomas	**277** *Cleopatra, Queen of Egypt*	26 Oct. 1638	1639 MS. BM. Royal 18 C. vii	Unknown	20	25	24/25	3	2,685

The Text of The Battle of Alcazar (1594)

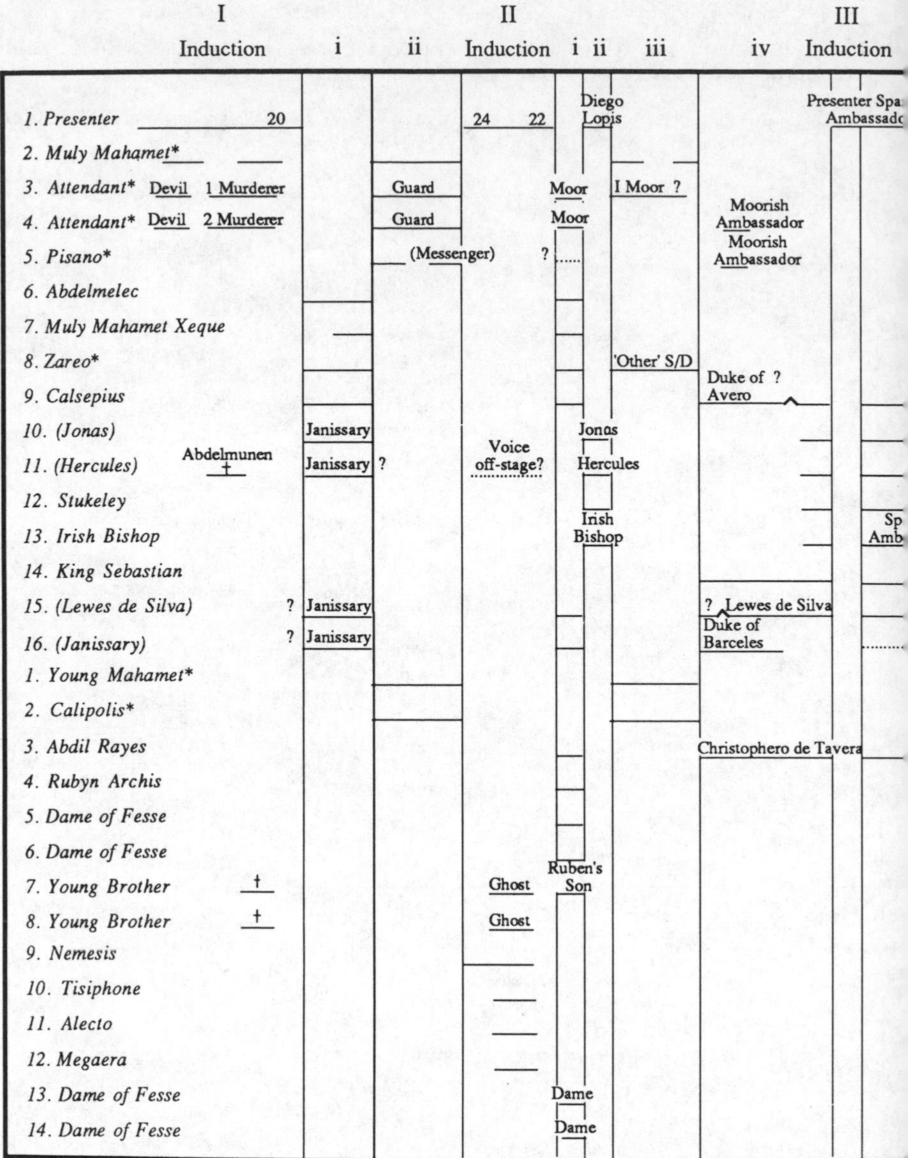

I
Induction
i
ii
II
Induction
i ii
iii
iv
III
Induction
1. Presenter
20
24
22
Diego
Lopis
Presenter Spa
Ambassado
2. Muly Mahamet*
3. Attendant*
Devil
1 Murderer
Guard
Moor
I Moor ?
4. Attendant*
Devil
2 Murderer
Guard
Moor
Moorish
Ambassador
Moorish
Ambassador
5. Pisano*
(Messenger)
?
6. Abdelmelec
7. Muly Mahamet Xeque
8. Zareo*
'Other' S/D
Duke of ?
Avero
9. Calsepius
10. (Jonas)
Janissary
Jonas
Abdelmunen
Voice
off-stage?
11. (Hercules)
Janissary ?
Hercules
12. Stukeley
Irish
Bishop
Sp
Amb
13. Irish Bishop
14. King Sebastian
15. (Lewes de Silva)
? Janissary
? Lewes de Silva
Duke of
Barceles
16. (Janissary)
? Janissary
1. Young Mahamet*
2. Calipolis*
3. Abdil Rayes
Christophero de Tavera
4. Rubyn Archis
5. Dame of Fesse
6. Dame of Fesse
7. Young Brother
Ghost
Ruben's
Son
8. Young Brother
Ghost
9. Nemesis
10. Tisiphone
11. Alecto
12. Megaera
13. Dame of Fesse
Dame
14. Dame of Fesse
Dame

* = Actor in black make-up; † = Character killed or reported dead; —^— =Actor leaves stage and returns imme
a dotted line = character doubtfully on stage or wrongly assigned.

11 Skeleton cast plan of the Text of *The Battle of Alcazor*

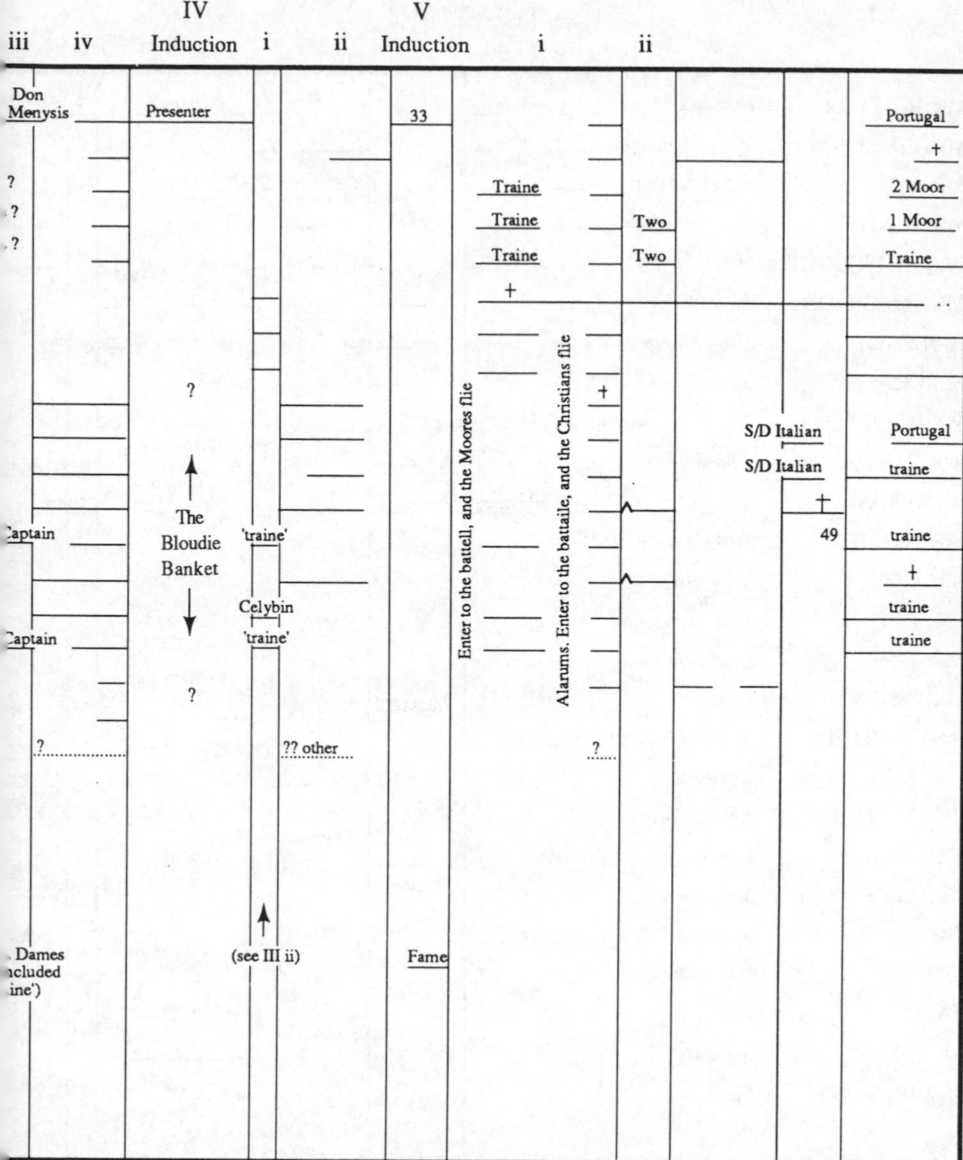

IV
V
iii
iv
Induction
i
ii
Induction
i
ii
Don Menysis
Presenter
33
Portugal
2 Moor
1 Moor
Traine
Traine
Traine
Two
Two
Traine
?
The Bloudie Banket
'traine'
Celybin
'traine'
Captain
Captain
Enter to the battell, and the Moores flie
Alarums. Enter to the battaile, and the Christians flie
S/D Italian
S/D Italian
49
Portugal
traine
traine
traine
traine
?? other
(see III ii)
Fame
Dames
ncluded
ine')

Plot of The Battle of Alcazar (1598)

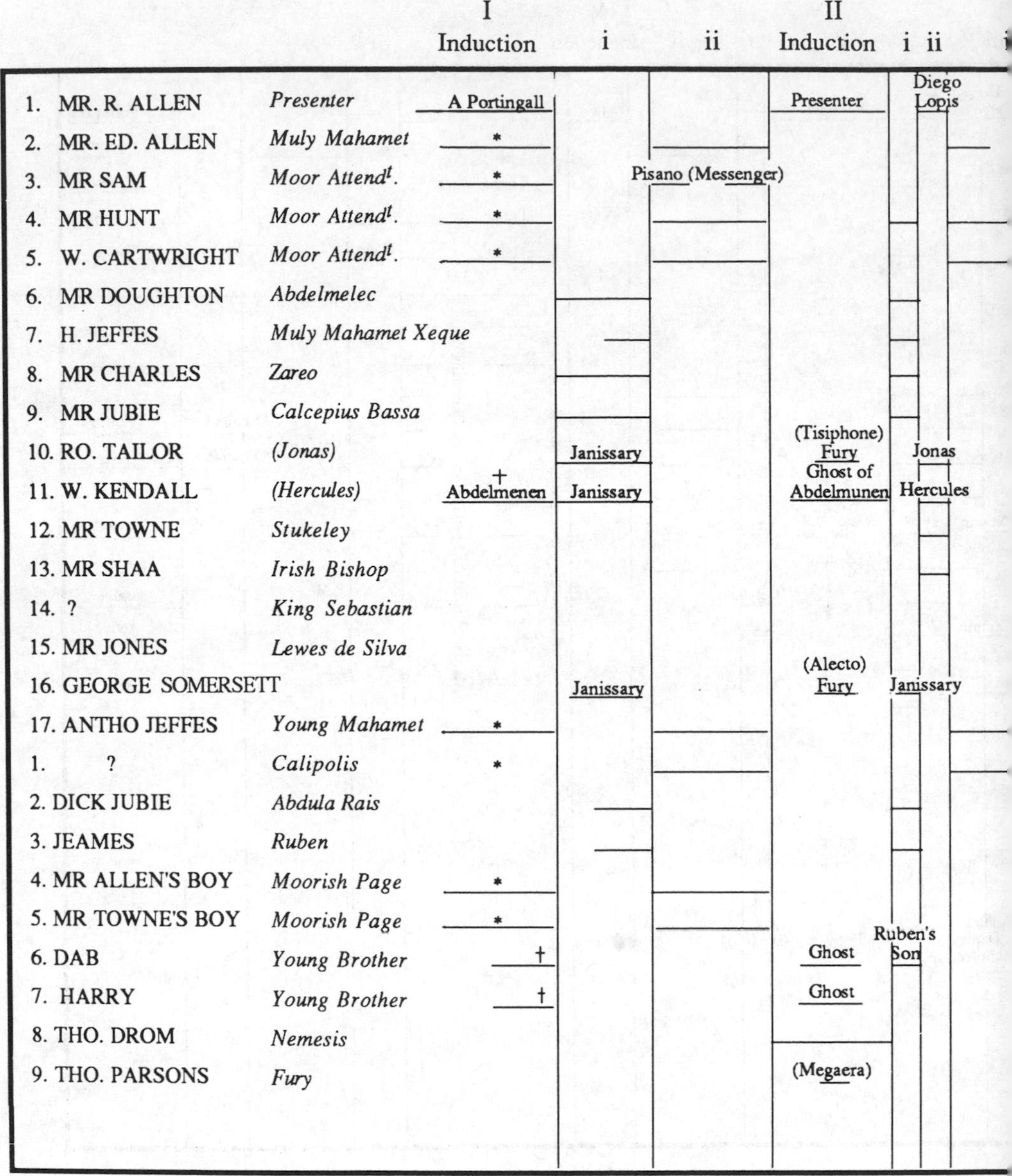

I
Induction
i
ii
II
Induction
i
ii
1. MR. R. ALLEN
Presenter
A Portingall
Presenter
Diego Lopis
2. MR. ED. ALLEN
Muly Mahamet
3. MR SAM
Moor Attend[t].
Pisano (Messenger)
4. MR HUNT
Moor Attend[t].
5. W. CARTWRIGHT
Moor Attend[t].
6. MR DOUGHTON
Abdelmelec
7. H. JEFFES
Muly Mahamet Xeque
8. MR CHARLES
Zareo
9. MR JUBIE
Calcepius Bassa
10. RO. TAILOR
(Jonas)
Janissary
(Tisiphone) Fury
Jonas
11. W. KENDALL
(Hercules)
Abdelmenen
Janissary
Ghost of Abdelmunen
Hercules
12. MR TOWNE
Stukeley
13. MR SHAA
Irish Bishop
14. ?
King Sebastian
15. MR JONES
Lewes de Silva
16. GEORGE SOMERSETT
Janissary
(Alecto) Fury
Janissary
17. ANTHO JEFFES
Young Mahamet
1. ?
Calipolis
2. DICK JUBIE
Abdula Rais
3. JEAMES
Ruben
4. MR ALLEN'S BOY
Moorish Page
5. MR TOWNE'S BOY
Moorish Page
6. DAB
Young Brother
Ghost
Ruben's Son
7. HARRY
Young Brother
Ghost
8. THO. DROM
Nemesis
9. THO. PARSONS
Fury
(Megaera)

* = Actor in black make-up; † = Character killed or reported dead;
‿ =Actor leaves stage and returns immediately; a dotted line = character doubtfully on stage or wrongly assi

12 Skeleton cast plan of the Plot of *The Battle of Alcazar*

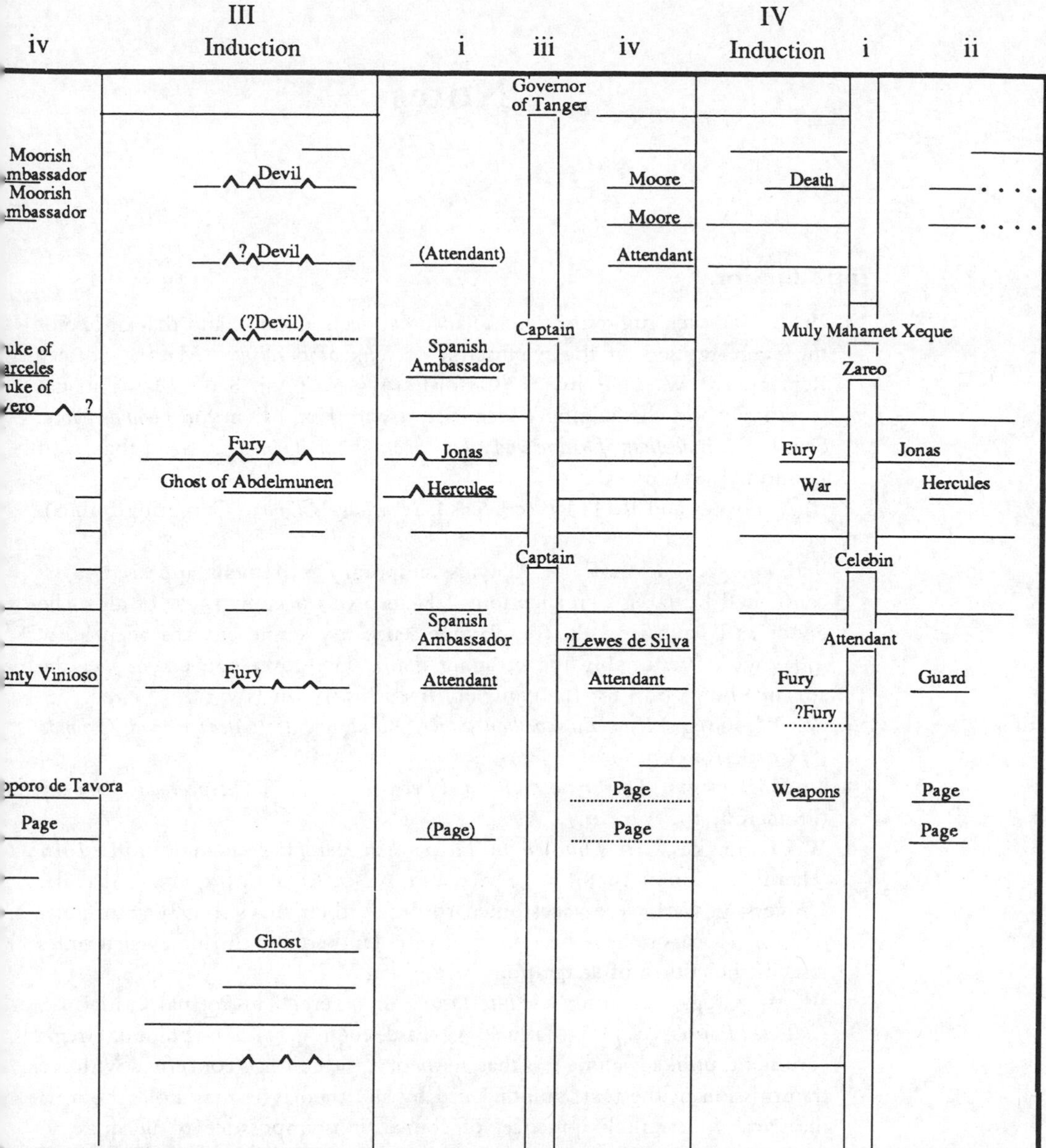

III
IV
iv
Induction
i
iii
iv
Induction
i
ii
Governor of Tanger
Moorish
mbassador
Moorish
mbassador
Devil
Moore
Death
Moore
?Devil
(Attendant)
Attendant
(?Devil)
Captain
Muly Mahamet Xeque
uke of
arceles
uke of
vero
?
Spanish Ambassador
Zareo
Fury
Jonas
Fury
Jonas
Ghost of Abdelmunen
Hercules
War
Hercules
Captain
Celebin
Spanish Ambassador
?Lewes de Silva
Attendant
nty Vinioso
Fury
Attendant
Attendant
Fury
Guard
?Fury
poro de Tavora
Page
Weapons
Page
Page
(Page)
Page
Page
Ghost

Notes

Introduction

1. W. L. Renwick suggests a resemblance between Hand C and that of one of the Stage-revisers of the manuscript of *John of Bordeaux*. Malone Society Reprint, ed. W. L. Renwick (Oxford, 1935–6), p.vii. Scott McMillin has tentatively and challengingly identified it with Hand D in *Sir Thomas More*. See *The Elizabethan Theatre and 'The Book of Sir Thomas More'* (Ithaca and London, 1987), p. 158.
2. R. A. Foakes and R. T. Rickert (eds.), *Henslowe's Diary* (Cambridge, 1968), pp. 16–19.
3. Ibid., p. 83. The myth of Alleyn's temporary retirement appeared to be confirmed by Greg's emendation of Henslowe's note in 1597 'of all suche goods as I haue Bowght for playnge sence my sonne edward allen leafte [p]laynge'. Presumably the meaning is that Henslowe had taken over the advance budgeting for the company from his son-in-law.
4. W. W. Greg, *Two Elizabethan Stage Abridgements: Alcazar and Orlando* (Oxford, 1923), p. 99.
5. T. W. Baldwin, *The Organisation and Personnel of the Shakespearean Company* (Princeton, 1927), p. 197.
6. W. T. Jewkes, *Act Division in Elizabethan and Jacobean Plays, 1583–1616* (Hamden, Conn., 1958), p. 40. See also, p. 50: 'The impression is that the University Wits were accustomed to divide their plays, but their original division appears to have been in some cases tampered with, and even at times lost, in the course of adaptation for the stage.'
7. W. W. Greg, 'Webster's *White Devil*. An Exercise in Formal Criticism', *Collected Papers*, ed. J. C. Maxwell (Oxford, 1966), p. 21. The point of Greg's comment, unlike Malone's, is that, in theory, the editor is concerned with the transmission of the text, uninfluenced by any theory he may hold about its theatrical function. In practice, of course, it is impossible to be quite so objective.
8. A. W. Pollard and J. D. Wilson, 'The "stolne and surreptitious" Shakespeare Texts', *Times Literary Supplement*, 1919 (*Henry V*, 13 March, p. 134; *Merry Wives*, 7 August, p. 420; *Romeo and Juliet*, 14 August, p. 343).
9. C. T. Prouty, '*The Contention*' *and Shakespeare's* '*2 Henry VI*' (New York, 1954).
10. J. K. Walton, *The Quarto Copy for the First Folio Shakespeare* (Dublin, 1971), p. 16.
11. H. Craig, *A New Look at Shakespeare's Quartos* (Stanford, 1961), p. 117.
12. See Cicero's paradox, attributed to Scipio: 'numquam se minus otiosum esse,

quam cum otiosus; nec minus solum quam cum solus est'. H. A. Hudson (ed.), *de officiis* (Cambridge, 1898). Noted by Mary Lord, who comments: 'That a complex linguistic pattern of this sort should survive when the meaning of the line is lost [in Q.2], is a phenomenon quite unlike the kind of variation commonly attributed to a reporter.' *The Relationship between Q1 and Q.2 of 'Romeo and Juliet'* (unpublished M.A. thesis, Monash University, 1976), p. 170.

13. Cited in E. Honigmann, *The Stability of Shakespeare's Text* (London, 1965), p. 2.
14. Ibid., p. 2.
15. F. Bowers, *On Editing Shakespeare* (Charlottesville, 1966), p. 11.
16. A. Hart, *Stolne and Surreptitious Copies* (Melbourne, 1942), p. 157.
17. Ibid., p. 152.
18. Greg, *Alcazar and Orlando*, p. 46.
19. P. Massinger, *Believe as You List*, ed. C. J. Sisson, Malone Society Reprint (Oxford, 1927), p. 99. It is important to note that this so-called 'properties' list is in fact a list of *writings* to be made out by the Plotter. Some of these are merely property letters, but one is 'a writing out of the booke', that is, a letter to be read on stage, containing the actual text. The list tends strongly to confirm the argument advanced in these pages that the making out of the Plot, in conjunction with the Book, had, as its first object, the preparation of the written documents concerned with the performance, including, of course, the actors' scrolls.
20. The manuscript is in the hand of Ralph Crane who acted as scribe for the King's Men for some years. Some of the casting annotations and alterations appear to be in his hand. Greg believed all may have been. Howard-Hill distinguishes fifty-three in a Stage-reviser's hand (these being distinct from the annotations of Sir George Buc, Master of the Revels), and suggests that there may have been close collaboration between the scribe and the book-keeper. (*Sir John van Olden Barnavelt*, ed. T. Howard-Hill, Malone Society Reprint (Oxford, 1979–80), pp. vi–vii.
21. D. Bevington, *From 'Mankind' to Marlowe* (Cambridge, Mass., 1962), p. 5.
22. Cited in E. K. Chambers, *The Elizabethan Stage* (Oxford, 1923), vol. II, p. 364 n. 1.
23. W. A. Ringler, 'The Number of Actors in Shakespeare's Early Plays', *The Seventeenth Century Stage*, ed. G. E. Bentley (Chicago, 1968), p. 121.
24. L. Glickfeld, *Interludes of Art* (unpublished Ph.D. thesis, Monash University, 1970), pp. 87–91.
25. There must, however, have been some very odd cases. In Day's *The Blind Beggar of Bednal Green* (1600), an Admiral's play, in which some of the principal characters must have made their first entrances in doubled minor roles, Gloster and the Cardinal of Winchester first appear *disguised* as their own servants. It is probable that Winchester would have had to appear at the end of Act III doubling genuinely as his own servant.
26. To extend this argument as far as the claim that the Princess of France in *Love's Labours Lost* was played 'not by a small graceful boy, but by a large ungainly man' (Ringler, 'Numbers of Actors', p. 130), is to stretch credulity to its utmost limits. The play is clearly written for a cast of twelve men and six boys.
27. Foakes and Rickert (eds.), *Henslowe's Diary*, pp. 287–8. The 'Plot' runs:

1. Sce Wm Wor: & Ansell & to them ye plowghmen
2. Sce: Richard Q. & Eliza: Catesbie, Louell, Rice ap tho: Blunt, Banester
3. Sce: Ansell Dauye Denys Hen: Oxf: Courtney Bourchierf & Grace to them Rice ap Tho: & his Soldiors
4. Sce: Mitton Ban: his wyfe & children
[6. Sce:]
5. Sce: K Rich: Catesb: Louell. Norf. Northumb: Percye

With the help of the chronicle and ballad material on which the story is based, it is possible to guess that this establishes an acting complement of sixteen men and four boys.

28. J. Wright, *Historia Histrionica* (1699), cited in Chambers, *The Elizabethan Stage*, vol. IV, pp. 370–2.
29. G. Sorelius, '*The Giant Race before the Flood*', Studia Anglistica Upsaliensia, 4 (Uppsala, 1966), pp. 37ff.

1 The logic of entrances

1. W. W. Greg, *Two Elizabethan Stage Abridgments, Alcazar and Orlando* (Oxford, 1923), pp. 142–200. Reproduced in facsimile in W. W. Greg, *Dramatic Documents from the Elizabethan Playhouses* (Oxford, 1931, rep. 1969), vol. II, Reproductions and Transcripts.
2. L. Hotson, *Shakespeare's Wooden O* (London, 1959).
3. The Stage Prologue to *The Staple of News*, C. H. Herford, P. Simpson and E. Simpson, *Ben Jonson* (Oxford, 1938, rep. 1954), vol. VI, p. 282.
4. R. A. Foakes and R. T. Rickert (eds.), *Henslowe's Diary* (Cambridge, 1968), pp. 319–21. See also T. J. King, *Shakespearean Staging, 1599–1642* (Cambridge, Mass., 1971), p. 2. Tom King's findings are that there were 'no significant differences in the staging requirements of the various companies, and that the stage equipment needed was much simpler than had been thought'.
5. *Epicoene or The Silent Woman*, IV, v, 29–34, ed. Herford and Simpson, *Ben Jonson*, vol. V, p. 236.
6. *Jonsonus Virbius* (London, 1638), ed. Herford and Simpson, *Ben Jonson*, vol. XI, p. 453.
7. T. Dekker, *The Guls Horn-Booke* (London, 1609). The Temple Classics (London, 1905, rep. 1941), pp. 32–3.
8. W. Poel, *Shakespeare in the Theatre* (London, 1913, rep. New York, 1968), p. 51.
9. Ibid., p. 41.
10. M. Doran, *Endeavors of Art. A Study of Form in Elizabethan Drama* (Madison, 1954), pp. 210ff.

2 Plotting from the texts

1. Scott McMillin's hope that the opening 500 lines of a play 'might be used as an index of each play's casting size' (*The Elizabethan Theatre and 'The Book of Sir Thomas More'* (Ithaca and London, 1987), pp. 86–90) turns out, according to the rules advanced here, to be illusory. I have not, unfortunately, seen his complete count up to 1610, but the limiting scene as I define it rarely occurs within the first quarter of any play. Very often major characters or sets of characters who cannot thereafter double have not even appeared by line

500. That is certainly the case, for example, with Sebastian and four members of the English party in the text of *Alcazar*, and of the very actors who play three of those roles in the Plot. It is also true, according to his method, which accounts only for speaking characters, of Northumberland, Ross, and Willoughby in *Richard II*. His appeal to the Plots of *1 Tamar Cam* and *2 Seven Deadly Sins* to confirm his figures is dubious at best. We have no way of distinguishing the speaking actors in any scene of those Plots, or of estimating the number of lines spoken; and his acceptance of the identification list of boys and men in Foakes and Rickert's *Henslowe* ignores the fact that in *2 Tamar Cam*, the latest of the Plots, at least three of the 'boys' play only adult male roles. Nevertheless, I believe McMillin is right in identifying *More* as originally a large-cast play, probably belonging to the Strange's-Admiral's company, and reduced in the process of revision; but my figures for the limiting scenes of both versions, taking account of all actors said to be on stage, do not suggest the probability either of its earlier possession by the Queen's Men or of its later association with the Admiral's. My guess is that the companies involved were the Strange's-Admiral's combination and Pembroke's company of 1597.

2. See Massinger, *Believe as You List*, ed. C. J. Sisson, Malone Society Reprint (Oxford, 1927–8), line 1,225; A. Munday, *The Death of Robert Earl of Huntingdon*, ed. J. C. Meagher, Malone Society Reprint (Oxford, 1967), lines 1760–70.
3. J. Tatham, *Knavery in All Trades*, Act III, D4^{v}, E1^{r}. Cited in G. E. Bentley, *The Jacobean and Caroline Stage* (Oxford, 1941–68), vol. I, p. 318.
4. *Histriomastix* (1610). Tudor Facsimile Texts
5. W. W. Greg (ed.), *The Book of Sir Thomas More*, Malone Society Reprint (Oxford, 1911, rev. H. Jenkins, 1961), p. 32.
6. E. K. Chambers, *The Elizabethan Stage* (Oxford, 1923), vol. II, p. 57.
7. Bentley, *The Jacobean and Caroline Stage*, vol. V, pp. 1,092–3.
8. J. T. Murray, *English Dramatic Companies 1558–1642* (New York, 1910, rep. 1963), vol. II, p. 356.
9. Bentley, *The Jacobean and Caroline Stage*, vol. I, pp. 286–7.

3 The travelling companies

1. W. W. Greg, *Two Elizabethan Stage Abridgements* (Oxford, 1913), p. 15.
2. The records are, of course, very incomplete. That is to say that records are missing in particular towns for many years together and in some towns, where the presence of troupes may be assumed, altogether. Giles E. Dawson has argued (Malone Society, *Collections VII*, pp. xxvi-xxvii) that in Kent, where 'a year that is without player payments in one town shows normal activity in other towns, the only probable explanation is that the blanks in the record were caused rather by the failure of the towns to pay than by failure of the players to appear or refusal of official permission for performance'. Payment of gratuities certainly seems to have been a matter of grace and favour, not of obligation, and companies that were not so rewarded would tend to leave no trace.

   It seems to me an unsafe inference to go further, as David Galloway and John Wasson do (Malone Society, *Collections XI*, p. xii) to suppose that 'some troupes with questionable credentials or reputation preferred not to present themselves to the authorities', if that is understood to be more than a general comment about human nature. The fact that companies are so frequently paid for *not* playing must mean that there was reasonably comprehensive control, at least in the major towns, and that all touring players must normally have been required to exhibit their licences. In 1639, R.Willis, recalling a youthful visit to a performance of a Morality Play in *Mount Tabor* or *Private Exercises of a Penitent Sinner*, set down the situation as it must have obtained in his memory over more than sixty years:

> In the City of *Gloucester* the manner is (as I think it is in other like corporations) that when Players of Enterludes come to towne, they first attend the Mayor to enforme him what noble-mans servants they are, and so to get licence for their publike playing; and if the Mayor like the actors, or would shew respect to their Lord and Master, he appoints them to play their first play before himselfe and the Aldermen and Common Counsell of the city; and that is called the Mayors play, where every one that will comes in without money, the Mayor giving the players a reward as hee thinks fit to shew respect unto them.

There are instances of fraudulent companies who did present bogus credentials. See below.

3. J. T. Murray, *English Dramatic Companies. 1558–1642*(New York, 1910, rep. 1963), vol. II, p. 316. At Norwich in 1584–5 Essex's Men took the town's reward for not playing, but played nevertheless. It was resolved never to give that company another reward. In 1590, in consequence of a similar incident, the leader of Beauchamp's troupe was gaoled (Murray, *Dramatic Companies*, vol. II, p. 336).
4. Ibid., vol. I, p. ix.
5. Ibid., vol. II, p. 285.
6. Ibid., vol. II, pp. 396–7.
7. Ibid., vol. II, p. 214. Other titles in the same year were *Myngs*, *The Queen of Ethiopia*, *The Court of Comfort* and *Quid Pro Quo*.
8. Murray, *Dramatic Companies*, vol. II, pp. 163–5.
9. Ibid., vol. II, p. 331.
10. Ibid., vol. II, p. 320.
11. The warrant of The Lord Chamberlain, the Earl of Pembroke, of 20 November 1622, recalling all expired licences, which also complains of the 'di^{vse} and sundry playes and shewes wch for ye most p^{t} are full of scandall and offence both against the Church and State', commands the corporations that 'to the utmost of yor power you doe forbid and suppresse all such playes shewes motions feates of actiuity sights and euery ofthem vnt^{ll} they shalbe approved lycensed and authorised by the said Sr John Astley or his said Deputy in man^{r} aforesaid who are appointed by his mâ^{tie} vnder the greate seale of England to that end and purpose Herein fayle not as you will answer the contrary at yo' p$^{'ills}$'. (Copy made by the Clerk at Norwich in the Mayor's Court Book. Murray, *Dramatic Companies*, vol. II, pp. 351–2.).
12. The special Patent of Commission for Edmund Tilney as Master of the Revels, dated 24 December 1581, remained in force as the formal declaration of the powers of the Master until at least 1622. See E. K. Chambers, *The Elizabethan Stage* (Oxford, 1923), vol. IV, pp. 285–7 (Appendix D).
13. Ibid., vol. II, p. 358.
14. The corporations quibbled wherever they could. In one town an 'Italian motion' was forbidden leave to exhibit because it was thought to have been made in London.

15. Murray, *Dramatic Companies*,vol. II, p. 252.
16. Pembroke's circular letter of 16 July 1616, recalling all duplicates or exemplifications of licences, names three companies (the Queen's Men, the Children of the King's Revels and the Prince Palatine's) who have separated and taken out duplicate patents, and 'severally ... with vagabonds and such like idle persons, haue and doe vse and exercise the quallitie of playinge in diuerse places of this Realme to the great abuse and wronge of his Maiesties Subjects' (Chambers, *Elizbethan Stage*, vol. IV, p. 344, Appendix D). The patents of these companies were to be confiscated and sent to the Lord Chamberlain and the players bonded to appear before hlm.
17. G. E. Bentley, *The Jacobean and Caroline Stage* (Oxford, 1941–68), vol. I, p. 14.
18. Murray, *Dramatic Companies*, vol. I, p. 168. Cf. Bentley, *Jacobean and Caroline Stage*, vol. I, pp. 50–1.
19. It has been assumed that the company of tumblers travelled under Symons and that the Duttons led the acting troupe (Chambers, *Elizabethan Stage*, vol. II, p. 111). Probably the reverse is true. The point is of some importance, for, on the assumption that Symons' (later Laneham's) company was the less dignified, the payments to the Queen's Men appear to fluctuate wildly and the players often to receive much less than the acrobats. Possibly both companies continued their feats of activity, but I suspect the company that gained smaller rewards (their standard reward was ten shillings) did no more than that. Certainly the satirical verses about the Duttons cited in Chambers, *Elizabethan Stage*, vol. II, p. 98, suggest that they were primarily fiddlers and rope-dancers, although Symons had also presented 'activities' at Court in the 1580s. If, however, the Duttons were the touring acrobats, the record would show some consistency. At Bath, 1588, a payment was approved to the Queen's Men on 29 July of 23*s*., and on 13 August of 17*s*. In the same year appears 'more given by Mr Mayor to the quenes men that were tumblers', 10*s*. At Leicester, 6 November 1588: 'certain of' the Queen's Men are paid 10*s*. and in the following May 'others moe' 10*s*. 8*d*., but in 1590 Queen's men are paid 40*s*. against Worcester's 20*s*. At Nottingham in 1588–9 both Symons's and Dutton's companies are paid 20*s*. At Dover one company is paid 10*s*., but other Queen's companies between 20*s*. and 40*s*. At Marlborough the payment in 1590 is 10*s*., but payments here were generally small. At Bridgnorth in 1590 is the record: 'Bestowed upon the Q. players at the dancing on the rop by debenter' 10*s*. At Cambridge, 1592, Queen's are paid 10*s*., against Strange's 20*s*., but in the following year receive 20*s*.and 26*s*. 8*d*. At Coventry, in 1591–2, Queen's receive between 20*s*. and 40*s*. for each of three visits, against 10*s*. to Strange's and Worcester's, but 'Mr Duttons players' get only 5*s*. At Southampton Queen's and Sussex's were given 30*s*. on Shrove Sunday, 1591, while, on 27 June, Dutton's was given 20*s*. At Faversham, 1590–1, Queen's and Essex's were paid 20*s*., and another Queen's company 10*s*. At Maidstone, likewise, one Queen's company was regularly paid about half as much as the other.
20. R. A. Foakes and R. T. Rickert (eds.), *Henslowe's Diary* (Cambridge, 1968), p. 7.
21. Chambers, *Elizabethan Stage*, vol. II, p. 14.
22. W. W. Greg, *The Editorial Problem in Shakespeare* (Oxford, 1942), p. 56.
23. Chambers, *Elizabethan Stage*, vol. II, pp. 247–60.

24. Ibid., vol. I, p. 12. For the petition below, see vol. IV, pp. 311–12.
25. Ibid., vol. II, pp. 312–13.
26. Ibid., vol. I, p. 121.
27. We do not know how many, if any, others of the later Admiral's company were also touring with Strange's. John Pyk (Pigg), Alleyn's boy, was certainly with him and wrote a charming letter to his mistress from Bristol. Thomas Downton may also have been of the party.
28. The Admiral's Men appear in 1592 at Bath, Ipswich (where they joined with Derby's), Leicester, Norwich, and Shrewsbury. At Leicester their reward was 8*s*., about half that of Pembroke's and a third of Queen's. They had 20*s*. at Norwich, where they are the only company recorded (but where Queen's regularly got 40*s*.), and 10*s*. at Shrewsbury. In 1593 we find them in combination with Mordern's (Morley's?) at York and with Strange's at Shrewsbury, where, as in the previous year, they also played independently for a reward of 10*s*. and, in 1594, with the players of 'L. Norris' at Bath.

    Strange's, meanwhile, visited Canterbury, Bath, Gloucester, and Coventry, in 1592, and appear to have done well everywhere but at Gloucester. Unless they are to be identified as 'therll of Darbys' company playing with the Admiral's at Ipswich, they did not amalgamate with others until the joint Shrewsbury performance in 1593. Chambers seems to have believed that all the above records relate to a single company, recorded under alternative names, but if the size of the town rewards means anything at all that is hardly possible. It is not unreasonable to assume that the depleted Admiral's may have been strongly tempted to adapt their repertory in these lean years, but, as we shall see, a depleted company could not have played *Alcazar*.
29. Murray, *Dramatic Companies*, vol. II, p. 392.
30. Bentley, *Jacobean and Caroline Stage*, vol. I, p. 14.
31. Chambers, *Elizabethan Stage*, vol. IV, p. 316.
32. Murray, *Dramatic Companies*, vol. II, p. 233.
33. Chambers, *Elizabethan Stage*, vol. IV, p. 247, citing Crosse, *Vertues Commonwealth* (1603).

4 The Plotter at work

1. J. Q. Adams, 'The Author-Plot of an Early Seventeenth Century Play', *The Library*, series 4, no.26 (1945–6), 17–25.
2. The scribe's copy for the manuscript of *John of Bordeaux* was written in verse (now copied as prose) which normally ran at about fifty lines to the page. This can be calculated from a number of accidentally repeated catchwords. The regular sequence of the verse pagination is dislocated by the prose comic scenes, which are clearly interpolated additions. These, in turn, contain matter that is lost, after having been deleted and replaced by variant phrases, thus showing that at least some of the additional material is original composition.
3. G. E. Bentley, *The Jacobean and Caroline Stage* (Oxford, 1941–68), vol. II, pp. 519–20.
4. D. Bradley, 'The Ignorant Elizabethan Author and Massinger's *Believe as You List*', *Sydney Studies in English*, 2 (1976–7), 98–125.
5. R. A. Foakes and R. T. Rickert (eds.), *Henslowe's Diary* (Cambridge, 1968), p. 100.

6. W. W. Greg, *Henslowe Papers* (London, 1907, rep. New York, 1975), pp. 73, 78.
7. G. E. Bentley, *The Profession of Dramatist in Shakespeare's Time. 1590–1642* (Princeton, 1971), pp. 242, 263.

5 Interpreting the Plots

1. W. W. Greg, *Dramatic Documents of the Elizabethan Playhouses* (Oxford, 1931), p. 123.
2. Ibid., p. 137.
3. W. W. Greg, *Two Elizabethan Stage Abridgements: Alcazar and Orlando* (Oxford, 1923), p. 45.
4. Ibid., p. 99.
5. Ibid., p. 47.

6 *Alcazar*: the text and the sources

1. W. W. Greg, *Two Elizabethan Stage Abridgments: Alcazar and Orlando* (Oxford, 1923), facing p. 122.
2. Ibid., p. 213. Greg perfectly well understood Poel's principle that an actor on stage at the end of one scene does not enter immediately in the next, and, in fact, uses it here to subvert the text. In his imaginary casting for a reduced company, it will explain both the cutting of the silent Moor attendant from II, iii, on the grounds that he will be needed to appear as Barceles in the following scene, and (we are led to assume) the reviser's intention to remove de Silva in particular from the Portuguese party, because he cannot have been the 'other'who remains on stage with Stukeley at the end of III, i. Both interpretations contradict the stage-directions, and are, of course, entirely hypothetical.
3. Peele's panegyrical *Farewell* to this expedition (1589) possibly refers to *Alcazar* as one of the delights the departing troops are leaving behind. See C. T. Prouty (ed.), *The Life and Works of George Peele*, vol. I, pp. 220–3.
4. Modern historians reckon the force as between 16,000 and 17,000, accompanied by an almost equal number of camp-followers, but the sources known to Peele give absurdly large figures.
5. The germ of the idea of Mahamet's hypocrisy is not hard to derive from the sources, but it is given particular emphasis in J. Centellas, *Les Voyages et Conquestes des Roys de Portugal* (Paris, 1578), pp. 48–9.
6. See *A True Historicall discourse of Muly Hamets rising to the three Kingdoms of Moruecos, Fes and Sus* (London, 1609): 'There is another title of dignitie termed Sheck, attributed to the chiefe man of everie familie or cast. Neither doth the Kings eldest sonne scorne the title, signifying that he is the prime or best blood of the royal kindred.'
7. The German translation of Conestaggio (1589) has 'Molucco'.
8. H. F. Conestaggio, *Dell'Unione del Regno di Portogallo alla Corona di Castiglia* (Genova, 1585), Lib. 2, Istoria di Portogallo, p. 41.
9. Ibid., trans. Edward Blount? *The History of the Uniting of the Kingdom of Portugal to the Crown of Castile* (London, 1600), p. 41.
10. *The Famous History of Captain Thomas Stukeley* has 'Sirus'(= 'Sus'?), Malone Society Reprint, line 2,373, but the names in that play are worse garbled in

the printing-house than those in *Alcazar*, although it is not a suspect text. The Trojan stories, or, perhaps, the lines of his own lost play of *Iphigenia*, were clearly running in Peele's head as he wrote. The birthplace of Achilles may naturally have presented itself as a place-name.

11. Greg, *Alcazar and Orlando*, p. 106.
12. See R. Simpson, *The School of Shakespeare* (New York, 1878), vol. I.
13. A. Munday, *The English Roman Life* (London, 1590), ed. P. J. Ayres (Oxford, 1980), p. 50.
14. William Pullen's report to Burleigh, P.R.O., State Papers Domestic, Addenda, Elizabeth, vol. XXV, no. 95.
15. Thomas Mansell, writing from Pisa to Ed. Mansell, 15 March 1578. Cecil MSS. Hatfield House, vol. CLX, f. 120.
16. Conestaggio, *Dell'Unione*, Lib. 1, p. 15. My translation.
17. A more specific account of the destruction of the city is in B.M. Sloane MSS. 61, ff. 3.4: 'the inhabitants being proud and exceeding in all other wickedness, the Lord sent an army of lyons upon them, whoe sparing neither man woman nor child, but consuming all ... took the city in possession to themselves.'
18. Ben Jonson, *Poetaster*, III, iv, 346–52. C. H. Herford, P. Simpson and E. Simpson (eds.), *Ben Jonson* (Oxford, 1932, rep. 1954), vol. IV, p. 256.
19. An African flavour for this Roman scene may have been prompted by a passage about oath-taking among the Abyssinians derived from Peter Pigafetta's translation of Leo Africanus. Povy's translation (1600), ed. Robert Brown, Hakluyt Society, Series I, vols. XCII-XCIV (London, 1896), runs: 'the partie to be deposed goeth accompanied by two priests, carrying with them fire and incense to the church-doore, whereon he layeth his hand; and then the priests adjure him to tell the truth, saying: If thou swear falsely, as the lyon devoureth the beasts of the forest, so let the divell devoure thy soule ... and as fire burneth up wood, so may thy soule enter into Paradise'. The passage is not in Leo.
20. Thus showing that Sebastian's 'aide that once was offered and refusde' (II, Ind., 353), contrary to Greg's opinion, never had any part in the play. The dramatic *given* of the scene is Sebastian's *mistrust*, inconsistent with the report of a previous offer of help that has crept in from the source material at the earlier point.
21. Greg's suspicions are aroused by the speech prefix *Legate* for the second Ambassador. A Papal Legate had, indeed, brought to Portugal the customary Bull for operations against the Infidel in 1573, but the Legate in the play speaks for King Philip. He is surely so called because the word in Freigius is always 'legatus', and 'legate' is so perfectly common an alternative in Elizabethan usage that examples ought to be needless. In *Alphonsus, King of Aragon*, the lords in Act IV are sent as 'Legats to god Mahomet', and recall a visit from 'the stately legate of the Persian King'. Even Milton recalls being received in Paris by 'the noble Thomas Scudamore, Viscount Sligo, legate of King Charles' (*Second Defence of the English People*, 1654).
22. What may be sufficient time for a costume change will, of course, vary according to the kind of action implied, and is, as Gary Taylor remarks in *Modernising Shakespeare's Spelling with Three Studies of Henry V* (Oxford, 1979), pp. 73–4, 'a matter of judgment'. He cites Ringler's observation that Jessica changes into boys' attire in seventeen lines between II, v and II, vi in

The Merchant of Venice. There are, however, twenty-five lines allowed for this change. One does not have to suppose, as Ringler does (having deducted, by some odd arithmetic, seven lines for the ascent), that the boy playing Jessica changes and *then* climbs the stairs. It is a hasty change, and it will not matter if it looks like it. Jessica, moreover, is not disguising herself from the audience or from the characters on stage. I have not found cases of genuine changes of identity under about twenty-seven lines. A test case is Face in *The Alchemist* (1610), who is an expert at disguising, and the faster the funnier; but is never allowed less than twenty-seven lines to change, unless Tim Mares is correct (F. H. Mares (ed.), *The Alchemist*, The Revels edition, London, 1967, note. p. 123.) in ignoring the break between Acts III and IV; in which case Face has to change on stage from his Captain's outfit to his 'Lungs' costume in only twenty lines. I think this strains the dialogue and that Jonson's act divisions are intended.

23. The eccentric time-scheme that Peele adopts suggests either careful calculation or great carelessness. I believe he wanted to play up the suggestions of Spanish deceit by prolonging the delay at Cadiz, and to waste no time in moving on to the battle once the army was in Africa.
24. J. Polemon, *The Second Book of Battailes* (London, 1587, rep. Amsterdam, The English Experience Series, no. 483, 1972), X2^{v}.
25. Ibid., Y2^{r}.
26. T. Freigius, *Historia de Bello Africano* (Nuremberg, 1580) A5^{r}. 'See, too, the crowns of three kings, fallen to the ground! Who was it urged the noble king to attack the infidel Moors with untried sword? What kind of faith was this? Did not the signs in the heavenly watchtower presage this disaster to any enlightened mind? Was the Comet a false prophet, with its blazing tail stretched out through the house of the celestial realm?' I am indebted to Professor David Rankin for the elucidation of this rather obscure poem.
27. Ibid., A4^{v}.
28. A. W. Pollard, 'The Manuscripts of Shakespeare's Plays', *The Library*, 3rd Series, no. 26., 7 April 1916, p. 214.

7 The Plotter under pressure

1. Anthony Jeffes is mentioned as a boy player in Europe in 1595, in the company of Robert Browne, under the protection of the Landgrave Maurice of Hesse. See J. Limon, *Gentlemen of a Company* (Cambridge, 1985), p. 107. If he is the Anthony Jeffes baptised on 14 December 1578 at St Saviour's Southwark, he was then presumably sixteen or seventeen years old, and would have been nineteen or twenty when he played Young Mahamet. See E. K. Chambers, *The Elizabethan Stage* (Oxford, 1923), vol. II, p. 324. Jeffes should perhaps be counted as a seventeenth man.
2. De Tavora is certainly described as Sebastian's favourite and bedfellow (*cameriero*) in Conestaggio, Lib. 1, p. 21. The translator of Blount's English edition (1600) gave it as chamberlain (*camerario*), perhaps a simple misreading. In order to allow the strictest possible comparison with the Plot, I have shown him on the casting plan of the text in the same position, doubling with Abdil Rayes, but he does not rightly belong there. I do not know whether, as I have jokingly suggested, the Plotter may have taken '*cameriero*', in conjunction with 'Efestian' (Hephaestion), to designate what Yoklavitch rather coyly

calls 'the royal friend'. I believe Peele was simply recording the facts as he found them in Conestaggio, and would have thought of de Tavora as of the same age as Sebastian. He had better reason for thinking of Barceles as a boy. In historical fact the latter was little more than twelve, and his 'toward youth' is pointed up in the dialogue.

3. Elizabethan Plotters, including our own, sometimes did little better. The golden statue scene in *Alcazar* is an obvious example. If the Plotter who worked on Q. 4 of *A Looking Glass for London and England* for a Jacobean revival followed his text with fidelity, the actors must have spoken a deal of nonsense. See C. R. Baskervill, 'A Prompt Copy of *A Looking Glass for London and England*', *Modern Philology*, 30 (1932–3). The sole surviving actor's scroll for Orlando's part in *Orlando Furioso* gives us no information on this score, for the greater part of the additional material is incoherent raving.
4. W. W. Greg, *Two Elizabethan Stage Abridgements: Alcazar and Orlando* (Oxford, 1923), p. 114.

9 The dumb-shows

1. See Natales Comes, *Mythologiae*, Lib.IX, pp. 1,007ff. 'De Nemisi'.
2. This scene may well be the one recalled in *A Warning for Fair Women* (1599), A2[v].

   a filthie whining ghost
   Lapt in some fowle sheete, or a leather pelch,
   Comes screaminge like a piggie halfe stickt
   And cries Vindicta, revenge, revenge.

   The leather pilch, of course, is a satirical reference to boys' breeches and indicates juvenile ghosts, but no doubt the plays of the children's companies could furnish many examples.
3. See *The Metamorphoses of Ovid*, trans. Mary McInnes (Harmondsworth, 1955), pp. 158–66.
4. The Scales of Justice are presumably intended. It may simply be a coincidence that the comet of 1578 appeared in the sign of Libra; but the Plotter, as we have seen, may have been something of a student of the sources of the play.
5. See *Locrine*, I, i, Prologue, where the death of Brutus is figured in a spectacle, thus: 'a Lion running after a Beare or any other beast, then come foorth an Archer who must kill the Lion in a dumbe show, and then depart'. Ate speaks the commentary, 'all in black, with a burning torch in one hand, and a bloodie swoord in the other'. (R. B. McKerrow (ed.), Malone Society Reprint (Oxford, 1908, rep. 1965), A3[r]). In *The Spanish Tragedy*, the Act V Chorus has a show of nuptial torches quenched in blood by Hymen.
6. M. J. Warren, '*Doctor Faustus: The Old Man and the Text*', *English Literary Renaissance*, 11 (1981), 111–47.

Select bibliography

Editions of *The Battle of Alcazar*

Bullen, A. H. (ed.), *The Works of Peele*, 2 vols. (London, 1888)

Dyce, A. (ed.), *The Works of Peele*, 3 vols. (London, 1829–30)

Greg, W. W.

(ed.), *The Battle of Alcazar*, Malone Society Reprint (Oxford, 1907, rep. 1963)

Two Elizabethan Stage Abridgements: Alcazar and Orlando (Oxford, 1923)

Yoklavich, J. (ed.), in Prouty, C. T. (ed.), *The Life and Works of George Peele*, 3 vols. (New Haven, 1961–70)

Sources of *The Battle of Alcazar* available to Peele and the Plotter of 1598

A dolorous discourse of a most terrible and bloudy battel, fought in Barbarie (London, 1578?)

Les Voyages et Conquestes des Roys de Portugal es Indes d'Orient ...receuilly de fideles tesmoings & memoires du Sieur Ioachim de Centellas, Gentilhomme Portugaiz (Paris, 1578)

Conestaggio, H. F., *Dell'Unione del Regno di Portogallo alla Corona di Castiglia* (Genoa, 1585)

[Nieto, L.], *Histoire Véritable des dernières Guerres advenues en Barbarie* (Paris, 1579. rep. de Castries, H., *Les Sources inédites de l'Histoire du Maroc*, 1st Series, Archives et Bibliothèques de France, Paris, 1905)

Nieto, L., trans. Thomas Freigius, *Historia de Bello Africano: in quo Sebastianus Serenissimus Portugalliae Rex, periit* (Nuremberg, 1580)

Nieto, L., trans. John Polemon, 'The Battaile of Alcazar, fought in Barbarie, betwene Sebastian King of Portugall, and Abdelmelec the King of Marocco', *The Second Book of Battailes, fought in our age* (London, 1587, rep. Amsterdam, The English Experience Series, vol. 483, 1972)

General references

Adams, J. C., *The Globe Playhouse, Its Design and Equipment* (London, 1942, rep. 1962)

Adams, J. Q., *Shakespearean Playhouses, A History of English Theatres from the Beginnings to the Restoration* (New York, 1917, rep. 1960)

'The Author-Plot of an Early Seventeenth Century Play', *The Library*, 26 (1945–6), 17–27

Allen, M. J. B. and Muir, K., *Shakespeare's Plays in Quarto* (Berkeley and London, 1981)

Ashley, L. R. N., *George Peele* (New York, 1970)

Bald, R. C., '*The Booke of Sir Thomas More* and its Problems', *Shakespeare Survey*, 2 (1966), 44–65

Baldwin, T. W., *The Organisation and Personnel of the Shakespearean Company* (Princeton, 1927)

Baskervill, C. R., 'A Prompt Copy of *A Looking Glass for London and England*', *Modern Philology*, 30 (1932–3), 29–51

Beckerman, B., *Shakespeare at the Globe: 1599–1601* (New York, 1962)

Bentley, G. E., *The Jacobean and Caroline Stage*, 7 vols. (Oxford, 1941–68)

The Profession of Dramatist in Shakespeare's Time. 1590–1642 (Princeton, 1971)

Bevington, D., *From 'Mankind' to Marlowe* (Cambridge, Mass., 1962, rep. 1968)

Bovill, E. W., *The Battle of Alcazar* (London, 1952)

Bowers, F., *On Editing Shakespeare* (Charlottesville, 1966)

'Marlowe's *Doctor Faustus*: the 1602 Additions', *Studies in Bibliography*, 26 (1973), 1–18

'*Beggar's Bush*: A Reconstructed Prompt-Book and its Copy', *Studies in Bibliography*, 27 (1974), 113–36.

Bradley, D., 'The Ignorant Elizabethan Author and Massinger's *Believe as You List*', *Sydney Studies in English*, 2 (1976–7), 98–125

Brown, J. R., *Shakespeare's Plays in Performance* (London, 1966)

Bullough, G., 'The Lost 'Troilus and Cressida'', *Essays and Studies*, 17 (1964), 24–40

Castries, H. de, *Les Sources Inédites de l'Histoire du Maroc de 1530 à 1845*, 1st Series, Dynastie Saadienne, 1530–1660, Archives et Bibliothèques de France, vol. I (Paris, 1905). Archives et Bibliothèques d'Angleterre, vols. I-III (Paris, 1918–35)

Chambers, E. K., *The Elizabethan Stage*, 4 vols. (Oxford, 1923)

William Shakespeare: A Study of Facts and Problems, 2 vols. (Oxford, 1933)

Craig, H., *A New Look at Shakespeare's Quartos* (Stanford, 1961)

Daborne, R., *The Poor Man's Comfort*, ed. K. Palmer, Malone Society Reprint (Oxford, 1954–5)

Davison, P. H. (ed.), *The Fair Maid of the Exchange 1607?, Malone Society Reprint* (Oxford, 1962–3)

Dawson, G., *Records of Plays and Players in Kent 1540–1642*, Malone Society Collections VII (Oxford, 1965)

De Banke, C., *Shakespearean Stage Production, Then and Now* (London, 1954)

Dekker, T., *The Guls Hornbook and the Belman of London*, Temple Classics (London, 1905, rep. 1941)

Diffie, B. W. and Winius, G. D., *Foundations of the Portuguese Empire, 1415–1580* (Minnesota and Oxford, 1977)

Fletcher, J., *Bonduca*, ed. W. W. Greg, Malone Society Reprint (Oxford, 1951)

Fletcher, J. and Massinger, P., *Sir John van Olden Barnavelt*, ed. T. H. Howard-Hill, Malone Society Reprint (Oxford, 1979–80)

Foakes, R. A. and Rickert, R. T. (eds.), *Henslowe's Diary* (Cambridge, 1968)

Freehafer, J., 'The Formation of the London Patent Companies in 1660', *Theatre Notebook*, 20, 1 (Autumn, 1965), 6–30

Frijlinck, W. (ed.), *The Tragedy of Sir John van Olden Barnavelt* (Oxford, 1922)

Galloway, D. and Wasson, J., *Records of Plays and Players in Norfolk and Suffolk 1330–1642*, Malone Society Collections XI (Oxford, 1980–1)

Gaskell, P., *A New Introduction to Bibliography* (Oxford, 1972)

Gerritsen, J., *The Honest Man's Fortune, a Critical Edition of MS. Dyce 9 (1625)*, Groningen Studies in English 3 (1952)

Glover, R. and Waller, A. R. (eds.), *The Works of Beaumont and Fletcher*, 10 vols. (Cambridge, 1905–12)

Greene, R., *Orlando Furioso*, ed. W. W. Greg, Malone Society Reprint (Oxford, 1906–7, rep. 1963)

Greene, R. and Chettle, H., *John of Bordeaux or the Second Part of Friar Bacon*, ed. W. L. Renwick, Malone Society Reprint (Oxford, 1935–6)

Greg, W. W. (ed.), *Henslowe Papers* (London, 1907, rep. New York, 1975)

The Book of Sir Thomas More, Malone Society Reprint (Oxford, 1911, revised Harold Jenkins, 1961)

Dramatic Documents from the Elizabethan Playhouses, 2 vols. (Oxford, 1931, rep. 1969)

The Editorial Problem in Shakespeare (Oxford, 1942)

(ed.), *Marlowe's Doctor Faustus 1604–1616.* Parallel texts. (Oxford, 1950)

The Shakespeare First Folio (Oxford, 1955)

Collected Papers, ed. J. C. Maxwell (Oxford, 1966)

Harbage, A., *Shakespeare's Audience* (New York, 1941)

Shakespeare and the Rival Traditions (New York, 1952)

Annals of English Drama 975–1700 (London, 1964)

Hart, A., *Stolne and Surreptitious Copies. A Comparative Study of Shakespeare's Bad Quartos* (Melbourne, 1942)

Herford, C. H., Simpson P., and Simpson E., *Ben Jonson*, 11 vols. (Oxford, 1925–52, rep. 1954–63)

Heylin, P., *Microcosmos, or a Little Description of the Great World* (Oxford, 1622)

Heywood, T., *The Captives*, ed. Arthur Brown, Malone Society Reprint (Oxford, 1953, rep. 1971)

The Escapes of Jupiter, ed. Henry D. Janzen, Malone Society Reprint (Oxford,1976–8)

Hinman, C. (ed.), *The First Folio of Shakespeare*, Norton facsimile edition (New York, 1968)

Hodges, C. W., *The Globe Restored. A Study of the Elizabethan Theatre*, 2nd edn (Oxford, 1968)

Honigmann, E. A. J., *The Stability of Shakespeare's Text* (London, 1965)

Hosley, R., 'The Playhouses and the Stage', *A New Companion to Shakespeare Studies*, ed. K. Muir and S. Schoenbaum (Cambridge, 1971), 15–34

Hotson, L., *Shakespeare's Wooden O* (London, 1959)

Howard-Hill, T. H., *Ralph Crane and Some Shakespeare First Folio Comedies* (Charlottesville, 1972)

'Buc and the Censorship of *Sir John van Olden Barnavelt* in 1619', *The Review of English Studies*, 39, no. 153 (February, 1988), 39–63

Jewkes, W. T., *Act Division in Elizabethan and Jacobean Plays (1583–1616)* (Hamden, Conn., 1958)

Jones, E., 'Racial Terms for Africans in Elizabethan Usage', *Shakespeare and England, Review of National Literatures*, 3, 2 (Fall, 1972), 54–89.

Kernodle, F., *From Art to Theatre: Form and Convention in the Renaissance* (Chicago, 1944)

King, T. J., *Shakespearean Staging, 1599–1642* (Cambridge, Mass., 1971)

Kuriyama, C. B., 'Dr. Greg and *Doctor Faustus*: The Supposed Originality of the 1616 Text', *English Literary Renaissance*, 5 (1975), 171–97

Lawrence, W. W., *The Elizabethan Playhouse and other Studies* (New York, 1913, rep. 1963)

Lever, J. W. (ed.), *The Wasp or Subject's Precedent*, Malone Society Reprint (Oxford, 1974–6)

Levinson, J. C., *The Famous History of Captain Thomas Stukeley*, Malone Society Reprint (Oxford, 1974)

Limon, J., *Gentlemen of a Company. English Players in Central and Eastern Europe, 1590–1660* (Cambridge, 1985)

Love, H. H. R., 'The Satirised Characters in *Poeta de Tristibus*', *Philological Quarterly*, 47 (October, 1968), 547–62

McKenzie, D. F., '"Printers of the Mind": Some Notes on Bibliographical Theories and Printing-House Practices', *Studies in Bibliography*, 22 (1969), 1–75

McKerrow, R. B., *An Introduction to Bibliography* (Oxford, 1927, rep. 1965)

'The Elizabethan Printer and Dramatic Manuscripts', *The Library*, 4th Series, 12, no.3 (December, 1931), 252–75

McMillin, S., 'Casting for Pembroke's Men: The *Henry VI* Quartos and *The Taming of A Shrew*', *Shakespeare Quarterly*, 23, no.2 (Spring, 1972), 141–59

'The Plots of *The Dead Man's Fortune* and *2 Seven Deadly Sins*: Inferences for Theatre Historians', *Studies in Bibliography*, 26 (1973), 235–43

The Elizabethan Theatre and 'The Book of Sir Thomas More' (Ithaca and London, 1987)

Massinger, P., *Believe as You List*, ed. C. J. Sisson, Malone Society Reprint (Oxford, 1927–8)

The Parliament of Love, ed. K. M. Lea, Malone Society Reprint (Oxford, 1928–9)

Maxwell, B., *Studies in Beaumont and Fletcher* (London, 1939)

Mehl, D., *The Elizabethan Dumb Show* (Cambridge, Mass., 1967)

Mulryne, J. R., 'Annotations in Some Copies of Two New Plays by Thomas Middleton, 1657', *The Library*, 5th Series, 30, no.3 (September, 1975), 217–21

Munday, A., *The Downfall of Robert Earl of Huntingdon. 1601*, ed. J. C. Meagher, Malone Society Reprint (Oxford, 1964–5)

The Death of Robert Earl of Huntingdon, ed. J. C. Meagher, Malone Society Reprint (Oxford, 1967)

Murray, J. T., *English Dramatic Companies. 1558–1642*, 2 vols. (New York, 1910, rep. 1963)

Nosworthy, J. M., *Shakespeare's Occasional Plays. Their Origin and Transmission* (London, 1965)

Orrell, J. and Gurr, A., 'What the Rose can tell us', *Times Literary Supplement*, June 9–15 (1989), 636

Poel, W., *Shakespeare in the Theatre* (London, 1913, rep. New York, 1968)

Pollard, A. W., 'The Manuscripts of Shakespeare's Plays', *The Library*, 3rd Series, no.26 (7 April, 1916), 198–226

Pollard, A. W. and Wilson, J. D., 'The 'stolne and surreptitious' Shakespeare Texts: *Henry V*, 1600', *Times Literary Supplement*, 13 March (1919), 134

'The 'stolne and surreptitious' Shakespeare Texts: *Merry Wives*', *Times Literary Supplement*, 7 August (1919), 420

'The 'stolne and surreptitious' Shakespeare Texts: *Romeo and Juliet*', *Times Literary Supplement*, 14 August (1919), 343

Povy, J. (trans.), *A Geographical Historie of Africa Written in Arabicke and Italian by John Leo a More* [Leo Africanus] (London, 1600), ed. Robert Brown, Hakluyt Society, Series I, 92–4, 1896

Prouty, C. T., '*The Contention*' *and Shakespeare's* '*2 Henry VI*' (New York, 1954)

Prouty, C. T. and Kokeritz, H., *Mr. William Shakespeare's Comedies, Histories, & Tragedies. A Facsimile Edition* (New Haven, 1954)

Reynolds, G. F., *The Staging of Shakespeare's Plays at the Red Bull Theatre, 1605–1625* (New York, 1940)

On Shakespeare's Stage (Boulder, 1967)

Rhodes, R. C., *The Staging of Shakespeare* (Birmingham, 1922)

Shakespeare's First Folio (Oxford, 1923)

Rice, W. G., 'A Principal Source of *The Battle of Alcazar*', *Modern Language Notes*, 58 (1943), 428–31

Righter, A., *Shakespeare and the Idea of the Play* (London, 1962)

Ringler, W. A., 'The Number of Actors in Shakespeare's Early Plays', *The Seventeenth Century Stage*, ed. G. E. Bentley (Chicago, 1968), 110–34

Rossiter, A. P. (ed.), *Woodstock*: *A Moral History* (London, 1946)

Sams, E., '"*Edmund Ironside*": A Reappraisal', *Times Literary Supplement*, 13 August (1982), 879

Simpson, P., 'The Play of *Sir Thomas More* and Shakespeare's Hand in it', *The Library*, 3rd Series, no. 8 (1917), 79–96

Simpson, R., *The School of Shakespeare*, 2 vols. (New York, 1878)

Smith, I., *Shakespeare's Blackfriars Playhouse. Its History and Its Design* (New York, 1964)

Sorelius, G., '*The Giant Race before the Flood*'. *Pre-Restoration Drama on the Stage and in the Criticism of the Restoration*, Studia Anglistica Upsaliensia, 4 (Uppsala, 1966)

Styan, J. L., *Shakespeare's Stagecraft* (Cambridge, 1967)

Urkowitz, S., *Shakespeare's Revision of King Lear* (Princeton, 1980)

Wallace, C. W., 'The Swan Theatre and the Earl of Pembroke's Servants', *Englische Studien*, 43 (1910–11), 340–95

Walton, J. K., *The Quarto Copy for the First Folio Shakespeare* (Dublin, 1971)

Warren, M. J., '*Doctor Faustus*: The Old Man and the Text', *English Literary Renaissance*, 11 (1981), 111–47

Wasson, J., 'Elizabethan and Jacobean Touring Companies', *Theatre Notebook*, 42, 2 (1988), 51–7

Watkins, R., *On Producing Shakespeare* (London, 1950)

Webster, M., *Shakespeare Today* (London, 1957)

Wells, S. and Taylor, G., *Modernising Shakespeare's Spelling, with Three Studies of the Text of Henry V* (Oxford, 1979)

Wilson, F. P., ed. Helen Gardner, *Shakespeare and the New Bibliography* (Oxford, 1970)

Index of plays

General index